Big Media, Big Money

Big Media, Big Money

Cultural Texts and
Political Economics

Second Edition

Ronald V. Bettig and Jeanne Lynn Hall

ROWMAN & LITTLEFIELD PUBLISHERS, INC.
Lanham • Boulder • New York • Toronto • Plymouth, UK

Published by Rowman & Littlefield Publishers, Inc.
A wholly owned subsidiary of The Rowman & Littlefield Publishing Group, Inc.
4501 Forbes Boulevard, Suite 200, Lanham, Maryland 20706
www.rowmanlittlefield.com

Estover Road, Plymouth PL6 7PY, United Kingdom

British Library Cataloguing in Publication Information Available

Library of Congress Cataloging-in-Publication Data

Bettig, Ronald V.
  Big media, big money : cultural texts and political economics / Ronald V. Bettig
and Jeanne Lynn Hall. — 2nd ed.
      p. cm.
  Includes bibliographical references and index.
  ISBN 978-1-4422-0427-0 (cloth : alk. paper) — ISBN 978-1-4422-0428-7 (pbk. :
alk. paper) — ISBN 978-1-4422-0429-4 (electronic)
  1. Mass media—Economic aspects. 2. Mass media and culture. 3. Corporate
power—United States. I. Hall, Jeanne Lynn, 1958- II. Title.
  P96.E25B48 2012
  384.0973--dc23

                                                                    2011045009

Printed in the United States of America

In Loving Memory

of

Jeanne Lynn Hall

2 December 1958–23 December 2011

Dedicated with love and gratitude to

Ron's mother, Lydia,

and

Jeanne's sister, Kathy

Contents

Acknowledgments

There are many people we wish to acknowledge, far more than we can name here. But we'd like to single out a few for special recognition.

First, I want to thank my support team: Timothy Free, E. Michael Johnson, Chris Mills, and Scott Rodgers. Special thanks are due to Tobin Bettivia and Chris Jordan for sharing their insights on the movie and music industries. I am grateful to my family for their consistent encouragement during the writing process. I am most thankful to my coauthor, Jeanne, without whom this book could not have been written.

Ronald V. Bettig

First and foremost, I want to thank Ron for collaborating with me on every step of this endeavor. All my love to my parents, Skip and Joy, who supported me throughout this journey. Special thanks to Rachel Guldin, Kelly Chernin, and Vanessa Sequeira, who were inspirations. Deep gratitude and utmost respect to Eileen Meehan and Robert McChesney, who have always been guiding lights.

Jeanne Lynn Hall

We both want to thank Neils Aaboe, Marissa Parks, and Alden Perkins of Rowman & Littlefield, whose patience and persistence helped us bring this project to fruition. Their belief in the book kept us going. Robert Hayunga was graceful and professional during the editorial process, and Meredith Nelson was thoughtful and creative in producing the cover design. Thanks also to the Center for Responsive Politics for use of its data from opensecrets.org and lobbying expenditures.

With this work, we hope to play our small part in making the world a better place through the advancement of media literacy and the struggle for democratic communications. All of the friends, family, students, colleagues, and editors mentioned above have helped more than we can say.

11 September 2011

1

Introduction: Beat the Press

This book began as a series of essays on media criticism titled *Beat the Press*. We'd like to begin with an explanation of that title: what it means to us to beat the press in terms of theory, method, and practice. By "press," we mean more than just journalism. We use the term to include our entire mediated environment: not only newspapers, but also broadcast and cable television, movies, music, books, the Internet, advertising, fashion, education, and the many other means we use to communicate. We use "beat" as a *sensitizing concept*, a qualitative research strategy suggested by Cliff Christians and James Carey, to "capture meaning at different levels and label them accordingly."[1] Christians and Carey liken this strategy to peeling "the onion of reality down to different layers."[2] Over the course of the twentieth century—and even more than ever at the dawn of the twenty-first—this "reality" has been defined by the mass media, which have in many ways usurped the traditional role of family, friends, and religion in shaping how we make sense of the events and experiences of our daily lives, so much so that we risk thinking of our mediated existence—and the particular form it has taken under global capitalism—as somehow natural or inevitable.

In the first section of this chapter, we use a number of different meanings of the word *beat* to examine the emergence and development of the mass media, from the invention of the printing press to the weaving of the World Wide Web. We explore the growing influence of the mass media on our shared perceptions of reality and investigate some deeply held beliefs about the free press in the United States. In the second section, we briefly outline the tradition of mass communications theory and research. This is important because communications scholars have sought to study the role of media in society in a number of different ways and toward a variety of

1

different ends. Our work is no exception. We conclude with a description of our approach and a survey of the wide range of local and global media texts we will examine as we attempt to "peel away the layers" in the chapters that follow.

MEET THE PRESS

Under capitalism, the media are structured so that their primary goal is profit. This means beating the so-called competition, whether at the news-stand, box office, search engine, social network, or *New York Times* best seller list. For the news media, beating the competition involves a long history of getting the scoop, as in "You saw it here first." The news business first emerged in the Italian city-states of the late fifteenth century with the rise of capitalism and the development of the modern printing press. Early printers found that there was a tidy profit to be made in providing merchant capitalists with news about markets and political conditions. The industrialization of the news business in the nineteenth century resulted in the transformation of news into a mass-produced commodity. With this development, the range and scope of news content expanded to cover a wider range of human events and social behaviors. Competition at the newsstand resulted in increased sensationalism and even fabrication of news. The motivation to get the scoop remains a dominant influence in the news business today, as evidenced by the premature projection of the results of the 2000 U.S. presidential election by television news networks. Although it is difficult to prove whether such broadcasts sway voter be-havior, the election was nonetheless followed by congressional hearings at which network news directors promised yet again to regulate their election coverage more rigorously.

The rise of the book publishing industry is also tied to the invention of the modern printing press and the rise of capitalism. As with the news busi-ness, book printing and publishing flourished in the capitalist city-states of late-fifteenth-century Italy, then spread throughout Europe. The earliest book publishers built their businesses with the publication of religious works, classic Greek and Roman texts, government documents, and educa-tional materials. As Elizabeth Eisenstein discovered, however, printers soon found that there was a lucrative market for "scandal sheets, 'lewd Ballads,' 'merry bookes of Italie,' and other 'corrupted tales in Inke and Paper.'"[3]

The book publishing industry became increasingly industrialized in the nineteenth century during what is known as the great age of the European novel. As in the newspaper industry, mass-produced novels took a new look at everyday human existence within the evolving social context of urbanization and industrialization. In the 1920s and 1930s, the book industry turned to the mass production of books based on formulas such as the western, detective story, science fiction, and romance. The modern publishing industry took shape in the 1960s, as large industrial conglomerates began buying up publishing houses and putting them on strict profit plans. This meant reducing risks by developing and promoting a stable of star authors—the Stephen Kings, Danielle Steels, Michael Crichtons, and J. K. Rowlings of the business. Prolific and predictable, such stars guaranteed best sellers—as well as television and movie deals—on a regular basis.

Celebrity authors are not the only ones who command million-dollar advances from publishers. Public figures who write or ghostwrite manuscripts do so as well. For example, Simon & Schuster agreed to pay $8 million for Hillary Rodham Clinton's autobiography, and Knopf Books (a division of Bertelsmann) promised Bill Clinton more than $10 million for his memoirs. The former president's advance was the largest ever for a nonfiction book. More recently, memoirs by former first lady Laura Bush and former Alaska governor Sarah Palin made the *New York Times* best seller list and brought in big bucks. (A characteristic headline said "Sarah Palin: *Going Rogue*, Making Dough.") The effects of the star system in publishing are highly significant. Paying a small number of authors large sums of cash makes the industry more concentrated, and the prospects for lesser-known authors much smaller. There is simply less money allocated to the development and promotion of their works.

Five global media corporations dominated the book publishing industry at the turn of the twenty-first century: AOL Time Warner, Bertelsmann, Viacom, Pearson, and News Corporation. After the first decade, the top five media firms in terms of capitalization, revenue, conglomeration, and general domestic and global reach were Time Warner, Walt Disney Company, News Corporation, National Amusements (Viacom and CBS), and Comcast (after taking control of NBC and Universal Pictures). These five firms form an oligopolistic core that dominates much of the content we receive. Each sector of the media industry is also controlled by oligopolies, as we will see in the movie and music chapters (chapters 3 and 4). Concentration at the retail level exacerbates the situation of mainstream media control; for example, chain bookstores and superstores drove independent bookshops out of business. Then chain bookstores gave way to large retailers. Brick-and-mortar stores came to face the competition of Amazon.com and iPads. Readers have fewer choices, since large retailers, like publishers, concentrate on best sellers. Any additional titles they offer are usually determined by buyers at corporate headquarters, rather than chosen by store employees or customers. The serendipitous discovery of a little-known gem on the shelves of a book superstore is growing increasingly rare.

According to Eisenstein, the printed book helped produce a revolutionary transformation in early modern Europe. The sheer abundance of texts proliferated new ways of thinking, leading Western civilization out of what was known as the Dark Ages. We may have an abundance of books today, but it takes work to find many that challenge existing ways of thinking or advance new ones. The book industry's reliance on a handful of genres and a stable of stars leads to the regular publication of all-too-familiar works. The same goes for movies and recorded music.

Both the movie and recorded music industries owe their origins to industrial capitalists of the late nineteenth century seeking to exploit new markets. They discovered the economic logic of capturing dramatic and musical performances on film or disc. The bulk of the costs of production went to staging and capturing the original performance; the costs of copying a movie or recording were miniscule by comparison. Film projection and recorded music quickly evolved from novelties found in arcades, nickelodeons, and vaudeville houses to become major entertainment industries in the mid-1920s. Motion picture palaces such as New York's Roxy Theater had more than six thousand seats. In the 1930s and 1940s, virtually every American between the ages of six and sixty went to the movies every single week. Like book publishing, movies and music came to depend on the star system, blockbusters, familiar genres, sequels, prequels, and outright imitations. Both industries also grew to rely on large production budgets and expensive promotion and marketing campaigns, though these costs are rarely associated with quality. Like the book publishing industry, the sale of DVDs and CDs became highly concentrated at the retail level, as video chains and independent stores gave way to megastores selling their products as loss leaders (less than wholesale price) to sell other more expensive products. Finally, all three industries are now adapting themselves to the Internet, which large media corporations first saw as a threat but soon began to view as an opportunity. The Internet maintains the potential to provide more diversity and variety of media sources, but what people do with the technology has largely been driven by those that can afford promotion of media products—the dominant media firms. It is also less work for audiences to attend to mainstream content than search out genuine alternatives.

Radio broadcasting comes next in the history of the mass media. Wireless telephony evolved as an alternative to the telephone around the turn of the twentieth century. Until the early 1920s, radio was primarily a hobby of amateurs based on the simple pleasures and practical uses of point-to-point communication, much as the Internet was originally used mainly for e-mail. The new technology put dollar signs in the eyes of industrial capitalists, who wrenched radio from the amateurs and transformed it into a source of profit. At first, radio broadcasters provided programming for free to promote sales of receiver sets. Soon, however, most U.S. households owned radio sets. The market for receivers was saturated, and revenues from the purchase of replacement sets were insufficient to cover the increasing costs of radio program production.

Looking to the newspaper industry as a business model, radio broadcasters turned to advertisers to support program production and distribution. They also copied the network model, enabling broadcasters to share programs and therefore program costs. By the early 1930s, radio broadcasting had evolved into a commercially supported and networked industry controlled by only two firms, the National Broadcasting Company (NBC) and the Columbia Broadcasting Company (CBS). Beating the competition grew to mean having the highest ratings, or the largest audiences to sell to advertisers.

Television broadcasters copied the radio broadcasting model wholesale, building a privately owned and operated, commercially supported, and tightly networked industry. They even borrowed or pilfered the same radio shows along with radio stars. At first the film industry saw television as a threat and responded with big-budget widescreen spectacles, Technicolor, and 3-D. In a good example of technology driving content, the studios produced biblical epics, Sirkian melodramas, and science fiction films in abundance. Soon, however, Hollywood capitalists saw profit-making opportunities in the new medium and began building their oligopolies. Since the rise of television, the content of filmed entertainment has not changed all that much, just the means of delivery—from cable and satellite television to videocassettes, DVDs, and the Internet. Meanwhile, the trend toward media concentration has accelerated, meaning more channels but not necessarily a wider range of voices.

The history of the mass media is intimately bound up with the history of advertising. While the book, movie, and music industries have traditionally relied more on direct consumer sales, the newspaper, magazine, and broadcast industries derive significant revenues from advertisers (around 50–60 percent for magazines, up to 80 percent for newspapers, and 100 percent for radio and television broadcasters). Advertisers exert two main influences over the programming they sponsor. First, advertisers determine the structure of media industries simply by choosing where to spend their money. They support media outlets that reach the right demographic groups—audiences that consume the most. Media producers seeking to serve "undesirable" audiences cannot count on advertising revenues to finance their operations and therefore remain marginalized. For example, advertisers have shunned urban radio stations with largely African American and Latino audiences, a practice known as "nonurban dictates." When advertisers do patronize such stations, they pay less for ads than they do for ads on stations with predominantly white audiences. In this way, advertisers contribute to the suppression of media diversity.

Second, advertisers exert direct influence over media content. There are many documented cases, and surely many more undocumented ones, of advertisers actually pulling or threatening to cancel their accounts because of critical reporting. This should not be surprising, because advertisers have a vested interest in keeping consumers uninformed or misinformed. They prefer for us to make decisions based on emotional bonds with their products. If the primary goal of advertising is to maintain brand loyalty and keep competitors out of the market, then the giant media companies are their own best advertisers. They launch extravagant promotional campaigns in print and television media promoting the latest blockbuster books, records, and movies, turning them into "must-buy" events. Again, advertising helps support an oligopolistic media structure by deluging audiences with information about a handful of media products and keeping them largely uninformed about alternatives.

Advertising is not only an economic institution operating for the benefit of a few major corporations and their owners; it is also an ideological institution that supports and negates certain ways of thinking. For example, advertisers had no interest in the vibrant working-class press of the nineteenth century, not only because working-class audiences had little to spend on manufactured goods, but also because the anti-capitalist sentiments these newspapers expressed were obviously contradictory to their goals. Advertisers therefore shunned publications that challenged consumerism as a lifestyle, especially as it became essential to sustaining the capitalist industrial system. First, people had to be convinced that there were an infinite number of unmet needs that consumption could surely satisfy. Advertisers began suggesting that social and personal relations could be improved by using new products such as deodorants and mouthwashes. Moreover, not just any brand of health or beauty aid would do; consumers also had to be persuaded that products manufactured by large national companies with famous brands were superior to those made at home or in town.

In the first few decades of the twentieth century, big brand advertisers began to use national magazines to spread the virtues of consumption, not only through the ads themselves but also through editorial content. Since then, advertiser-supported media have been expected to promote consumerist lifestyles, largely based on credit, to enrich the capitalist class so that its members can enjoy consumption at the level of luxury. Such are the rewards of ownership and control of the few hundred multinational corporations that account for most of the world's advertising expenditures.

The advertising industry has proven itself voracious in its search for new venues and attractive demographics. Advertisers have even taken their anthem of consumption into the once-sacred realm of public education, where they have found a most lucrative captive audience. In the United States, elementary and secondary education belongs to the public sector.

It is seen as both a guaranteed right for all citizens and the responsibility of a democratic society to provide. Increasingly, however, public schools strapped for cash are turning to the private sphere for sponsorship of academic and athletic programs and for donations of educational materials.

Education funding shortages have long been a problem in the United States due to the unequal distribution of tax money and the contradictory way the public thinks about taxes. The largest portion of public school revenues is generated from local property and income taxes, creating large gaps between rich and poor school districts. Although everyone wants their children to have a good education, those living in poor neighborhoods cannot afford it and those living in richer neighborhoods do not want to pay for it. Taxes reduce personal income and so are seen as an invasion of the right to consume. State and federal education funds have not been sufficient to close the gap, and advertisers have been all too willing to step in. Students are subjected to ads on school buses, in hallways and cafeterias, and in educational materials such as textbooks and news programs. The parameters of science projects are subject to the dictates of corporate sponsors. Market researchers have even bought class time to conduct taste tests and surveys, all to establish lifelong brand loyalties in children while they are still young.

While education in the United States is primarily a public institution, journalism has evolved as a private institution working under a general mandate to serve the public. Journalists are expected to "beat the bushes" (to return to our sensitizing concept) but more routinely they are relegated to "working the beat." The difference here is crucial. Beating the bushes, or searching out stories that are not advertised or announced, requires time and effort. This raises the costs of news production. Working the beat usually entails covering the courthouse, police station, city hall, the White House, Wall Street, and so on. This ensures stories on a predictable timetable and at low cost. The result is that news and public affairs are defined by authority figures such as politicians, corporate spokespersons, and readily available experts from think tanks and research institutes. Such officials are prone to beating around the bushes—withholding information, spreading half-truths, or just plain lying. It was not the press corps working the White House beat that broke the Watergate story; they were being misled by President Richard Nixon's press agents. It took investigative reporting from outside to get the real scoop.

This leads to the most obvious referent in the title of our newspaper column and this chapter of our book, the NBC Sunday morning news show called "Meet the Press," the longest-running television show in worldwide broadcasting history (since 1947). Along with other Sunday news shows "Meet the Press" has served as a site where Washington's elite meet to set government and media agendas for the week. The topics discussed on these

Sunday shows invariably become the subjects of newspaper reports and analyses on Monday. Far from challenging authority figures, journalists have come to rely on them. The media thereby become the means by which officials define public issues and set the parameters of policy debates. Those in power also use the media to determine what is not news and therefore what will not be debated. Important arguments are often left unspoken; significant news is unreported, buried, or banished to the last paragraph of a column or the final minutes of a broadcast. An analysis of the guest lists and topics of four Sunday morning news talk shows concluded decisively that issues of corporate power are not on the agenda.[4]

Finally, we use "beat" as a sensitizing concept to invoke reflection on the long history of violence against journalists and other media workers. In *Violence against the Press*, John Nerone documents the history of violent censorship and suppression of journalists seeking to expand the public sphere from the Revolutionary War to the late twentieth century.[5] Both Nerone and Jon Bekken cite violence as a routine means of suppressing the working-class press.[6] Around the world, journalists continue to sacrifice their lives for the expression of ideas and the dissemination of information that threatens the status quo. In the 1940s and 1950s, Hollywood studio owners caved in to national anticommunist hysteria, blacklisting writers, directors, and actors deemed "un-American" by virtue of their involvement in radical or merely liberal political organizations. Authors have endured book burnings, book bans, and even death threats. The suppression of nonmainstream music also has a long history. Conservative groups and government officials have consistently attacked alternative music genres, from early rock 'n' roll to heavy metal and rap.

Why the violent response to the press? Most of the time the marketplace filters out threatening ideas and information, but there are leaks in the system and the media can play a role in effecting social change. The muckrakers of the early twentieth century exposed corrupt and dangerous corporate practices. Their efforts contributed to laws and regulations governing corporate behavior, ranging from product safety standards to the oversight of mergers and acquisitions. Investigative journalism continues to have an effect, but there is not enough of it, and its findings are seldom put into broader social, political, and economic contexts. In the spring of 2001, for example, Knight Ridder Newspapers published a series of investigative reports on the use of child slave labor in the cultivation of cocoa beans, the essential ingredient in chocolate. The reports prompted responses from both the chocolate industry and the federal government.[7] After first denying that child slaves were cultivating cocoa beans, the Chocolate Manufacturers Association agreed to finance a study of such business practices. Hershey Food Corporation, the largest chocolate manufacturer in the United States, pledged financial support for the study. The Labor Department began an investigation into the government's cocoa purchasing practices. The House of Representatives voted to direct the Food and Drug Administration to develop disclaimers guaranteeing that chocolate products sold in the United States did not come from child slave labor.

The publication of the two-month Knight Ridder investigation is in itself exceptional, and the political action it prompted even more so. The reports stop short, however, of any kind of critique of the larger global economic context that forces many more millions into slavery and billions to work at poverty or below-poverty levels of income. The idea of boycotting the purchase of chocolate products was dismissed by the series reporters, who echoed the industry line that a boycott could harm slaves.[8] In doing so, the reporters ignored the long history of successful boycotts in the struggle for human rights. These include the bus boycott by African Americans in Montgomery, Alabama, in 1955; the international economic, political, and cultural boycott of South Africa under apartheid; and the global boycott of Nestlé that forced the company to revise its marketing practices for infant formula to mothers in the Third World.

Instead of a boycott, the reporters recommended that readers express their concerns to the chocolate companies, U.S. Congress, and president. Meanwhile, the chocolate industry moved to quell any further action by Congress, with lobbying efforts led by former Senate majority leaders Bob Dole, a Republican, and George Mitchell, a Democrat. The industry also enlisted major food manufacturers such as Kraft and General Mills to lobby lawmakers with operations in their home districts to help thwart the "slave free" label movement.[9] Ultimately, bad publicity forced chocolate manufacturers to create an action plan that sought to halt the practice, which took ten years to implement due to the chocolate industry's lobbying power and foot-dragging.[10]

Although this example hints at the potential power of the press in effecting social change, it also reveals the limitations imposed by political and economic forces. Throughout human history, the control of knowledge and culture has been inextricably bound up with the control of wealth and political power. Therefore, in order to understand the communications system at any point in history, we must place it in its political-economic context. Not doing so can lead to misleading arguments, such as the one often made about freedom of expression within the U.S. media system.

It is commonly held that since the government does not directly control the media in the United States, and in fact is prohibited from doing so by the First Amendment, freedom of expression prevails. This ignores the role government officials play in setting media agendas, as well as more direct forms of intervention from laws and regulations, from laws regarding libel and obscenity to the allocation of radio and satellite frequencies. More importantly, it ignores what Edward Herman calls "market system constraints on freedom of expression,"[11] or the ways in which profit-making goals result in the suppression of diversity. If indeed the marketplace of ideas is prone to failure, then the assumption that "truth" will prevail becomes problematic. This raises the larger normative question guiding our analysis: Can a system in which culture and information are treated as commodities fully meet the needs of a self-governing, democratic polity?

MEDIA TEXTS IN CONTEXT

Our criticism of the media is rooted in the tradition of mass communications theory and research. From this tradition, we draw upon the political economy approach to examine the production and dissemination of information and culture. This approach provides the context that informs our interpretations of media content. In this section, we briefly review the mass communications research tradition and explain what we mean by political economy and interpretive textual analysis.

The dramatic expansion of the mass media in the 1920s and 1930s led to questions about their effects on society. Government, business, religious, and parent organizations began funding research on media effects in hopes of using the media to better promote their interests and causes. Government officials were most interested in mass mobilization of the public during wartime. The U.S. military used media research to improve motivation of troops. Politicians sought polling data and studies of voter behavior in hopes of influencing election outcomes. Business was most interested in understanding consumer behavior to create more effective marketing and advertising campaigns. Religious groups and parent associations prompted research on the potential threat of the media to traditional morals and values. These efforts were often barely disguised attacks on minority or working-class media. In sum, the entire foundation of mass communications research was oriented toward better control and manipulation of audiences. This administrative research orientation dominated the field of mass communications studies well into the 1960s.

The rise of a critical challenge to administrative research paralleled the larger challenges posed by the civil rights, feminist, environmental, and anti-imperialist movements in the 1960s. Critical communications research dramatically reversed the focus, studying the ways in which the media perpetuated institutional racism, sexism, imperialism, and other forms of oppression. This required an inquiry into the relationship between the media and economic and political systems, prompting the development of a political economy approach to the study of communications. Concurrently, critical media researchers sought to expand the range of methods for the study of media content.

Traditional content analysis relied on quantitative methodology, basically counting obvious things such as the number of articles or column inches the press devoted to each candidate in an election and deciding whether the coverage was more or less favorable. Content analysts worked on a basic assumption that press coverage ultimately affected voter behavior, although research did not always prove that this was the case. Effects researchers found that, more often, the media reinforce preexisting dispositions, attitudes, and opinions. They therefore concluded that the effects of the media were limited. Critical communications researchers challenged this idea, arguing that the capacity of the media to reinforce existing beliefs is a powerful effect to the extent that it mitigates social change.

Critical communications research on audiences shifted the focus of administrative research from the study of how media texts affect behavior to the study of how audiences make meaning of media texts. Using qualitative methods such as focus groups and ethnography, critical audience researchers found that responses to media texts varied according to audience demographics including class, race, and gender. They found that audiences generally respond to media texts as producers intend them to but may also miss the point if it is not clear. Some audiences understand the producer's intent, but they resist it and replace it with an opposing meaning.

Most students of mass communications are familiar with the traditional model of sender, message, and receiver. Although not entirely breaking from this model, interpretive theories break the communications process down into phases of making meaning. They begin by analyzing the context within which the sender operates: how meaning is shaped at the point of production. Interpretive textual analysis examines how various levels of meaning are expressed—intentional meanings, but, more importantly, the hidden and often unintended meanings found in media content. Interpretive studies of audiences focus on how meaning is produced by receivers. By treating the making of meaning in phases, we are able to concentrate on both the context of production and the messages we find in the texts. That is, we can examine how media ownership, media control, and the profit-making motive affect what we read, hear, and see.

THINKING LOCALLY AND GLOBALLY

We draw on a wide range of media to inform our analysis of the press. Our daily newspaper, the *State College (Pa.) Centre Daily Times (CDT)*, served as the source of our initial inquiry into many of the local, national, and global issues and events we use to examine how media structures and practices affect content. The newspaper serves the community of State College, Pennsylvania, site of the main campus of the Pennsylvania State University and the surrounding townships and boroughs. When we wrote the first edition of this book, the *CDT* was part of the second-largest newspaper chain in the United States, Knight Ridder, whose flagships included the *Philadelphia Inquirer* and the *Miami Herald*. In 2006, Knight-Ridder was purchased by McClatchy, which operates thirty newspapers in fifteen states with an average daily circulation of 2.2 million. Because it is a chain newspaper and serves a diverse university and local population, the *Centre Daily Times* provides a good sample of local, national, and international news for textual analysis. When we use the term "sample," we mean representative rather than random, as traditional content analysis requires. National and international news in the *Centre Daily Times* comes from wire services, notably the Associated Press. The local press helps inform our study of the larger structure of media and educational institutions.

As the issues and events we study become more national and international in scope, we expand the range of our sample to include more national media, including the major broadcast and cable television news networks; upper-tier newspapers such as the *New York Times, Washington Post,* and the *Wall Street Journal*; the primary wire services and syndicates, the trade press both offline and online, corporate reports, government data and so on. Our analysis of media merger mania, for example, takes the merger of America Online (AOL) and Time Warner as an opportunity to examine how the national news media reported facts and opinions about the event. From mergers and acquisitions to going-out-of-business sales, we find that immediate economic ramifications, rather than long-term political or cultural implications, tend to be prioritized in the news. Side stories on big mergers focus on the personalities of chief executive officers and the effects on stock market prices. This is to be expected of the business press, but we should expect news media to be more vigilant in their coverage of concentrations of power—including within their own industry—as part of their normative mission of serving the public. Since this is not the case, we are often left with a handful of alternative media sources to put current events into perspective.

By alternative media, we mean the nonprofit, largely ad-free newsletters, magazines, and periodicals operating on the margins of the media marketplace. Because they are primarily reader-supported publications, they have greater freedom to provide a wider range of views, but because they are not a part of the mainstream distribution system, they are nearly impossible to find at the local newsstand. In terms of methodology, our use of the alternative press provides a comparative dimension that is also a key qualitative research strategy. We compare, for example, mainstream coverage of protests against the World Trade Organization (WTO) and the International Monetary Fund (IMF), written by reporters sent to the scene, to accounts in alternative media, written by activists actually involved in the scene. The differences are striking, and the reasons for this will become more apparent in the following chapters.

Chapter 2 examines the process of media merger mania, as well as the logic behind it and news coverage of it, using two millennial megamergers, Viacom with CBS and AOL with Time Warner, as case studies. Chapter 3 discusses the structure of the Hollywood film industry and its relationship to the larger political economic system. It also examines how the structure of the film industry oligopoly affects its performance and output. Chapter 4 follows with an analysis of the music industry, again examining its structure and how it has evolved in the Internet age. Chapter 5 examines advertising and journalism as ideological and economic institutions, exploring the effects of the symbiotic relationship between them on the structure and content of the news. Chapter 6 explores the phenomenon of "ad creep," or the hypercommercialism of contemporary culture. Chapter 7 extends this analysis with an examination of the commercialization and privatization of public education as advertisers invade the classroom. Finally, in chapter 8, we turn to media coverage of those struggling to expand news agendas or to challenge the parameters of public debate. Specifically, we examine a surge of protest against global capitalism at the turn of the twenty-first century and media attempts to symbolically contain it. We argue that alternative voices will be more important than ever in the struggles to come.

2

Media Merger Mania: Concentration in the Media Industry

Many have argued that media concentration has increased since the 1990s and has negatively influenced the industry's performance and output. Douglas Gomery defined oligopoly as "controlled competition with a few players" and noted that oligopoly was "the most common market structure for mass media ownership in the 1990s."[1] This oligopolistic structure continues to be predominant in the twenty-first century. The players share common interests, allowing them to more easily agree on standards and practices. They appear competitive on the surface because they allow some entry by independent companies operating on the margins, but their profit-maximizing and risk-minimizing strategies ultimately govern the majority of what gets produced and sold in the so-called media marketplace and affects what we read, see, and hear.

In *The New Media Monopoly*, Ben Bagdikian argued that five transnational media firms, "operating with many of the characteristics of a cartel," owned most of the media outlets in the United States in 2004: Time Warner, the Walt Disney Company, News Corporation, Viacom, and Bertelsmann.[2] In 2006, *The Nation* produced a centerfold titled "The National Entertainment State," that listed six dominant firms in the media sector: News Corp., General Electric (NBC/Universal), Disney, Time Warner, Viacom, and CBS.[3] That same year, *Advertising Age* found that 55.6 percent of net media revenue in the United States was earned by the top ten firms.[4] Another study of concentration in the copyright industries concentrated on another top five: General Electric, Time Warner, Disney, News Corp., and National Amusements (owner of Viacom and CBS).[5] Media Owners, a media industry tracking firm that excludes telecommunications and cable companies from its top twenty list in 2007 had these as its top ten: Time Warner, Disney,

Viacom, News Corp., CBS, Cox Enterprises, NBC, Universal, Gannett Co., Inc., and Clear Channel Communications, Inc.[6] By 2011 the top five were: Time Warner, Disney, National Amusements, News Corp., and Comcast/ NBC Universal.

Not only is the media sector as a whole concentrated, so are individual media industries. They are branches of a family tree that grows from the Big Media trunk. The Center for Public Integrity list of the top ten pay-television programming companies in 2006 (USA Network, the Disney Channel, TNT, ESPN, Lifetime Television, TBS, Cartoon Network, Nickelodeon, Fox News Channel, and FX) were owned by General Electric, Disney, Time Warner, Viacom, and News Corp.[7] The Center listed the top five television station owners as News Corp., CBS, GE-NBC, Disney-ABC, and the Tribune Company. Tribune was a distant second in terms of number of daily newspaper subscribers with 3.3 million to Gannett Co., Inc.'s leading total of 7.3 million in 2006. Two companies controlled the radio industry, Clear Channel and CBS Radio in terms of revenues. Two cable companies far outpaced their competitors in 2006: Comcast Corporation, with 26.8 million subscribers, followed by Time Warner Cable Inc. with 14.4 million. The top two satellite television companies were the DIRECTV Group Inc., then controlled by News Corp. and Echostar Communications Corporation, and XM Satellite Radio Holdings Inc. and Sirius Satellite Radio Inc. claimed satellite radio for themselves. By 2011, six companies controlled the film industry and four dominated the music industry (see chapters 3 and 4).

One reason we write this book is to call attention to the biases, distortions, and gaps in mainstream media coverage of contemporary issues and events. In this chapter we focus on the way in which the media "cover" themselves. There are, of course, occasional acts of self-flagellation and *mea culpas* when news operations are caught fabricating stories or distorting facts and images to support a particular take on a news report. One need only recall the outcry surrounding flights of fancy in a Pulitzer Prize–winning "news" story in the *Washington Post*, written by Janet Cooke about a nonexisting eight-year-old heroine addict, published in 1980. There was the infamous *Time* magazine cover "photo illustration" of O. J. Simpson at the time of his murder trial in 1994, with darkened skin tone.[8] Then there was the incident that came to be called "Rathergate," when CBS anchorman Dan Rather was accused of using fake documents in a report on George W. Bush dodging National Guard duty. CBS apologized to Bush, and Rather left the anchor chair earlier than he wanted to. Critics within the media often condemn their colleagues' speculative and sensationalistic coverage of scandals and tragedies involving politicians and celebrities. But this kind of internal "flak," to use Edward Herman and Noam Chomsky's term,[9] only serves to reinforce the public's belief that the media are vigilantly policing themselves and that the media marketplace is free and competitive enough to ensure that the truth generally prevails.

Unfortunately, such self-criticism leaves serious gaps in mainstream coverage of media issues. Most notable, perhaps, is the lack of any systematic analysis of the processes and effects of media concentration. Media mergers have implications that resonate far beyond Wall Street, but these are seldom explored, merely announced. Such is the case of news coverage of Viacom's announcement in September 1999 of its intent to acquire the CBS Corporation for $37.3 billion, creating the second-largest transnational media conglomerate in the world, as well as the announcement by America Online (AOL) in January 2000 of its intent to acquire Time Warner for $165 billion. These two mergers were the largest in the media industry's history. Therefore the ways in which these mergers were covered or not covered warrant closer examination. In this chapter, we take a look at each.

THE VIACOM-CBS MERGER

This transaction continued a trend that began in the mid-1990s when the Federal Communications Commission (FCC) repealed regulations that prohibited the major television networks—ABC, CBS, and NBC—from producing and syndicating their own prime-time programming. The FCC had imposed the Financial Interest and Syndication Rules (FISRs) on the networks in the 1970s when their viewing audience still attracted about 95 percent of U.S. households. At that time, the FCC found that the networks were forcing producers of prime-time television shows to give up portions of their revenues and their syndication rights to gain access to the airwaves. Also, prime-time schedules tended to favor the scheduling of shows in which the networks had a financial interest. By the mid-1990s, however, the FCC found that the decline in the share of network audiences to cable television, as well as the rise of a competing fourth network, Fox, made the FISRs unnecessary. The rules had also prevented the merger of major film studios with the networks when such vertical integration seemed necessary to improve the global competitiveness of U.S.-based media companies. Indeed, even before the rules were repealed, the Walt Disney Company announced its intent to purchase ABC, confident of the federal government's approval. Disney's film and television studios planned to provide in-house programming for ABC's national broadcast network. Similarly, Viacom's takeover of CBS gave Paramount film and television studios direct access to the prime-time network audience at both CBS and the United Paramount Network (UPN). The repeal of the rules essentially revived the practice of utilizing vertical integration to favor in-house programming on the prime-time broadcast schedules.[10]

Programming the Audience from Cradle to Grave

Media concentration is an ongoing trend that follows the predominant tendency within capitalism toward centralization of economic power in the hands of oligopolies. The 1996 Telecommunications Act, which lifted a number of restrictions on media ownership and control, accelerated further concentration, as the industry-written law freed the logic of capitalism from public control by shifting it to the private sector. CBS, for example, directly benefited from the removal of restrictions on the number of radio stations a single company could own. Until the mid-1980s, FCC rules permitted a single company to own seven AM and seven FM radio stations. In 1985, the FCC raised the limit to twelve AM and twelve FM stations. The 1996 act removed most restrictions on radio ownership and set off what Douglas Gomery called "the greatest merger wave in history."[11] The CBS-owned Infinity Broadcasting chain owned 160-plus radio stations when the Viacom takeover was announced. Many of these stations were concentrated in the same cities, giving Infinity up to 50 percent of the advertising revenues generated in these markets.[12] Clear Channel Communications took a commanding lead of the industry by acquiring over 1,200 radio stations.

The Viacom-CBS marriage included the consolidation of a number of media operations in addition to the CBS and UPN networks and Infinity Broadcasting. The deal involved cable programming (MTV, VH1, Nickelodeon, Comedy Central, ShowTime, and country music stations TNN and CMT); seventeen owned-and-operated television stations; copyrights to the Paramount film and television libraries and to more than a hundred thousand songs; Spelling Programming; Blockbuster Video; five amusement parks; billboard advertisers TDI Worldwide and Outdoor Systems Inc., with 210,000 billboards nationwide; and the Simon & Schuster publishing company. New media outlets included MTV Networks On Line, Marketwatch .com, CBS.com, and Country.com.[13] The estimated combined value of the advertising revenue generated by all Viacom-CBS outlets in 1999 was $11 billion,[14] far ahead of its nearest rival, Australia-based News Corp. At the time the deal was announced, the audience demographics of the merged Viacom-CBS literally ranged from the cradle to the grave, from *Rugrats* to *Touched by an Angel.*

Joined at the Hip

So what about news coverage of this media megamerger? The *State College (Pa.) Centre Daily Times (CDT)*, signaled the significance of the merger with a front-page story from the Associated Press (AP).[15] The headline, "Giants of Media Join at the Hip," acknowledged the magnitude of the deal while playing on the dominant theme of the story—the merger of "hip properties like MTV and VH1" with the "old line network" known for

60 Minutes and *Murder She Wrote.*[16] The report cited two sources. The first was Viacom Chairman Sumner Redstone, who ranked fourteenth on the *Forbes 400* 2001 list of the richest people in the United States, worth an estimated $10.1 billion.[17] Redstone controlled National Amusements Inc., a family-owned, private company that began with a single theater owned by his father. (By 2007 National Amusements controlled over fifteen hundred screens across the United States, Britain, Latin America, and Russia. Its theater chains included Showcase Cinemas, Multiplex Cinemas, KinoStar, and Cinema de Lux. It also operated IMAX theaters in the United States and Argentina.) Viacom and CBS would be controlled by National Amusements, which held roughly 70 percent of the combined company's voting stock. This received only passing mention in the press, if any.

In the AP story, Redstone declared that Viacom-CBS "will be the global leaders in every facet of the media and entertainment industry, financially strong from day one, with an enviable stable of global brands." The second source, an analyst from PaineWebber, gave his approval: "It's a good deal for everybody. . . . You need to be big. You need to have a global presence."[18] No sources questioning the political and cultural implications of the deal are cited. This is typical of the mainstream news media and reflects their reliance on a "golden Rolodex" of sources for expert commentary.

Since the AP account of the merger was framed as a business story, it is not surprising that CEOs and Wall Street experts were the first consulted, but the *CDT*'s follow-up story—provided by Knight Ridder and buried in the back of the Sunday business pages—was just as disappointing.[19] Again, the commentary flows entirely from media analysts and executives, while the entire process of media concentration is treated as natural and inevitable—as "part of an evolutionary process leading to a day in the near future when four to six companies control most of what the world hears on radio, watches on television and sees on the big screen."[20] The report does not even begin to touch upon the significance of this reality. It was written by a reporter for the *Atlanta Journal-Constitution*, which published an extended version on the front page of its business section, but the additional text narrowly focused on the emergence of Melvin A. Karmazin, CBS's chief executive, as a "new media kingpin."[21] This is in keeping with the mainstream media's tendency to favor personality profiles of CEOs or hierarchies within organizations over substantive analyses of institutional structures.

Network news coverage of the Viacom-CBS deal followed the same formula. We focused our attention on *NBC Nightly News*, since the merger left NBC as the only network not owned by a major Hollywood studio. NBC news producers left it up to anchor Tom Brokaw to raise the question of the impact of media concentration on diversity, creativity, democracy, and freedom of expression. His expert witness, however, was yet another Wall Street analyst, who quickly dodged the question and returned to the economic dimensions of the deal.[22] Foremost for Wall Street, of course, is how the integration of the two companies could potentially reduce costs by increasing "efficiency" and hence raise returns to company shareholders and lenders. As Herman argues, such mergers produce no real benefits to society, only to investors.[23]

The *New York Times* coverage of the Viacom-CBS merger also cast the story as a business matter. Almost all of the reporting on the merger was printed in the business pages. The front page of the "Business Day" section was dominated by two articles featuring the biographies of Redstone and Karmazin.[24] Only a very careful reader might catch a glimpse of the economic, political, and cultural implications of the deal. One article, for example, predicted another round of major cuts at the CBS news division and a further erosion of the line between news and entertainment. The conglomerate owners of the major news networks expect these divisions to be profit centers. In order to cut costs, they favor the cheaper news magazine genre over more costly foreign, investigative, and documentary news.[25] Another suggested that the deal would enhance the likelihood of privileged access for Paramount productions to CBS's prime-time schedule to the exclusion of more creative independent producers.[26]

A report on the impact of the deal on the music business hinted that the combination of MTV, VH1, TNN, and CMT with Infinity Broadcasting's 160-plus radio stations would give the company a dominating presence in the music industry, and that this domination would extend to the Internet, given the brand recognition that had made MTV's websites among the most popular.[27] Stuart Elliott, advertising columnist for the *New York Times*, cited sources expressing concerns that Viacom's control over so many media outlets would drive up advertising rates, as the company extracted a premium for access to its many audiences.[28] Finally, the day after the deal was announced, the *New York Times* ran an editorial written by an in-house "editorial observer," who concluded that the deal promised benefits for stockholders but merely "more of the same" for audiences.[29] The editors of the *Times* effectively dissociated the paper from this opinion by including the author's byline and placing the piece beneath the unsigned editorials, separated by a black border.

Despite the apparent concerns, a *New York Times* report on how federal regulators would respond to the deal found "a widespread consensus that at the end of the day Washington will bless the acquisition."[30] Immediately after announcing the deal, Redstone and CBS president Karmazin headed to Washington, D.C., to seek exemptions from the remains of the FCC regulations that the merger would violate, confident that these hurdles could be cleared. Karmazin declared that ownership limits on broadcasters were outdated and needed to be modified due to the proliferation of cable and satellite television and the Internet.[31] Viacom also challenged broadcast ownership limits on First Amendment grounds, arguing that they constituted an arbitrary regulation that violated the company's freedom of expression. When the FCC approved the deal in May 2000, the *New York Times* quoted an "ebullient Mr. Redstone" as saying, "This has really worked perfectly. We basically got everything we had wanted."[32]

Not quite. Existing FCC rules still required Viacom-CBS to sell off some of its television stations. The merged company would control more than 40 percent of the national television audience, exceeding the 35 percent limit. FCC rules also prohibited a single company from owning two national broadcast networks, in this case CBS and UPN. Viacom's challenge to the rule limiting its share of broadcast households to 35 percent gained momentum when News Corp. (controlled by Rupert Murdoch, number twenty-one on the 2001 *Forbes 400* list at $7.5 billion) announced its $3.5 billion acquisition of Chris-Craft's ten television stations from Herbert Siegel (211th on the *Forbes* list with $1.1 billion).[33] The acquisition also put News Corp.'s share of the U.S. broadcast audience over the limit and violated FCC cross-ownership rules prohibiting one company from owning television and newspaper outlets in the same media market.

Like the Viacom-CBS merger, the FCC approved News Corp.'s takeover of Chris-Craft under the condition that certain properties be sold or traded to reduce its broadcast reach to 35 percent of U.S. households. Meanwhile, Viacom and News Corp. took their case to the U.S. Court of Appeals for the District of Columbia. The court is responsible for ruling on the legality and constitutionality of FCC procedures and regulations. In April 2001, the D.C. court of appeals granted Viacom's request for a suspension of the date by which the company was to divest some of its television stations. The FCC had to defend the rules before the court in September 2001, but it was clear that under President Bush's newly appointed chair of the commission, Michael K. Powell, son of Secretary of State Gen. Colin L. Powell, the rules already were on their way out. Powell, called the "Great Deregulator" by the *Washington Post*, was criticizing the rules even as FCC attorneys were obligated to defend them.[34] The *New York Times* concluded that the sharp tone of the judges' commentary during oral arguments suggested that the FCC was going to lose this case.[35]

On February 19, 2002, the D.C. court of appeals handed what a front-page story in the *New York Times* called "a huge victory to the nation's largest television networks and cable operators."[36] The rule prohibiting a broadcast television network from reaching more than 35 percent of U.S. households was sent back to the FCC for reconsideration. The court struck down another rule preventing companies from owning a cable system and broadcast station in the same market. Given FCC Chairman Powell's open skepticism of the need for ownership restrictions, the *New York Times* predicted that the 35 percent rule was all but certain to be watered down or abandoned. Instead, the FCC raised the National Television Ownership limits to 45 percent in June 2003. The decision was a setback for smaller owners of broadcast stations and consumer groups advocating more diversity in media ownership. Congress responded with a threat to withhold FCC funding to enforce the rule, likely in part because the scenario of concentrated ownership of TV stations had larger implications for their access to and image on the local television stations back home. The result was a compromise, in which household reach would be capped at 39 percent, hence ratifying the status quo. Congress turned the rule into statutory law as an attachment to a $37 million omnibus spending bill. As the *New York Times* noted, the FCC's deregulatory moves with court approval were likely to "open the door for a new wave of mega mergers in the entertainment and media industries and a continued concentration of power among the biggest media companies."[37] Broadcast chain ownership rules date back to the 1930s, when NBC and CBS dominated radio airwaves. The court's action therefore called into question seventy years of government regulation of broadcast network concentration.

Viacom had more immediate success with the abolition of the rule preventing ownership of two television networks. In April 2001, the FCC voted 3–1 to repeal the fifty-year-old rule preventing a single company from owning more than one national television broadcast network. The decision primarily hinged on Viacom's claim that the two-hundred-affiliate UPN network would not survive if divested, and diversity would be lost since the network targeted African American audiences and employed African American talent. Following this logic, only the deep pockets of a major media conglomerate could enhance diversity. Robert L. Johnson (172nd on the 2001 *Forbes 400*, at $1.3 billion)[38] argued the same when he sold his BET Holdings II Inc., which owned Black Entertainment Television (BET), to Viacom for $2.9 billion in 2001. Johnson received $1.3 billion in Viacom stock from the deal and a five-year contract to remain head of BET. At the time of the acquisition in January 2001, BET reached 70 million homes and had become a major medium for reaching black consumers. More than half of its schedule was made up of free programming—music videos supplied by record companies. Most of the remaining schedule was made up of reruns of black situation comedies and monologues by black stand-up comedians. Johnson expected to draw on Viacom's resources to enhance the quality of the programming and silence those who criticized the network for exploiting African American audiences with cheap programming.[39] For Viacom, the takeover of BET gave the company a lock on music television from urban to country, with MTV, VH1, and its two country music networks, CMT and TNN.

A year after the announced Viacom-CBS merger, it was confirmed that the deal was about synergy rather than diversity. The *New York Times*, reporting on the scene of the 2000 MTV video awards, noted that while a "rap artist hip-hopped around with the back of his pants worn at thigh level, revealing his gray undies in all their glory" on stage, Viacom executives up in the first mezzanine were sipping champagne and dining on lobster, "fully attired in business suits, pants belted at their waists," apparently enjoying the show.[40] Rather than a culture clash, the report found that the Viacom executives had much to celebrate as the first fruits of the deal began to pay off. Thus far, CBS had run promotions for the MTV awards during its season finale of *Survivor*, Nickelodeon planned to provide children's programming for CBS's Saturday morning schedule, VH1 would rerun CBS concert specials, and Viacom regularly promoted its programming on Infinity radio stations.

Separate Bedrooms

The marriage was consummated in 2000 (by that time worth $112 billion). The wedding gift from shareholders came through the market, driving up stock prices to a high of $71.13 a share in August of that year. Viacom and CBS remained under the control of Redstone's National Amusements Holdings. Redstone remained chairman of the board and chief executive of Viacom with around 70 percent of the company's stock. Karmazin stayed on as president of CBS. Redstone's son Brent joined the Viacom board, while daughter Shari served as director and president of National Amusements. The honeymoon proved to be short-lived. Redstone and Karmazin immediately clashed; Karmazin wanted more independence to run the company on a day-to-day basis while Redstone wheeled and dealed. As the tensions grew and became more public, outside board members led by Ivan Seldenberg, president and co-CEO of Verizon, demanded that the two settle their differences because their feud was affecting the company's stock price and long-term financial outlook. The board's intervention was seen as highly unusual, but demonstrated the power of investors to intervene in situations where their broader interest in making money may override the specific interests of corporate ownership and leadership. Nevertheless, Redstone prevailed. The *New York Times* attributed Karmazin's exit to the different styles of the two; Karmazin kept his business and personal lives separate while Redstone wanted him to socialize with his top executives.[41] Karmazin walked away in 2004 with $35.4 million, as guaranteed by his contract, along with a significant amount of Viacom stock. Redstone replaced Karmazin with two copresidents: Les Moonves from CBS and Tom Freston, the founder, board chair, and CEO of MTV Networks since 1978.

By the mid-2000s, Viacom's only major deal had been the sale of Blockbuster, one that actually ended up costing the company a total of $2.9 billion due to changes in accounting rules in 2002 regarding the valuation of a company. The sale of Blockbuster, a division that had generated 10 percent of Viacom's revenues, also cut the vertical cord that tied Paramount studios to the retail market. Since the acquisition of Blockbuster in the late 1990s, the sale or rental of any Paramount production ended up directly in the pockets of Viacom. This synergistic strategy appeared to be working but was not seen as a good fit with Viacom's focus on the production of content. Wal-Mart, Netflix, and video-on-demand posed enough of a future threat to let the nation's largest video chain go. In the final quarter of 2004, Viacom's stock had dropped from $46.30 before the merger with CBS to $30.00 a share, a 35 percent decline over the first five years of the union. A write-down of $18 billion that quarter alone, to pay off two other 1990s acquisitions, Infinity ($10.9 billion) and the outdoor advertising unit ($7.1 billion), revealed that Viacom had again overpaid for them.

By early 2005, the business press began speculating that Viacom and CBS were heading for a divorce. Redstone had gone through his own divorce, and his personal wealth had fallen by nearly half to $6 billion. With Wall Street's encouragement, Redstone became eager to split the company in order to "unlock" its shareholder value (in Wall Street terminology). Earnings at CBS had put a drag on Viacom's revenues.[42] By March 2005, Redstone proposed splitting Viacom into two companies: Viacom, which would include the cable networks and Paramount; and CBS, which would keep the broadcast networks and stations, the Paramount television production unit and theme parks, outdoor advertising, and Simon & Schuster publishing. To sell the plan to Wall Street, Redstone characterized Viacom as a growth stock and CBS as a mature steady-earning stock. Viacom was officially split into two companies at the beginning of 2006 and began trading on the stock market as separate entities.

The separation of Viacom was like moving into separate bedrooms of the National Amusements mansion. Les Monvees of CBS would get one room, Tom Freston of Viacom would take another, while Redstone resided in the master suite. Freston began to feel the heat as Viacom's stock dropped, largely due to reduced advertising income from the cable networks and slower subscriber growth in the cable industry, while CBS share prices performed well. This set off fierce competition between the two companies rather than the planned synergies. A *Wall Street Journal* article blamed the competition and tension between Moonves and Freston on the "sins of the parent."[43] Meanwhile, Redstone's personal wealth had risen to $7.6 billion, putting him at number 41 on the *Forbes 400* list in 2007.[44] By the end of September 2007, Viacom's assets totaled $21.37 billion[45] and CBS's $41 billion[46], a $60 billion media empire (see table 2.1). It also had joint ventures with Cingular, Sprint, Verizon Wireless, Motricity, Virgin Mobile USA, Amp'd Mobile, Apple iTunes and Music Store, YouTube Inc., On Broadband Networks, Universal, Time Warner (50-50 share of the CW network), Sundance Channel (37 percent), and the Quetzal Group Inc. (34 percent).

Table 2.1. National Amusements Holdings: Viacom Inc. and CBS Corporation Subsidiaries, 2006

- CBS Corporation
  - CBS Broadcasting Inc.
    - King World Productions, Inc.
  - CBS Outdoor
    - CBS Outdoor International
  - CBS Radio Inc.
    - CBS Radio Altitude Group
  - CBS Television Distribution Group
    - CBS Interactive
    - SportsLine.com Inc.
  - CSTV Networks Inc.
  - CW Television Network (50%)
  - Midway Games Inc.
  - MovieTickets.com Inc.
  - Quetzal (34%)
  - Showtime Networks Inc.
  - Simon & Schuster Inc.
    - Simon & Schuster Children's Publishing
    - Simon & Schuster UK Ltd.
  - Sundance Channel (37%)
- Viacom, Inc.
  - BET Holdings Inc.
    - BET.com
    - BET Digital Media Group
    - Black Entertainment Television Inc.
  - CBS Cable Networks Inc.
  - Famous Music
  - Harmonix Music Systems Inc.
  - MTV Networks Company
    - Atom Entertainment Inc.
    - Caballero Television
    - Comedy Partners
    - Country Music Television Inc.
    - IFILM Corporation
    - Logo
    - MTV
    - MTV2
    - MTV.com
    - MTV Games
    - MTV Networks Europe Ltd.
    - MTV Networks Global Inc.
    - MTV Networks Latin America Inc.
    - MTV Networks On Campus Inc. (mtvU)
    - MTV Networks South Africa Inc.
    - MTV Russia Holdings Inc.
    - MTV Shopping Networks Inc.
    - MTV Songs, Inc.

(continued)

Table 2.1.   (continued)

- MTVN Direct Inc.
- MTVN.Online Inc.
- Neopets Inc.
- Nickelodeon Networks
  - Nick at Night
  - Nickelodeon Australia Inc.
  - Nickelodeon Brazil Inc.
  - Nickelodeon UK Ltd.
- Noggin LLC
- Paramount UK Partnership
- RateMyProfessors.com
- Spike TV
- TNN Classic Sessions Inc.
- TurboNick
- Urge
- VH1
- Xfire Inc.
- Paramount Pictures Corporations
  - BET Pictures II
  - DreamWorks
  - MTV Films
  - Nickelodeon Movies
  - Paramount Classics Paramount Pictures
  - Paramount Home Entertainment Group
- Y2M: Youth Media and Marketing Networks

Sources: www.hoovers.com, Viacom and CBS Forms 10 K 2006

In addition to their vast range of joint ventures and interlocks with other media corporations, the companies also had ties to *Fortune 500* companies, trade associations, law firms, government, education, and charities and philanthropies. The interlocks between the companies' top officers and board members and such organizations fit nicely with G. William Domhoff's description of the "power elite," the working arm that looks after the wealth, power, and class-consciousness of the ruling class.[47] Among the board of directors in 2007 was Phillipe P. Dauman (who replaced Freston as president and CEO of Viacom), a cofounder of the private equity firm DND Capital Partners LLC, which specialized in taking publicly owned media and telecommunications firms private. Private equity firms are free of the scrutiny of Wall Street and the Securities and Exchange Commission, which only requires reports from publicly traded companies. Dauman also sat on the board of National Amusements and served as a trustee of the Boston Museum of Fine Arts. The cofounder of DND, Thomas Dooly, became senior executive vice president of Viacom. Another inside board member, George Abrams, had served as general counsel to the U.S. Senate Judiciary

Committee. In 2008, Abrams served as an attorney at a Boston firm and on the boards of National Amusements and Sonesta International Hotels corporations. Also on the board, listed as "Not independent," was Redstone's daughter Shari, president and second-largest shareholder of National Amusements. She also served as a member of the board of the National Association of Theater Owners to protect the interests of the theater chains and was a board member of CBS.

Among the "Independent" board members, Alan Greenberg had ties to Bear Stearns Companies Inc. and the Kraft Group; he was owner of International Forest Products and several other companies, plus the New England Patriots. Greenberg also served as a member of the National Football League's finance committee and director of the Dana Farber Cancer Institute (to which several Viacom and CBS board members belonged) and the Federal Reserve Bank of Boston. Other members had ties to Pepsi, the Travelers Companies, Oracle, Morgan Stanley, Verizon, Akamai Technologies, Consolidated Edison, and Yeshiva Law School.

The CBS board included Sumner Redstone as executive chairman and Leslie Moonves, president and CEO of CBS. Moonves was a member of the NCAA Advisory Board (CBS carried the "Final Four" college basketball championship) and served on the board of the Los Angeles Free Clinic and the board of trustees of the Entertainment Industries Council, National Council for Families and Television (both industry trade groups), and the American Film Institute; he was cochair of the board of the Museum of Television and Radio. Other interlocking directorates included Columbia University; former U.S. secretary of health, education, and welfare and assistant for domestic affairs to Lyndon B. Johnson; a former secretary of defense, senator, and house representative; American International Group, Liberty Mutual Group, and Bank of America; the former president and CEO of the National Association for the Advancement of Colored People (NAACP; helpful to BET); Southern Company, City National Bank, and Southwest Water Company; a member of the advisory board of the RAND Corporation Center for Middle East Public Policy (RAND is a government-financed military think tank); and a former president of Warner Music U.S. In 2006, sixteen board members of Viacom and CBS also sat on the board of National Amusements[48] (see table 2.2).

The power elite utilize these organizational interlocks to influence government through the policy-planning process. These are the sites of the positions and consensus that protects and extends the long-term general interests of the capitalist class as a whole. They help unify separate divisions of capital that might otherwise engage in destabilizing behaviors in the marketplace in pursuit of their specific, shorter-term interests. Domhoff addresses two additional processes through which the ruling class influences government in its favor. One is the lobbying process, through which

Table 2.2. Viacom Inc. and CBS Corporation: Organizational Interlocks, 2008

- Banks, Financials
  - Bank of America
  - Bear Stearns Companies Inc.
  - City National Bank
  - Cohen Group Financial Partners
  - DND Capital Partners LLC (2)
  - Federal Reserve Bank of Boston
  - Griego Enterprises Inc.
  - Intercontinental Exchange Inc.
  - International Finance LLC
  - Kraft Group
    - Kraft Group International Forest Products
    - Kraft Private Equity Funds
    - Kraft Real Estate Group
    - New England Patriots (National Football League)
    - New England Revolution (Major League Soccer)
    - Rand Whitney
  - Morgan Stanley (2)
  - Popular Inc.
  - Willis Group Holdings Ltd.
- Business Policy-Planning Groups and Thank Tanks
  - Public Policy Institute of California
  - RAND Corporation
- Education
  - Columbia University
  - Yeshiva University
- Insurance Companies
  - American International Group Inc.
  - Liberty Mutual Group
  - Travelers Companies
- Foundations and Philanthropies
  - Advisory Council, Academy of Television Arts and Sciences Foundation
  - Boston Museum of Fine Arts (2)
  - Cedars Sinai Medical Center
  - Combined Jewish Philanthropies
  - Dana Farber Cancer Institute (4)
  - John F. Kennedy Foundation
  - Los Angeles Board of Governors of the Museum of Television and Radio (2)
  - Massachusetts General Hospital
  - NAACP
  - National Center on Addiction and Substance Abuse
  - Packard Foundation
  - United Way of New England
  - Will Rogers Motion Picture Pioneers Foundation
- Government (former)
  - Assistant to U.S. President Lyndon B. Johnson
  - Deputy Mayor of Los Angeles
  - U.S. House of Representatives

- U.S. Secretary of Defense
- U.S. Secretary of Health, Education, and Welfare
- U.S. Senate
- U.S. Senate Judiciary Committee
- Law Firms
  - Cadwalader, Wickersham & Taft
  - Lourie & Cutler (Boston)
  - Winer & Adams (Boston)
- Other Corporations
  - AECOM Technology Corporation
  - Consolidated Edison Inc.
  - Northstar Neuroscience Inc.
  - Oracle Corporation
  - Pepsi Bottling Group Inc.
  - Southern Company
  - Southern Water Company
  - Tyco International Ltd.
  - Verizon Communications Inc.
- Other Media Corporations
  - CBS Corporation (Viacom, 3)
  - CineBridge Ventures Inc.
  - Kopelson Entertainment
  - Midway Games Inc.
  - National Amusements Inc. (16)
  - Universal Music Group
  - Viacom (CBS, 2)
- Trade Associations
  - Entertainment Industries Council
  - National Association of Theater Owners (2)
  - National Council for Families and Television

Source: CBS and Viacom Proxy Reports, 2007

individuals, companies, or corporate sectors seek special treatment from Congress and administrative agencies. Viacom's lobbying expenditures between January 1998 and June 2004 totaled more than $16 million. Its influence extended into the lobbying process via membership in trade associations such as the National Association of Theater Owners (NATO), the National Association of Broadcasters (NAB), and the Motion Picture Association of America (MPAA). During the same period it was involved in the candidate-selection process, with contributions to politicians totaling $2.36 million.[49] About 70 percent of its contributions went to Democrats, as its bottom line was directly hit by the Republican-led FCC in 2004, with fines for Janet Jackson's "wardrobe malfunction" during the 2005 Super Bowl half-time show produced by MTV and for indecency by Howard Stern on its Infinity stations.

So, all was not peaceful in the National Amusements mansion. The ouster of Freston in September 2006 was a bit of a surprise, but Redstone was unhappy that the company's stock continued to drop even after the acquisition of Dreamworks SKG live action unit. Redstone dumped Tom Cruise, who had a long-term deal with Paramount. Then the public really began to learn about Redstone's ruthlessness. His nephew, Michael Redstone, filed a lawsuit that Sumner had cheated him and his late sister out of their inheritance of National Amusements stocks, which had been left to them by Sumner's father through two earlier stock transactions among Sumner and the grandchildren. A Massachusetts court dismissed the suit on the basis of statute limitations. In 2006, Brent Redstone sued his father for misuse of National Amusements' funds and complained that Sumner was favoring his sister in the family business. Sumner settled by buying out his son's one-sixth interest in National Amusements.

Finally came his falling out with his daughter, the heir apparent, apparent no more. Relations between father and daughter began to deteriorate as Sumner waded into the video game business to the point of being over his head. Shari sought to stop the bleeding and reportedly stood up to her father as no one ever had.[50] She was publicly humiliated by Sumner in a letter to *Forbes*, in which he took credit for the improvement of corporate governance that she had initiated. The *Los Angeles Times* called the letter a "public slap" to his daughter.[51] Sumner also showed disdain for the theater chain that Shari had built up over the years, as a nongrowing industry and a poor fit with Viacom and CBS. Additionally, the letter to *Forbes* turned good governance against her by stating that succession would be determined by the boards of Viacom and CBS.

Age eighty-six in 2011, Redstone seemed intent on running things his own way until his death. However, the Great Recession did not spare him. His wealth in 2009, according to the *Forbes 400*, was down to $2 billion. He was forced to sell $200 million worth of stock in his companies Viacom and CBS, as their prices dropped below levels set by lenders. Redstone also lost big on video-game maker Midway Games both financially and directly, as his daughter gained control of Midway stock and took over as its chair. CBS and Viacom were kept afloat by loans from National Amusements, which in turn owed lenders $1.6 billion in 2010. Nevertheless, the media empire he built would carry on in one form or another, as the company's content and brands fueled the rapid growth of digital outlets.

THE AOL–TIME WARNER MERGER

While Viacom pursued government approval of its acquisition of CBS, in January 2000 America Online (AOL) announced its intention to acquire

Time Warner for an estimated $165 billion. Following the Viacom-CBS merger, it was the largest merger in world history, not just in media history. The estimated value of the combined companies was $350 billion. As one industry analyst put it, only a merger of AT&T, Yahoo, and Disney would have been of equal significance.[52] This merger brought AOL's 20 million Internet subscribers together with Time Warner's 35 million HBO pay-cable subscribers, 13 million cable system subscribers, and 120 million magazine readers, including readers of *Time, People,* and *Sports Illustrated.* Time Warner's cable news network, CNN, reached a global audience of 1 billion at the time. Its Warner Brothers' film and television division and Warner Music, with more than forty labels, were global leaders in their respective industry sectors.

The deal involved converting Time Warner and AOL to AOL Time Warner stock, with Time Warner shareholders receiving one-and-a half shares of AOL Time Warner for each share of Time Warner stock they owned, and AOL shareholders receiving one share of AOL Time Warner stock for each share of stock in AOL. This gave AOL shareholders 55 percent and Time Warner owners about 45 percent of the new company. It seemed like the perfect marriage, and Wall Street gave its blessing. The courtship lasted a year before the nuptials commenced.

Merging to Make a Better World

The significance of the AOL–Time Warner merger made front-page headlines. The *State College (Pa.) Centre Daily Times* reported that the merger between the world's largest Internet service provider and the world's largest media empire "means whenever you pick up a magazine, turn on the TV, flip to a cable channel, go to the movies or log on to the Internet, AOL Time Warner will probably be there with you."[53] It's possible that the reporter was alluding to AOL's penchant for monitoring the proclivities of its customers, but considering the total lack of any critical assessment of the deal, this is doubtful. Rather, the sole sources, AOL chairman and CEO Steve Case (211th on the 2001 *Forbes 400* list, worth $1.1 billion)[54] and two financial analysts, celebrated the merger as a historic transformation of the media and Internet landscape. A follow-up article from Knight Ridder further celebrated the deal as a boon to Silicon Valley.[55]

On the PBS *NewsHour with Jim Lehrer*, Case and Time Warner CEO Gerald M. Levin put a similar history-making spin on the merger.[56] The script, according to *New York Times* television critic Walter Goodman, cast the merger as an altruistic endeavor that had nothing to do with power and money. "This is not trying to have control for some self-serving reason," Case was quoted as saying. "In business, you can have a social commitment." Levin agreed: "This company is going to operate in the public interest." When

Case announced his commitment to creating "the most respected company in the world," Levin did him one better: "We want to make a better
world."[57] In their universe, this meant integrating Time Warner brands
with the marketing and delivery power of AOL. As Goodman concluded,
nothing in the script suggested improving the quality and diversity of the
merged company's output.

Merging as Mating

Despite the global implications of the merger for media and democracy,
much of the *New York Times* reporting and commentary remained superficial. The dominant themes involved fashion, cuisine, and romance. For
example, the day after the merger was announced, the front page of the
paper included a large color photo of Case and Levin. In identifying the
two CEOs, the photo caption accompanying the lead story described Case
as "with tie" and Levin "without tie."[58] Another accompanying story, also
on page 1, explained how strange it was for Case to wear a suit and tie while
announcing the takeover of Time Warner, since he was known "for clinging
to his casual costume of denim shirts and khakis on even the most formal
occasions."[59] A third front-page story noted that Case had once appeared in
a Gap ad.[60] Levin, it was noted, removed his tie before the news conference,
then welcomed the "suits from Virginia," home of AOL's headquarters. A
next-day lead article in the *New York Times* business pages described an
AOL senior executive as expressing relief that Time Warner had casual dress
days five days a week.[61] The article is accompanied by a large color photo
of AOL's president, Robert W. Pittman, without tie—an accessory that, the
reporter notes, was required at Time's editorial offices in New York until
the beginning of the 1990s. A senior executive from the Time Inc. division
predicted the merger would be smoother than the one with Warner back in
1989, since the AOL management was made up of "Dockers guys" rather
than "Hollywood killer types."[62]

In addition to the fashion hook, *New York Times* reporters used a cuisine
theme to interpret this merger of "old" and "new" media and to speculate
upon the potential clash of corporate cultures. The AOL model is cast in
the image of Case, who once worked for Pizza Hut,[63] was known to hold
"regular beer parties" on Fridays at AOL headquarters, and had a penchant
for popping jellybeans during interviews.[64] Time Inc. once exuded an image
of Ivy League gentility. In the 1950s and 1960s, the closing of an issue of the
magazine was heralded by a waiter with "a cart of wine and hard liquor for a
celebration."[65] The ascension of Levin to the top of Time Warner, however, is
said to have "brought about a certain anodyne quality, almost a neutral environment," and there was reportedly no drinking at the "big, rather bland"
Time Warner headquarters at Rockefeller Center in midtown Manhattan.[66]

The cuisine and beverage theme reemerged when AOL announced its profit forecasts. One article quoted "people who know both Time Warner and America Online," who predicted the first culture clash between the two companies would be in the advertising sales area. A former Time Inc. president stated that Time Warner had developed "an implied code of civility," while at AOL civility was frowned upon. She compared AOL's pursuit of advertisers to "the bar scene in Star Wars: everyone is a character, and a tough one."[67] The same Time Warner senior executive who commented on the pants worn at AOL did not foresee such a conflict, describing his future colleagues as "latte-drinking nice guys."[68]

The most prevalent metaphor for the merger in the *New York Times* was that of romance. Reporters typically described the deal in terms of courtship and marriage. The courtship process, we were told, included regular dinners between Levin and Pittman along with their spouses.[69] In an article headlined "The Online Generation Courts the Old Guard," Case is described as a "prickly suitor." He rebuffed overtures from AT&T but was still "on the prowl" for a "major-league partner" in media or telecommunications, though "unwilling to get together with just any admirer."[70] Case was attracted to Time Warner and was said to have had long phone conversations with Levin, "wooing him with his vision of the wired future."[71] Time Warner had had its chance to merge with AOL when it made its promising debut in the mid-1980s. Now, with AOL's far greater stock value, it was Time Warner shareholders who, as the *New York Times* reported, "leapt in celebration, like some waif rescued by a wealthy benefactor."[72] Not everyone approved of the marriage, however. One article cast investors as skeptical parents seeking to rend the couple asunder, believing each had greater value as a single entity.[73]

Within three days after the announcement, AOL investors signaled their disapproval by selling off their stock, dropping its value by one-fifth. This, in turn, reduced the value of the deal to Time Warner shareholders, who were to be paid off in AOL stock. Under the terms of the merger contract, however, Time Warner was altar-bound regardless of the price of AOL shares, locking the companies into going forward "for richer or for poorer."[74] Additionally, the marriage had the blessings of Janus Capital, an institutional investor that owned $12 billion worth of AOL and Time Warner stocks. Finally, a key partner in the marriage was Ted Turner (62nd on the 2001 *Forbes 400* list at $6.2 billion), then the largest individual shareholder in Time Warner with 6.7 percent of the company's stock. Bringing together the themes of money and romance, Turner approved the deal, later declaring: "When I cast my vote for 100 million shares, I did it with as much excitement as I felt the first time I made love some 42 years ago."[75]

A closer analysis of the *New York Times* coverage of the merger does reveal some strains of criticism of the merger and the trend it exemplifies, beginning with columns by reporters on the media beat. From the "Arts/ Culture Desk," for example, Walter Goodman mocked the cuisine metaphor, describing Levin as "carried away by a strange image of gobbling up all the information and entertainment" that he foresaw "flooding America, digitally or otherwise." Levin is quoted as saying: "I want to ingest it" and "consume it," to which Goodman responded: "He sounded like a commercial for Pepcid AC."[76] In a "Digital Commerce" column, Denise Caruso burlesqued the courtship metaphor that likened AOL's proposed purchase to "a snapshot of the new economy versus the old." The merger was not, she insisted, "a slightly sordid wedding between a luscious nubile and her tottering trophy husband, shuffling to the altar on his last hormonal surges." Rather, it was "more like two very wealthy old men doing combovers on their balding pates, trying to look hip and zippy but not quite willing to let go of the past," while gaining as much control over the evolving online entertainment distribution system as possible.[77] On the advertising beat, Stuart Elliott cited a CEO of a leading interactive advertising agency who praised the "union" of Time Warner's database and "amazing knowledge of the American consumer" with AOL's "amazing knowledge" of its 20 million members.[78] He acknowledged that some advertising agency executives had concerns about "overconcentration and oligopolistic control" of the media industry, but he did not quote them or explain why: because advertisers would be forced to pay higher rates, as a smaller number of companies charge more for access to their growing range of media outlets. Indeed, these concerns were summarily dismissed with a quote from a Saatchi and Saatchi media director: "I don't think those issues pertain here."[79]

The Big Media Debate

The *New York Times* ran a lead editorial following the merger announcement, acknowledging anxiety about the potential societal effects of the monopolization of the media market in the hands of a few companies. Finally, however, the editorial suggested that the deal would increase access to high-speed Internet services and lead to "broader choice."[80] For *New York Times* editors, the more serious threat posed by such economic concentration was to the U.S. political system: the ability of such "corporate behemoths" to "buy political influence." The editors concluded that there was no need to scuttle such mergers but rather to reform campaign finance laws.

Cartoonists and Other Critics

Appearing opposite the *New York Times* editorial, a piece of op-art by cartoonist Tom Tomorrow depicts a clueless middle-class U.S. couple celebrating the merger as the world takes "one step closer to the single source of news, information and entertainment" and dreaming about the day when AOL Time Warner merges with Microsoft.[81] Below the cartoon is a serious op-ed piece by Robert H. Frank, a Cornell University economist, who argues that the merger is driven by "the technological imperative" to either "dominate or perish." In his view, AOL Time Warner's ability to dominate the market therefore promises to benefit stockholders and consumers alike.[82]

The *State College (Pa.) Centre Daily Times* also relied on syndicated political cartoons to provide its readers with critical views on the merger. One drawing, by Kevin Siers, imagines an outer space view of planet Earth slapped with a label stating: "Contents: Copyright AOL Time Warner."[83] Another, by Tom Toles, envisions a series of morphing computer screens, beginning with the words "Microsoft Inc." and ending with something called "Soft-CBS-Viacom Inc."[84] Both were welcome commentaries on the ramifications of media concentration. The only extended analysis of the deal was a guest editorial written by Henry Giroux, then a Pennsylvania State University professor of cultural studies and education. In it, Giroux criticized AOL Time Warner for seeking to harness culture, entertainment, and information "to unfettered consumerism" at the expense of more important noncommercial values necessary for a healthy democracy, such as "a respect for freedom, equality, liberty, cultural differences, constitutional rights and economic justice."[85] This "My View" column, prefaced with an authorial byline and biographical blurb, was carefully placed on the "Viewpoints" page of the paper under the aforementioned morph cartoon—lest readers assume it in any way reflected the opinions of the *Centre Daily Times*.

No Cause for Alarm

Nonetheless, there was nothing approaching even this level of critique in the *New York Times*. A concerned reader had to scour the middle pages of the business section to find two articles raising questions about the effects of the deal on media autonomy and democracy. The journalists consulted their golden Rolodex for critics of Big Media and dutifully cited Ralph Nader (identified as a "consumer advocate"); Ben H. Bagdikian (author of *The Media Monopoly*); Robert McChesney (communications professor at the University of Illinois and cofounder of Free Press); and Jeff Cohen, founder of Fairness and Accuracy in Reporting (FAIR), described as "a liberal-leaning media watch group."[86] These sources made strong arguments concerning the threats posed by media concentration to journalistic independence and information diversity. In a "News Analysis" article, Laurence Zuckerman noted a seeming paradox: Public debates over media concentration have diminished since the 1980s, even as media concentration has increased. He subtly acknowledged that the lack of public discussion over Big Media is only apparently paradoxical, since the media themselves, as powerful shapers of the public agenda, have conveniently ignored it. He finally suggested that the ambiguities of the issue may simply have "sapped many people's sense of outrage."[87]

Perhaps the sapping of people's outrage is precisely due to the mainstream media's coverage of media mergers. Traditional journalistic practice is to reduce complex issues to two sides (see chapter 5). However, when it comes to covering events concerning the media business, journalists seem compelled to discover ambiguities that resist such reduction. Hence, Zuckerman suggests four reasons for why the AOL–Time Warner merger was not as alarming as the critics he quotes warn. First, he argued that concentration of media ownership and control is not a problem because of the proliferation of new media outlets, from cable networks to the Internet. Second, Big Media do not crowd out alternative voices; they enhance the diversity of the marketplace because they have the resources to launch new media products and absorb losses generally incurred by such ventures (for example, the millions spent by the Gannett Company before *USA Today* became profitable). Third, Zuckerman claimed that concerns that media conglomerates will use their outlets to protect or promote their own interests are overstated; attempts by these companies to stifle embarrassing news coverage in their subsidiaries will eventually come to light when they are "pounced upon by competitors, often owned by rival conglomerates." Additionally, owners and editors committed to editorial integrity will not allow their media outlets to promote personal causes, because, Zuckerman quotes Norman Pearlstine, editor in chief of Time Inc., as saying, "then you are going to have bad journalism."[88]

Finally, Zuckerman suggested, critics of Big Media may merely be "blinded by nostalgia" for some "golden age 30 or 40 years ago" when broadcast and newspaper companies were independently owned and operated. In fact, he claims, journalists working for such firms were often beholden to advertisers such as car dealers and supermarket and department store chains, or constrained by the interlocking economic and political interests of the company's owners. He concludes that only global media conglomerates have the clout to stand up to threats from advertisers, big business, or national governments.[89] Zuckerman does not allow his sources to provide counterarguments to his claims. Instead, Nader is cast as an alarmist for being "extremely critical of the deal" and an elitist in his hopes that mainstream media will finally collapse by boring audiences to tears. Bagdikian is cast as the blinded nostalgic. To find such counterclaims, a critical reader had to turn to the alternative media. They have the least to lose for criticizing media concentration and the most to lose as a result of this process.

The Technology Fix

The first claim, which holds that media concentration is not a serious problem because of the proliferation of new media outlets, can be countered by the rebuttal that the very purpose of such mergers is to create closed systems in which content and delivery systems are internally linked. Until the AOL–Time Warner merger, AOL supported open systems, since it required access to phone and cable lines to provide its Internet service, reaching 54 percent of U.S. households at the time. By acquiring Time Warner's cable system, with 22 percent of the nation's cable subscribers, the combined companies created a natural incentive to bundle their services and restrict access to their cable systems.[90] AOL promptly dropped its commitment to open access after announcing the merger. So although the combination of the Internet and broadband cable services had the potential to deliver content from millions of sources, it made more sense for a media monolith to deliver that which it already owned. AOL–Time Warner was tapping into a trend pointed out by Joel Bleifuss, editor of *In These Times*, in which Internet traffic was already being routed to fewer and fewer sites. Already by the year 2000, the one hundred most-visited websites accounted for nearly half of all pages viewed.[91] Jupiter Media Metrix reported that between March 1999 and March 2001, the total number of companies controlling half of U.S. user minutes online shrank 64 percent, from eleven to four. Even more drastic was the drop in the number of companies controlling 60 percent of all U.S. minutes spent online during the same period, from 110 to 14, an 87 percent decrease.[92] According to Bleifuss, the average online user in 2000 spent almost 20 percent of his or her time on the Internet at the top ten websites. AOL–Time Warner's goal was to have its sites among them.[93]

In another *In These Times* editorial, Pat Aufderheide described ways this could be done, such as rigging the speed of transmission of favored websites or making sure AOL–Time Warner services pop up first on the computer screen.[94] Hence, rather than giving people greater ability to produce, distribute, and receive information via the Web, the Big Media continued to seek to reproduce a captive consumer audience. This is inherent to the logic of vertical integration and is confirmed by the media's historical record. Each new medium is introduced with high hopes and expectations of increasing diversity and communications democracy. However, existing economic and political forces always seem to undermine these promises. Brian Winston called this recurrent historical pattern the "'law' of the suppression of radical potential,"[95] meaning there was no reason to believe that the future of the Internet would be any different.

Those who claim faith in the technology fix are determinists who see technological advances as progress in motion. They fail to consider or they ignore the unintended consequences of new technologies, or they believe that problems caused by new technologies can be fixed by more technology. Big Media coverage of solutions to the Gulf of Mexico oil spill in May 2009 revealed its general bias toward the technology fix, while having to finesse its overall tendency to reinforce the use of fossil fuels. Furthermore, the Big Media fuel consumption by celebrating the latest products being brought to the market with occasional tidbits scattered in the press that obscure consistent patterns of unintended consequences. Consider these news items: In South Korea a boot camp/rehabilitation center was established to help young people kick their addiction to the Internet and gaming. The *New York Times* reported on its front page that more and more workers use their lunchtimes to watch YouTube, news sites, or other sources.[96] Web producers had specifically provided content designed for lunchtime viewing. Already alienated workers become more alienated, with the screen replacing the water cooler or cafeteria.

The Big Media and consumer electronics companies convinced almost everyone that digital photography and videography were an essential product for capturing, storing, and distributing pictures and videos when they were first introduced. Yet columnist David Carr, who writes the "The Media Equation" for the *New York Times*, reported that the average number of times a computer-stored digital photo was actually viewed had dropped rapidly from once[97] to none. The only advantage was that they did not have to be stored in shoeboxes taking up space in the closet. No one figured that cell phones would cause so many unintended consequences, beginning with the subtle disappearance of pay phones, down 2.6 million between 1997 and 2007 and in phase-out mode by 2010.[98] Enough research on the unintended consequences of driving while talking or text messaging led certain cities and states to ban the use of handset cell phones on the road. There is a technology fix—voice-responding automobile systems. However, one cannot replace the face-to-face communication with a cell phone, and one does not face the yet unknown risk of getting cancer from the device. This issue is of sufficient concern that it became a research topic for the World Health Organization's International Agency for Research on Cancer.

The toll that new technology is taking on our planet and our species can hardly be measured. Regarding waste, a McClatchy wire release cited Environmental Protection Agency (EPA) estimates that 130 million phones loaded with all sorts of toxic materials are sent into the trash can each year.[99] Tons of electronic waste is exported to China and other Southeast Asian countries, where workers disassemble them for salvageable substances that at the same time are destroying their health. Other unintended consequences of the digital age include loss of privacy; the proliferation of spam and its waste of work time; sexual predators; the waste produced by disposing of analog television sets in the change to high-definition television; higher crime rates (flash mobs); the substitution of virtual reality for healthy fantasy; interruption of vacation time; a ten-year-old girl who received an MP3 video player bought as a gift at Wal-Mart that was preloaded with pornography and explicit songs about drugs; and the transformation of Craigslist to a resource for both prostitutes and police.[100]

Deep Pockets and Diversity

This brings up the second claim, that critics of Big Media need not worry since conglomerates have the resources to develop and sustain new media outlets and therefore foster media diversity. This claim is defeatist and concedes to oligopolistic control of the media while buying into AOL–Time Warner executives' claims that they understood the significance of the social and political power they wielded and promised that they would do so with responsibility. It is true that only Big Media can afford the huge losses that often accompany the launching of new media products such as Gannett's *USA Today*, or the sustaining of existing unprofitable operations such as News Corp.'s conservative *New York Post* or *Weekly Standard* (sold by News Corp. in 2010). The *Standard* lost its mission with the election of Barack Obama, but it served as the bible of the G. W. Bush administration. It is impossible to imagine these companies doing the same for genuinely alternative voices and views. If this were the case, more than 1 percent of U.S. communities would have competing newspapers, instead of one-newspaper monopolies, and more than just 1 percent of box office revenues would be generated by foreign movies. These situations are not caused by a lack of audience demand but rather are due to the fact that these markets do not achieve the levels of profitability demanded by media investors.

The deep-pockets argument is more often seen by economists as a threat than an opportunity. Large conglomerates are able to engage in predatory pricing (charging prices below actual costs), because their deep pockets allow them to afford the temporary losses that small and mid-sized firms cannot. Additionally, predatory pricing is usually accompanied by large advertising budgets that cannot be matched by smaller competitors. As smaller firms are forced to leave the business, further concentration of the economy occurs, leading to higher prices and less variety. Although predatory pricing practices are harder to find in the media business, since audiences tend to choose media based on taste rather than price, the large media conglomerates nonetheless maintain significant advantages in the marketplace. They can cultivate tastes for their own products with their enormous advertising and marketing power.

Media corporations are among the top national advertisers. According to *Advertising Age*, among the leading national advertisers in 2008, the first year of the Great Recession, Time Warner ranked eighth, spending $2.2 billion on pitching its products and services. Walt Disney Co. spent a little over $2.2 billion in advertising, General Electric (NBC/Universal) ranked ninth at $2 billion, and the Sony Corporation (including Sony Pictures and Sony Music Group) spent $1.46 billion. News Corp. ranked twenty-first at $1.3 billion and Viacom thirty-third, with U.S. advertising spending at $1.8 billion.[101]

The arguments that new media technologies or socially responsible media conglomerates should mitigate concerns about merger mania are both essentially flawed, since they confuse what British communications scholar Graham Murdock has called multiplicity with genuine diversity. "More does not necessarily mean different."[102] In its editorial comment on the AOL–Time Warner merger, *The Nation* feared that the rush of media mergers and joint ventures had already "created the worrisome prospect" that the Internet would go the way of television: "500 channels and nothing worth watching, while the cacophony of independent voices that makes for vibrant public discourse will be pushed to the margins where hardly anyone will even know to look for them."[103]

Fear of Exposure

The third reason that critics of the AOL–Time Warner merger were cast as alarmists focused on their supposedly undue concerns about the effects of conglomeration and concentration on media content, particularly journalism. In fact, critics have compiled a long list of episodes in which big media have tried to suppress news and information detrimental to their corporate interests.[104] The usual response is that concerns are unwarranted precisely because such a list could be produced. The oligopolistic competition among the big media offers assurances that such episodes eventually come to light, embarrassing any company caught violating journalistic ideals. Yet, as Zuckerman grudgingly admitted, "It is impossible to know how many articles have not been pursued because journalists felt it could limit their careers to challenge their corporate parents."[105]

Actually, surveys of news professionals suggest that they routinely take such factors into consideration. In a 1980 survey, 33 percent of editors working for newspaper chains admitted they would not run stories reflecting negatively on their parent firm.[106] A 2000 poll conducted by the Pew Research Center for the People and the Press along with the *Columbia Journalism Review* found that 35 percent of the nearly three hundred reporters and news executives surveyed said that news stories that would hurt the financial interests of a news organization go unreported either often or sometimes. More importantly, nearly 80 percent of those surveyed claimed market pressures led to the avoidance of stories deemed newsworthy but seen as too boring, while more than half claimed avoidance of stories considered too complicated for their audiences.[107] A Pew study found that in

2003, 66 percent of journalists at national media outlets and 57 percent of local journalists had come to believe that bottom-line pressure was "seriously hurting" the quality of the news.[108] Such surveys no longer need be conducted, as job cuts in the news industry have become a frequent story on the business pages, often in the same paper making the lay-offs. The effects on content extend from the institutionalization of self-censorship to news as infotainment. Under such conditions, the Big Media cannot perform their essential role in keeping the public fully informed.

Critics of Big Media have also compiled a long list of incidents in which media owners have used their outlets to promote their political and economic interests. The counterargument here is that audiences see such self-promotion as poor journalism and reject it. Accordingly, Time Inc.'s Pearlstine points out that *Forbes* magazine never openly supported the presidential candidacy of its owner, Steven Forbes, since the magazine's readers were more interested in the mind-sets of CEOs than those of presidential candidates (which shows where real power lies).[109] Although *Forbes* may not have directly plugged its publisher, this self-proclaimed "capitalist tool" did help legitimize his radically conservative economic policies, such as a regressive flat tax on income. Similarly, Rupert Murdoch's repurchase of the money-losing *New York Post* was evidence not of some altruistic effort to preserve another editorial voice, but rather an expansionary move to combine the property with his local television station (even though this was against FCC regulations) and increase his political clout in New York City. This is the same reason for establishing the money-losing *Weekly Standard*, led by neoconservative editors William Kristol and Fred Barnes, and the Fox News Network, where Kristol served as a frequent guest commentator. Michael Bloomberg, mayor of New York City used his own money to buy his way into the position.

Clearly, Big Media critics can make a solid case demonstrating that media owners routinely find ways to promote and protect their economic and political interests. However, as Robert H. Lande, professor of law at the University of Baltimore, explained in *The Nation*, "These problems could exist without any improper intent on the part of the media barons."[110] Therefore, the critique becomes stronger when the focus is shifted from how the behavior of individual corporations and their owners affect media content to the institutional level of how media are used to protect and promote the political and economic interests of the capitalist class as a whole. Once again the historical record shows that the communications system has generally served the dominant class. Although force and coercion have always been central to class domination, gaining the consent of the dominated has generally proven more efficient in maintaining the status quo.

Despite whatever oligopolistic competition exists among the Big Media, they continue to serve their historical function of maintaining the wealth and power of the current ruling class. As our parenthetical references to the *Forbes 400* are designed to suggest, media owners are among the richest individuals in the United States. According to the 2009 *Forbes 400*, twenty-five of those listed by industry were in the Media category, three in Entertainment, two in Information Technology, ten in Internet, eleven in Software, and three in Telecommunications.[111] *Forbes'* categorization of source of income leaves out those who made a fortune in the media and then sold out, such as John Kluge, owner of Metromedia (number thirty-five), who made his fortune selling his television stations to Rupert Murdoch; Thomas Hicks (number 371), with $1 billion made from selling Clear Channel; or Wayne Huizenga (number 154), worth $2.1 billion from selling Blockbuster to Viacom. Many of the *Forbes 400* were listed simply as investors, yet held significant stakes in media and communications companies. An example is Phillip Anschutz, number 37 in 2009 at $6 billion, who owned half of Regal Cinemas, the largest U.S. theater chain in 2010, with 6,739 screens at 545 theaters. Cross-ownership, investor relations, interlocking boards of directors, and joint ventures result in the thorough integration of Big Media with Big Business.

Benjamin M. Compaine rightly concluded that most media investors are most concerned with a company's long-term profits and do not concern themselves "with the controversial—or lack of controversial—content of movies or books or television shows"[112]—although they do expect management to avoid controversial content to protect the corporate image. Big Media critics do not claim otherwise. Indeed, as Thomas Guback concluded after examining the ownership and control of the filmed entertainment industry, institutional investors are most concerned with "sound financial results." However, Guback pointed out that there are indirect and structural influences on content, since media owners "share a class interest that shapes their posture toward social resources: how they are used, by whom, for what purpose and in whose interest."[113]

More important, though, is the role of the power elite in promoting the long-term stability and goals of the ruling class as a whole. Interlocking boards of directors provide a site where such interests can be pursued. Outside board members, those not involved in day-to-day operations, serve precisely that purpose. Thus, AOL's board at the time of the merger included General Alexander M. Haig Jr., President Ronald Reagan's former secretary of state; General Colin Powell, the chair of the Joint Chiefs of Staff under President George H. W. Bush; Franklin Raines, chair and CEO of Fannie Mae; and Marjorie M. Scardino, CEO of Pearson PLC, one of the world's largest publishing companies.[114] Time Warner's board also included outsiders from finance, big business, government, and arts and entertainment. Ties to finance included East-West Capital Associates, an investment banking boutique helping Time Warner find acquisitions, and the Bank of

New York Company. Big business links included Hilton Hotels Corporation, UAL Corporation (United Airlines), Colgate-Palmolive Company, and Philip Morris Companies. Former U.S. Senator John C. Danforth and former U.S. Trade Representative Carla Hills provided the company with access to government. Representing arts and entertainment were Beverly Sills Greenough, chair of the Lincoln Center for the Performing Arts, and Francis T. Vincent Jr., former commissioner of Major League Baseball.[115]

Like institutional investors, members of boards of directors are expected to protect the interests of stockholders. Their presence alone can make media executives think carefully about running stories that may offend certain economic interests. More important is the power directors have to hire, fire, and discipline upper-level management. Since the trend has been toward an increase in the number of other corporate executives and directors, the ties among the members of Big Business continue to become more intertwined. Interlocking directors can do favors for one another as their business interests cross paths. Boards of directors also advise stockholders on how to vote on shareholder proposals—and control the proxy vote of those who don't. For example, in Disney's 2002 Notice of Annual Meeting of Shareholders, the board of directors advised shareholders to vote against proposals that would prevent the company's accountants from also serving as consultants; compel the company to follow a set of widely accepted human and labor rights standards for its operations in China; require the company to disclose its policies on amusement park safety and fully report all injuries; and limit the stock options received by individual executive officers.[116] A "no" vote on these proposals was virtually predetermined, given the millions of Disney stockholders who own only a handful of shares and the handful of Disney stockholders who own millions of shares and control the proxy vote by default. Disney eventually did adopt the proposal to sever its accounting and consulting services—but only in response to threats by labor unions to drop the company's stock from their pension fund portfolios. In the wake of the Enron, WorldCom, and Global Crossing accounting scandals that came to light in 2001–2002, boards of directors were forced to become even more active in company oversight and even more independent of company management to look after class interests as a whole.

Still, in cases where the owner is also the majority stock owner, as in the case of Redstone at Viacom, owners retain the power to block resolutions put forward by stockholders. Redstone urged shareholders to vote no on a resolution introduced in the 2007 Proxy Statement by the As You Sow Foundation, Maryknoll Sisters, and Saint Joseph of Capuchin Order that Paramount Pictures refrain from depicting tobacco use in "youth friendly" movies, as Disney and Warner Brothers had already agreed to do.[117]

The most important function of boards of directors is the role their institutional connections play in forging the unification of the capitalist class around its common stake in preserving the existing unequal distribution of wealth and power. Accordingly, unlike the textbook version of capitalism, nominally competitive and independent firms are formally linked into a "network of relationships that makes cousins of entire broods of economic giants"[118] including the Big Media, which play a central role in protecting and promoting the family business. Such a critique of the effects of Big Media on news and information runs the risk of being seen as a conspiracy. However, as Bagdikian explained, "in modern times actual conspiracy may not be necessary," since large media corporations "have shared values" that "are reflected in the emphasis of their news and popular culture. They are the primary shapers of American public opinion about events and their meaning."[119]

False Nostalgia

Ironically enough, Bagdikian's reference to "modern times" leads to a fourth way in which critics of Big Media have been summarily dismissed. The argument is that contemporary media critics harbor a false nostalgia for some "golden era" when independently owned newspapers put public service before profit. Jon Katz, writing for *The Netizen*, epitomizes this nostalgia in his "Media Rant": "What a truly amazing transformation of American journalism, founded by raggedy outcasts, misfits, idealists, and quarrelsome colonial pamphleteers, none of whom would be allowed to drive Michael Eisner's limousine today."[120] The 2001 *Forbes 400* listed Eisner, then chair and CEO of Walt Disney Co., at number 359, worth an estimated $720 million.

Defenders of Big Media counter that there never really was a golden era. Family-owned newspapers and broadcasting companies often stifled news that would offend major advertisers. Editors and reporters learned not to pursue stories that might embarrass their companies' owners or the owners' friends. Indeed, the apologia goes, as large chains began to gobble up independents in the 1960s, publishers and editors gained greater autonomy, since distant parent companies had less concern about the actual content of the news, provided profit plans were being met. With big parent companies behind them, little papers in news media chains could supposedly stand up to advertisers, business interests, and government officials, serving their communities with stronger local reporting. Compaine dismisses so-called nostalgists with academic research supporting defenders of chain-owned newspapers. Based on "snapshots taken over several decades," Compaine finds that the "overwhelming weight of the research has shown that . . . corporately owned newspapers and 'monopoly' newspapers are, overall, either indistinguishable from family-owned newspapers or, by some accounts, superior."[121]

In fact, critics of Big Media are well aware of the dangers of romanticizing market competition.[122] There are inherent problems in a system in which news is produced to sell audiences to advertisers and produce profits for their owners. Yes, journalists have always faced constraints generated by the system, whether working for family-owned operations or large national newspaper chains. However, Robert McChesney identified a substantial change as a result of concentrated media ownership. Whatever autonomy journalists once had, which was not used very effectively for the most part anyway, has diminished significantly, resulting in "a softening of news stories and a reluctance now to attack major advertisers."[123] For Katz, the problem was that the Big Media had turned editorial content over to mass-marketers. "They have to avoid content that's controversial, idiosyncratic, or too brainy. In the 1990s, the people running the media ape one another in the most important ways: They value market research, profits, status, and expansion."[124] Ultimately, Bagdikian continues, if Big Media do have a record of improvement in service to the public or independence from government, it is "not sufficiently impressive to counter the dangers of tightening control of public information."[125]

Consumer and public interest advocates, such as the Consumers Union, Consumer Federation of America, the Media Access Project, and the Center for Media Education, opposed the AOL–Time Warner merger on precisely such grounds. Internet service providers (ISPs), regional Bell telephone companies, AT&T, NBC, and the Walt Disney Company also opposed the deal, but due to concerns about market power rather than media democracy. In one of its last major decisions under the Clinton administration, the Federal Trade Commission (FTC) approved the merger in December 2000, after requiring America Online and Time Warner to sign a five-year consent decree promising access to its cable systems to competing ISPs, including the nation's second-largest ISP at the time, Earthlink Inc. This guarantee, as well as the promise that AOL–Time Warner would not favor its own content or discriminate against others when transmitting content over its cable systems, including interactive television services, assuaged opponents of the deal. Without such concessions it is unlikely the merger would have been approved, but by making them, the two companies signaled their belief that cross-marketing opportunities produced by the combination were more important. While the deal was pending, a test of this assumption proved successful when AOL's promotion of Time Inc.'s magazines resulted in 600,000 new subscriptions in just six months.[126] Demonstrating its same belief in the power of branding, the Walt Disney Company issued a statement approving the FTC agreement as a "huge victory for consumers and for competition."[127]

The final site of resistance to the merger was before the FCC. Consumer advocates, media access advocates, and competing firms had petitioned the commission to block the deal. Among the five commissioners was Michael Powell, who refused to recuse himself from the deliberations even though his father served on the AOL board. One year and one day after America Online and Time Warner announced their union, the FCC approved the merger, subject to conditions, and rejected all petitions to deny.[128] The FCC's order required AOL to open its instant messaging service to Internet rivals once the companies began integrating the service with Time Warner's high-speed cable systems. The *New York Times* reported that "consumer groups hailed" the FCC's decision, but only Gene Kimmelman, codirector of the Washington, D.C., office of the Consumers Union, is quoted.[129] In his view, the combined actions of the FTC and FCC had averted "enormous dangers to consumers" and "transformed a merger that threatened competition into one that could actually expand consumers' choices for high-speed Internet and interactive TV services." A Time Warner spokesman called the FCC's order "a tremendous win for consumers worldwide."[130]

Post-Merger: Unhappy Marriage, Seeking Counseling

AOL and Time Warner were officially joined in January 2001. Steven Case took over as executive chairman and Gerald Levin as CEO. It was an expensive affair, and by the end of the year AOL–Time Warner was $21 billion in debt. Two thousand workers were laid off immediately, a total of 3 percent of the workforce.[131] Revenue and sales failed to match projections, and the value of the company's stock went into a free fall starting in 2002. Levin "retired" as CEO at the end of 2001 but was actually ousted by board members led by Ted Turner and according to a *New York Times* report was left with "a reputation tattered by the transaction."[132] He was replaced by Richard Parsons, who beat out co-chief operator Robert Pittman, marking the ascendance of Time Warner over AOL. Parsons presided over what was to be the worst year in U.S. corporate history. The first historic occasion was a corporate record-breaking $54 billion write-down in the first quarter of 2002. The value of the company dropped to as low as $61 billion, and AOL–Time Warner share prices dropped below $10 a share (Time Warner's shares alone were worth $71 before the merger). Pittman was forced out by the board mid-year as the fortunes of AOL began to decline. The year ended with a notorious $98 billion paper write-down to reflect the decline in share prices, *the largest in U.S. corporate history*. It still had revenues of $41 billion that year, up 7 percent from the year before. But declines in growth at AOL due to the bursting of the dot-com bubble negatively affected the unit's advertising revenue, much of it from dot-com companies themselves. Also, subscriptions to AOL's dial-up service had begun to slow due to household saturation and new services, including broadband. There was also competition from Microsoft with its Netscape Internet service. While

AOL had introduced millions to the online world, its luster was starting to tarnish.[133]

The year 2003 started off with the announced resignation of Steven Case as chair of the board, who had drawn the ire of investors with Pittman gone.[134] Richard Parsons was named to succeed Case in May. Ted Turner quit as vice chairman of AOL–Time Warner shortly after but remained on the board of directors. AOL–Time Warner had to borrow another $7 billion when it was forced to buy back Bertelsmann's half of AOL Europe according to the terms of the joint venture. Aside from cross-promotion, the anticipated synergies had not materialized. Time Warner's debt was at $29 billion when it agreed to buy back AT&T's 27 percent stake in Time Warner Entertainment for $3.6 billion, $2.1 billion in cash and the remaining $1.5 billion in AOL–Time Warner cable stock. These proceeds ended up in the hands of Comcast as it was buying out AT&T's cable business to become the largest cable operator. Comcast ended up with a 21 percent stake in a newly formed Time Warner Cable company.[135] Meanwhile, the SEC began an inquiry into an advertising deal between AOL and Vivendi regarding suspicious accounting practices.

AOL–Time Warner's debt had become a straitjacket on further expansion, so it began to sell off assets to bring it down. There was also a change in the company's name. AOL–Time Warner sold Comedy Central to Viacom in July 2003. Viacom's interest was increasing its leverage with cable operators by expanding its stable of cable networks and programming. AOL–Time Warner raised another $800 million from the sale of its stake in DIRECTV, owned by Hughes Electronics, a unit of General Motors (later bought out by Rupert Murdoch's News Corp.). Cinram International Inc. bought the CD and DVD manufacturing division of the company for $1.05 billion. Another $750 million came from Microsoft to settle an antitrust suit. Still, the company continued to struggle. In August 2003, AOL executives asked to have AOL dropped from the corporate title, claiming the association with Time Warner's troubles was tarnishing its image. The board agreed to rename the company Time Warner Inc. and changed its stock ticker from AOL to TWX. In November 2003, Time Warner announced the sale of the once mighty Warner Music Group to Edgar Bronfman Jr. and a group of private equity investors including Thomas H. Lee Partners, Bain Capital, and Providence Equity Partners for $2.6 billion. Other sales continued through the years, including its book unit and its sports franchises in Atlanta.

The price of Time Warner stock eventually settled in at around $18 a share at the beginning of 2005. It was not good enough for investors. Corporate raider Carl C. Icahn, who owned 1.3 percent of the company's stock, joined with three other hedge funds to bring the total to 2.6 percent. Icahn and friends began to pressure Time Warner to spin off its cable television business and buy back $20 billion worth of its stock.[136] Parsons fended the group off when he agreed to the $20 billion stock buy-back to be completed in 2007 but held firm on selling the cable division. Parsons had too much support from institutional investors after rescuing the company from the merger debacle, selling off Warner Music before the music industry decline, fending off government investigations, easing out Stephen Case, and putting an end to the culture wars within the company.[137] He did stand by while AOL was broadsided by Google, Yahoo, and Microsoft's MSN. In August 2006, AOL transformed itself to a purely ad-supported service. Its 17.7 million remaining subscribers no longer had to pay for the service. Five thousand AOL workers lost their jobs, roughly three thousand with the sale of AOL Internet access businesses in Britain, France, and Germany and two thousand in the United States, mainly in customer service.[138]

In December 2007, Parsons retired and chief operating officer Jeffrey Bewkes, with a long history at Time Warner, took over as chair and CEO of Time Warner. He inherited a company with assets of $132 billion in 2006, with total revenues that year of $44.2 billion, net income of $6.55 billion, and outstanding debt of $35 billion.[139] Bewkes suggested that Time Warner would not look the same after 2007 (see table 2.3).[140] The implication was that Time Warner Cable would be sold off and possibly AOL as well, leaving the company to focus on the production of content and letting others take care of distributing it throughout the media system. These two units provided one-half of Time Warner's value. Therefore, one risk of the spin-offs was that the smaller company would be ripe for takeover itself.

Separation and Divorce

Despite the risk of becoming too small and a takeover target, Time Warner spun off Time Warner Cable (TWC) to Time Warner stockholders in March 2009. The parent company distributed 0.083710 a share of TWC common stock for each share of Time Warner common stock.[141] The split-off was a $9.5 billion windfall for Time Warner, while TWC had to borrow $9 billion for a syndicate of banks that raised its total debt load to $24.2 billion. Still, by the first quarter of 2010, TWC remained second to Comcast's 25 million video subscribers with 14.8 million of its own. In total, it served 26 million video, voice, and high-speed data subscribers.[142]

Although there are no longer formal ties between Time Warner and TWC, there are informal ones via the TWC board of directors, including the former chairman of Time Warner's Media and Communications Group, who also served as its executive vice president and chief financial officer. Other board members are connected to Big Business (e.g., Proctor & Gamble), private investors, business policy groups (e.g., the World Economic Forum), government (former U.S. Senator John E. Sununu), and higher education. The board had a definite conservative tilt.[143] Time Warner overhauled its

Table 2.3. Partial List of Time Warner Inc. Subsidiaries, 2007

- America Online LLC
  - Advertising.com
  - AIM
  - AOL
  - AOL Canada
  - AOL Europe
  - Compuserve
  - GameDaily.com
  - MapQuest
  - Moviefone
  - Netscape
  - Spinner.com
  - TMZ.com
  - Truveo
  - Winamp
  - Xdrive
- Home Box Office Inc.
  - Cinemax
  - Cinemax On Demand
  - HBO
  - HBO Independent Productions
  - HBO Mobile International (11 countries)
  - HBO On Demand
  - HBO On Demand International
- New Line Cinema Corporation
  - New Line Cinema
  - New Line Distribution
  - New Line Home Entertainment
  - New Line International Releasing
  - New Line Merchandising/Licensing
  - New Line New Media
  - New Line Records
  - New Line Television
  - New Line Theatricals
  - Picturehouse
- Time Inc.
  - *Entertainment Weekly*
  - *Essence*
  - *Fortune*
  - *Fortune Asia*
  - *Fortune Europe*
  - *Golf*
  - *In Style Money*
  - *People*
  - *People en Español*
  - *Sports Illustrated*
  - *Time*

(continued)

Table 2.3. *(continued)*

- Grupo Editorial Expansion
- IPC Media
  - Special Niche Magazines (81 titles)
- Southern Progress Corporation
  - *Coastal Living*
  - *Cooking Light*
  - *Health*
  - *Southern Accents*
  - *Sunset*
  - *Sunset Books*
- Time Inc. Business Units
- Time Inc. South Pacific
- Time Warner Cable Inc.
  - Cable Franchises (23 cities)
  - Local News Programming (9 cities)
  - Road Runner High Speed Online
  - SportsNet New York
  - Time Warner Cable
- Turner Broadcasting System Inc.
  - Adult Swim
  - Cartoon Network
  - CNN
  - CNN Airport Network
  - CNN Headline News
  - CNN International
  - Court TV
  - NASCAR.com
  - PGA.com
  - TBS
  - Turner Classic Movies
  - Turner Network Television
  - Veryfunnyads.com
  - Williams Street Studio
- Warner Bros. Entertainment Inc.
  - DC Comics
  - Warner Bros. Consumer Products
  - Warner Bros. Home Entertainment Group
    - Warner Bros. Advanced Digital Services
    - Warner Bros. Anti-Piracy Operations
    - Warner Bros. Games
    - Warner Home Video
    - Warner Premiere
  - Warner Bros. International Cinemas
  - Warner Bros. Pictures
  - Warner Bros. Pictures International
  - Warner Bros. Studio Facilities
  - Warner Bros. Television Group
    - The CW Television Network (50%)

- Kids WB
- Telepictures Productions
- Warner Bros. Animation
- Warner Bros. Television
- Warner Horizon Television
- Warner Bros. Theatre Ventures
- Warner Independent Pictures Group

Source: Time Warner Fact Sheet 2007, www.timewarner.com

board of directors in 2009 to make it appear more "independent" than that of 2007 (see table 2.4) meaning that it would be able to assert greater control of corporate operations. It was largely a publicity stunt to regain the confidence of investors; despite the new names and faces, the institutional networks listed in table 2.4 remained in place. This included Time Warner's continued role in affecting public policy and opinion.

Time Warner involved itself significantly in the lobbying process during the 1998–2004 period, including some of its roughest years of marriage, with expenditures of $46 million.[144] Its campaign contributions for the period totaled $4.6 million. Like Viacom-CBS, it favored the Democratic Party with 63 percent of its contributions, but it also contributed 36.5 percent to the Republican Party. Between 1989 and 2012, it ranked thirty-first among the "heavy hitters," donating $20 million to candidates, with 72 percent going to Democrats.[145] In the 2008 election cycle, Time Warner contributed over $3 million to federal candidates and parties, 81 percent of that going to Democrats.[146] Time Warner's Political Action Committees contributed $2.11 million to federal candidates in 2008. That year television, movie, and music companies donated nearly $50 million. Also that year, Time Warner spent over $8 million on lobbying government agencies and elected officials.[147] Lobbying expenditures by the TV, film, and music industries as a whole totaled $102,585,026.[148] Both lobbying and campaign contributions are multiplied further through contributions by trade associations to which the Big Media belong. This political spending must be put into the context of the George W. Bush administration and its open hostility to the entertainment industry as a whole. This suggests that using money to influence politics is both defensive and offensive. Defensively, the Big Media give according to potential threatening government legislation and rules that may disturb their oligopolistic status or curbs on content. Offensively, lobbying and campaign contributions allow Big Media to influence federal agencies and write the laws that are to their benefit, such as tax breaks, subsidies, and self-regulation. The Great Recession underscored the nature of capitalist greed and how self-regulation becomes the central means to exploit it.

Table 2.4. Time Warner Board of Directors Interlocks, 2007

- Banks, Financials
  - Appleton Partners Inc.
  - Barksdale Management Corporations
  - Carver Bancorp Inc.
  - Collins & Aikman Corporation
  - Gordon Brothers Group
  - Forstmann Little & Company
  - JER Investors Trust Inc.
  - J. E. Roberts Companies (2)
  - KPCB Venture Capital
  - Kleiner, Perkins, Caulfied & Byers
  - Oak Grove Ventures
  - TIAA-CREF
  - Vincent Enterprises
  - World Bank/International Monetary Fund (former)
- Business Policy-Planning Groups and Think Tanks
  - American Assembly
  - Bilderberg Group
  - Center for Global Development
  - Center for Law and Renewal
  - Committee to Encourage Corporate Philanthropy
  - Council on Foreign Relations (2)
  - Institute for International Economics
  - National Bureau of Economic Research
  - Partnership for New York City
- Education
  - Harvard
  - Johns Hopkins
  - Northwestern
  - Stanford
  - Yale
- Foundations and Philanthropies
  - American Museum of Natural History
  - Apollo Theatre Foundation
  - Barksdale Reading Institute
  - Central Connecticut State University
  - Children's Defense Fund
  - Combined Jewish Charities
  - Committee to Encourage Corporate Philanthropy
  - Conservation International
  - Creative Coalition
  - Harvard University
  - Howard University
  - Markle Foundation Task Force on National Security in the Information Age
  - Mayo Foundation
  - Memorial Sloan-Kettering Cancer Center
  - Museum of Modern Art
  - Museum of Television and Radio

- Rockefeller Brothers Fund
- Simon Wiesenthal Center
- Tufts University
- Yale University (St. Thomas More Chapel and Center)
- Government (former and current)
  - Foreign Intelligence Advisory Board (Bush appointee)
  - New York City Housing Authority
  - TechNet (lobbying firm)
  - U.S. Deputy Secretary of Defense
  - U.S. Securities and Exchange Commission
- Law Firms
  - Mintz, Levin, Cohn, Ferris, Glovsky & Popeo PC
  - Ropes & Gray
- Other Corporations (former and current)
  - AMR Corporation (American Airlines)
  - AT&T Wireless
  - BBN Technologies Inc.
  - Cabela's Inc.
  - Coca-Cola Company
  - Colgate-Palmolive
  - Dell Inc.
  - FedEx Corporation
  - Hilton Hotels Corporation (co-chair/CEO retired 2007)
  - KB Home
  - Kentucky Fried Chicken Corporation
  - Kraft Foods Inc. (2)
  - Marriott Corporation
  - Netscape Communications Corporation
  - Paratek Pharmaceuticals Inc.
  - Philip Morris Companies Inc.
  - Prematics Inc.
  - Sun Microsystems Inc.
- Other Media and Entertainment Companies (former and current)
  - Axel Springer AG
  - Brillant 310 GmbH
  - Citadel Broadcasting Corporation
  - Columbia Pictures Industries Inc.
  - Deutsche Presse Agentur GmbH
  - Harrah's Entertainment Inc.
  - Leipziger Verlags-und Druckereigesellschaft mbH & Co. (books)
  - Major League Baseball (commissioner)
  - Omnicom Group Inc.
  - ProSiebenSat.1 Media AG, dpa
  - Walt Disney Company

Sources: Time Warner Inc. Proxy Statement 2007; corporate and organization websites

Epilogue

Ten years after the celebrated wedding announcement, the *New York Times* changed its tone. With a combined value of just $50 billion (compared to its original stabled value of $350 billion) and only 5 million subscribers (compared to 26 million in 2000), *Times* online beat reporters called "the divorce a healthy decision." Time Warner could concentrate on its core media businesses, while AOL could "move forward without the shackles of a bureaucratic corporate parent."[149] Finally, the *Times* interviewed the major players in 2010, as the sub-headline read, to "Reflect on a Debacle": how the two got together and what went wrong.[150] Levin reminisced about the beginning of the courtship at the fiftieth anniversary of the Peoples Republic of China at Tiananmen Square in 1999 when he was seated in front of Case and his wife. One thing that Levin registered was that the two seemed "to have a very sweet relationship and I like that."[151] Eduardo Mestre of the investment bank Salmon Smith Barney commented on the exuberance of the press at the time by hailing "the triumph of the New Economy":

> If you go back and read what was written in the *Journal* and was written in the *Times* about this transaction, you would have thought it was the second coming of the messiah. I'm sure that if one were to read those words today one would find it amusing, maybe dated, but it was, for financial reporting, it was as soaring and this is the great epiphany-of-life kind of journalism and you read it and it brought tears to year eyes.[152]

Ted Turner said he would "like to forget it . . . and that it should pass into history like the Vietnam War and the Iraq and Afghanistan wars. It's one of the biggest disasters that have occurred to our country" (the audacity of comparing a failed corporate merger to the devastation of war notwithstanding).[153] Turner lost 80 percent of his net worth ($8 billion) and was ousted as a company executive and finally resigned from the board. Case still insisted on "the core value of the idea," while Levin turned to technological determinism, in that Google came along with a better design and business plan for search engines. Parsons stressed the "cultural matter," questioning in retrospect his "abilities to figure out how to blend the old media and the new media culture. They were like different species, and in fact, they were species that were inherently at war."[154] In 2010, Time Warner remained atop the Big Five media companies that controlled the output of mainstream content. AOL, spun off as a public company, remained but a shell of its former self.

CONCLUSION

Our analysis of the institutional structures and media coverage of the two largest media mergers in history leads to several conclusions. First, media merger mania is inherent in the structure of capitalism, as is economic concentration in general. Capitalists would rather plan and control markets than actually compete. As we have shown, this leads to buy-outs, mergers, price discrimination, predatory pricing, and a heavy reliance on advertising and marketing. The media oligopoly seeks above all to minimize risk and maximize profits. The old media have crept their way into the new—along with commodification, commercialization, and concentration. The "core strategic value of the idea" of merging the two has come to fruition. In an early response to the AOL–Time Warner merger published in *The People*, Ken Boettcher argued that for any "real student of the media it should come as no surprise that new media are being commercialized just like older means of communication." Nor is it a surprise that "the capitalist-owned media are subject to the same laws of competition that lead to greater and greater concentration of capital—and control—in every industry." Furthermore, it doesn't seem to really matter "whether few capitalists or many own and control the mass media," since the so-called information they convey has "not brought the working class one inch closer to knowing what to do about the dire problems capitalism creates." Therefore, Boettcher recommends leaving the antitrust reforms to competing elements of the capitalist class and turning our energy and support to alternative, independent media.[155]

Second, media coverage reflects a bias in favor of mergers and acquisitions, sometimes even celebrating them if it seems they will lead to greater efficiencies and higher profits. Third, the business pages tend to focus on the individual and organizational levels of analysis, looking at the players and the game plan without putting mergers and acquisitions within an institutional context. We also find that the business pages can be explicitly ideological, as when the *Times* dismissed critics who questioned the potential negative implications of the AOL–Time Warner merger. Finally, the Big Media are generally silent when it comes to the implications of media mergers for the genuine artistic, journalistic, and intellectual diversity and creativity essential to a genuine democracy.

3

The Hollywood Movie Industry: Do We Really Need It?

In 2000, two eminent media scholars, Benjamin Compaine and Douglas Gomery, published a revised edition of *Who Owns the Media?*[1] The authors' respective chapters set up a debate about whether the media marketplace was competitive, diverse, and dynamic or rather an industry of "controlled competition with a few players."[2] The players are oligopolies that share common interests, allowing them to more easily agree on standards and practices. They appear competitive on the surface because they allow some entry by independent companies operating on the margins, but their profit-maximizing and risk-minimizing strategies ultimately govern the majority of what gets produced and sold in the so-called media marketplace and ultimately affect what we read, see, and hear.

In *The New Media Monopoly*, Ben Bagdikian concluded that the media industry had all the characteristics of a cartel controlled by just five companies.[3] In 2006, *The Nation* produced a centerfold titled "The National Entertainment State," which listed six dominant firms in the media sector.[4] That same year, *Advertising Age* found that 55.6 percent of net media revenue in the United States was earned by the top ten firms.[5] Media Owners, a media industry tracking the top twenty U.S. media owners in 2009, listed its top ten as Time Warner, Disney Viacom, News Corp., CBS, Cox Enterprises, NBC Universal, Gannett Co. Inc., and Clear Channel Communications Inc.[6] In 2010 the top tier of the media oligopoly was down to five: Time Warner, Disney, News Corp., National Amusements (Viacom and CBS), and General Electric (GE), which owned NBC Universal.[7] In 2010, GE was in the process of selling its media unit to Comcast, in a deal that gave Comcast 51 percent of NBC Universal stock with GE retaining 49 percent.

Hence, in 2010 Comcast became a member of the Big Five media oligopoly, as GE returned to its core businesses.

Not only is the media sector as a whole concentrated, but so are individual media industries. They are branches of a family tree that grow from the Big Media trunk. The Center for Public Integrity listed the top ten programming companies in 2006 as USA Network, The Disney Channel, TNT, ESPN, Lifetime Television, TBS, Cartoon Network, Nickelodeon, Fox News Channel, and FX—all owned by the Big Five. The Center found that just five television broadcast companies owned most of the local television stations in the United States. The newspaper industry's top dog was the Gannett Company, with 7.3 million subscribers, followed by the Tribune Company, a distant second with 3.3 million. Since the passage of the 1996 Telecommunications Act, just two companies gained control of the radio industry in terms of revenues and number of stations: Clear Channel and CBS Radio.[8] Two cable companies far outpaced their competitors in 2010: Comcast Corp., with roughly 25 million subscribers, followed by Time Warner Cable Inc. (TWC), with around 14 million. Also in 2010, only two satellite television companies claimed most of the market: the DIRECTV Group Inc., controlled by Liberty Media, and Dish Network. Satellite radio became a monopoly when XM Satellite Radio Holdings Inc. and Sirius Satellite Radio Inc. merged in 2008.

In this chapter, we want to focus on the oligopolistic structure of the Hollywood film industry and its links to the broader political economic power structure. We want to question why we all go to see the same movies and to wonder what we might be missing.

MONEY AT THE MOVIES: FILM INDUSTRY STRUCTURE

Most of our news about the movie industry comes from celebrity gossip columns or similarly formulaic news-entertainment television shows and film reviews. Indeed, in a parasitical way, the various media that cover the film industry are dependent upon its very existence. Much of this coverage lacks any kind of substantive consideration of the movie business, but sometimes there are revealing tidbits that give a glimpse of how things work. For example, the Associated Press syndicated a daily column to newspapers around the nation titled "People in the News." In May 1999, Sean Connery made "People in the News" for doubling as star and "tightfisted producer" of the movie *Entrapment* (John Amiel, director). The news was that Connery produced the film, budgeted at $68 million due to "complicated stunts" and "exotic locations," for only $66 million. Apparently Connery set the frugal tone "by shunning such usual star perks as private aircraft."[9]

The Academy of Motion Picture Arts and Sciences does not give an annual award for "Tightfistedness on the Set of an Important New Action-Adventure Film," but certainly Connery would have been in the running. The point, of course, is that making a movie for less than $68 million in the late 1990s had somehow become a complicated stunt in Hollywood (when the average cost of producing a film was $50 million). The message to moviegoers was that they should be grateful for tightfisted producers. Nevertheless, the cost of making and marketing a movie continued to rise. According to the Motion Picture Association of America (MPAA), the industry's trade association, the average cost of producing a movie in 2006 was $65.8 million. Marketing expenditures averaged an additional $35.4 million, for a total investment of $100.3 million per picture.[10] Blockbuster movies with production budgets of more than $200 million became more frequent by the end of the decade. For example, *Avatar* (James Cameron, 2009) cost at least $300 million to produce with an additional global marketing budget of $150 million.[11]

The exorbitant costs of producing, distributing, and marketing films have historically created high barriers to entry into the industry. In the so-called Studio Era, from about 1930 to 1950, five companies dominated the industry: Twentieth Century Fox, Warner Bros., Loew's/MGM, Paramount, and RKO (owned by the Radio Corporation of America). The Studio Era established the performance of the Hollywood film industry. With minor restructuring such as having to sell off theater chains and deal with the rise of television, oligopoly has characterized the industry's historical economic structure.

In 2010, six movie production/distribution companies dominated the domestic box, video, and DVD sales, and other ancillary markets such as television broadcast and cable. A snapshot of the North American (U.S. and Canadian) box office for 2009 demonstrates the level of control by the Big Six. In total, this so-called domestic box office generated revenues estimated at $10.6 billion.[12] Only Universal failed to break the $1 billion mark in terms of gross revenues. Using rounded numbers from Box Office Mojo, our picture shows that Time Warner led the pack with Warner Bros., accounting for 19.8 percent of the domestic box-office gross for a total of $2.1 billion. National Amusements' Paramount unit pulled close to 14 percent for a total gross of nearly $1.8 billion. Sony/Columbia was right behind with 13.7 percent of domestic market share with 13.3 percent and total gross of about $1.5 billion. At number four in 2009 was News Corp.'s 20th Century Fox, with 13.2 percent of the box office, grossing $1.4 billion. The Walt Disney Company's motion picture distribution unit, Buena Vista ("nice view" in Spanish), slid to number five, with a box office share of 11.6 percent and gross of $1.3 billion. GE's Universal studio placed last in 2009, taking in $890 million with 8.2 percent of the domestic box office.

Although it appears as if the Big Six controlled about 80 percent of the market, when one includes News Corp.'s Searchlight unit and Universal's Focus Features division, we can add another 4 percent to the Big Six market share for 2009. Even so, many of these so-called boutique studios were phased out as the Great Recession hit Hollywood.

In sum, since the 1990s the major producer/distributors have regularly taken 85 percent of the total market share, leaving independents with the rest. The movie industry has a dual economic structure: the core, made up of a handful of dominant firms, and a periphery, where numerous small and medium-sized businesses are found.[13] As Janet Wasko pointed out, through the late 1970s and 1980s, production/distribution had a three-tiered structure, with midsize firms operating between the core and periphery.[14] These companies were either bought up by the majors or driven from the business. We will first profile the Big Six and then discuss the enormous advantages that the core firms have over those on the periphery.

PROFILES OF THE BIG SIX

Warner Bros.: Big Kid on the Block

We begin with Time Warner, since its Warner Bros. film unit led the 2009 box office with nearly 20 percent of the total gross revenues. In 2009 Time Warner ranked as the 82nd-largest U.S. firm among the Fortune 500, with revenues of nearly $29 billion and profits of $2.47 billion.[15] Globally it ranked 259th, with revenues of $47 billion and losses of $13.4 billion.[16] By 2010, Time Warner turned its focus to providing content, after selling off Time Warner Cable (TWC) and AOL. Still, the filmed entertainment unit produced content for the company's Network division, including the CW Television Network (half-owned with National Amusements' CBS Corporation) and cable networks such as HBO and Cinemax. Its Picture House movie company was an internal joint venture between HBO Independent Productions and New Line Cinema. Furthermore, Time Warner's studios could count on exhibition at its twenty-one theaters and 223 screens in the United States and also through Warner International Cinemas with operations in Japan, Spain, and Taiwan.[17] Its joint venture in Italy, Warner Village Cinemas, was the nation's leading theater circuit. By April 2007, it had pulled out of the Chinese theater business due to regulations passed by the government in 2005 that prevented it from taking a majority stake in Warner-branded cinemas but continued other media operations there. At the same time it signed a deal with Abu Dhabi's leading real-estate developer to build a theme park, shopping center, hotel and jointly owned multiplex cinemas and announced plans to enter the theater business in India.

In the early 2000s, Time Warner had become a leader in the production and distribution of so-called franchise films, taking inspiration from Disney's long tradition of turning films into brands. In 2002, for example, Time Warner had around twelve franchise films in the works, including the lucrative Batman franchise. As Eileen Meehan rigorously demonstrated in her analysis of the history and synergies surrounding the development of the Batman franchise, Time Warner, through its ownership of DC Comics, had already established the roots of the franchise before the first Batman movie was released in 1989.[18] By 2002, after the release of four Batman films, the franchise had generated $2 billion. Worldwide, 30 percent came from the box office, 29 percent from home video, and 19 percent from licensing and merchandising. An additional 10 percent came from domestic television rights and 8 percent from foreign television rights.[19] By 2008, the seven Batman films had generated $1.5 billion at the domestic box office.[20]

In 2002, media beat reporters at the *New York Times* examined the intensification of the franchise strategy. They consulted the golden Rolodex (so-called experts cited to interpret media business news) and found a media analyst at Morgan Stanley who stated: "The movie industry has learned that they are, in essence, producing a consumer product" and "that shareholders expect to see returns, given the capital companies are committing to the movie business."[21] One result of franchising was that making a film took on an even more factory-like process. For example, screenwriters at Warner Bros. began writing multiple scripts based on a single character, sometimes two teams working on different scripts for the same film. The *Times* reporters found another result, citing no one in particular, that the franchise phenomenon "has led to the frequent complaint in Hollywood that the major studios seem to be abandoning the business of making Oscar-caliber movies in favor of more fiscally predictable fare" and cited "critics" who said the company had "retreated into mass-market safety."[22] The rather lengthy article ended by letting Warner Bros. president Alan Horn, "more auditor than auteur," have the last word: "Our job is to make movies that make money for shareholders. . . . We are producing entertainment. These are not teaching tools. We're providing mass entertainment for mass consumption."[23]

How could it be that Horn is being so very honest about what Hollywood is all about and at the same time be so wrong? Henry Giroux's concept of cultural pedagogy helps clear this up:

> Films do more than entertain, they offer up subject positions, mobilize desires, influence us unconsciously, and help to construct the landscape of American culture. Deeply imbricated with material and symbolic relations of power, movies produce and incorporate ideologies that represent the outcome of struggles marked by the historical realities of power and the deep anxieties of the times; they also deploy power through the important role they play

connecting the production of pleasure and meaning with the mechanisms and practices of powerful teaching machines. Put simply, *films both entertain and educate*.[24]

At the same time that movies entertain and educate us, they also generate profits that enhance the wealth and power through the control of cultural and intellectual creativity in film via their oligopolistic production, distribution, and marketing practices.

Disney: The Recycle Bin

We turn our attention to the second-largest transnational media conglomerate and member of the Big Six movie club, the Walt Disney Company. In 2009, the *Fortune 500* ranked Disney at number 60 with revenues of nearly $38 billion and profits of $4.5 billion, and it ranked 201 on *Fortune Global 500*.[25] The revenue came from Disney's four divisions: Media Networks, Parks and Resorts, Studio Entertainment, and Consumer Products. The *Fortune 500* reported that Disney's total revenues in 2010 were $36 billion, with profits of $3.3 billion.[26] Disney's studio entertainment division included Walt Disney Pictures, Touchstone Pictures, Miramax, Walt Disney Animation Studios, and Pixar Animation Studio.

Disney took out its main competitor, Pixar, in a classic example of horizontal integration. Horizontal integration involves buying out competing firms in the same line of business, in this case a competing animated motion picture studio. Such integration, along with vertical integration and conglomeration, underscores the overriding tendency of capitalism toward concentration and the control and planning of markets to avoid competition. The deal involved a stock transaction that gave Pixar shareholders 2.3 shares of Disney stock for one of their Pixar shares, for a total worth $7.4 billion.[27] Steven Jobs (number 54 on the *Forbes 400* in 2009, worth $5.1 billion), co-founder of Apple and of Pixar, became the company's largest stockholder.[28] By 2010, Jobs controlled 138 million shares, or 7 percent, of the company's total public stock traded on the New York Stock Exchange. Through 2010, Disney belonged to the Dow Jones 500 Industrials index, a key measurement of stock performance of 500 select companies, which signified the media sector had become part of big business.

Disney created Touchstone, Dimension Films, and Hollywood Pictures as in-house studios while acquiring or merging with independent studios such as Miramax and Pixar to extend the range and number of movies Disney could bring to the screen while protecting Disney's family-friendly image. By 2010, Disney began cutting back on smaller films and announced it had a buyer for Miramax, a private equity firm Colony Capital, so it could return to concentrating on more blockbusters rather than boutique films.

With the closure of the deal pending at the end of 2010, Disney integrated parts of Miramax into its Disney Touchstone unit. Disney's studios have sought to attract a wider audience demographic, including older teens and adults. However, it also maintained its formula of targeting younger teens by building stars from scratch such as Miley Syrus, also known as Hannah Montana, who started with a television show on Disney's cable network that soon became a motion picture event in 2009.

Disney has also long exploited the franchise strategy, recognizing its power in attracting preconstituted audiences. Its popular Pirates of the Caribbean amusement-park ride became one of its most lucrative franchises, bringing in $1 billion for three films. The 2006 release of *Dead Man's Chest* (Gore Verbinski) topped the domestic box office, shattering box-office records at $405 million in the first six days of its North American release and $960 million total worldwide. The film earned 40 percent of its revenues domestically and 60 percent abroad and became the fifth-biggest global release of all time.[29] Even though the domestic box office generally accounts for about only one-fifth of a film's total gross revenues, it is still the premiere site that determines how a film performs financially in ancillary markets such as DVDs, television, on-demand cable, and the Internet.

Disney's recycling of its film library at theaters and on videocassettes and DVDs became enormously profitable after the 1984 Betamax case. Disney, already the master of creating artificial scarcity in the theatrical market, stretched the strategy into video and DVD sales. For example, Disney's 1937 feature animation *Snow White and the Seven Dwarfs* (William Cottrell, William Hand) sold 27 million video copies when it was released in 1994. Disney released a restored DVD version of the film in October 2001, loading two discs with the movie plus extras, including a newsreel and thirty-minute radio broadcast from the world premiere; production timelines; storyboards, clips, and trailers; and a new performance of "Some Day My Prince Will Come," sung by Barbra Streisand.[30] Disney's artificial scarcity strategy involves withdrawing certain titles from distribution for certain periods of time. In 2007 it once again dipped into its library, re-releasing *Peter Pan* and *The Jungle Book* as a limited-edition Platinum DVD series. In search of new markets, Disney discovered an old medium: theatrical productions. Disney's invasion of Broadway has changed the character of the medium from one that often pushed the cultural envelope to one that features theatrical productions based on movies such as *The Lion King* (Roger Allers, Rob Minkoff, 1994), *Mary Poppins* (Robert Stevenson, 1964) and *The Little Mermaid* (Ron Clements, John Musker, 1989). Disney took artificial scarcity to new heights with the Disney Channel's *Hannah Montana*, moving it through a synergistic system from a television show into a one-time concert event charging monopoly prices, followed by the concert film. The company originally stated the film would be only in theaters for only one week but then exploited fan demand and extended its theatrical run.

Disney also showcases feature films on its ABC broadcast network, its owned-and-operated broadcast stations, and its cable networks, including the Disney Channel and the Family Channel. Touchstone teamed up with Disney's ESPN sports cable network in 2002 to produce the network's first-ever feature film for large-format theaters. *Ultimate X: The Movie* is based on footage from ESPN's 2001 winter and summer "X Games." This is a twist on an earlier Disney project in which life imitated art, when the company formed a National Hockey League team, the Anaheim Mighty Ducks, named after its 1992 movie *The Mighty Ducks* (Sam Weisman). From 1997 to 2005, Disney also owned the Anaheim Angels Major League Baseball team. Other media conglomerates also bought sports teams to provide content for their outlets. The Fox Entertainment Group owned 82 percent of the Los Angeles Dodgers from 1998 to 2000. Time Warner acquired the Atlanta Braves when it bought the Turner Broadcasting System in 1996, then sold the team to Liberty Media in 2007. While these companies no longer directly own sports teams, many among the *Forbes 400* and large media do. The hypercommercialization of sports is one result, for example, the sponsorship of lineups, plays of the game, television time-outs—all advertising within the delivery format of a sports event, not just the ads surrounding it.

Aiming at adolescents, the Disney Channel, a cable network, scored enormous success with the 9–14 age group with its made-for-television movie *High School Musical* (Kenny Ortega, 2006). The show attracted 7.8 million viewers and generated $100 million in profits from the DVD, sound tracks, touring concerts, and ice shows, among other uses of the brand. *High School Musical 2* made history as the single most-watched show of any kind on basic cable, with a debut audience of 17.2 million.[31] The film was offered as a special preview to subscribers of Disney Channel on Demand through Cablevision and Verizon. The Disney Channel jumped past Viacom's Nickelodeon Channel in the kids' cable ratings chase in 2006, as it continued to build stars from scratch and cycle them through its ancillary capillaries. In 2010, the Disney Channel topped the USA Network as the top prime-time cable network. Still, Nickelodeon held the number one spot for day-time cable that year.[32]

Rides in Disney theme parks in California, Florida, Japan, France, and Hong Kong are designed to remind visitors of the treasured properties in Disney's vaults. For example, Disneyland in Anaheim, California, has long featured rides such as Dumbo's flying elephants and the Mad Hatter's spinning teacups. In 2007, Disney revived its world-famous underwater submarine ride at Disneyland, this time as the *Finding Nemo Submarine Voyage*. One could also find a *Pirate's Lair* on *Tom Sawyer Island* within the park. The theme parks serve as a continual reinforcement of the company's internal projects, as well as the brands of other Fortune 500 corporations who sponsor rides and exhibits. Disney's Filmed Entertainment division produced only one-fifth of the company's revenue. The rest came from licensing of merchandise and a vast range of domestic and international subsidiaries, including the ABC broadcast network and ESPN sports cable networks (see table 3.1).

Michael Eisner served as Disney's CEO from 1984 to 2005 and built the company into a corporate empire. Roy Disney Jr., Walt's nephew, and the oil-rich Bass family (Robert M., number 65, worth $4 billion; Lee, number 158, worth $2 billion; and Edward, number 236, worth $1.5 billion, on the 2009 *Forbes 400*) put Eisner in charge. The Bass family bet big and gained control of up to 18 percent of Disney's stock. The family found itself exposed after the dot-com bubble burst, forcing it to sell its Disney shares in 2001 to raise cash to shore up sagging portfolios. After taking the Disney helm, Eisner went from movie mogul to media tycoon. In 1988, he became the highest compensated CEO for the year with salary, cash bonuses, and stock options for a total of $40 million.[33] Eisner eventually made it to the *Forbes 400* only to miss the cut in 2004; in 2007 he ranked with 82 billionaires who did not make the top 400, and by 2010 had moved on to hosting a cable news show on MSNBC.[34]

In addition to running the Disney empire, Eisner served as a so-called active member of the Business Council from 2001 to 2005, bringing the company into the arms of the corporate elite. The Business Council, founded in the early 1920s, is an invited membership club made up of 100 or so of the CEOs and chairpersons of leading U.S. companies.[35] The group has evolved into one of the major organizational sites through which the ruling capitalist class builds a general consensus regarding public policy that may affect capital as a whole. The Business Council is one of a handful of business policy organizations such as the Business Roundtable, the Chamber of Commerce, the Club for Growth, and others that belong to the permanent government made up of unelected capitalists and their paid ideologists. Their mere existence underscores the point that both the Republican and Democratic parties are merely two branches of the Business Party, the same party that pumped billions into the 2010 mid-term elections in support of business-friendly candidates.

Despite Eisner's personal financial gains and his fundamental role in building Disney into a major media conglomerate, Roy Disney Jr. (then number 361 on the 2007 *Forbes 400*, worth $1.4 billion) began a shareholder revolt as Disney stock prices stalled in the early 2000s. In 2003, Roy (then worth $900 million[36]) led a shareholder revolt, encouraging 43 percent of Disney shareholders to withhold their proxy votes for Eisner, an exceptionally high number for such a vote and a signal that Eisner's welcome was wearing out. Shareholders had expected more profits along with the

Table 3.1. The Walt Disney Company, Third Quarter 2007

- ABC Television Network (231 affiliates)
  - ABC Television Stations
    - KABC-TV (New York)
    - KFSN-TV (Fresno, Calif.)
    - KGO-TV (San Francisco)
    - KPVI-TV (Philadelphia)
    - KTRK-TV (Houston)
    - WJRT-TV (Flint, Mich.)
    - WLS-TV (Chicago)
    - WTVD-TV (Raleigh-Durham)
    - WTVG-TV (Toledo, Ohio)
- ABC Television Production and Distribution
  - ABC Family Productions
  - ABC Movies of the Week
  - ABC Studios
  - Buena Vista Productions
  - Disney-ABC Domestic Television
  - Disney-ABC International Television
  - Walt Disney Television
- Walt Disney Cable/Satellite Networks
  - A&E International (37.5%)
  - A&E Network (50% with the Hearst Corporation)
  - ABC Family Channel
  - BASS (BASS Federation Nation)
  - The Biography Channel
  - CTV Specialty Television Inc. (50%) (Canada)
  - Disney Channel
  - ESPN (80%)
  - ESPN2 (80%
  - ESPN Classic (80%)
  - ESPN Deportes
  - ESPN HD
  - ESPN2 HD
  - ESPNNEWS (80%)
  - ESPN Regional Television
  - ESPN Radio Network (750 station affiliates)
  - ESPN Radio Stations (5 stations: New York, Los Angeles, Chicago, Dallas–Fort Worth, Pittsburgh)
  - ESPN the Magazine
  - The History Channel (37.5%)
  - International Disney Channels (in order of launch date: Taiwan, U.K., Australia, Asia, France, Middle East, Spain, Italy, Germany, Latin America, Brazil, Portugal, Scandinavia, Japan, India)
  - Jetix Europe (73.6%)
  - Jetix Latin America
  - Lifetime Movie Network (50%)
  - Lifetime Real Women (50%)
  - Lifetime Television (50%)

- Radio Disney Network (54 markets)
- SOAPnet
- Star Sports (30%) (Asia)
- Toon Disney
- Walt Disney Consumer Products
  - Character Merchandise Licensing
  - The Children's Place (franchised)
  - Disney Interactive Studios (video games)
  - Disney Publishing Worldwide
    - Disney Global Book Group
    - Global Disney Magazines
    - U.S. Consumer Magazines
  - DisneyShopping.com
  - Disney Store (franchised in United States and Japan; owned and operated in Europe)
- Walt Disney Internet/Mobile Networks
  - ABC.com
  - ABCNews.com
  - ABCFamily.com
  - Club Penguin
  - Disney.com
  - Disney Mobile Studios
  - Disney Online
  - ESPN.com
  - ESPN360.com
  - Mobile ESPN
- Walt Disney Parks and Resorts
  - Disney Cruise Lines
  - Disney Vacation Club (8 resort facilities)
  - Disneyland Resort (California)
    - Disneyland
    - Disneyland Hotel
    - Disney's California Adventure
    - Grand Californian Hotel & Spa
    - Paradise Pier Hotel
  - Disneyland Resort Hong Kong (43%)
    - Hollywood Hotel
    - Hong Kong Disneyland
    - Hong Kong Disneyland Hotel
  - Disneyland Resort Paris (51%)
    - Disneyland Park
    - Walt Disney Studios Park
  - ESPN Zone
  - Tokyo Disney Resort (licensor)
    - Disney Ambassador Hotel
    - Disney Sea Hotel
    - Disneyland Hotel
    - Tokyo Disneyland

(*continued*)

Table 3.1. (*continued*)

- Tokyo DisneySea
- Walt Disney Imagineering
- Walt Disney World Resort (Florida)
  - Blizzard Beach
  - Disney-MGM Studios
  - Disney's Animal Kingdom
  - Disney's Wide World of Sports
  - Epcot
  - Magic Kingdom
  - Typhoon Lagoon
- Walt Disney Studio Entertainment
  - Disney-ABC Domestic Television (Broadcast, PPV, Pay TV, satellite, Web licensing)
  - Disney-ABC International Television (foreign licensing)
  - Disney Music Group
    - Buena Vista Concerts
    - Disney Music Publishing
    - Hollywood Records (incl. Mammoth and BV Records)
    - Lyric Street Records
    - Walt Disney Records
  - Disney Theatrical Group
  - Hollywood Pictures (and Home Video)
  - Miramax Film Corp. (and Home Video)
  - Pixar Animation Studios (and Home Video)
  - Touchstone Pictures (and Home Video)
  - Walt Disney Pictures (and Home Video)

Source: The Walt Disney Company, 10K Report, 29 September 2007

company's expansion. Eisner was pushed out the door in 2005. In 2006, George Mitchell was brought in as chairman of the board in order to give it a greater appearance of independence from senior management. Mitchell had served in the U.S. Senate for fifteen years, the last six as Senate majority leader. He established himself as a global troubleshooter for a number of multinational corporations or corporate sectors, including lobbying for big chocolate against a bill that would have required labels on chocolate products indicating whether the cocoa beans were harvested by child slave labor in West Africa. While he chaired the Disney board from 2006 to 2007, he was also a director at FedEx, Staples, and Starwood Hotels and Restaurants, and served as a member of the Council on Foreign Relations. Robert Iger, who had been a company man, having spent many years at ABC, came to Disney with its $19 billion takeover of Capital Cities/ABC in 1995. Iger was restored to the kingdom, earning him $30.6 billion in salary, stock options, and other financial stakes in the company in 2008.[37]

In 2010, Steven Jobs also served on the board of directors to protect his shares. Among institutional stockholders, FMR LLC, controller of Fidelity Management and Research Company, owned 92.3 million shares, worth $3.2 billion in mid-2010.[38] Fidelity was controlled by members of the family of Edward C. Johnson III (number 30 on the 2009 *Forbes 400*, worth $8 billion) only to be outranked by his daughter, Abigail, at number 17, worth $11 billion. In 2008 Disney's board of directors was interlocked with corporations such as Boeing, Estée Lauder, FedEx, Proctor & Gamble, Siemens Nixdorf (owned by the German consumer electronics giant Siemens), Visa, and Yum! Brands (see table 3.2). Another outside member serving to mollify shareholders was Father Leo J. O'Donovan, a professor of theology at Georgetown. Wall Street sees outsiders as independent of senior management and therefore more vigilant regarding shareholders' interests. While not a member of the capitalist class, O'Donovan's service, as with that of other interlocking board members, was the same: to protect and advance the specific interests of Disney as well as the interests of capital as a whole. In other words, boards of directors are never independent of the logic of capital: to generate profits.

The ties that bind Disney to centers of wealth and power are reinforced through its lobbying efforts and campaign contributions. These efforts are supplemented through membership in trade associations with deep pockets and powerful lobbying organizations such as the Motion Picture Association of America and the National Association of Broadcasters. In 2008, Disney alone spent almost $6 million on lobbying.[39] During the 2008 election cycle, the company spent $1.4 million on campaign contributions.[40] Disney's lobbying and campaign contributions have been multifold. It has primarily used its power and influence via the power elite and the state to gain access to global markets and to protect its intellectual property. In 1997, the company sent Henry Kissinger to China to smooth over its relationship with Chinese government officials after they showed disapproval of Disney's distribution of Martin Scorsese's *Kundun* (1997) about the Dalai Lama. Disney feared reprisals that would inhibit its operations in China, including its theme park in Hong Kong. Warner Brothers had passed on the film for the same reason, as did Universal, owned by Seagram and concerned about access to the Chinese liquor market.[41]

Disney has been a major combatant in the war on film piracy. Its lobbying and campaign money have resulted in legislation supporting trade sanctions against countries that fail to protect U.S. intellectual property rights. Each year the U.S. Trade Representative must report the status of the level of protection of U.S. intellectual property rights on a country-by-country basis. Those who fail to enforce intellectual property rights become subject to trade sanctions or the repeal of trade benefits. Other Disney-supported legislation included the No Electronic Theft Act, criminalizing

Table 3.2. The Walt Disney Company, Board of Director Interlocks, 2008 (Number of Ties)

- Banking, Financials
  - Bank of America Corp.
  - Deloitte & Touche
  - Morgan Stanley Group
  - The Shinsei Bank Ltd.
  - Visa Inc.
  - Washington Mutual Co.
  - Western Asset Management Co.
- Business Policy-Planning Groups and Think Tanks
  - California Business Roundtable
  - California Health Care Foundation
  - Catalyst Organization
  - Chamber of Commerce
  - Conservation International
  - Council on Foreign Relations (3)
  - Foreign Policy Association
  - National Academy of Engineering
  - Natural Resources Defense Council
  - Ohio Business Roundtable
  - Pacific Council on International Policy
  - World Technology Network
- Education
  - California Institute of Technology
  - Stanford University
  - University of California
  - University of Southern California
  - Xavier University
  - Yale University
- Government
  - Advisory Committee for Trade and Policy Negotiations
  - Bush-Cheney '04 (2)
  - California Public Utilities Commission
  - California State Board of Education
  - California State Water Resources Control Board
  - Committee of 100 (top G. W. Bush campaign donors)
  - Friends of Hillary
  - George W. Bush for President (2)
  - Hillary Clinton for President
  - John McCain 2008
  - Romney for President
- Foundations and Philanthropies
  - Children's Safe Drinking Water Net
  - Cincinnati Youth Collaborate
  - Cincinnati Zoo and Botanical Garden
  - Clinton Global Initiative
  - Japan Society
  - Lincoln Center for the Performing Arts

- Los Angeles County Museum of Art
- National Campaign to Prevent Teen Pregnancy
- Partnership for a Drug-Free America
- San Francisco Symphony
- W. M. Keck Foundation (USC Medical School)
- Weingart Foundation
- Insurance Companies
  - American International Group
  - Transamerica Corporation
- Other Corporations (former and current)
  - Apple
  - Boeing Company
  - Boston Scientific Corp.
  - Cisco Systems Inc.
  - Clorox Company
  - Edison International
  - Estée Lauder Companies Inc.
  - FedEx
  - Goodyear Tire & Rubber Co.
  - Halliburton Co.
  - Kmart Holding Corporation
  - McKesson Corporate
  - Motorola Inc.
  - Nike Inc.
  - Proctor & Gamble Company (2)
  - The Seagram Company Ltd.
  - Sears Holdings Corporation
  - Siemens AG
  - Starbucks Corporation
  - Sun Micro Systems
  - Sybase Inc.
  - Tenet Healthcare Corp.
  - Unisys Corp.
  - Yum! Brands Inc. (A&W, KFC, Long John Silver's, Pizza Hut, and Taco Bell)
  - Xerox Corp.
- Other Media Corporations (former and current)
  - ImpreMedia LLC
    - La Opinion (largest Spanish-language newspaper in the United States)
  - LivePerson Inc.
  - Times Mirror Company
  - USA Networks Inc.
- Trade Associations
  - Cosmetic, Toiletry, and Fragrance Association
  - Motion Picture Association of America

Sources: The Walt Disney Company, 2008 Proxy Statement, corporate and organization websites

the distribution of copyrighted works over the Internet, and the Digital Millennium Copyright Act in 1998, preventing decoding of encrypted formats, and stiff fines for copying or possessing illegitimate Disney products.

Copyrights cease to be private property when their statutory term of protection expires. In the late 1990s, Disney characters were headed for the freedom of the public domain. Disney exerted its political power in Congress to save its intellectual property from passing into the public domain by gaining the quick action of Congress in passing the Sonny Bono Copyright Extension Act, also known as the Mickey Mouse Extension Act. Disney's Mickey Mouse was set to enter the public domain, to be freely copied in 2003 (seventy-five years after the cartoon character became a popular cultural icon in the late 1920s). The act extended copyright for an additional twenty years for cultural works, protecting them for a total of seventy years after the death of an individual author and for ninety-five years from publication in the case of works created by or for corporations. The Supreme Court heard arguments against the Copyright Extension Act in late 2002. Opponents of the legislation argued that the U.S. Constitution sets limits on the terms of intellectual property rights to encourage intellectual and artistic creativity. In sharp contrast to the claim that copyright serves as an incentive to creative expression, those opposing the Copyright Extension Act argued that the vitality of the public domain is the key to creativity. Nevertheless, the Court decided in favor of the extension and stronger protection for private intellectual property rights.[42]

Disney is notorious for its aggressive protection of its intellectual rights, even though founder Walt freely mined characters and stories from classic fairy tales and novels in the public domain since they were free. The company has actively fought to protect its film vault and its characters. For example, it joined Universal Studios in a suit against Sony in 1976 to halt the distribution and sale of Betamax videocassette recorders on the grounds that home taping from broadcast television was an infringement of their copyrights. The Supreme Court ruled in 1984 that home taping was a fair use of a copyrighted work, but as the ruling came down Disney discovered a then new market in the sale of prerecorded video cassettes. Disney has often used copyright as censorship. In 1975, it used copyright claims to stop importation of Armand Mattelart and Ariel Dorfman's book *How to Read Donald Duck*, a critique of Disney's imperialist ideology. In 1978, the publishers of an underground comic book *Mickey Mouse Meets the Air Pirates* were shot down by a federal district court that found them guilty of copyright infringement for the depiction of Mickey and Minnie situated an urban milieu in which they encounter drugs and violence. Canadian artist Carl Chaplin created a *Wishing on a Star* free postcard series in 1983, one of which depicted the Magic Kingdom being vaporized by a nuclear bomb. Disney threatened an infringement suit unless he surrendered his 250 copies of the postcard to the company. He did.

Disney's actions contribute to a chilling effect where artists engage in self-censorship to avoid so-called unauthorized uses. Again, creativity is stifled rather than encouraged. The Disney film *Enchanted* (Kevin Lima, 2007) took ten years to produce from when the company bought the original script, as it was seen as not fitting of the company's image, that is, the likelihood of being rated "R." After several rewrites the film became a Disney celebration.[43] The company's first black princess finally made it to the screen, appearing in *The Princess and the Frog* (Ron Clements, John Musker, 2009), in the twenty-first century as Disney sought to exploit an untapped market in young black girls. The effort was based on economics, not inclusiveness, as historically Disney has offered significant quantities of racist, sexist, and classist content. This also makes its content prime material for parodies, especially mash-ups, largely protected by the First Amendment. Online parodies are abundant, and Disney chose not to pursue infringement suits because of the fine line between parody and an illegal use of a work and the bad publicity such an effort would generate. Disney could make them part of its revenue stream as the independent film company Lionsgate did in a deal with Google's YouTube. Lionsgate announced it would leave up posted do-it-yourself videos that used its intellectual property, as YouTube runs ads and even pop-ups on where to buy the film or television show being parodied. Lionsgate gets half of the ad revenues and potential sales.[44]

In 2004, Disney's aggressive protection of its brand and economic interests led to direct suppression: the company refused to fund the release of Michael Moore's *Fahrenheit 9/11* (2004) through its Miramax unit, even though it had put money into production of the film. This intervention by corporate headquarters did make the news. An Associated Press story appeared on the front page of the *State College (Pa.) Centre Daily Times* in the bottom left corner.[45] The film was clearly critical of the Bush administration, therefore too political for Disney's high-level decision makers. The reporter cites Moore, who suggests Disney did not want to endanger tax breaks it receives from the state of Florida, where Bush's brother, Jeb, was then governor. But it was then CEO Eisner who revealed the deeper political economic interests at stake, stating that the company "did not want a film in the middle of the political process where we're such a nonpartisan company and our guests that participate in all our attractions do not look for us to take sides."[46] The suggestion that Disney does not take sides masks the larger ideological influence held by this member of the Big Media.

News Corp. and Twentieth Century Fox

In 2010, News Corp. ranked 76 on the *Fortune 500* list of the largest U.S. corporations with revenues of $30.4 billion—but due to the Great

Recession also lost $3.4 billion.[47] It ranked 126 on the *Forbes Global 2000* based on revenues and assets in 2009.[48] In 2009, News Corp. was structured into six segments for reporting and managing purposes: filmed entertainment, television, cable network programming, direct broadcast satellite television, publishing, and other. Filmed entertainment consisted of the production and acquisition of live-action and animated motion pictures and television programming for distribution and licensing worldwide, mainly through Twentieth Century Fox. Its television division consisted of thirty-five television stations, including two TV stations in nine U.S. cities, and the Fox Television Network in the United States and Asia. Its cable network programming segment included the Big Ten Network, the Fox Business Network, and the top-rated cable news channel, Fox News. The direct broadcast satellite television used to include DIRECTV in the United States. In 2010 its satellite services included SKY Italia, British SKY Broadcasting (39 percent), SKY Deutschland (38 percent), TATA SKY in Asia (20 percent), and 20 percent of FOXTEL in Australia and New Zealand.

Its print and online operations included the Magazine and Inserts unit, which published free-standing inserts for Sunday newspapers in the United States, and an in-store marketing service, primarily for consumer-packaged goods manufacturers, in the United States and Canada. Its newspaper operations consisted of four national newspapers in the U.K. (*London Times, The Sun, News of the World, Sunday Times*), *European Wall Street Journal, Wall Street Journal Asia,* nearly 150 local newspapers in Australia—and in the United States, the *New York Post* and the *Wall Street Journal.* The publishing division also owned one of the major global book publishers, HarperCollins. Other operations included open end-to-end digital technology and services to digital pay-television operators and content providers; the News Outdoor Group, primarily operating in Russia and Eastern Europe; and Fox Interactive Media, which ran News Corp.'s Internet activities.[49] In a letter to shareholders in 2007, CEO Rupert Murdoch wrote that segmentation had a purpose: "It guarantees that we always have at least one generation of assets that can be considered our growth assets."[50] In other words, owning and controlling a wide variety of media outlets helps maintain regular revenue flows in the media sector, in which income tends to ebb and flow.

Murdoch maintained control of News Corp. in 2010; his total wealth put him at number 37 on the *Forbes 400* list, worth an estimated $6 billion in 2009.[51] The Murdoch Family Trust controlled 29 percent of the company's voting stock. Its second-largest shareholder in 2010 was Prince Alwaleed bin Talal al-Saud of Saudi Arabia (number 19 on Forbes Billionaire list, worth $19.4 billion in 2009) with 7 percent of News Corp. stock.[52] This connection came to light in 2010 when Talal al-Saud was revealed as one of the investors in the proposed Cordoba House, an Islamic-based ecumenical worship center two blocks from where the World Trade towers stood. Jon

Stewart of *The Daily Show* pointed out the irony that News Corp. subsidiary the Fox News Channel was helping lead the opposition to its construction with no one mentioning its second-largest owner. Before Talal al-Saud, Liberty Media, owned by cable TV mogul John C. Malone (number 141 on the *Forbes 400* 2009, with $2.3 billion), had been the second-largest shareholder. Murdoch felt his control threatened as Malone bought up to 19 percent of News Corp. shares. To get rid of Malone, News Corp. sold its 34 percent stake in the DIRECTV Group to Liberty in exchange for Malone's stock in the company. Malone ended up with 48 percent of the News Corp.'s DIRECTV in exchange for ensuring Murdoch's control of the company, with 29 percent of its stock.[53]

Twentieth Century Pictures became a film industry powerhouse in the 1930s, among them two Academy Award nominated films, *House of Rothschild* (Alfred L. Werker, 1934) and the screen version of Victor Hugo's novel, *Les Misérables* (Richard Boleslawski, 1935). That year it merged with the Fox Film Corporation. The merged Twentieth Century Fox Film Corporation (TCF) joined the ranks of the Big Five oligopoly that dominated the industry into the 1950s. By the end of the 1960s, TCF was struggling and near bankruptcy. Two films helped TCF get back on its feet, *Patton* (Franklin J. Schaffner) and *M*A*S*H* (Robert Altman), both released in 1970. After these hits, TCF launched the first episode of the Star Wars franchise in 1977. Its mistake was to let George Lucas (number 97 on the 2009 *Forbes 400*, worth $3 billion) retain control of licensing and merchandising rights. Still, with the Star Wars franchise, TCF moved back into Hollywood's top ranks. Marvin Davis, an oil tycoon, took over TCF in 1981 and sold it to Rupert Murdoch in 1985. Murdoch used TCF to launch and program the Fox television network, cable channel networks, and satellite programming around the world. In 2009, the Filmed Entertainment segment generated one-fifth of News Corp.'s revenue.[54] The 2006–2007 Annual Report stated the company's essential goal: "a business model . . . faithfully followed that keeps costs relatively low while minimizing risk."[55] Still, nothing could stanch the negative effects on News Corp. that came with the Great Recession. Its $5.4 billion profit in 2008 turned into losses of $5.65 the fiscal year ending in June 2009.[56] Table 3.3 lists News Corp.'s holdings as of 30 June 2009, listed in its annual report.

As the chart indicates, News Corp. was a transnational media corporation, part of a global media system controlled by the same companies that produce U.S. domestic intellectual and artistically creative works distributed to the public. Its broad range of media holdings requires constant vigilance over government policies. Ben Bagdikian wrote that Murdoch was driven by two basic motivations: "the accumulation of as much media power as possible and the use of that power to promote his deep-seated conservative politics."[57] He used his media outlets to support both Margaret Thatcher

Table 3.3.   News Corporation, as of 30 June 2009

- Filmed Entertainment
  - Balaji Telefilm (26%) (Asia)
  - Canal Fox (Latin America)
  - Fox Filmed Entertainment
    - Blue Sky Studios
    - Fox 2000 Pictures
    - Fox Atomic
    - Fox Music
    - Fox Searchlight Pictures
    - Fox Television Studios
    - Regency Television Studios (50%)
    - Twentieth Century Fox Entertainment
    - Twentieth Century Fox Film Corp.
    - Twentieth Century Fox Licensing and Merchandising
    - Twentieth Century Fox Television
    - Twentieth Television
- Television
  - ANTV (20%) (Asia)
  - Fox Broadcasting Company
  - Channel [V] Asia
  - Channel [V] (50%) (Thailand)
  - Cine Canal (33%) (Latin America)
  - ESPN Star Sports (50%) (Asia)
  - Fox Television
  - Fox Television Stations
    - WNYW (New York)
    - WWOR (New York)
    - KTTV (Los Angeles)
    - KCOP (Los Angeles)
    - WFLD (Chicago)
    - WPWR (Chicago)
    - WTXF (Philadelphia)
    - KDFW (Dallas)
    - KDFI (Dallas)
    - WFXT (Boston)
    - WTTG (Washington, D.C.)
    - WSCA (Washington, D.C.)
    - WAGA (Atlanta, Ga.)
    - WJBK (Detroit, Mich.)
    - KRIV (Houston)
    - KTSH (Houston)
    - KMSP (Minneapolis)
    - WFTC (Minneapolis)
    - WTVT (Tampa Bay, Fla.)
    - KSAZ (Phoenix)
    - KUTP (Phoenix)
    - WJW (Cleveland, Ohio)
    - KDVR (Denver)

- WRBW (Orlando, Fla.)
- WOFL (Orlando, Fla.)
- KTVI (St. Louis, Mo.)
- WDAF (Kansas City, Mo.)
- WITI (Milwaukee, Wis.)
- KSTU (Salt Lake City, Utah)
- WBRC (Birmingham, Ala.)
- WHBG (Memphis, Tenn.)
- WGHP (Greensboro, N.C.)
- KTBC (Austin, Tex.)
- WUTB (Baltimore)
- WOGX (Gainesville, Fla.)
- MyNetworkTV
- Phoenix Satellite Television (18%) (Asia)
- Premium Movie Partnership (20%) (Australia and New Zealand)
- STAR (Asia)
- STAR ANANDA (26%) (Asia)
- STAR CHINESE CHANNEL (Asia)
- STAR CHINESE MOVIES (Asia)
- STAR GOLD (Asia)
- STAR MOJHA (26%) (Asia)
- STAR MOVIES (Asia)
- STAR NEWS (Asia)
- STAR One (Asia)
- STAR PLUS (Asia)
- STAR WORLD (Asia)
- STAR UTSAV (Asia)
- Telecine (13%) (Latin America)
- VIJAY (Asia)
- XING KONG (Asia)
- Cable Network Programming
  - Fox News Channel
  - Fox Cable Networks
    - Big Ten Network (49%)
    - FSN
    - FX
    - Fox College Sports
    - Fox Movie Channel
    - Fox Pan American Sports (38%)
    - Fox Reality
    - Fox Regional Sports Networks (15 owned and operated)
    - Fox Soccer Channel
    - Fox Sports Net Bay Area (40%)
    - Fox Telecine (13%)
    - Fox Telecolumbia (51%)
    - National Geographic Channel–Domestic (67%)
    - National Geographic Channel–Europe (25%)
    - National Geographic Channel–International (75%)

(continued)

Table 3.3. *(continued)*

- National Geographic Channel–Latin America (67%)
- Premier Media Group (50%) (Australia)
- STATS LLC (50%)
- Direct Broadcast Satellite Television
  - British Sky Broadcasting (39%)
    - Sky Movies
    - Sky News
    - Sky One
    - Sky Sports
    - Sky Travel
  - The DIRECTV Group (39%)
  - Sky Italia
    - Sky Calcio
    - Sky Cinema
    - Sky Sport
    - Sky TG 24
  - TATA SKY (20%) (Asia)
- Newspapers and Information Services
  - Asia
    - *The Wall Street Journal Asia*
    - *The Far Eastern Economic Review*
  - Australia
    - *The Advertiser*
    - *The Australian*
    - *The Weekend Australian*
    - *The Courier-Mail*
    - *Sunday Mail (Brisbane)*
    - *Sunday Mail (Adelaide)*
    - *The Daily Telegraph*
    - *The Sunday Telegraph*
    - *The Herald Sun*
    - *Sunday Herald Sun*
    - Plus 135 additional metropolitan, suburban, and regional titles
  - Fiji
    - *The Fiji Times*
    - *Sunday Times*
  - Papua New Guinea
    - *Post-Courier (63%)*
  - Europe
    - *eFinancialNews*
    - *thelondonpaper*
    - *love it!*
    - *News of the World*
    - *STOXX (33%)*
    - *The Sun*
    - *The Times*
    - *The Sunday Times*
    - *Times Literary Supplement*
    - *The Wall Street Journal Europe*

- United States
  - Barron's
  - Community Newspaper Group
  - Dow Jones Client Solutions
  - Dow Jones Financial Information Services
  - Dow Jones Indexes
  - Dow Jones Local Media Group
  - Dow Jones News Wire
  - Factiva
  - *New York Post*
  - *Wall Street Journal*
- Magazines and Inserts
  - News American Marketing
    - FSI (Smartsource Magazine)
    - In-Store
    - News Marketing Canada
- Book Publishing
  - HarperCollins Publishers (United States, Canada, Europe, New Zealand, and Australia)
- Other
  - United States
    - Fox Interactive Media
      - AmericanIdol.com
      - AskMen
      - Flektor
      - Fox.com
      - Fox Mobile Entertainment
      - hulu (32%)
      - IGN Entertainment
      - kSolo
      - Myspace
      - RottenTomatoes
      - Scout
      - Slingshot Labs
      - WhatIfSports
    - Jamba (50%)
  - Europe
    - Broadsystem Ventures
    - Convoys Group London Property News
    - London Property News
    - Milkround.com
    - NDS (73%)
    - News Corp. Europe
      - Multimedia Holdings (50%)
      - NCE Television Group
    - News Outdoor Group
    - Propertyfinder.com (58%)

(*continued*)

Table 3.3.   (*continued*)

- Asia
  - China Network Systems
  - Hathway Cable and Datacom (22%)
  - STAR DEN (50%)
- Australia and New Zealand
  - FOXTEL (25%)
  - National Rugby League (50%)
  - News Digital Media
  - realestate.com.au (58%)
  - Rugby Union
  - Sky Network Television Ltd. (44%)

Source: News Corporation, 2009 *Annual Report.*

and Ronald Reagan. However, Murdoch has demonstrated that opportunism overrides political loyalty. As Eric Alterman put it: "When news values and business interests clash, business wins."[58] Murdoch abandoned the British Conservative party in support of Labour candidate Tony Blair, who made it clear that the party would not impose restrictions on British media ownership. He supported Hillary Clinton in her bid for the U.S. Senate by holding a money-raising party. News Corp. has deep pockets and will take losses if it means extending its conservative politics (such as the *New York Post* or the *Weekly Standard*—the latter having been sold to Clarity Press in 2009, or for many years the Fox News Channel).

Media scholars, critics, and activists reacted highly negatively to News Corp.'s takeover of Dow Jones & Company and the *Wall Street Journal* in 2007. In defense of the deal, Murdoch pointed to the autonomy of the elite *London Times* and declared that the public had nothing to fear about the loss of integrity in the *Journal*'s reporting. Still, the Bancroft family insisted on an agreement to limit Murdoch's control of the *Journal*'s newsroom and its pages, but it did not go as far as the family wanted.[59] News Corp. does produce film and video content that run counter to Murdoch's rebel conservativism, with content ranging from *The Simpsons* animated series to the barely clad women found in the pages of the *London Sun.*

The connection between ownership and content is not always direct. In the Fox News Channel, however, media owners can shape the content, form, and delivery of news, public opinion, and popular culture. At the same time, a film such as TCF's *Avatar*, with its alleged critical proenvironmental stance, may be not correlated to Murdoch's conservatism. Its profit-generating potential was obvious. The film's use of a 3-D spectacle did indeed attract mass audiences. Yet on a mid-screen analog television via a rather dated DVD player, it becomes apparent that the film actually has very little to say and special effects efface its potential subversiveness. The economic and cultural impact of this film cannot be dismissed. The film shattered global box office records,[60] had much more to earn in ancillary markets, and had at least two sequels in the works in 2010. Its production budget remained a mystery, with estimates ranging from $250 million to $500 million, plus another $150 million in marketing and advertising costs.[61] Its box office take as of 24 June 2010 was $749.5 billion domestic and nearly $200 million from foreign box offices.[62]

Murdoch's corporate supporting cast includes U.S. and global capitalists and politicians. The News Corp. board in 2008 had seventeen members, including Murdoch, who was chair; Peter Chernin, president and COO; David F. DeVoe, chief financial officer; and Arthur M. Siskind, senior advisor to the chairman, who served as insiders (board members who actually work for the company). Family members included James Murdoch, chair and CEO, Europe and Asia; and Lachlan Murdoch, another son. Stanley S. Shuman, a director emeritus, was also managing director of Allen & Co., an investing firm that had found that "there's no business like financing show business."[63] The investment bank has been involved in the financial dealings of some of the biggest media and technology companies, often facilitating mergers such as Disney and Capital Cities, and Seagram and Universal. It is run by Herbert A. Allen (number 239 on the 2008 *Forbes 400* list, worth $2 billion), who has held annual retreats for a "secretive gathering of media kingpins, technology geniuses, billionaire investors . . . [and] the occasional star athlete" in Sun Valley, Idaho.[64] For example, attendees in 2004 included Michael Eisner, Richard Parsons, Bill Gates (number 1 on the 2009 *Forbes 400*, worth $50 billion), Warren Buffett (number 2 on the *Forbes 400*, worth $40 billion in 2009), and Rupert Murdoch, who welcomed newcomer California governor Arnold Schwarzenegger.

Sites such as this one, off the map and out of public view, allow for both formal business dealings and also building a consensus regarding the primary mutual concerns of Big Media and big business as a whole. The 2007 retreat signaled the changing media environment, with Google and a number of computer software companies joining the gang. David Carr, *New York Times* media columnist, argued that Murdoch lacked respect among elites on both the East Coast of the United States and in London, but on the West Coast at Silicon Valley he "is truly among friends" and seen as a fellow "pirate" and "folk hero."[65] He really did not need to bother with what the establishment thought, since he was so well connected to them. Outside board members ranged from the author of the Patriot Act, the implementer of the No Child Left Behind Act, and a knighted subject of the British Empire to the former prime minister of Spain (see table 3.4).

In 1985, Murdoch entered the U.S. market big time via the purchase of the Metromedia Group, which included six television stations in major

Table 3.4. News Corporation Board of Directors Interlocks, 2008 (Number of Interlocks)

- Banks, Financials (current and former)
  - Allco Financial Group Ltd.
  - American Express Co.
  - Centaurus Capital
  - ChoicePoint
  - Commonwealth Bank of Australia
  - Fund Evaluation Group (2)
  - Goldman Sachs
  - Industrial and Commercial Bank of China
  - JPMorgan Chase Banks N.A. (Australia and New Zealand)
  - Kleiner Perkins Caulfield & Byers
  - Leeds Equity Partners LLC
  - Morgan Stanley
  - NAI Global (2)
  - Pacific Century Group Inc.
  - Rothschild Investment Trust Capital Partners PLC
  - Templeton Emerging Markets Investment Trust
- Business Policy Planning Groups and Think Tanks
  - Asia Society
  - Bancroft Associates PLC
  - Bilderberg Group
  - Brookings Institute
  - Cato Institute
  - Club of Madrid
  - Council on Foreign Relations (2)
  - Ditchly Foundation
  - Federalist Society
  - Foundation for Analysis and Social Studies
  - Hoover Institute (at Stanford University)
  - National Committee on US-China Relations
  - Technology CEO Council
  - Washington Legal Foundation
  - World Technology Network
- Education
  - Cornell Law School
  - Georgetown University (4)
  - Howard University
  - Stanford University
  - Tsinghua University (Beijing)
  - Woodrow Wilson International Center
  - Yale University
- Government (current and former)
  - Al Franken for Senate
  - Assistant Attorney General of the United States
  - Bush-Cheney '04 (2)
  - Clinton Climate Initiative
  - Financial Control Board (City of New York)

- Friends of Dick Durban (Senate D-IL)
- Hillary Clinton for President (4)
- Knight of the British Empire
- News America–Fox Political Action Committee
- Obama for America (2)
- Order of Australia
- Our Common Values PAC
- PAC for Change
- President's Foreign Intelligence Advisory Committee
- Prime Minster of Spain (1996–2004)
- Straight Talk America (McCain PAC)
- Transition Committee for California Governor Arnold Schwarzenegger
- U.S. Department of Labor
- U.S. Justice Department
- U.S. Secretary of Education
- Foundations and Philanthropies
  - American Judicature Society
  - Brain and Spine Foundation
  - Carnegie Hall
  - China Institute of America
  - Eisenhower Fellowships
  - Harlech Scholars' Fund
  - Jerwood Charity
  - Kirov Opera and Ballet
  - Liberty's Promise
  - Malaria No More
  - Markle Foundation
  - Motion Picture and Television Fund
  - Museum of Television and Radio
  - NAACP
  - San Francisco Ballet
  - Shipston Home Nursing
  - Stanley S. Shuman Foundation
- Other Corporations (current and former)
  - Ansell Ltd. (Australia)
  - Ansett Australia Group
  - Applied Materials Inc.
  - CLP Holdings (Hong Kong) (Asian electricity distributor)
  - Cathay Pacific Airways Ltd.
  - Chartwell Education Group LLC
  - China Netcom Communications Group
  - Compaq Computer Corp
  - Corning Glass
  - Educational Broadcasting Corp.
  - Ford Motor Company
  - Genentic Inc.
  - Hewlett-Packard Co. (2)
  - Higher Ed Holdings LLC

(continued)

Table 3.4. **(continued)**

- Intel Corp.
- Intermilling Ltd. (Malaysia)
- LSI Logic
- Laura Ashley
- Metcash Ltd. (Australia)
- NCR Corp.
- Philip Electronics
- Philip Morris International Inc. (2)
- Rio Tinto Ltd.
- Rio Tinto PLC
- Rolls Royce Group PLC
- Samuel Smith & Sons Ltd. (Australia)
- Tandem Computers Corp. (2)
- Other Media Corporations
  - *The Economist*
  - Independent Newspapers Ltd.
  - London Daily Telegraph Group
  - Lorimar Filmed Entertainment
  - NDS Group PLC (2)
  - PMP Ltd.
  - Reuters
  - Showtime/The Movie Channel
  - St. Martin's Press
  - Victorian Major Events Ltd.
  - Warner Books
- Trade Associations
  - Motion Picture Association of America (2)

Source: News Corporation reports, organization and corporation websites, www.muckety.com, www.nnbd
.com.

markets, from John Werner Kluge (number 35 on the 2009 *Forbes 400*, worth $9 billion). He used the broadcast stations to expand his global empire. Murdoch became a U.S. citizen to comply with Federal Communication Commission (FCC) regulations that limited foreign ownership of U.S. broadcasting stations to 25 percent. Before then, the FCC had granted Murdoch a waiver of the 25 percent rule to help grow a fourth national television network to compete with ABC, CBS, and NBC. It granted the waiver in the so-called public interest.

Ronald Reagan also helped Murdoch along by having the FCC waive the Financial Interest and Syndication Rule passed by the agency in 1972, which limited the number of hours the three major networks could use programming produced in-house for broadcast during prime time. The FCC's intent was to increase the number of independent television producers and create wider diversity. It worked for a while, as a number of new entrants brought programs such as *All in the Family* (1971–1979) and *Maude* (1972–1978), created by Norman Lear; *Soap* (1977–1981), created by Susan Harris; *The Mary Tyler Moore* Show (1970–1977), created by James L. Brooks and Alan Burns; and *Lou Grant* (1977–1982), also created by Brooks and Burns, along with Gene Reynolds. However, by the 1980s, the Big Six film companies had driven out independent television producers through direct control of the broadcast networks. By 2002, studio-owned networks (ABC, CBS, NBC, Fox) controlled nearly 80 percent of prime-time television production.[66] Murdoch had one regulatory setback, when he was forced to sell the *New York Post* in 1988 to satisfy FCC cross-ownership rules preventing one company from owning a television station and newspaper in the same market. It was only temporary, as he was allowed to repurchase the *Post* in 1993, when it planned to shut down—which would have left New York City with a single tabloid newspaper, the *New York Daily News*, owned by Mortimer Zuckerman (number 236 on the 2009 *Forbes 400*, worth $1.5 billion).

Murdoch received additional waivers when the penetration of News Corp.-owned-and-operated television stations into U.S. households exceeded the 35 percent cap under the National Television Station Ownership Rules (see chapter 2). News Corp., National Amusements, and other Big Media have sought to sweep away regulations that prevent newspaper and broadcast owners from belonging under one corporate umbrella in the same market. Nevertheless, News Corp. owned both media in New York City. Murdoch's flouting of U.S. law extends to the company's tax payments. Between 1987 and 1999 it earned hefty profits in Britain yet paid no income tax. News Corp.'s effective tax rates in the United States ran between 1 and 8 percent throughout the 1990s, compared to 20 percent being paid by the other members of the Big Media. News Corp. parked its profits offshore in order to avoid paying the taxes, and huge streams of profit flowed through more than seventy-five News Corp. companies in the British Virgin Islands, the Cayman Islands, and the Dutch Antilles.[67]

News Corp. has been heavily involved in both the lobbying and candidate-selection processes. Its lobbying expenditures reached $3.9 million in 2003, when Congress began looking at the activities of the deregulatory Republican-led FCC. Total lobbying expenditures from January 1998 to June 2004 approached $16 million. Campaign expenditures during this period totaled nearly $2.6 million, roughly $2.1 million of that going to the Democratic Party.[68] In the 2010 mid-term elections, Murdoch made a sharp right turn in his campaign donations, giving $1 million donations to the Republican Governors Association and the Chamber of Commerce, allegedly because President Barack Obama attacked *Fox News* in an interview in *Rolling Stone* magazine. In reality, Murdoch was just joining the "make government more business friendly" movement. That does not mean that News Corp. always gets its way. The Supreme Court upheld the government's powers to fine broadcasters who permit "fleeting expletives" such as "fucking" and "shit" in *FCC v. Fox Television*—words uttered during a Fox broadcast of the Grammy music awards during acceptance speeches. The Media Access Project called the 5–4 ruling unconstitutional under the First Amendment.[69] The case was remanded and a lower court threw out the FCC "fleeting expletive" policy as overbroad. At this writing, Murdoch has refused to pay the fine, while the FCC tries to refine its broadcast television obscenity rules.

The hands-on management style of Murdoch has led to several notable instances of direct censorship or distortion of news. In 1993, News Corp. and Time Warner launched STAR TV in Asia, its footprint covering Hong Kong, Taiwan, and the People's Republic of China. In 1994, the Chinese government banned satellite dishes in response to negative coverage by the BBC's World Service Television. Murdoch dropped the BBC shortly thereafter so STAR TV could continue operating in the region. In 1995, News Corp.'s HarperCollins book division dropped plans to publish the memoirs of Chris Patten, the last British governor of Hong Kong, who had offended the Chinese government regarding reforms in the former British colony. Murdoch admitted he did not want to offend Beijing. In 1999, an investigative reporter for a Fox television affiliate in Kansas City quit the company after editors watered down his expose about a pesticide made by Dow Chemical Company. In 2000, a local Fox reporter in Florida was fired for refusing to falsify a story on bovine growth hormone that implicated the powerful Monsanto Corporation.[70] It has also used its advertising dollars to punish other media outlets. In 1999 Fox dropped its film advertising from the *Hollywood Reporter*, an industry trade magazine, in retaliation for negative comments about the studio's movie *Fight Club* (David Fincher, 1999).[71] Back in 1992, Paramount Pictures had used the same tactic, threatening to pull its advertisements from *Daily Variety* after the industry trade magazine published a scathing critique of its movie *Patriot Games* (Phillip Noyce, 1992). *Variety*'s editors apologized to Paramount for the review, which they conceded was "unprofessional," and promised that the critic would no longer review the company's films.[72] Certainly such flak influences film critics. Only a few such incidents are necessary to lead to their own self-censorship. Furthermore, movie reviews often run in media outlets owned by the same parent company.

News Corp. also served as a powerful voice in the run-up to the 2003 Iraq invasion, forcing all 175 of its newspapers to support it. Fox News misled its viewers along the way and the effects were palpable, according to a survey of viewers for whom Fox was a primary news source. Fox reinforced three misperceptions that the Bush administration wanted the public to believe: (1) that there was solid evidence of an Iraq–Al Qaeda link; (2) that weapons of mass destruction had been found in Iraq; and (3) that the majority of the world supported Bush's decision to go to war. Eighty percent of Fox viewers agreed with one of the misperceptions, while 45 percent believed in all three.[73] In the first quarter of 2007, the Project for Excellence in Journalism conducted a content analysis comparing coverage across media of the Iraq War, the presidential campaign, and the death of Anna Nicole Smith. During the daytime hours, CNN's war coverage totaled 20 percent, MSNBC 18 percent, and Fox 6 percent. Coverage of Smith totaled 5 percent at CNN, 19 percent at MSNBC, and 17 percent at Fox.[74] Indeed, Paul Krugman, opinion columnist for the *New York Times*, argued that Murdoch "did more than anyone in the news business to mislead this country into an unjustified, disastrous war." If there were "justice," he "would be a discredited outcast. Instead, [with the purchase of Dow Jones & Co.] he's expanding his empire."[75] This all emanated from a man whose biographer for the Museum of Broadcast Communications called "perhaps the single most powerful media magnate ever."[76]

Paramount Pictures: All in the Family

Paramount Pictures is the next of our Big Six. In 2009, it was a unit owned by Viacom Inc. and controlled by National Amusements (see chapter 2). In this section we will focus on Viacom's two primary sectors: *Media Networks*, which included the cable networks, BET, CMT, Comedy Central, MTV, Nickelodeon, and TV Land, among others; and *Filmed Entertainment*, which included Paramount Pictures Corporation, producer and distributor of films by Paramount Pictures, BET Pictures II, DreamWorks Pictures, Dreamworks Animation, MTV Films, Nickelodeon Movies, and Paramount Vantage Pictures. Paramount Home Entertainment (PHE) was responsible for international sales of DVDs of these films and the cable network's television shows. And until 2006 the Filmed Entertainment sector also included the global distributor United International Pictures, jointly owned with Universal Pictures and one of the world's most powerful film industry distribution companies for decades.[77] We will also take a glance at its sister subsidiary, CBS, and its efforts to enter the filmed entertainment market.

Viacom's *Media Networks* derived its income through advertising sales, affiliate fees, and ancillary sales, such as sales of home entertainment products and licensing of consumer products. The division accounted for about 60 percent of the company's overall revenues in 2009.[78] The Filmed Entertainment division brought in most of the rest of the company's revenues from theatrical release, home entertainment products, and distribution to pay and basic cable, and from broadcast and syndicated television exhibition of its movies.[79] In 2007, its domestic box office numbers were boosted by its DreamWorks Studios rather than Paramount's own production output. DreamWorks Animation's *Shrek the Third* (Chris Miller, Rama Hui, 2007) grossed $322.8 million at the domestic box office, playing in 4,172 theaters. The foreign box office was $475 million for a total of $797.7 at theaters worldwide. Paramount/DreamWorks also had a hit with the $150 million film *Transformers* (Michael Bay, 2007), which earned $319 million and $387 million at the domestic and foreign box office respectively, for a total of $706.5 million. Both franchises remained lucrative through 2010 via sequels. Both films, with their characters already or easily adaptable to toys, also generated higher licensing and merchandising revenues for the company. Other Paramount/DreamWorks Animation projects in 2007 included *Bee Movie* (Steve Hickmer, Simon J. Smith) and *Norbit* (Brian Robins). The Paramount production *Beowulf* (Robert Zemekis) was the thirty-fourth-highest-grossing film in 2007, with $82 million in domestic box-office revenues.[80] Paramount's acquisition of DreamWorks included animated film titles plus fifty-nine live action films produced by the studio before its takeover. A 51 percent stake in these films was sold to two private-equity firms, Soros Equity Partners and Dune Entertainment II LLC, from which Viacom earned $675.3 million profits on a film library valued at $900 million. Plus, Paramount kept the distribution rights to the films.[81]

Paramount has been around second-longest of the Big Six. Adolph Zucker founded it in 1912 in New York, and in 1914 his Famous Players Film Company merged with the Jesse L. Lasky Company to form Paramount Pictures, based in Hollywood. It was one of the Big Five during the Studio Era and controlled a vertically integrated operation that included production, distribution, and exhibition. In 1948, the Supreme Court found the Big Five to have violated antitrust laws through control of theaters, the practice of block booking (whereby exhibitors had to rent a block of movies including the duds in order to get the hits), and the practice of blind buying (whereby exhibitors were forced to rent films not yet made). The court's decision forced the major companies into settling with the Department of Justice through a set of so-called Paramount Consent decrees, by which the studios admitted no guilt to collusive behavior but promised never to do it again. The decrees forced the studios to sell off their theaters and cease block booking and blind buying practices.

In 1966 the giant conglomerate Gulf + Western Industries Inc. bought Paramount during a wave of buy-outs of movie and music companies by large conglomerates. Wall Street had discovered that the music and film libraries were undervalued and encouraged the conglomerates to add the properties to their many lines of business to increase revenue streams. The logic behind conglomeration has always been to even out revenue flows as various industry sectors cycle up and down, so investors can count on steady returns. Wall Street also promoted media conglomeration, since these industries are naturally prone to cycle up and down based on big hits and expensive duds. At the time, Gulf + Western owned a wide array of unrelated lines of business, from auto parts to zinc mills. It also owned the Simon & Schuster book publishing house, which suppressed Mark Dowie's book *Corporate Murder*, even though Gulf + Western was not mentioned in the book, because it made all Big Business look bad.[82] Making movies and publishing books was not the same as making lingerie or running steel mills, and Gulf + Western sold off its assets to focus on the entertainment industry, renaming itself Paramount Communications Inc. Paramount then merged with Viacom Inc. in 1994 and became part of Sumner Redstone's media conglomerate. Paramount owned total rights to over a thousand films and various rights to another twenty-five hundred in 2008. Its film library contained many evergreen titles produced since World War II, including *Shane* (George Stevens, 1953), *White Christmas* (Michael Curtiz, 1954), *The Ten Commandments* (Cecil B. DeMille, 1956), *Romeo and Juliet* (Franco Zeffirelli, 1968), *True Grit* (Henry Hathaway, 1969), *The Godfather* films (Francis Ford Coppola, 1972, 1974, 1990), *Saturday Night Fever* (John Badham, 1977), *Ordinary People* (Robert Redford, 1980), *Raiders of the Lost Ark* (Steven Spielberg, 1981), *Reds* (Warren Beatty, 1981), *Patriot Games* (Phillip Noyce, 1992), *Terms of Endearment* (James L. Brooks, 1983), *Beverly Hills Cop* (Martin Brest, 1984), *Top Gun* (Tony Scott, 1986), *Ghost* (Jerry Zucker, 1990), *The Hunt for Red October* (John McTiernan, 1990), the *Star Trek* franchise, *Indecent Proposal* (Adrian Lyne, 1993), *Forrest Gump* (Robert Zemeckis, 1994), *Braveheart* (Mel Gibson, 1995), *Mission: Impossible* (Brian De Palma, 1996), and *Titanic*, coproduced with Fox (James Cameron, 1997).

Viacom entered the home video market in 1984, when it bought 82 percent of Blockbuster. By the early 2000s it was the dominant video rental-retail chain in the United States by a wide margin, with more than five thousand stores in twenty-seven countries. Viacom's entry into home video gave the company an advantage over other studios by allowing the company to profit directly from video rentals. Other studios sold their videos to retail outlets but did not benefit beyond that from the store's rental fees due to the First Sale Doctrine, codified in U.S. copyright law in 1909. The First Sale Doctrine was originally designed for permitting the resale of printed works, for example at a garage sale or used book store. Videos bought by retailers fell under the doctrine, meaning that they owed no more money to the studios after the initial purchase of the video cassette. For that reason, the studios charged $100 to $120 per prerecorded videocassette and deterred the rise of a home-video sales market. Hence, for National Amusements' Paramount it was like the Studio Era all over again, as it controlled production and distribution of movies, and had its own theater chains as well as the Blockbuster video stores.

Blockbuster had a profound effect on the video rental marketplace. Its buying power and brick-and-mortar rental stores entirely drove the original mom-and-pop video rental stores out of business. By 2010, a vibrant college town such as State College, Pennsylvania, home of Penn State University, had only one movie rental/sales outlet—a Blockbuster, a good distance from campus. This university town at one point had had at least seven video rental/sales outlets.[83] Why does this matter? Blockbuster stores provided mainstream film and video entertainment. The local mom-and-pop video rental/sales stores offered a much greater variety, since the choices of titles carried were made autonomously rather than determined by Viacom headquarters.

In 2004, National Amusements used a tax-free spin-off transaction giving Viacom shareholders a stake in the new Blockbuster, by then a corporation with more than eight thousand stores worldwide. The company's exit from the video rental/retail business came as a sign that the industry was facing challengers, such as Wal-Mart and Best Buy, which sold DVDs at deep discounts to attract shoppers for consumer electronics goods; rent-by-mail services, such as Netflix; online distribution of movies; video on demand; and rental kiosks. The well-known corporate raider, Carl C. Icahn (number 22 on the 2009 *Forbes 400*, worth $10.5 billion) immediately began buying up shares and by 2006 had effectively taken control of the company, joining the board of directors and becoming its largest shareholder. His renowned "magic touch" failed him this time, as his stake (once worth $300 million) shriveled by three-fourths by April 2010.[84] His losses reflected declining sales of DVDs, down 50 percent from 2000 to 2010. The introduction of DVD rental kiosks, particularly Redbox, also cut into DVD rental revenues.[85] The DVD rental company, formerly owned by McDonald's, became popular among retail stores for increasing foot traffic. Paramount set up a revenue-sharing deal, not a general practice of Redbox, along with the latter's agreement to destroy its DVDs rather than resell them.

In 2007 its box office share was bolstered by the success of *Paranormal Activity* (Orin Peli). Its marketing strategy was based on a traditional economic practice used by capitalists to raise prices by creating artificial scarcity. The film was first offered to a dozen college-town students, who worked to sell the film via social networking. Paramount then exploited the buzz by encouraging audiences to create demand to see the film by voting on the Internet. *Paranormal* became the highest-grossing R-rated film in a decade and brought in over $100 million in the first five weeks at the theater. The film itself cost $15,000 to make and only cost Paramount and DreamWorks $300,000 for distribution rights. Paramount began planning a sequel in late 2009. A long-time Hollywood lawyer noted that the sequel was not a "given" because it would be turned into a Hollywood film; the original earned its dollars precisely because "it was not a Hollywood film."[86] However, *Paranormal Activity 2* (Tod Williams), released in 2010, stuck with the formula, with a $3 million budget, and broke the weekend box office record for highest-grossing R-rated horror film. A cheap R-rated horror film may not be family friendly, but unlike Disney, the producers did not need to worry about synergies with a family-friendly image. Viacom was releasing 14 to 16 films per year domestically, including two to four films from DreamWorks Animation and Marvel. Paramount also kept the rights to *Iron Man 2* (Jon Favreau, 2010) in a deal made before Disney bought Marvel Comics, its effort to challenge Warner's DC Comics. In its report to stockholders in 2010, Viacom said that it would keep "focusing on key tent pole films" along with capitalizing on synergies for "smaller productions or acquisitions" as well as more fully exploiting its *Media Networks* unit, including MTV, Nickelodeon, and Comedy Central.[87]

When Viacom and CBS became separate companies in 2006, certain ties remained. For example, Viacom provided Paramount films at a discount to CBS's Showtime movie pay channel via a nonexclusive licensing agreement. When the agreement expired in 2008, CBS Feature Films announced it would produce four to six pictures a year for under $50 million. Its first acquisition was the rights to a best-selling series of espionage novels by Vince Flynn, published by CBS's Simon & Schuster/Atria Books. The plan was to build a franchise out of the main protagonist, CIA operative Mitch Rapp.[88] In 2010, CBS announced it was going to begin producing films in the mid-range of production costs, for about $50 million, falling between low-budget and blockbuster films. One example would be an adaptation of the classic TV western, *Gunsmoke*.[89]

Meanwhile, over at Viacom there was talk about entering the television program production business. The two companies, now in separate houses, had become competitors within the National Amusements family, as they remained sister subsidiaries. In October 2009, Viacom launched a multiplatform premium entertainment service called EPIX. Its partners were MGM Studios/United Artists and Lionsgate, and third-party films slotted to be made available through pay TV channels (an exclusive license that shut out HBO and Showtime), video-on-demand, and an Internet site. EPIX was primed to bring films from Paramount, Paramount Vantage, MTV Films, and Nickelodeon Movies, all within the Sumner Redstone mansion.

General Electric, NBC Universal, and the Universal Studios Group

In 2009, NBC Universal (NBCU), a unit of the General Electric Company, was another of the film industry's Big Six. GE ranked sixth on the *Fortune 500* and twelfth on the *Fortune Global 500* that year, with revenues of $183 billion and profits of $17.4 billion.[90] General Electric acquired 80 percent of Vivendi Universal Entertainment in 2004, while Vivendi kept 20 percent.

In 2007 Universal had settled to be at the bottom of the Big Six—an intentional strategy, with the aim of forgoing expensive blockbusters and focusing on mid-range budget films. In 2009, Universal garnered 8.2 percent of the domestic box office share and earned only $867 million, according to Box Office Mojo. This was after the most successful year in the studio's history, with three films surpassing the $100 million mark in domestic ticket sales: *The Incredible Hulk* (Louis Leterrier), *Mama Mia!* (Phellida Lloyd), and *The Mummy: Tomb of the Dragon Emperor* (Harold Young). In 2009, its third franchise film, *Fast and Furious* (Justin Lin), earned $350 million in worldwide box-office revenue. Universal created a separate studio, Illumination Entertainment, dedicated to family-friendly entertainment and run by billion-dollar producer Chris Meledandri. At the same time, its Focus Features division distributed works it called "original and daring films . . . that challenge mainstream movie goers."[91] Its most lucrative film/video division was Universal Studios Home Entertainment, with a catalog of more than four thousand films ready to be released from its vaults to feed new media outlets. The home video division also had a unit to distribute home video for nonmedia companies such as Mattel.

Universal is the oldest of the Big Six, tracing its roots back to 1909. Founder Carl Laemmle started up a production studio in New York, and by 1925 the company was vertically integrated with control of film production and distribution. In 1936, Standard Capital Corporation took over the company when the Laemmle family could not repay $750,000 it had borrowed from Standard. During the Studio Era, Universal belonged to what was called the Little Three, along with United Artists and Columbia. These were not fully integrated studios and focused mostly on providing "B" movies with low production and marketing budgets to supplement the output of the Big Five and maintain a constant supply of new product to exhibitors. Decca Records, one of the music industry's oligopolists at the time, took full control of Universal in 1952.

In the late 1950s, Universal was in bad shape and sold its studio lot to Music Corporation of America (MCA), a talent agency and television production studio controlled by Lew Wasserman. MCA took over Universal in the 1960s, and Wasserman turned it into a respectable competitor throughout the 1970s and 1980s, with major hit films such as *Jaws* (Steven Spielberg, 1975), and *E.T.* (Spielberg, 1982). It also controlled production of over one-half of all prime-time programs. In 1990, the world's largest consumer electronics firm, Matsushita Electric Industrial Co. Ltd., took over Universal Pictures. The deal occurred on the heels of Sony's purchase of Columbia and "prompted near-panic in the national press" that Japan would take over the U.S. media.[92] These acquisitions occurred simultaneously with Japanese investors buying up high-priced works of European art at U.S. auctions, upsetting the U.S. art world that had originally appropriated them from Europe. Many of the Japanese investors were corporations that had purchased expensive works for purposes of financial engineering; assets in art were used to conduct loan transactions and evade taxes.[93] The collapse of the Japanese stock market took care of any threat to U.S. economic hegemony and Matsushita. Indeed, Matsushita turned around and sold 80 percent of Universal to Canadian liquor manufacturer Seagram Ltd., while keeping the other 20 percent.

Edgar Bronfman Jr. ran Seagram at the time, and in a highly criticized move sold the company's 25 percent stake in the DuPont Company, which was generating 70 percent of Seagram's revenues. He took the $9 billion gained on the sale and branched out into media, buying up Polygram and Deutsche Grammophon, in addition to MCA/Universal. Bronfman's tenure as media mogul was a rough one. In 2000 Seagram sold itself to Vivendi in a $34 billion deal, creating the world's second-largest media conglomerate after Time Warner. Vivendi was in the water utilities business but its media interests included 49 percent of Canal+, Europe's largest pay-television company; 23 percent in British Sky Broadcasting Group; Havas, a major publisher of software, video games, books, and magazines; and Cegetel, France's second-largest cell-phone company at the time. With this acquisition Vivendi came to control the world's second-largest film library.[94] Vivendi also gained control of Seagram's stake in the USA Network, Sci-Fi Channel, and Home Shopping Network, along with theater chains in Europe and theme parks in Southern California, Florida, Japan, and Spain.

The deal was seen as Europe's answer to the AOL–Time Warner merger. Like AOL–Time Warner, the combination of Universal with Vivendi's cable systems gave the company control over both media content and the pipes that deliver it. Also like the AOL–Time Warner merger, the Vivendi-Seagram deal attracted the attention of government regulators, in this case the European Commission (EC). The EC set three conditions before allowing the deal to go through. First, it required Vivendi to sell its 23 percent stake in News Corp.'s BSkyB satellite television service. Second, the company had to agree to offer rival pay-television operators access to Universal films, while also guaranteeing that its cable service, Canal+ Group, would not hold first rights to more than 50 percent of the studio's film output. The third dictate concerned Vivendi's multi-access Internet portal, Vizzavi, a joint venture with the Vodafone Group PLC of Britain. In order to gain the EC's approval, the merged company agreed to offer rival portals access to its music library over the next five years. At the end of 2001, Vivendi announced its intent to acquire full control of USA Networks' film and television units in a complex deal through which John C. Malone (then number 90 on the *Forbes 400* list, with $2.1 billion), chairman of the Liberty Media Group, ended up with a 3.6 percent stake in Vivendi.[95] At the beginning of 2002, Liberty also held stakes in AOL–Time Warner (4 percent), Viacom (1 percent), and News

Corp. (18 percent), giving the company equity interests in four of the top six movie companies.[96]

By 2003, investors began dumping Vivendi stock, and the conglomerate began selling off assets to ease its severe cash crunch. After saying at first that Universal assets were not on the block, Vivendi turned around and sold 80 percent of Universal Pictures to General Electric while holding on to the Universal Music Group. General Electric's history in the media goes back to the early twentieth century, when it founded the Radio Corporation of America along with AT&T, Westinghouse, and United Fruit in 1919 and started the NBC radio network in 1926. FCC regulators put pressure on GE to sell RCA, which it did in 1932, but in 1986 GE repurchased RCA for its NBC television network and stations, while spinning off RCA records to Bertelsmann AG and the electronics division to Thomson SA. GE merged NBC and Universal into a media subsidiary called NBC Universal, with an estimated value of $43 billion.[97] The merger brought together Universal's film and TV vault and film and television production studios with NBC's broad range of media outlets, such as its broadcast network, cable networks, and television stations.

The GE conglomerate integrated NBC Universal into its vast range of unrelated lines of business. Table 3.5 offers a brief look at the sources of GE's other revenues in 2008, which include appliances, military hardware, financial services, medical equipment, transportation, and water.

GE's links to the capitalist power structure and government are vast. Because it is involved in so many lines of business, it maintains a large lobbying force in Washington, D.C., as there is hardly a day when legislation or regulations do not confront the company. It had particularly strong ties to the U.S. military via former head of the Senate Armed Forces Committee Sam Nunn. Other board connections included directors from Sustainable Performance Group A.G., advertising oligopolist Young & Rubicom, Avon Products, Penske Automotive Group, General Catalyst Partners, Wellcome Trust, John Deere Credit Company, ConocoPhillips, Loews Corporation, and from academia, a director from Massachusetts Institute of Technology. GE's CEO and chairman of the board, Jeffrey Immelt, alone had direct or indirect ties to Goldman Sachs, Federal Reserve Bank of New York, GEFS (Suisse) A.G., JPMorgan Chase, Oak Hill Capital Partners, Allstate, Campbell Soup, Dow Chemical Kimberly-Clark, Coca-Cola, PepsiCo., McDonald's, Merck, Pfizer, Citigroup, Eastman Kodak, Texas Instruments, Microsoft, a major philanthropy The Robin Hood Foundation, universities such as Columbia, Rochester, New York University, and media outlets including DIRECTV and Bloomberg, along with another two hundred or so affiliations.[98]

The merger of NBC Universal with Comcast, with general approval by Congress, the Department of Justice, and the FCC, closed in early 2011. It

Table 3.5.   General Electric Company, 2008: Nonmedia Holdings (Partial)

- Infrastructure
  - Bently Nevada LLC
  - Cardinal Cogen Inc.
  - Caribe GE International of Puerto Rico Inc.
  - Everest VIT Inc.
  - GEA Parts LLC
  - GE Aviation Service Operation LLP (Singapore)
  - GE Caledonian Limited
  - GE Drives & Controls Inc.
  - GE Energy Europe B.V. (Netherlands)
  - GE Energy Holding SAS (France)
  - GE Energy Parts Inc.
  - GE Engine Services Inc.
  - GE Gas Turbines (Greenville) LLC
  - GE Generators (Pensacola) LLC
  - GE Infrastructure Inc.
  - GE Ionics Inc.
  - GE Jenbacher GmbH (Austria)
  - GE Keppel Energy Services Pte. Ltd. (50%) (Singapore)
  - GE Military Systems
  - GE Osmonics Inc.
  - GE Packaged Power Inc.
  - GE Transportation Systems Global Signaling LLC
  - GE Water & Process Technologies Canada
  - GE Wind Energy LLC
  - MRA Systems Inc.
  - Nuclear Fuel Holding Co. Inc.
  - PII Limited
  - Panametrics Ltd.
  - Reuter-Stokes Inc.
  - Unison Industries LLC
- Commercial and Consumer Finance
  - Bank of Aydhya (33%)
  - GE Funding Finland KY
  - General Electric Capital Corporation
  - General Electric Capital Services Inc.
  - General Electric Financing C.V. (Netherlands)
  - Granite Services Inc.
  - Vetco Gray U.K. Ltd.
- Healthcare
  - Datex-Ohmeda Inc.
  - GE Healthcare AS (Norway)
  - GE Healthcare Bio-Sciences AB (Sweden)
  - GE Healthcare Finland Oy (Finland)
  - GE Healthcare Ltd. (U.K.)
  - GE Medical Systems Inc.

(continued)

Table 3.5. (*continued*)

- GE Medical Systems Global Technology Company LLC
- GE Medical Systems Information Technologies Inc.
- GE Medical Systems Société en Commandite Simple (France)
- GE Medical Systems, Ultrasound & Primary Care Diagnostics LLC
- GE Yokogawa Medical Systems Ltd. (Japan)
- IDX Systems Corporation
- OEC Medical Systems Inc.
- Viceroy Inc.
- Industrial
  - GE Canada Company
  - GE Druck Holdings Ltd. (Northern Ireland)
  - GE Fanuc Intelligent Platforms Inc.
  - GE Hungary Co. Ltd.
  - GE Inspection and Repair Services Ltd (U.K.)
  - GE Security Inc.
  - GE Transportation Parts LLC
  - GEA Products LP
  - GEAE Technology Inc.

Source: General Electric Company, Annual Report 2008.

became the largest media firm in the United States. At hearings in Chicago in July 2010, FCC chair Michael Copps raised concerns regarding the deal, estimated at between $15 and $30 billion, especially the potential of the Internet to become a "province of gatekeepers and toll-gate collectors."[99] Comcast acquired a 51 percent stake in NBC Universal, with GE holding on to the remaining 49 percent. Opponents of the deal pointed to the fact that Comcast would control both content and the pipelines that deliver it, discriminate against other content providers, and raise what are already monopoly prices. Furthermore, Comcast's power in the cable market also meant that it need not worry about quality of its service. In 2010 it reached 23.2 million via cable television services, 16.4 million via high-speed Internet, and 8 million by telephone.[100] Its cable segment provided analog cable franchises to full digital services, such as On Demand offering more than seventeen thousand movies and television shows over the course of a month. XFINITY TV, introduced in 2009, combined both video and high-speed Internet services.[101] Content providers included SportsNet (with eleven regional sports networks) and cable channels such as E! (Entertainment Network), G4, TV One, The Style Network, PBS Kids Sprout, Exercise TV, Fearnet, Versus, and the Golf Channel. Its Interactive Video Media included Comcast.net, Fancast, Fandango, Daily Candy, video service manager the Platform, and the address book Plaxo. Its Comcast-Spectacor unit owned the Philadelphia Flyers National League Hockey team, and until 2011 the Philadelphia 76ers National Basketball team, Global Spectrum, a public assembly management firm, Ovations Food Services, Front Row Marketing, and New Era Tickets. Comcast Spotlight was the advertising sales division of Comcast Cable that served advertisers, with a presence in approximately 30 million owned and represented subscribers in ninety markets providing "a wide range of advertising solutions that help advertisers harness the enormous power of cable advertising."[102]

Brian L. Roberts, son of Ralph J. Roberts, founder of Comcast, served as its president, CEO, and chairman of the board in 2010. He was also the company's largest sole shareholder with 33 percent of its voting stock and the 47th-highest-paid chief executive in 2009 according to *Forbes*, at $16.4 million.[103] He also served as the director of the National Cable Television Association, the cable industry's trade association. Other board members had direct ties to Fannie Mae, Tyco International, Aegis, International Flavors and Fragrances, Catalyst, the Bank of New York Mellon, PepsiCo., AMR Corporation, Citigroup, the Rockefeller Foundation, Sotheby's, and even Time Warner Cable through secondary links (the NCTA and Cable Television Labs). The combination of Comcast and GE's powerful connections to other major corporations, banks, business policy groups, philanthropies and charities, trade associations, government, and so on was significantly extended. Comcast spent about $3 million on campaign contributions in the 2008 election cycle, half from individuals and half from its political action committees. By August of the 2010 election cycle the figure was already at $2.5 million, much of it targeted at key members of Congress who need to approve the merger. Lobbying expenditures neared $7 million by late summer 2010; an additional 196 lobbyists had been hired, with 15 of them coming through the revolving door from the public to the private sector, including several former chiefs of staff to key legislators and policymakers.[104]

The acquisition of NBC gave Universal a huge advantage, with the vertical integration of production and film and television libraries; the NBC television network and its owned-and-operated television stations; and cable networks such as CNBC, MSNBC, USA, Bravo, Syfy, the Weather Channel, A&E, Lifetime, and the History Channel. NBC Universal and its affiliated units had sunk $1.7 million into congressional coffers by August 2010. GE's total lobbying expenditures by the end of July 2010 were $17 million, of which $250,000 came from NBC Universal.[105] By fall 2010, it already appeared that the merger would gain government approval and Comcast would get what it wanted: "*to build a moat around its business* so that it could avoid being treated like a commodity transport provider."[106] Josh Silver of Free Press predicted that the approval of the merger "would trigger a new wave of mega-mergers, as other giants like News Corp. and Disney bulk up to exert more control over new media" and merely provide more of what is already given: "higher prices, fewer independent and local voices, and the same cookie-cutter content wherever we go."[107] What this reminds us, once again, is that though we see that capitalism is dynamic, its overall tendency is toward concentration, as capitalists would rather control markets than compete, imposing the marketplace restraints of freedom of expression that comes naturally to the system.

Sony: From Cinema Screen to Home Theater

In 2010 the Sony Corporation of Tokyo, Japan, controlled the subsidiary Sony Corporation of America. Its principal U.S. business divisions included Sony Electronics, Sony Computer Entertainment America, Sony Pictures Entertainment, and Sony Music Entertainment. Sales revenue for Sony Corporation consolidated at the fiscal year ending in March 2010 was $78 billion. The company boasted 1,006 consolidated affiliates worldwide. This put Sony at number 69 on the *Fortune Global 500* list of top companies.[108] Sony's motion picture unit took in $7.2 billion in 2009, with a domestic box office market share of 13.7 percent and gross revenues of $1.45 billion.[109] Sony Pictures also had a vast reach within the global media market. Filmed entertainment accounted for 9.8 percent of the company's overall revenues; 7.1 percent came from music, and 21 percent from video gaming. Sony's film division, Columbia TriStar Motion Picture Group, released about twenty-four films in fiscal year 2009.[110]

In 2010, Sir Howard Springer served as Sony Corporation's CEO and chairman of the board, a position he had held since 2005. He was also CEO and chairman of Sony Corporation of America, a position he occupied since 1998. In 1999, he was confirmed as a Knight Bachelor by Queen Elizabeth II. The Welsh-born Stringer served as chairman of the board of trustees for a number of charities, arts organizations, and philanthropies, including the American Film Institute. He was the U.S. chairman of the British Army Benevolent Fund, and member of the boards of the Paley Center for Media, New York Presbyterian Hospital, the American Theater Wing, Lincoln Center, Carnegie Hall, and Teach for America. His corporate connections included chairman of a Sony-Ericson fifty-fifty joint venture for developing mobile phones.[111] In 2010, Stringer had 274 ties to other major corporations, banks, and private investment firms, such as Allen & Co. (see News Corp. above) via the charity/philanthropy network. Indeed, meetings at these power-structure sites brought Stringer face-to-face with competing media companies including GE, Walt Disney, Time Warner, CBS and Viacom, News Corp., New York Times Co., Nielsen, Random House, and IAC/Interactive.[112] Other Sony board members included the chair of Toyota, vice-president of British Quality Foundation (a corporate strategy consultant company), Vail Resorts, the CEO and chair of Berlitz International, the Carlyle Group (a private-equity firm), the CEO and chair of

Chugai Pharmaceutical (a subsidiary of Roche Holding AG), and the CEO and chair of Mitsubishi.

Like the other film majors, Sony has long been involved in seeking assistance from the U.S. government when its special interests or those of its corporate allies are threatened. Sony was the plaintiff in the Betamax case (see above) when Universal and Disney sued to halt the distribution of Sony's Betamax videocassette recorder. While Disney withdrew from the case, Universal fought Sony all the way to the U.S. Supreme Court. Sony won with a ruling in 1984 that upheld the rights of VCR users to record and watch broadcast television programs at a later time (known then as time-shifting). Sony also showed its clout in Congress while the case was pending in the courts, where it lobbied for home-recording rights legislation that would make time-shifting illegal. Like all content providers, Universal regards the protection of its intellectual property rights as imperative. Thus Sony must seek legislation through lobbying and campaign contributions to gain congressional legislation to protect these rights, for example in the fight against audio and video piracy. According to the Center for Responsive Politics, in 2009 Sony ranked tenth among TV/movie/music companies and trade associations, spending nearly $3.6 million. Sony's lobbying expenditures in 2004 were just over $1 million but jumped to nearly $4 million in 2007.[113] In the 2009 election cycle, Sony contributed $1.1 million to federal and state candidates via its PACs, employees, and owners. Sony Entertainment kicked in an additional $64,000 in state-level contributions, to garner state funding to subsidize filmmaking.[114]

Sony charged into the media content industry when it bought CBS records in 1988 for $2 billion and Columbia Pictures from the Coca-Cola Company in 1989 for $4.9 billion. Coca-Cola had tried various ways to insert its products into Columbia films in an early attempt to use product placement as a way of exploiting the captive film audience. The effort was premature compared to the massive quantities of such placements by 2010, although the effects of Coca-Cola's ownership on content are evident in "*Missing*" (Costa-Gavras, 1982), a film about two U.S. citizens caught up in the military coup d'état in Chile that ousted the democratically elected president, Salvador Allende. Coca-Cola was cinematically associated with the resistance to the coup, while Pepsi was associated with the brutal dictatorship of Augusto Pinochet. Still, after several expensive flops, Coca-Cola shareholders did not see any significant value to owning a major movie producer/distributor. Sony's purchase of Coca-Cola led to the acquisition of the rights to 3,500 movies and 23,000 television episodes. It intended to use its media software to drive the sale of its consumer electronics hardware. Its first effort to use content to win electronic format wars flopped with the Betamax video recorder. Sony's refusal to license the technology to other manufacturers and lack of Betamax pre-recorded videocassettes at rental shops allowed the VHS standard to become dominant.

At the same time, Sony accelerated a trend toward vertical reintegration that began when major studios started buying theater outlets in the 1980s. In 1948 this form of integration was found to be illegal by the Supreme Court. To settle the antitrust suit, the major production/distribution/exhibition firms were banned from owning theaters. Enforcement of the consent decrees lapsed after the election of President Ronald Reagan, who sought to pay off the film industry for financially supporting his political career. In 1997, Sony merged its Loews theater exhibition group with the Cineplex Odeon theater chain, partially owned by Universal Pictures' parent company Seagram. At the time, the deal created the second-largest theater chain in North America. Sony and Universal sought to re-create the illegal vertical integration of the studio era of the 1930s and 1940s, when just five companies controlled movie production, distribution, and exhibition. By 1997, according to Standard & Poor's, the major movie companies had gained control of 8 percent of U.S. movie screens, with many in prime locations.[115] However, vertical integration did not pay off for Sony and Universal, and in early 2001 Loews filed for bankruptcy. The problem was not with the vertical model but rather a matter of overbuilding theater complexes when actual theater admissions failed to increase. Between 1995 and 1999, the number of movie screens increased 34 percent, while admissions increased by only 16 percent.[116]

In addition to Loews, a number of other large theater chains filed for bankruptcy beginning in 1999, including United Artists Theatre Co., General Cinema Theatres, Carmike Cinemas Inc., and Regal Cinemas. Regal Cinemas was one of the world's largest theater chains in 2002, with 350 theaters and four thousand screens. Small theater chains filed for bankruptcy as well. These included the nation's oldest family-owned-and-operated theater chain, Wehrenberg Theaters, with 199 screens, and the closely held Edwards Theater Circuit Inc. of Newport Beach, California.[117] Commercial developers and their financial backers could take partial blame for the dire straits of the theater business. Before lending money to developers of large suburban shopping malls, bankers required guaranteed tenants, including national retail stores and movie chains. While the movie chains went on a building spree, many older urban theaters went into decline and were closed to cut costs and pay off creditors. Vivendi Universal cut its ties to Loews in 2001, selling its entire 25.6 percent stake (15 million common shares) for a nominal payment of one dollar to the Goldman Sachs Group. Vivendi then qualified for a tax write-off that offset its capital gains for taxes for the year.[118]

As the theater chains came out of bankruptcy, ownership and control of the industry shifted to finance capital. In late 2001, Canada's Onex Corp., a publicly traded buyout firm based in Toronto, and Oaktree Capital Management LLC, a "distressed-debt specialist" based in Los Angeles, announced their intent to acquire General Cinema Theatres as it came out of bankruptcy.[119] The most striking development involved the fire-sale acquisitions of the cinema chains Edwards Theater Circuit, United Artists, and Regal Cinemas by Philip Anschutz, chairman of Quest Communications International Inc. (then number 16 on the 2001 *Forbes 400* list, with $9.6 billion).[120] When the dust from bankruptcy proceedings began to settle at the beginning of 2002, Anschutz had parlayed his oil, rail, and fiber-optic wealth into ownership of 20 percent of U.S. theater screens. Anschutz also owned the Los Angeles Kings National Hockey League team, part of the Los Angeles Lakers National Basketball Association franchise, the Staples Center in which the teams play, and a concert promotion company. He also founded two movie production companies, Crusader and Walden Media, with the goal of producing "films with a family bent."[121] With 20 percent of the nation's theaters poised to screen them, these films had a better chance of being seen, and Anschutz had an opportunity to impose on Hollywood the kinds of films he believed should be produced. In 2010, Regal remained the largest theater chain, with 6,800 screens at some 550 theaters in nearly forty states. Anschutz controlled 78 percent of its voting stock, and by August 2010 ranked number 34 on the *Forbes 400*, worth $7 billion. The privately held Anschutz Corporation controlled 78 percent of REG, with more than 120 entertainment venues worldwide, and sponsored many of the performances inside by underwriting tours such as the Black Eyed Peas, Cher, Jon Bon Jovi, and others.

Once out of the theater business, Sony took a different direction, exploiting vertical relations via the use of its movie, television programming, video games, and music in home entertainment systems. Sony had fallen behind in the production of television sets, having focused primarily on the Triniton, but the company jumped back quickly with its own high-definition televisions. It also won the format war for high-definition DVDs with Blu-ray against Toshiba's HD DVD system, despite the latter having the support of three Hollywood studios. Ultimately, it was Wal-Mart, the largest retailer of DVDs, which put the final nail in the HD DVD coffin when it chose to exclusively sell Blu-ray, following similar decisions by Best Buy and Netflix in early 2008. The Blu-ray DVD player accelerated changes in the way, place, and times audiences experienced film. The convenience and sophistication of home entertainment systems threatened earnings at the theatrical box office, yet for Sony it was a win-win situation.

As with the rapid increase in household penetration of television in the 1950s, producers of theatrical films, as well as exhibitors, had to make movies spectacular to keep audiences coming to the theater. The same strategy reemerged in the first decade of the twenty-first century, including the revival of 3-D films. Theaters charged more for 3-D films; Disney's *Meet the Robinsons* (Steven J. Anderson, 2007) and the Paramount–Warner Bros. joint production *Beowulf* (Steven Zemeckis, 2007) earned twice as much at the box office at 3-D venues than at regular venues.[122] Admission to Disney's 3-D film *Hannah Montana/Miley Cyrus: Best of Both Worlds Concert Tour*, released in early 2008, cost $15. The success of these films forced exhibitors to convert more screens to digital, of course at a cost. In 2007, Imax and AMC Entertainment's theater chain announced that they would open one hundred new Imax theaters for large-format 3-D films. Imax provided the projectors, at $500,000 each, and AMC picked up the costs of reconfiguring the seats and enlarging the screens.[123] The trend toward special effects and higher ticket prices went hand in hand. For Sony, however, success at the box office led to even more revenues from the DVD market, video games, and digital delivery of its content. For the rest of the studios, 3-D allowed for increases in ticket prices and created event movies such as *Alice in Wonderland* (Tim Burton, 2010) from Disney and of course *Avatar*, off-setting declining theater attendance. Meanwhile, Sony was working on a video-game console that would tie Hollywood with the Internet for home viewing of its film and television libraries, while also exploiting them on portable communications devices without making it easier to copy illegally.

Hollywood's response to movie pirates—undercutting the market for pirated films with lower-priced, higher-quality products—is a well-rehearsed strategy that also includes litigation and legislation aimed at outlawing the theft of intellectual property. The strategy can be traced back to the early 1970s, when the International Federation of Phonographic Industries attempted to stop music cassette piracy in Hong Kong. Faced with increasing videocassette piracy in the early 1980s, Hollywood also targeted Hong Kong in an effort to protect its copyrights. The studios, along with other major copyright owners, worked with the Hong Kong legislature to secure increased criminal penalties for videocassette piracy, and then with local enforcement agencies (police, customs, and tax agents) to crack down on duplicating labs and exporters of illegal videos. Disney supplemented these efforts with its own investigative force, leading to dozens of copyright infringement lawsuits against Hong Kong's video pirates. At the same time, Hollywood sought to undercut videocassette piracy by establishing "legitimate" relations with video producers and dealers, and by cutting prices on prerecorded videocassettes to reduce the differential between pirated and studio-released copies.[124] The introduction of digital video discs moved the piracy problem to a higher level. The digitalization of film and video content allowed copies to be made at a rapid and high quality-level. It also opened the door to illegal uploading and sharing of copyrighted works in the MP3 format.

At the dawn of the digital age, Hollywood joined other copyright owners to protect their intellectual property using four basic strategies: legislation, encryption, litigation, and market penetration. It first sought legislation through Congress, which passed the No Electronic Theft Act (NETA), aimed at criminalizing the distribution of copyrighted works over the Internet. The Digital Millennium Copyright Act of 1998 (DMCA) made Internet service providers (ISPs) responsible for policing the distribution of copyrighted materials. The ISPs would be exempt from copyright infringement if they followed the "notice and take down" procedures, essentially removing the infringing material from their servers. Another key aspect of the DMCA made it illegal to decode encrypted DVDs or to wash out watermarks used to block and trace the unauthorized use of copyrighted works. Several constituencies, including libraries, universities, and computer programmers, protested this provision of the DMCA, arguing that encryption technologies limited freedom of expression and therefore violated both fair use and First Amendment principles. Matthew Jackson concluded that the "DMCA as a whole was a significant step toward the reprivatization of copyright" and that its primary purpose was to promote the development of e-commerce.[125] The two acts provided copyright owners with the legal protection they needed to proceed with the development and deployment of encryption technologies through digital rights management (DRM) programs.

As the filmed entertainment industry had already learned with its war on videocassette piracy, copyright laws are useless unless they are enforced. With the backing of the state and the implementation of DRM systems, copyright owners turned to their third strategy, litigation. In 1999, the Motion Picture Association of America (MPAA) successfully sued the publisher of a hacker publication, forcing him to take down links publicizing a DVD descrambling system called DeCSS, which enabled users of the open source Linux program to play DVDs on their home computers. The MPAA's main concern was that DeCSS not only violated the DMCA, but also served as the platform for massive sharing of movies online. The MP3 digital format led to the explosion of websites dedicated to sharing music files such as MP3.com, Napster, and Aimster, until they were shut down through litigation or forced to adopt legal business practices. These services were then supplanted by peer-to-peer (P2P) services such as Morpheus, KaZaA, and Grokster that bypassed a central server by transforming every online computer user into a potential distributor of unauthorized digital works. The copyright industries, led by the music industry, fought back by gaining court permission to subpoena ISPs to acquire names of individuals suspected of infringing copyrights in order to proceed with litigation against them. This in turn, imposed a system of panoptic surveillance in order to "territorialize the Internet in the service of corporate capital."[126]

Legislation, encryption, and litigation are the basic means by which copyright owners seek marketplace legitimatization, to force out intellectual property pirates. Hollywood's efforts to capture the Internet as an ancillary outlet began in August 2001, when five of the major studios announced a joint venture to deliver movies over the Internet. A front-page article in the *San Diego Union-Tribune* cited studio executives predicting that this was the "first step to the coming world of true video-on-demand when consumers will be able to watch any movie they want, whenever they want."[127] The players included Paramount, Warner Brothers, Universal Pictures, MGM, and Sony Pictures. Sony's Moviefly subsidiary (later named Movielink), an Internet movies-on-demand service, was to provide the platform for the new venture. The studios planned to release a hundred or so recent movies from their libraries for computer users with broadband connections to download and view at their leisure. The system was designed so that a downloaded movie would stay on the computer hard drive for thirty days or until the file was opened. Then the clock would start ticking. Within twenty-four hours of opening the file, viewers could watch the film as often as they pleased and reverse, pause, or fast-forward at will. Twenty-four hours after the initial download, the film would erase itself.

The release of such a small number of titles from studio vaults holding thousands of movies betrayed the consortium's concern about the security of online film distribution. The studios saw no choice, since piracy of movies on the Internet was just beginning and the technology for illegal downloading of films, as opposed to music, was also in its infancy. In July 2001, Media-Force, a digital copyright enforcement firm, listed its top ten movies pirated online, including films that had yet to be released in home video formats, such as *Dude, Where's My Car?* (Danny Leiner, 2000) from Fox and *Crouching Tiger, Hidden Dragon* (Ang Lee, 2000) from Sony Pictures Classics.[128] The studios hoped that by offering easy access and high-speed delivery of their own movies they could preempt the emerging digital piracy industry.

Sony extended its efforts to preempt digital piracy a week after the Moviefly deal was announced by striking another deal with the New York–based inDemand, a cable pay-per-view network then owned by four of the largest cable companies in the United States (AT&T Broadband, AOL–Time Warner, Comcast, and Cox Communications). The service was designed to allow subscribers to choose from a selected list of movies to watch at their convenience. In the deal, Sony sold rights to movies such as *Crouching Tiger, Hidden Dragon* and *The Wedding Planner* (Adam Shankman, 2001) to inDemand, which had already obtained rights to Universal Pictures films including *The Mummy Returns* (Stephen Sommers 2001) and *The Sting* (Gregory Roy Hill, 1973), as well as *The Blair Witch Project* (Joe Berlinger, 2000) distributed by Artisan Entertainment.[129]

In September 2001 the two remaining major movie companies, Disney and Fox, unveiled a joint venture named Movies.com that drew upon both companies' films to create an exclusive window for a limited period of time before making them available to other outlets, including cable video services such as inDemand. Movies.com was launched as an Internet-only service. Both the Moviefly and Movies.com deals caught the attention of federal regulators and prompted the Department of Justice to begin an antitrust investigation. Studio heads acted unconcerned on the grounds that they were fighting digital piracy, and the historical logic of copyright as private property was on their side. Hollywood had seen these threats before with the introduction of broadcast television, cable television, and the videocassette recorder.[130] Though each new medium *apparently* posed a threat to the filmed entertainment oligopoly, each became a major ancillary outlet for the movie companies. By 2000, the studios were earning more than 45 percent of their revenues from home video, nearly 29 percent from television, and only about 25 percent from the box office.[131]

In 2002, Fox abandoned its joint venture with Disney, and in 2004, the Antitrust Division found that the "evidence did not support a finding that [Movielink] had adversely affected competition through increased prices or decreased output."[132] Meanwhile, MGM Studios, with the backing of the MPAA and the music recording industry, filed a suit against Grokster and Streamcast (makers of Morpheus), two P2P file-sharing services, for contributing to copyright infringement. The case tested the Supreme Court's finding in the 1984 *Sony* case on the limits of fair use. The federal district and appeals courts decided that P2P networks had legitimate uses, not just infringing ones, and that the defendants were not liable for contributory infringement. However, in 2005 the Supreme Court weighed in with a unanimous ruling in favor of MGM, finding that Grokster and others could be held liable for copyright infringement since they functioned and indeed willfully marketed themselves as sites for illegal downloads. While the Supreme Court did not overturn *Sony*, it did find that any producer of technologies that facilitated the unauthorized copyright of intellectual property could be held liable. It was a strong enough message to intimidate future software and hardware developers of digital copying technologies. Grokster announced in 2006 that it would return as a legitimate file-sharing site.[133]

In 2005, Apple introduced video iPods that pushed the film industry to begin making its films available through the Internet. Movielink began offering movies to be purchased for download, and it was joined by CinemaNow in offering download-to-burn services. However, many of the most valuable movies remained in the copyright owners' vaults. The industry continued to milk the DVD rental and sales market, even as brick-and-mortar video stores began to disappear (although Blockbuster seemed invincible in 2005). Netflix bypassed expensive retail outlets by setting up a subscription service that allowed consumers to rent movies by mail ("clicks, with no bricks").[134] Blockbuster established its own version of the service and seemed poised to capture the market. Netflix's execution strategy had been flawless, while Blockbuster bungled and the former became the industry leader. By September 2010, Blockbuster filed for bankruptcy after becoming a penny stock. Also by then, the film release window had significantly changed. Still, the theater venue remained a film's primary showcase and determined its value in downstream markets.

On average, theaters enjoyed a 120-day exclusive period for showing new movies. Then the releases appeared on video-on-demand services at a price of around $5. With new copy-blocking technology, the studios moved to close that window to 45 days after a film opened at the theater. This allowed the studios to charge a premium price of $25 for on-demand exclusivity. More important, it allowed them to combine marketing campaigns for each window. Opponents of the plan included Best Buy and Wal-Mart, which would lose DVD sales, already down by 30 percent from the DVD market's peak in 2005. Revenues for DVDs dropped to about $10 billion in 2010, despite the introduction of Blu-ray discs, which cost twice as much as the DVD format.[135] Of course, those most upset by narrowing of the release window were theater owners. The National Association of Theater Owners took out full-page ads in *Variety* and *Hollywood Reporter* opposing the move, fearing that theatrical attendance, already on the decline, would be adversely affected by would-be theatergoers who realized that heading out to the cineplex cost more than waiting a few weeks to watch the movie on the couch—which was precisely what 3-D movies sought to prevent.

The next battle over the release window involved online streaming of television shows and movies. The key was the transition of movie and TV program downloads or streaming that audiences were watching on the computer to a television set. Sony's Playstation video-game consoles were transformed into the nerve center for downloading TV shows and movies, directing them to television home entertainment centers and multiple other digital devices. In 2010, Netflix was reaching subscribers who paid $8 per month to load content onto their personal computers, video-game consoles, and Internet set-top boxes such as Roku and Apple TV. The service gave consumers a license permitting them to download movies to their portable digital devices. Netflix claimed that it could support more than one hundred digital screens of various sizes nationwide. Its main problem was lack of major Hollywood hits in its streaming-video catalog of twenty thousand movies. The winner in this infant industry would be determined by who gained the greatest access to Hollywood's vaults. In that case, Hulu.com, a joint venture of Disney, News Corp., GE, and Providence Equity Partners, benefited from in-house vertical integration, providing access to each film partner's vaults and television networks ABC, Fox, and NBC, plus programming from Comedy Central, Lionsgate, MGM, MTV Networks, National Geographic, Paramount, BBC, Sony Pictures Television, and Warner Bros Television Group. CBS distributed its own streaming video via its online portal, TV.com, purchased from Apple's iTunes in 2008. Google's YouTube dominated the market at the time with its advertiser-supported model, making shows available at no immediate cost. It also offered movies and television programs from BBC Worldwide, CBS, Discovery Networks, Lionsgate, MGM, National Geographic, PBS, Sony's Crackle, and Starz, among others. In 2009, it announced a partnership with Sony Pictures and other Hollywood studios as part of an effort to transform the site from a user-contributed amateur-video outlet into a more professional venue.[136]

Theater owners began barking louder as the film release window was winnowed. The smaller the window between theatrical release and downstream outlets, the less theater owners stood to earn, as their gross domestic box office increased the longer a picture played in the theater (from a fifty-fifty split between them and the distributors in the first week to a seventy-thirty split after three weeks). By narrowing the ancillary release windows, the studios were looking to take the biggest bite from the apple in the shortest amount of time. Hence their efforts to rush Blu-ray formatted DVDs, video-on-demand, and digital streaming to increase the rate of amortizing the costs of production, distribution, and marketing, while still providing the spectacle-event films theater owners traditionally seek. Another strategy by theater owners to attract customers, begun in 2008, was to plow money into upgrading venues to merge dinner and a movie by including high-profile restaurants, bars, and lounges in the theater.[137] The theater companies kept all the revenues from concessions, be they popcorn or filet mignon. Of course, with all of these changes, including questioning the release window model itself, the experience of watching filmed entertainment was bound to change: Compare the large-screen Imax to the small-screen cell phone.

MORE MONEY AT THE MOVIES: FILM INDUSTRY PERFORMANCE

The economic and power structure analysis of the Big Six film companies that dominated the industry before and since the new millennium, provided above, is intended to demonstrate how they are owned and controlled. Together they had a box office market share in 2009 that totaled 84.4 percent (including News Corp.'s Fox Searchlight and Universal's Focus Features). The remaining studios that made the Box Office Mojo chart in 2009 included Summit Entertainment, a subsidiary of E1 Entertainment, the largest independent music, television, and film distributor in North America, ranking seventh with 4.6 percent of the box office; Lionsgate, film producer/distributor with 3.8 percent; the Weinstein Company (1.9 percent); and Overture Films, a subsidiary of John Malone's Liberty Media, with 1.5 percent. There were also some ten thousand working producers in Hollywood in 2010, many of them working for and at the mercy of the Big Six.[138] The number of producers on retainer was sharply cut, as was the number of films they produced over the decade. Independent producers put their own money at risk or borrowed from major banks, private equity firms, and hedge funds. They still needed a distribution deal, primarily with one of the Big Six. The total number of films released in 2009, according to Box Office Mojo, was 521, down from the peak year (2007), when 631 films were released. Before 1982, Box Office Mojo data only includes major releases—161 in 1980 and 173 in 1981.[139] What is striking is precisely that of the 500 films or more released each year, most filmgoers see only a handful, primarily those involving the Big Six, due to their major advantages over would-be competitors that have films with the potential to significantly diversify what we see in theaters.

The first advantage of the majors over would-be competitors is their economic structure. These firms are vertically and horizontally integrated conglomerates. The goal, as stated in Viacom's 2006 annual report, is "developing synergies across our brands[, which] permits us to leverage the core . . . audiences."[140] In addition to financing and distributing their own movies, they also serve as the primary financiers and distributors of coproductions. The majors borrow money from investors by selling them a partial ownership interest in the copyrights for a slate or a group of films or a single film. The sale of a piece of the movie's copyright is therefore used to raise revenue to produce movies. The goal is to improve the investment returns on films and reduce economic risks by spreading them around.[141] Movies financed and distributed by the core firms are hardly independent. Their budgets, talent lists, and story ideas must meet the approval of those who hope to profit from the film. In addition, the major distributors charge a 30–35 percent fee for getting the movies into theaters. Usually, these deals are designed so the studio will not lose money, or will at least minimize its exposure by taking its share of the gross revenues first. For example, Disney strong-armed *Pearl Harbor*'s (2001) producer Jerry Bruckheimer and director Michael Bay into a "backend" deal, in which the producer and director would not earn a cent until Disney recovered its production costs.[142] In exchange for financing and distributing a movie, the majors can also insist on obtaining ancillary rights, such as home video, pay cable, broadcast television, and foreign distribution. As Gomery concluded, for the Hollywood oligopoly "distribution has always been a key to corporate longevity" and worldwide distribution has been the basis for its power.[143]

To get a movie financed and distributed by a Hollywood major typically requires pulling talent together, including star directors and actors. A second advantage the majors have is that they can create barriers to entry with their deep pockets to build and pay stars. As the level of stardom for directors and actors has increased, so has the price for their services. Stars increase the budget of a film according to their *apparent* box office value. In the 1980s and 1990s, the triumvirate of action-adventure film stars—Arnold Schwarzenegger, Sylvester Stallone, and Bruce Willis—were among the first stars able to demand as much as $20 million for appearing in a movie. In the late 1990s, Jim Carrey and Julia Roberts joined the $20 million club. Star budgets increased the chance of a big payback at the box office and downstream outlets. Between 1986 and early August 1997, of the 104 movies that topped $100 million at the domestic box office, 35 percent starred one or more of just seven performers (the five noted above plus Tom Cruise and Robin Williams).[144]

By 2000, the value of star power seemed to be declining, with the same seven stars accounting for only 30 percent of 149 films earning $100 million or more between 1990 and 2000.[145] Nevertheless, in December 2001, Schwarzenegger signed a $30 million contract to star in *Terminator 3* (Jonathan Mostow, 2003).[146] In 2006, Paramount ended a fourteen-year relationship with Tom Cruise that the *New York Times* media beat reporters interpreted as "the latest sign that media conglomerates that control Hollywood are growing impatient with the megastars who earn the highest salaries."[147] For Paramount, that meant a savings of $10 million a year, the reported cost of Cruise's contract. Still, the star system remained essential, with Hollywood's increasing dependence on the global box office, foreign home video, and television sales to earn back the high costs of production and marketing. Again, only 20 percent of a film's total gross revenues are generated by the U.S. domestic box office.[148] As revenues generated in the global marketplace increase, the types of films that get made are adjusted accordingly. The simplistic dialogue and intensive use of extravagant special effects make the action-adventure movie a genre that easily transcends cultural and linguistic boundaries. Hence, although big action stars were no longer breaking U.S. domestic box office records by 2002, their global exchange value made the high star salaries and production costs well worth the expense. Even a film such as *Godzilla* (Roland Emmerich, 1998), trashed by critics and earning only $136 million at the domestic box office, finished as the fourth-biggest worldwide hit in 1998, earning an additional $248 million in overseas markets.[149] Other global hits rely on focusing on genres that have universal appeal, such as weddings. IFC's *My Big Fat Greek Wedding* (2002), produced by Tom Hanks, was one such film. Made for a mere $5 million, it grossed nearly $370 million at the global box office. The film ranked first in Box Office Mojo's genres Cinderella Complex, Romantic Comedy, and Wedding.[150]

Stars are used to attract preconstituted audiences minimize the level of risk and create a higher potential for profits. However, only about 2 percent of actors earn more than $200,000 a year, 8 percent make between $10,000 and $30,000, and 90 percent are unemployed. In 2007 the top ten women in the star system included (in descending order): Reese Witherspoon, Angelina Jolie, Cameron Diaz, Nicole Kidman, Renee Zellweger, Sandra Bullock, Julia Roberts, Drew Barrymore, Jody Foster, and Halle Barry, with the top three making $15–$20 million per film and the rest making $10 million or more.[151] The top ten male actors with the highest income in 2007 were Will Smith ($80 million), Johnny Depp ($72 million), Eddie Murphy ($55 million), Mike Myers ($55 million), Leonardo DiCaprio ($45 million), Bruce Willis ($41 million), Ben Stiller ($40 million), Nicholas Cage ($31 million), Will Ferrell ($31 million), and Adam Sandler ($30 million).[152] Bankable stars do not necessarily generate higher gross revenues. Among those named as most overpaid stars in 2007 were Russell Crowe, Nicole Kidman, Jim Carrey, Will Ferrell, and Adam Sandler.[153] Some stars have tried the producer route, such as Tom Cruise, who partnered with Paula Wagner with the backing of MGM seeking to revive United Artists, a subsidiary of the latter. The privately held MGM was controlled by a private consortium including Sony, Comcast, TPG Capital, L.P., and Providence Equity. Its film vault contained four thousand movies, along with a half stake in the James Bond franchise. Though Tom Cruise served as part owner of United Artists, he was hardly independent. Rather, United Artists became a vehicle for his own films.

Hollywood's core film companies also maintain their market power through exploitation of their film libraries. Movie rights represent valuable assets. They can be used as collateral to finance new projects. They can also be split in a variety of ways and used to generate cash or support the growth of new media outlets. A case of the latter occurred in 1986, when Ted Turner bought broadcast and videocassette rights to MGM movies from Kirk Kerkorian for $1.5 billion to provide programming for his growing cable network operations. The deal included classic movies such as *Gone with the Wind* (Victor Fleming, 1939), *Casablanca* (Michael Curtis, 1942), *2001: A Space Odyssey* (Stanley Kubrick, 1968), *The Wizard of Oz* (Victor Fleming, 1939), and *Singin' in the Rain* (Stanley Donen, Gene Kelly, 1952). Recognizing the exchange value of old movies and famous movie stars, Turner remarked, "We've got Spencer Tracy and Jimmy Cagney working for us from the grave."[154] In 1990, Turner acquired broadcast rights for an additional eight hundred MGM movies, as MGM sought to raise cash for its big comeback. MGM regained control of the rights to most of these movies in 1999, in hopes of rebuilding the MGM library and launching its own cable television network. In March 1999, MGM paid $225 million to Warner Brothers to repurchase video rights to the movies it once produced and owned.[155] By rebuilding its filmed entertainment library, MGM hoped to rejoin the Hollywood oligopoly to which it once belonged and regain the status it enjoyed in the Studio Era.

In addition to using star actors and directors to attract and retain moviegoers, Hollywood has a long tradition of exploiting star authors. The studios can bank on a best-selling author's fans to show up at the theater. For example, in 1993 both Michael Crichton's *Jurassic Park*, produced by Universal and directed by Steven Spielberg, and John Grisham's *The Firm*, produced by Paramount and directed by Sydney Pollack, became blockbusters. In 2001, the adaptation of books to movies drove the box office to new heights with Warner Brothers' *Harry Potter and the Sorcerer's Stone*, written by J. K. Rowling, and New Line's *Lord of the Rings*, written by J. R. R. Tolkien. Both film companies were subsidiaries of AOL–Time Warner, but the parent company put much more of its money and effort behind the *Harry Potter* franchise while leaving New Line to set up its own global distribution, marketing, and merchandising network for *Lord of the Rings*. Warner Brothers recognized the broad appeal of the *Harry Potter* children's books to readers of all ages. By 2001, the four *Harry Potter* books in print had already produced sales of 116 million copies in two hundred countries and had been translated into forty-seven languages.[156] Warner Brothers transformed the literary work into what its executives described to *Variety* as "a prime example of corporate synergy [in] the brave new world of vertical integration, in which a film becomes 'product' and every department works itself into a cross-promotional frenzy."[157]

The frenzy involving *Harry Potter and the Sorcerer's Stone* (Chris Columbus, 2001) was fueled by the widest North American theatrical release of any movie ever. The movie premiered in November 2001 at 3,672 theaters on 8,200 screens, nearly one out of every four screens in the United States and Canada. The film, with an estimated $120 million budget, broke the box office record for a weekend opener, with $93 million in its first three days.[158] Hoping not to overexpose the brand or alienate Harry Potter fans, the studio decided to skip fast-food tie-ins, but did sign an exclusive $150 million deal with the Coca Cola Company on the condition that characters in the movie would not be shown actually using the product. Following the wishes of J. K. Rowling, Warner Brothers further insisted that Coca-Cola promote literacy in its ads.[159] The number of licensees for the movie and book series totaled eighty-five, much less than the 150 licensees signed up for Warner Brothers' *Batman* movie series a decade before. Nonetheless, merchandising was expected to generate as much as $150 million.[160] The merchandise included dozens of toys from Mattel, including a levitating game and science kit for potion-making, a 682-piece Lego version of Hogwarts Castle ($89 listed retail price), sheets and pillowcases, collectible dolls and trading cards, action figures, and computer and Gameboy games.[161] To further fuel frenzy for the theatrical release, AOL–Time Warner subsidiaries HBO, TBS, Cartoon Network, the WB network, and the Warner Music record division promoted the movie through ads and special promotions. Its Internet subscribers were deluged with interactive ads for the film.[162] By February 2002, *Harry Potter*'s global box office revenues approached $1 billion, of which $313 million came from the North American market.[163]

For the release of *Harry Potter* on videocassette and DVD in May 2002, Warner Brothers Home Video mounted its largest marketing campaign ever, with a $25 million blitz seeking to make more than 12 billion "impressions" on potential consumers through television, magazines, websites, billboards, and in-store displays.[164] AOL–Time Warner sold the network broadcast rights for the first two *Harry Potter* films to its competitor, Disney, for $130 million, in the most expensive deal of its kind to date. *Lord of the Rings* stayed in-house when New Line sold the rights to the trilogy for $160 million to AOL–Time Warner's WB network and sister cable networks TNT and TBS.[165] The broadcast window for the first movie was set for fall 2004, after the movie's pay–cable television run on Liberty Media's Starz!/Encore. The sequels were aired on broadcast television in 2005 and 2006, respectively.

By 2009, the first five *Harry Potter* sequels had generated $4.5 billion. All had opened at number one in revenues earned in the first three days, including *Harry Potter and the Half-Blood Prince* (David Yates, 2009), until the release of *Transformers: Revenge of the Fallen* (Michael Bay) later that same year.[166] They also generated another $10.7 billion from global sales of DVDs ($2.7 billion, 211.4 million units), merchandise ($7 billion), and video-games ($1 billion, 40 million units).[167] The six *Harry Potter* films earned $1.7 billion at the domestic box office, for an average of $286 million per film; led by *Harry Potter and the Sorcerer's Stone* (Chris Columbus, 2001), which grossed $317 million at the domestic box office and $974 million worldwide. Together, the films were the highest-grossing franchise of all time (unadjusted for inflation) making it number one of all time. The final film in the series, *Harry Potter and the Deathly Hallows*, was released in two parts, with part 1 in 2010 and part 2 in 2011. The Potter franchise expanded beyond leading the box office. The books alone, translated into sixty-seven languages, sold 400 million copies, second only to the Bible, and made its author, under the pen name J. K. Rowling, the highest-paid literary figure in history. The brand was further extended via a mini theme park, Islands of Adventure, which opened in 2010 at Universal's theme park in Orlando.

Sequels have long been a Hollywood staple, relied on to attract a preexisting audience generated by the original film. However, the film industry oligopoly dramatically intensified its use of sequels and franchise pictures in the first decade of the twenty-first century. Between 1999 and 2008, each year's top-grossing film worldwide was a sequel or prequel.[168] This, in turn, determines what kinds of films are produced and their production and marketing budgets. The *Harry Potter, Batman, Pirates of the Caribbean, Star Wars,* and *Lord of the Rings* franchises have established a global presence based on content that has been exposed to audiences around the world, either a comic book character, a theme-park ride, theatrical plays, a television show, popular novels, or other preexisting formats. The *Star Wars* formula is based on the classic western genre, which has long traveled well at the box office. It is worth noting that some franchises are not entirely dependent upon using the same stars (e.g., James Bond and Batman), hence reducing the cost of talent. *Harry Potter* actors threatened to hold out unless given bigger paychecks, as by then they were the vehicles most identified with the film. All sequels are made with bigger budgets, even though sets can be recycled. The franchise phenomenon also affects the way in which films are perceived by their creators, as a profit vehicle expected to keep on running. This implied smaller budgets for films that are not viable for serialization, intended to be experienced as single works and no more. They do not easily transfer into merchandise. They are complex and difficult and often more bound to domestic cultural identities. Here we see a clear link between the industry's structure and performance and the content they produce.

In addition to sequels, the studios hedge their bets with remakes of classical Hollywood films as well as movie versions of hit television shows. Hollywood's obsession with sequels and remakes is perhaps best epitomized by its recycling of Alfred Hitchcock's legendary thriller *Psycho* (1960). Universal produced two sequels, *Psycho II* (Richard Franklin) in 1983 and *Psycho III* (Anthony Perkins) in 1986, before signing up star director Gus Van Sant to make what *Variety* referred to as a "faithful-unto-slavish" remake of the original in 1998. A small sampling of other movie remakes includes *King Kong* (RKO, 1933; Paramount, 1976), *D.O.A.* (United Artists, 1950; Touchstone/Disney, 1998), *Angels in the Outfield* (MGM, 1951; Disney, 1994), and *Cape Fear* (Universal, 1962 and 1991).[169] Other strategies for minimizing risk and maximizing profits include making movies from television series or vice versa, drawing upon historical catastrophes such as the sinking of the *Titanic* or the bombing of Pearl Harbor. *The Titanic* (James Cameron, 1997) was also a remake that cost Paramount and Fox $200 million to make (a record at the time) and had the highest box office gross of all time ($1.8 billion box office gross worldwide) until it was knocked off by *Avatar* in 2010. A 3-D rerelease of the film was expected in 2012. This process of recycling films was mastered by Disney, which used its valuable film vault to rerelease its theatrical blockbusters to create artificial scarcity to reach generation after generation. The practice was extended to Disney DVDs released for retail sales for limited periods of time. Disney films on Blu-ray cost twice as much as those on the DVD format, but prompted a new round of consumption as home video shoppers replaced their old libraries.

The advantages enjoyed by the dominant filmed entertainment companies make for nearly impenetrable market barriers for potential competitors. Meanwhile, the Hollywood oligopoly hypes event movies to such an
extent that they instill a social obligation to participate. Writing in the
1940s, Frankfurt School scholars Max Horkheimer and Theodor Adorno
observed that the universal criterion of a movie's cultural merit had become
equated with how much was spent on it—what they called "conspicuous
production." As they recognized, and as audiences sometimes do also, "The
varying budgets in the culture industry do not bear the slightest relation to
factual values, to the meaning of the products themselves."[170] They meant
that moviegoers had become used to the formulas of movie spectacles
because the content of the films themselves did not require any kind of
real thought. Since movies are produced as commodities, Horkheimer and
Adorno argued that they could no longer be art. In their view, art challenges
its audiences to question the status quo and the things they tend to take for
granted. However, the products of the movie oligopoly provide no room
for independent thinking. In Horkheimer and Adorno's view, if movie
theaters were shut down tomorrow there would be no great loss. Once the
movie hype disappeared, people would no longer feel obligated to go. Then
the enormous resources, time, and energy spent producing, distributing,
and consuming films could be used to do something capitalism refuses to
do: "abolish hunger."[171]

4

The Music Industry:
The Payer Calls the Tune

The music recording industry resembles the movie industry in both structure and performance. In fact, some of the players are involved in both sectors. In this chapter, we examine the structure and performance of the recorded music industry. The period we examine is the first decade of the new millennium. We will also examine the changes in the industry as well. While much has changed in the industry over the last ten years, certain features of the industry remain the same as it pursues the same goal as most U.S mass media, which is to make a profit by selling cultural commodities. Hence, the music industry follows the logic of capitalism, resulting in specific structures and practices. The commodification of music and music video content affects what is produced. The industry also reflects the overriding tendency within capitalism toward concentration and oligopoly. Oligopolies follow specific practices to maintain their dominant status. Oligopolies must adjust their practices according to technological developments in order to survive. The music industry has had to adjust to how technology drove the audience's practice of listening to it. This has generated new strategies by the industry to make music-listening ubiquitous, accessible from anywhere on any portable communications device. The music to which we listen shapes part of our identities and has an enormous emotional power. The question is: Where does this process begin, and how well does this industry serve the normative goals of a democratic communications system that provides room for creativity and exploration for the purposes of enlightenment and enrichment of life.

Five music distribution companies accounted for 83.3 percent of the total sales of record albums in the U.S. market in 2001.[1] Vivendi's Universal Music unit led the way with 26.4 percent of total record sales. Universal

Music topped the 2001 charts for the third straight year after its acquisition of Polygram Music in 1998. At the time, the Universal Music Group was owned by the Canadian liquor firm Seagram Co., in turn controlled by the Bronfman family (then led by patriarch Edgar Bronfman Sr., number 24 on the 2001 *Forbes 400* list, with $6.8 billion).[2] Seagram acquired Polygram Music from Philips Electronics, a Netherlands-based manufacturer of electronics for military, industrial, and consumer use. Polygram's labels included many formerly independent labels such as A&M, Motown, and Island. Its major labels included Decca, Mercury, Polydor, and Deutsche Grammophon. It was the third-largest music publisher, with 375,000 copyrights, along with a 30 percent stake in Really Useful Holdings, which owned the copyrights to the Andrew Lloyd Webber catalog. Polygram also owned music clubs in Britain and France.[3] After the merger, thousands of employees were terminated, a number of bands found themselves without contracts, and some artists were required to buy back their own music.

The Universal Music Group's holdings included MCA and full or partial ownership of nearly forty additional record labels. Universal also distributed music for a number of independent labels, including Chess (Muddy Waters, Chuck Berry), Margaritaville (Jimmy Buffett), and Nothing (Nine Inch Nails, Marilyn Manson). Its music publishing division, MCA Music Publishing, generated roughly $250 million a year from 155,000 copyrighted songs, including "I Want to Hold Your Hand," "Hound Dog," and "Strangers in the Night."[4] Universal also owned a concert promotion company and several concert halls, including the Universal Amphitheater in Los Angeles. Vivendi's takeover of Seagram in 2000 launched Universal Music to the top of the record charts. To gain the EC's approval of the deal, Vivendi agreed to license its online music catalog to competitors of its Vizzavi multiaccess Internet portal service.

Next on Billboard's 2001 list of top music distributors was AOL–Time Warner's record division, the Warner Music Group, with 15.9 percent of total U.S. album sales.[5] The Warner Group owned more than forty labels, including Atlantic, with artists such as Tori Amos, Brandy, Phil Collins, matchbox20, and Tim McGraw; Elektra, with Jackson Browne, Tracy Chapman, Metallica, and Phish; and Warner Brothers Records, with Eric Clapton, Madonna, R.E.M., Red Hot Chili Peppers, Paul Simon, Steely Dan, and Neil Young.[6] Like Universal Music, the Warner Music Group held labels spanning a range of music genres, including rock, pop, rap, country, rhythm and blues, jazz, classical, and gospel. With such a stable of music labels, the company can hedge its bets from year to year. So, for example, when rap music sales are down, gospel music sales may be up. AOL–Time Warner's music group was a fully vertically integrated operation. Its holdings included a division that manufactured the tapes, CDs, and DVDs for its labels. The company owned or controlled the copyrights to more than a million songs through its Warner/Chappel Music publishing house and subsidiaries. On the retail level, the music division shared a 50 percent stake in the Columbia House record club with Sony.

Sony Music Distribution ranked third on Billboard's 2001 list of total U.S. album sales, with 15.9 percent.[7] Sony entered the music business in the 1980s when it bought CBS Records in hopes of finding synergies between music software and hardware. Sony's major labels included Columbia (Bruce Springsteen, Neil Diamond), Epic (Oasis, Pearl Jam), Crescent Moon (Gloria Estefan), and Associated (Rage Against the Machine). Sony Music Independent Labels included MJJ Music, co-owned with Michael Jackson.[8] Sony also manufactured tapes and discs and owned music copyrights through its publishing division. A separate label, Soundtrax, produced the sound track for the movie *Men in Black*. The label highlights the synergy between Sony's movie and music divisions and suggests the ways in which movie sound tracks have become vehicles for a company's other interests. Thus, film producers at Sony would be encouraged to promote a company's contract artists rather than carry the tunes by artists that a filmmaker might have wanted.

Bertelsmann's BMG Distribution ranked fourth in 2001, with 14.7 percent of the total U.S. album market share.[9] The German-based company generated revenues of $16.5 billion that year, putting it among the Big Ten of global media conglomerates.[10] Bertelsmann was Europe's biggest broadcaster, with stakes in twenty-two television channels. It was also the largest U.S. book publisher, including imprints such as Random House, Knopf, Vintage, Modern Library, Bantam Doubleday Dell, and Delacorte, as well as one of the world's largest magazine publishers, with eighty titles. Its music division controlled more than two hundred labels, including RCA and Arista, distributed in fifty-four countries. These labels produced and distributed music by artists such as 'N Sync, Britney Spears, Dave Matthews Band, and the Grateful Dead. BMG also distributed records for a number of other labels and controlled the rights to 700,000 songs, including 100,000 Famous Music copyrights co-owned with Viacom's Paramount Pictures. Finally, Bertelsmann owned the BMG Music Service with record clubs serving the United States and Canada, giving it direct access to the retail market.

The last of the Big Five recording companies at the beginning of the twenty-first century was EMI Music Distribution, which finished fifth in total album sales in 2001 with 10.6 percent.[11] EMI, based in England, owned major labels including Capitol (Beastie Boys, Bonnie Raitt), Chrysalis, Grand Royal, Virgin (Rolling Stones, Smashing Pumpkins), and Pointblank (John Lee Hooker, Isaac Hayes). Additional labels covered the rap, country, R&B/blues/jazz, classical, gospel, and Latin categories. EMI also served as distributor for Apple records. Its best-selling titles in 2001 included *Beatles I*, Janet Jackson's *All for You*, and Garth Brooks's *Scarecrow*. From the recycle bin, EMI scored best sellers in 2001 with *Now That's What I Call Music! 7* and *Now That's What I Call Music! 8*.[12] EMI's music division was a fully vertically integrated operation: It owned the world's largest music catalog, with over a million titles; it manufactured compact discs, with plants in Britain, Holland, and Japan; and it controlled 231 retail outlets in Britain and the United States, including the Virgin Megastores in New York and Philadelphia. Although it was a major player in the music business, EMI's other media holdings were minuscule compared to those of the rest of the Big Five. This made the company a constant target for takeover.

Such was the case in January 2000, when Time Warner announced its intent to acquire the EMI Group to create the world's largest record company, soon after the announcement of its intended merger with America Online. The combined music divisions would have owned the rights to nearly 2 million songs.[13] In October, Time Warner and EMI withdrew the proposed merger after the European Commission raised concerns about concentrated control over music copyrights, which it feared could be extended into domination of the online music delivery business. America Online already had a distribution agreement with BMG to deliver its music online. Time Warner improved its chances of gaining the EC's approval of its pending merger with America Online by forgoing the EMI acquisition. EMI therefore remained a major music force and also an enticing acquisition for a global media conglomerate.

Another major player in the music industry at the time was Viacom, by virtue of its control over the dominant cable television music networks: MTV, VH1, BET, and CMT (Country Music Channel). Music videos are basically ads for music recordings. Music video channels such as MTV serve the same role as radio stations: They sell audiences to advertisers while their programming promotes sales of music. MTV once had an enormous influence on the sale of a recording simply by putting the video into high rotation. An album that might have sold only 100,000 copies might make gold (500,000 copies) with enough exposure on MTV.[14] For established stars, MTV helped sell millions of albums.[15] Despite its hip image, however, MTV's division of standards and practices took a hard look at each video, helping homogenize music to downright censorship. From 1989 to 1994, every single winner in the Best Video category of MTV's Video Music Awards was initially rejected for cable play and sent back to its director for reediting.[16] Similarly, MTV refused to play Madonna's "Justify My Love" video released in the mid-1980s, because it found the nudity and images of bisexuality too extreme. MTV's impact on the music marketplace in the 1980s and 1990s was twofold: What it promoted sold, and what it failed or refused to promote generally did not (although Madonna took her video directly to retail and opened a new market for music video singles).

THE RECORDED MUSIC INDUSTRY TEN YEARS AFTER

The music recording industry of the 1990s was based on sales of CDs promoted through broadcast television such as late night talk and variety shows, such as "Saturday Night Live"; music videos on cable; and radio. The legal market for digital music was in its infancy. By 2010 the digital share of the industry was 29 percent, up more than 1000 percent between 2003 and 2010, amounting to $5.2 billion the last year.[17] Total legal downloads passed one billion that year. Total worldwide revenues of the music industry in 2010 were $66.4 billion, which included revenues generated by record labels, music publishers, recording artists, composers, concert venues, and merchandise companies. Of that, $34.1 billion came from recorded music in both physical and digital formats.[18] Overall North American recorded music industry revenues, both physical and digital, amounted to $12.6 billion in 2010.[19] Nevertheless, the music industry was seen as a declining sector of the media, primarily due to the collapse of the CD market (worth $11.9 billion in 2003, down to $6.2 billion by 2010), as well as the enormous number of illegal music downloads despite all industry efforts to curtail this practice.[20] This led to cutbacks throughout the industry of both operations and employment. However, while certain models used by the industry evolved with the rise of digital music, the basic structure remained the same, except instead of five dominant firms it was down to four: Universal Music Group (UMG), Sony Music Entertainment (SME), Warner Music Group (WMG), and EMI.

Universal Music Group

Universal Music Group was literally universal, as the world's largest recording company. Its Universal Music Publishing Group was also the world's largest, and the company controlled the world's largest catalog of recorded music. Its U.S. market share in 2010 was 31.4 percent.[21] UMG was a subsidiary of Vivendi S.A., and the giant French media conglomerate ranked number 189 on the *Fortune Global 500*.[22] Among its subsidiaries was Activision Blizzard, which controlled digital channels and video games (61 percent owned). It was the number one worldwide producer of online and video console games, including *Black Ops*, which had earned the company more than a billion dollars by 2010. Other UMG subsidiaries were a French telecommunications operator, SFR (56 percent owned); the mobile telephone company Moroc Telecom Group, the leading telecommunications company in Morocco (53 percent owned); GVT, the largest private telecommunications operator in Brazil (100 percent owned); and Canal+Group, the number one pay-TV service in France (100 percent owned), as well as a film production and distribution company operating throughout Europe.[23]

It sold its 20 percent share of NBC/Universal to GE in 2009, clearing the way for the eventual Comcast/NBCU merger. Revenues for Vivendi reached nearly $29 billion in 2010. Of that, UMG earned roughly $4.5 billion, the largest amount coming from sales of physical and digital music that totaled around $3.6 billion. Other music revenues came from music publishing, synchronization rights (for sound tracks, television shows, commercials, and so on), and artist services and merchandising. Its top ten best-selling artists in 2010 were Eminem, Lady Gaga, Taylor Swift, Rhianna, Justin Bieber (twice), Take That, Black-Eyed Peas (twice), and Bon Jovi's *Greatest Hits—The Ultimate Collection.* The 2010 breakdown of recorded music revenues by geographical area was 41 percent from Europe, 40 percent from North America, 13 percent from Asia, and 6 percent for the rest of the world. [24] The company's record labels are listed in table 4.1. Each of these labels had its own sublabels and subsidiaries throughout the world, covering every genre of music: rock, rap, pop, alternative, Latin, gospel, and sound tracks.[25]

UMG was not always the giant music company as it stood in 2010. A brief recent history explains how it got that way. The company was acquired by Universal Studios and MCA Records by the Japanese electronics conglomerate, Matsushita, in 1990. This followed the lead of Sony, which had recently bought Columbia Pictures and CBS Records in search of hardware-software synergies. Under Matsushita's ownership, the division was seen as underperforming and in 1995 sold 80 percent to the Seagram Company, the Canadian liquor and juice conglomerate led by dominant stockholder Edgar Bronfman Jr. Bronfman went on a spending spree in the late 1990s, including the purchase of Polygram N.V. in 1998 for $11 bil-

Table 4.1. Universal Music Group Record Labels

Decca
Deutsche Grammophon
DreamWorks Nashville
DreamWorks Records
Geffen Records
Interscope A&M Records
Island Def Jam Music Group
Lost Highway Records
MCA Nashville
Mercury Records
Philips
Polydor
Universal Motown Records Group
Verve Music Group

lion from Philips N.V., a Dutch electronics firm. The combined company instantly moved up in annual distribution share charts. The deal included Philips labels such as A&M Records, Island Records, Mercury, Motown, Polydor, and Deutsche Grammophon. The spending spree ate up much of the Bronfman family fortune and eventually led to the acquisition of Universal by Vivendi, then a water and waste utility conglomerate. That year Vivendi also bought Canal+ and began its transformation into a telecommunications and media conglomerate, Vivendi Universal Entertainment. Bronfman became Vivendi Universal's largest shareholder and its board chairman, but he soon stepped down to vice chairman of the board of directors. The company's CEO was Jean-Marie Messier; he was forced out by the board in 2002, and Bronfman left the company in 2003. (In January 2011, a French court convicted Bronfman and Messier of misusing company funds and misleading investors, and both were forced to pay fines). Jean-René Fourtou became CEO and chair of the board from 2002 to 2005. Jean-Bernard Lévy took over as chairman of the board in 2005, a position he continued to hold in 2011, while Fourtou served as chairman of the supervisory board. After dramatic declines in the company's stock value (75–80 percent), Vivendi began selling off assets. In 2006, Vivendi sold 80 percent of Universal Pictures to General Electric, synergizing the filmed entertainment company with NBC. Vivendi retained the music division of Universal, which eventually became its largest media subsidiary. That year it also bought out the remaining 20 percent of the company held by Matsushita, giving it 100 percent share in UMG.

A power structure analysis of Vivendi's connections to other corporations, banks, philanthropies, business policy groups, and so on begins with its chairman, Jean-Bernard Lévy. In 2011, Lévy was connected to ninety-eight board members in six different organizations across eight different industries.[26] Among his notable positions and functions were board directorships of Société Générale, a major European financial services company; Vinci (made up of the water and utilities subsidiaries once belonging to Vivendi); Institut Pasteur; Viroxis, a bio-pharmaceutical company; Institute Telecom, a business policy organization that manages higher education establishments; and Paris Europlace, a company that provides marketing services to the Parisian financial industry. Other members of what it calls its supervisory board were tied to pharmaceuticals; a global energy management firm; the investment firm AXA; the automotive industry; a leading manufacturer of carbon products; the University of Pennsylvania; a private online education firm; Chanel, the perfume company; a real estate investment trust; a liquor company; a cosmetics company; Total, investors in the gas industry; another financial investment firm, Patrimonial Conseil; and an online shopping service. While most board members were French, their related business interests spanned the globe. The company's top six shareholders were private equity firms, banks, and a sovereign fund: Black-Rock Inc. with 5 percent, Capital Research Management with 4.64 percent, Amundi (Credit Agricole AM/Société Générale AM) with 4 percent, Groupe Société Générale with 4 percent, CDC/FSI with 3.8 percent, and Emirates International Investment Company LLC with 2.8 percent.[27] Outside capital puts extra financial pressure on UMG, as investors demand returns. Again, profit prevails over art, as investors have no interest in the product anyway, as long as it sells.

UMG was among the first labels to sell digital versions of its music and video content, but it maintained constant concern about the security of its crown jewels, its music library. As it adapted to the various digital formats, UMG created a system known as the Huge Asset Library in order to hold its assets and automate the process by which they would be distributed via various online music services, each with its own unique format. It partnered with Savis to support its distribution of content to third parties such as iTunes, the legal Napster, Verizon, T-Mobile and others. In January 2010, UMG introduced Free All Music, its own music website that allowed music listeners to download free music in exchange for viewing short advertisements. This is hardly a new model; it follows the commercial broadcast practices of radio. It is just another way to turn audiences into commodities to be sold to advertisers. UMG digital service also set a new record of six million downloads of the Black-Eyed Peas song "I Got a Feeling." It also signed a deal with 19 Entertainment, creator of "American Idol," to market, promote, and distribute music spun off from the show. Lady Gaga became the first artist to surpass one million streaming listeners, followed by Justin Bieber, also a UMG artist. It also entered into a partnership with eMusic to provide U.S. members of its Digital Music Club access to the 250,000 songs in its music catalog, bringing eMusic's total library to ten million songs.[28] Its music video site, Vevo, a joint venture with Sony Abu Dhabi Media was established to distribute music videos. With the world's largest music catalog, UMG would continue to be a major player in the transformation of music from physical formats to all digital while seeking to maintain its oligopolistic status and the relevance of music labels.

Sony Music Entertainment

Sony Music Entertainment (SME) ranked second in terms of music distribution in 2010, with 27.4 percent.[29] SME was a subsidiary of the Sony Corporation of America, itself a subsidiary of Sony Corporation of Japan (see chapter 3). Sony's involvement in the music industry began in 1988, when it bought CBS Records with its flagship labels Columbia and Epic music for $2 billion. It became the second-largest music group when it merged with the Bertelsmann Music Group (BMG) in 2003, creating Sony BMG

Entertainment. In 2006, the group signed deals with Google and YouTube for digital distribution of its music and continued making deals with other online media servicers. In 2008, Sony bought out BMG's 50 percent share of the joint venture, eliminating BMG from the record label oligopoly and leaving the Big Four profiled here. In 2010, SME earned revenues of $5.7 billion out of Sony Corp.'s total revenues of $88 billion. Sony lost $3.2 billion during the fiscal year ending March 2010, the largest loss in sixteen years.[30] A small part of this was due to declining sales of DVDs and CDs. SME controlled several labels and sublabels covering all music genres, with operations around the world in some forty-four countries (see table 4.2).

Among Sony's leading artists were Aerosmith, Avril Lavgne, Beyoncé, Britney Spears, Bruce Springsteen, Christine Agulera, Dave Matthews Band, Dixie Chicks, Foo Fighters, Glee, Kenny G, Madonna, Pearl Jam, Ricky Martin, Santana, Shakira, and Tori Amos, along with a number of international

Table 4.2. Sony Record Labels, 2010

American Recordings
Arista Nashville
Arista Records
Battery Records
Beach Street Records
BNA Records
Columbia Nashville
Columbia Records
Day 1
Epic
Essential Records
Flicker Records
J Records
Jive Records
LaFace Records
Legacy Recordings
MASTERWORKS
Polo Grounds
RCA Nashville
RCA Records
RCA Red Seal
RCA Victor
Reunion Records
Roc Nation
Sony Classical
Sony Music Latin
Star Time International
Verity Gospel Music Group
Volcano Entertainment

music acts. Its back catalog also included several famous deceased artists, such as Michael Jackson. UMG's success with Jackson's CDs and a motion picture after his death led it to sign a lucrative deal worth $250 million in 2010 with the Jackson estate to continue to repackage released music as well as unreleased music and any other use of his work in all platforms including video games. In 2009, immediately after Jackson's death, works released in the first nine months of sales of his music totaled 31 million albums, with two-thirds coming from overseas.[31] Nielsen SoundScan reported that Jackson's catalog sold 8,285,000 albums in the fiscal year ending 31 March 2009, dropping to 2,118,000 units in 2010. Still, dead artists can generate large revenues over time as the record labels continually promote them.

Sony/ATV Music Publishing was established as a joint venture with trusts formed by Michael Jackson that owned the melody and words to 750,000 songs by legendary artists. It led the country music publisher market share with 12.8 percent of the nation's airplay. It included catalogs acquired from Famous and Leiber & Stoller in 2007, acquiring rights to film scores such as *The Godfather* (Francis Ford Coppola, 1972), *Braveheart* (Mel Gibson, 1995), and the theme to the television show *Mission Impossible*. Songs that came with the catalogs included "Stand by Me" and more than twenty of the greatest songs recorded by Elvis Presley, including "Houndog" and "Jailhouse Rock." A publishing division owns, manages, and exploits this music as copyright permission is required for the use of words or music in songs. It does not own the right to the master recordings, which belong to the labels. Music publishers also earn revenues by licensing writers the right to use their own songs in radio airplay or sell their own CDs and/ or a digital song/album, and from music used in films, TV shows, and TV commercials.[32]

Like UMG, Sony joined the transition from physical formats to digital delivery of music. Sony spent much of the decade trying to protect access to its catalog through digital rights management (DRM). By 2008, Sony moved to a DRM free format—the last of the majors to do so—and began licensing its music catalog to third-party digital music services. Sony BMG signed a license agreement with advertiser-supported we7, based in the United Kingdom, for streaming its catalog of one million tracks. The deal signaled that music distribution would continue to be tied to advertising, with the Internet again turning audiences into commodities to be sold to the industry. That year also, Sony licensed its catalog to Amazon's MP3 store but continued to hold out with the other majors to sign with iTunes due to its dominance of the digital download market with up to 88 percent of the market since 2006 and due to Apple's refusal to introduce variable pricing per song. Instead, it searched for other partners such as the ad-supported music service Qtrax, which already had deals with EMI and UMG. Qtrax was to share ad revenue with labels and publishers of those works, with the goal of being able to legitimately offer thirty million songs. In 2009 Sony became the first major to license its music video catalog to YouTube. Once Apple decided to make its iTunes Store DRM free, Sony and the other majors signed on. Under pressure from the majors, Apple eventually introduced variable pricing. Also in 2009, Sony signed a deal with eMusic, a service that charged a subscription fee for a specific number of songs for download. The deal was a step away from eMusic's primary focus on delivery of independently published music.[33] The independents worried that they would be marginalized. Sony also expanded its global digital presence by signing deals in Italy, Russia, and Germany. In 2010 Sony partnered with others to create Music Choice, a multiplatform video and music network delivering music to millions of consumers through televisions, cell phones, and the Internet. This service illustrated the interconnectedness of the industry, as it involved partnerships among subsidiaries of Microsoft, Motorola, EMI Music, and the top three U.S. cable providers: Comcast, Cox, and Time Warner Cable.[34]

After years of third-party partnerships, Sony launched its own fee-based streaming digital music service in 2011, called Music Unlimited.[35] Its partners included the other three majors, and its goal was to cut out the middleman and gain more control and revenues over the retail market dominated by iTunes, Wal-Mart Stores, and Amazon.com. BMI, the music royalty collection society, signed on with more than 6.5 million musical compositions in its vault. The service was powered by Qriocity, a cloud-based music service that gave music consumers access at any time to its 7 million songs and generated competition with Spotify, another ad-supported service.[36] The service was first rolled out in Europe and could be used via Sony's Playstation 3 game consoles, Blue-ray disc player, and its network-enabled BRAVIA televisions. It was slated to become available on a wide range of Sony's portable devices, Android-based mobile devices, and other portable devices. The service therefore utilized a number of Sony's hardware devices, culminating its hardware-software synergies. Hence Sony received revenues from both the music and the hardware.

With the launch of Music Unlimited and its almost instant success, Sony threatened to terminate its licensing agreement with iTunes Store but signed on with Apple's cloud service, along with EMI and WMG (though the service was not yet up and running), realizing it could not untie the knot with the number one digital music service. Apple was following Google and Amazon's lead with a streaming service from the cloud instead of having to download it to a hard drive—again, allowing consumers to access music via handheld devices or directly to Web browsers and cell phones. In 2011, Apple formally launched its cloud service iTunes Match, a $25-a-year service that scans users' devices and hard drives for music acquired in other ways. Apple stores the music on central computer servers to allow its subscribers access to their music anywhere, including ripped or swapped songs. Apple reached the deal by giving recording companies more than 70 percent of the new fees generated by the service, which allowed them to make more on digital music and slow overall revenue declines. Amazon had led the way by developing a digital music locker service so that consumers could have ready access to their music collections stored in a central server. During this period, many streaming services failed, but Sony's Music Unlimited had an advantage—again due to its hardware, which were predicted to total 350 million Sony devices by the early 2010s.[37]

Another advantage came with Sony's enormous marketing power. In 2009, Sony was the nineteenth leading advertiser in the United States, spending $1.46 billion to promote its movies, music, video games, and hardware.[38] Nevertheless, Sony's transition to digital music did not offset declines in physical sales and only indirectly affected digital music piracy by opening up what the industry calls a legitimate service. It remained a global force in developing artists and promoting them, which was still the key to success for artists in the music business and profits for the firm. Musicians complained all along that while digital music profits rose, they were receiving very little of it.

Warner Music Group

The Warner Music Group (WMG) finished the year 2010 with 14 percent of the music distribution share. Its full year revenue in the fiscal year ending September 30, 2010, totaled almost $3 billion, down 9 percent from the year before. Recorded music was down 7.1 percent to about $2.5 billion from 2009, with 48 percent of that coming from the domestic market and 58 percent from international sales. Music publishing at Warner/Chappell, the owner of "Happy Birthday to You" and copyrights to one million songs, was also down to just $556 million, 38 percent domestic and 62 percent international. The only bright spot was digital revenues, which rose 6 percent for the year to $759 million, roughly a quarter of total revenues.[39] Major artists for the year 2010 included Michael Bublé, Jay-Z, Linkin Park, Muse, and the sound track for *New Moon* (Chris Weitz, 2009). Some of WMG's many labels are listed in table 4.3. WMG also provided sales, marketing, and distribution services for physical and digital, and audio and video products, both to its own labels and to leading independent labels, through Warner-Elektra-Atlantic Corporation (WEA Corp.), Alternative Distribution Alliance (ADA), and Ryko Distribution. In addition, WMG operated through numerous affiliates and licensees in more than fifty countries.[40]

In 2000, WMG was folded in with the merger between AOL and Time Warner (see chapter 2). In 2003, AOL–Time Warner sold off WMG, including Warner/Chappell Music Publishers, to Edgar Bronfman Jr. for $2.6 mil-

Table 4.3.   Warner Music Group Labels

Asylum
Atlantic
Cordless
East West
Elektra
Nonesuch
Reprise
Rhino
Roadrunner
Ryko
Sire
Warner Bros.
Warner Music Nashville
Word

lion in order to reduce its $30 billion debt load incurred after the merger. Several other properties were sold off in what has been aptly called a giant "corporate garage sale."[41] For Bronfman, it was an opportunity to polish his tarnished image from his time at UMG. Bronfman's investors included the private equity firms Thomas H. Lee Partners, Bain Capital (co-founded by Mitt Romney), and Providence Equity Partners. Their offer topped that of EMI. For Time Warner it meant losing the synergies between music and filmed entertainment, a system that had existed since the introduction of sound motion pictures in the late 1920s. At that time Warner Brothers sought to reduce licensing fees for sound tracks by buying Chappell Music Publishing in 1929. The terms of the sale of WMG left Time Warner with the corporate title "Warner Music" and the right to buy back up to 19 percent of WMG under certain conditions. This never happened. Most importantly, WMG went from a publicly traded company under Time Warner, as Bronfman and his investors took it private.

Doug Henwood defines private equity funds as "pools of capital raised from institutional investors such as pension funds and very rich individuals, all gathered together to do deals" to take publicly traded firms private.[42] In the 1980s, they were referred to as leveraged buyouts (LBOs), until the term took on understandably negative connotations as depicted in the film *Wall Street* (Oliver Stone, 1987). The primary strategies of private equity managers involve serious cost-cutting, including eliminating jobs, and selling off unprofitable assets, while squeezing out as much profit as they can from what is left. After turning so-called distressed companies around, the private equity firms sell them wholesale to other buyers, yielding proceeds much higher than the initial costs of the buyout. In other cases, they sell the company back to the public through initial public offerings (IPOs) through the stock market. As the cost cutting and sell-offs occur, private equity managers pay themselves large fees (on which they pay only 15 percent in income taxes, the capital gains rate, rather than the 35 percent income rate), waiting for what Henwood calls "the magic" to kick in.[43]

Many members listed on the *Forbes 400* Richest Americans list have included private equity owners. These billionaire investors held investments in almost every sector of the U.S. economy, including the media. Private equity firms, using partnerships, seek to leverage their buyouts by using banks for debt financing. The more private equity firms borrow from banks, and the less they have to use of their own money, the richer the payoff in the end. However, the banks are owed returns on the capital they invested. The first thing private equity firms do is cut jobs. WMG eliminated 2,000 of its 6,500 workforce, cutting back on workers in global operations by 20 percent, cutting back on artists by 30 percent, cutting back on signing new artists, and producing fewer releases, reducing costs by $250 million.[44] By 2009, the workforce was down to 3,400. In early 2005, investors began asking for their money back as the company's performance was dragged down by general industry woes—declining CD sales and piracy—and concern about WMG's heavy debt load. In 2005, WMG announced that it was going public with an IPO of 32.6 million shares to be traded on the New York Stock Exchange. WMG initially set the price between $22 and $24 per share but was forced to drop down to $17 per share as investors saw its capitalization as over-valued. Its plans to allocate $574 million to debt fell short by $20 million.[45] The stock closed at $16.40 a share at the end of its first day. However, WMG could boast about its status as the largest free-standing, publicly owned recording company.

After the IPO, WMG's stock continued to decline to as low as $5 per share. For Bronfman and his private equity partners the magic was not kicking in. Meanwhile, WMG pursued integration with various digital platforms, offering to release its music DRM-free in 2007. Bronfman pioneered a new approach toward musicians by treating them in a manner "almost like [the] venture capital business."[46] If artists seemed to be asking too much, they could simply go elsewhere, as did Madonna, who signed with Live Nation with a $250 million advance. Rather, Bronfman followed the practices of the popular music industry of the 1930s and 1940s. By going with new bands, the company could leverage its bargaining power with bands from the outset, rather than deal with established stars. WMG struggled with the strategy for the rest of the decade, but it became the dominant model in the industry with the emergence of so-called 360-degree deals that the labels were making, through which musicians gave up all their rights to the labels in exchange for development, distribution in all formats, and promotion.

In January 2011, WMG announced it was taking bids to sell all or part of the company. The announcement led to a bidding frenzy during a three-month auction period. Among the early bidders were music companies Live Nation and BMG Rights Management (a joint venture between Bertelsmann and private equity firm Kohlberg Kravis Roberts and Co.) and the Sony Corporation, which was especially interested in WMG's song-publishing unit. Other bidders included Platinum Equity; Yucaipa Co., controlled by Ron Burkle (number 98 on the 2010 *Forbes 400*, worth 3.2 billion), Len Blavatnick (number 31, worth $7.5 billion), and investor Ron Perelman (number 24, worth $11 billion).[47] By April, WMG decided it would sell the company as a whole unit. The most controversial bid was Live Nation's bid on WMG's recorded music operations. The Live Nation–Ticketmaster merger had come under intense year-long scrutiny by federal antitrust officials of a deal that would bring together the largest owner and operator of concert venue events and the largest seller of tickets. After approval of the deal by the Department of Justice, Live Nation sought reverse vertical integration by signing Madonna, Nickelback, and Jay-Z to 360 deals that included touring, merchandising, and any publishing rights. Live Nation stopped making the deals as the concert industry and CD sales declined, but had it bought WMG's recorded music division it could have released its own artists' albums rather than building them from scratch. Once WMG insisted on selling the company as a whole, Live Nation left the bidding war.

The winner was Russian American Len Blavatnik's Access Industries, which paid $3.3 billion in an all-cash transaction including the assumption of $1.9 billion of WMG's debt. Access Industries held diverse assets in natural resources, chemicals, media, telecommunications, and real estate. Blavatnik had served on WMG's board of directors between March 2004 and January 2008, and by 2011 already owned 2 percent of the company's stock. Among Access Industries other media and telecommunications holdings were Top UP TV; Scandanavian mobile and voice services provider ice. net; and Amedia, a Russian television series producer. For Edgar Bronfman Jr., it was another unsuccessful effort to revive his image as a music mogul. Blavatnik did not say whether Bronfman would stay on as CEO. For Thomas H. Lee partners, the magic did indeed set in, as its 2004 private equity investment doubled while the company struggled.

The primary issue Access Industries faced with the acquisition of WMG was how to increase its digital presence, as it had long lagged behind the other three majors. It had joined the three other majors in 2008 by going with the Dupral management system that began offering DRM-free music. That year it also joined UMG and Sony BMG in launching MySpace Music, a service that offered DRM-free MP3 downloads, as well as ad-supported video and audio streams, ringtones, merchandise, and concert tickets. Yet it refused to renew its license with Last.fm to use its music and had still not permitted Vevo to use its artists' music videos or license to ad-supported services. But in 2011, it signed with Apple's cloud service in hopes of squeezing out more revenues from digital music. The takeover by Access Industries offered new opportunities with its various media outlets. There were hints that Blavatnik was not finished with his music acquisitions, as Citigroup put EMI up for sale in 2011.

EMI

EMI, based in London, had the smallest share of the music distribution market in 2010, with 10.2 percent.[48] It regularly lagged behind the other three majors throughout the first decade of this century. EMI's history is interesting, as it was a creation of Thorn PLC, a vast British media and manufacturing conglomerate. In this case, Thorn was looking for a way to promote the sale of its record players, televisions, and radios. So it developed its own music division. When it acquired Capitol Records, it became highly profitable from sales of records, including works by artists such as the Beatles and Pink Floyd. Thorn spun off EMI in 1996, and it has been at the bottom of the rankings since then, although it managed to get by with a small number of major artists focusing on blockbusters. It did control the world's largest music publishing division, with some 1.3 million songs. Its major label groups, all of which have sublabels, are listed in table 4.4. Its stand-alone labels included EMI Music and Capitol Music Nashville, among others. It also had subsidiaries in Europe, Africa, South America, and Asia. Among the artists in its publishing catalog were Lily Allen, Bat for Lashes, the Beatles, Beastie Boys, Luke Bryan, Coldplay, Depeche Mode, Gorillaz, David Guetta, Iron Maiden, Norah Jones, Lady Antebellum, Massive Attack, Kylie Minogue, Katy Perry, Pink Floyd, Corinne Bailey Rae, Sir Simon Rattle, Snoop Dogg, Tinie Tempah, Thirty Seconds To Mars, KT Tunstall, Keith Urban, and Robbie Williams, as well as international artists such as Amaral (Spain), Air and Camille (France), Empire of the Sun (Australia), Tiziano Ferro and Vasco Rossi (Italy), Flex (Mexico), LaFee (Germany), and Hikaru Utada (Japan).[49]

The company's small size relative to the majors made it attractive for takeover by one of the other majors. Instead, EMI agreed to be taken private by Terra Capital Partners in July 2007 for $4.8 billion, largely by borrowing funds from Citigroup. The British-based Terra Firma was a private equity firm controlled by Guy Hands. Speaking to the Royal Television Society in

Table 4.4. EMI Major Record Groups

Blue Note
Capitol Music
Caroline Distribution
EMI Christian Music Group
Virgin

September 2007, Hands proclaimed that Terra Firma's strategy was to "look for the worst business we can find in the most challenged section, and we're really happy if it's really, really bad. We're just hoping that EMI is as bad as we think it is."[50] The first step in Terra Firma's business plan for EMI was to oust existing management and members of the board of directors, replacing them with its own people. The company was restructured to make operations more centralized and streamlined. Some divisions were merged and others cut back or eliminated. The second strategy involved considerable cost cutting, including two thousand jobs (one-third of its workforce). EMI reviewed artists' contracts with the bottom line in mind. Like WMG, it allowed several major acts—including the Rolling Stones, Radiohead, and Paul McCartney—to sign elsewhere. One of the industry's perks was that artist and repertoire (A&R) personnel had been able to scout freely for new talent nationwide and globally. Such talent searches were severely curbed, as EMI became fixated with minimizing costs and maximizing revenues in evolving music markets. A third strategy involved so-called partnering with artists selling less than 200,000 albums; that is, providing initial production, distribution, and marketing services, all while billing musicians for them. Partnering helps expose artists, who take all the risks. The record label was covered for its services by the artist, avoiding any losses should the recording not sell. Finally, EMI admitted that it would continue to focus on blockbusters: the multimillion sellers, which remain the industry's real cash cows. This suggested, of course, that listeners could expect more of the same.

Terra Firma held a wide range of businesses, owning thirty companies in the United States and Europe, including Waste Recycling Group, Phoenix Inns, Annington Homes (seller of refurbished homes), and the world's third-largest airline leasing company, and it was Europe's largest movie theater owner, including the Odeon Cineplex chain. Such conglomeration gave EMI the room to continue losing money until it became profitable or salable, which is the logic behind the formation of conglomerates. If certain divisions are down for the year, there are others to make up for losses, thereby maintaining steady annual revenue flows. However, the EMI deal did indeed end up being really, really bad and had exposed 30 percent of Terra Firma's total portfolio. In February 2011, Terra Firma's main creditor, Citigroup, took over 100 percent of EMI by putting Maltby Investments Ltd., the parent company of EMI, into bankruptcy. Even though EMI had not breached loan covenants at the time, Terra Firma's equity had been wiped out.[51] In November 2011, Citigroup announced the sale of EMI's recorded-music unit to UMG for $1.9 billion and its music publishing division to a group headed by SME for $2.2 billion. SME was to become a minority partner in a consortium including the Michael Jackson estate, Mubadala Development Co. sovereign fund of Abu Dhabi, Jynwel Capital Ltd., Blackstone Group, and the billionaire media mogul David Geffen (number 58 on the *Forbes 400* in 2001).[52]

EMI was a pioneer in the transition to digital. Its first websites were launched in 1993 and 1994. It was the first to stream an entire digital album, *Mezzanine* by Massive Attack, in 1998. A year later it was the first major to release an album for download—David Bowie's *Hours*. In 2001, EMI made the first digital video single "Dig In" by Lenny Kravitz. EMI was the first of the major labels to release its music DRM-free in 2007 and signed up with iTunes. In November 2010, EMI licensed the Beatles to iTunes, a long-awaited development. The next year it signed with Apple's cloud service iTunes Match. It expanded its partnerships with digital services to more than one hundred outlets by 2010, along with its own website available around the world.[53] Some of these arrangements may be terminated if EMI is sold off in pieces. Otherwise, it was positioned to make the transition from physical to digital.

"The Independents"

In 2010 the so-called indie sector combined for an 11.6 percent share of music distributed in the United States. This figure does not take into account independent labels that were distributed by major-label-owned indie distributors such as WMG's ADA.[54] The industry's trade tracker Nielsen SoundScan therefore underestimates the percentage of independently produced music market sales because it is folded into the total distribution market share. This underscores how high the barriers to entry in the music industry really are. Even major media conglomerates have tried to enter the business with little success. News Corp. sought to build its own music label in 1996. The synergy potential was high, with a wide range of media outlets including television, film, books, and other media. Its intent was to build acts in-house under the Festival label. In 1999, it expanded horizontally by buying out Australia-based Mushroom Records, creating Festival Mushroom Records under the control of Rupert Murdoch's son James. Despite his efforts, the label never evolved into the major that News Corp. once envisioned, and it was sold in 2006 to Warner Music Australia. In 2008, News Corp. signed up the Big Four for Myspace Music, an advertiser-supported digital music service. UMG was an investor in Myspace Music, the part of the social network that streamed songs online. By 2011, the social networking site Myspace's popularity gave way to Facebook; it lost 29 percent to 62.6 million visitors, from 88 million in February 2011.[55] In mid-July 2011, the advertising network Specific Media acquired Myspace for $35 million, less than one-tenth of what News Corp. paid for the company in 2005 at $580 million. Five hundred workers were laid off. As part of the deal, News Corp. took a private equity stake in Specific Media. Justin Timberlake also took an ownership stake in the company, promising to revitalize the site.

The Walt Disney Company, also included in the "independent" category, has been in the music business since 1955 with the creation of Disneyland Records. The focus has been on synergies with its film and television products. Disney sought to broaden its presence in the music industry when it established Hollywood Records in 1990, signing deals with rappers and alternative rock musicians. In 1996, Hollywood Records was pressured to pull the rap act Insane Clown Posse's disc from stores after complaints regarding obscene lyrics. Disney still had to maintain its family-friendly image. The label did not produce a blockbuster artist until 2003 as the synergies between the Disney Channel and Radio Disney. Disney's formula was to build stars from scratch with massive promotion. Hillary Duff was the label's first success, with her first album selling 5 million copies and her second 13 million. Then along came a string of major artists, including the Cheetah Girls, Vanessa Hudgens, Raven Symoné, Miley Cyrus, Demi Lovato, Selena Gomez and The Scene, and the Jonas Brothers, many aimed at the so-called tweeners, consumers between the ages of thirteen and nineteen, but some as young as six. However, Hollywood Records still relied on the Big Four for distribution, primarily UMG.

A distinction must be made between so-called boutique or vanity labels and the indies. The former usually involve an already-established artist who signs with a major label. Usually the artists were promised more artistic freedom and expected to sign new artists to the label. In 1992, Madonna and two partners formed Maverick Records with Time Warner. Though the label had broken some successful artists, including Alanis Morrisette, it was losing money. In 2004 Maverick sued the Warner Music Group, claiming the parent company's poor management of resources and questionable bookkeeping was to blame. WMG countersued, claiming the losses were by Maverick itself. WMG then bought out Madonna and her partners, keeping the label for itself. Another traditional strategy used by the majors was to sign successful independent artists away from an indie, or in the case of WMG, buy out the entire label as it did with Sub Pop, the Seattle label that brought grunge into the spotlight. The indies have always been large in number but small in sales. Dischord Records had one of the simplest business models in the CD days: Send $10 to the label and get the CD postage-free. There are other models, but indies still rely on independent distributors in order to avoid dealing with the music oligopoly, those not owned wholly or in part by one of its members. For the majors, indies have served largely as test markets where the high risks are taken by someone else—that is, the costs of production, distribution, and especially marketing and promotion. In essence, the majors have learned to scrape the cream off the top.

Obviously, the Internet has become an active site for musicians, including many independent artists. Studio-quality production is now widely available to those who can afford the technology and learn how to use the programs. Do-it-yourself (DIY) musicians have used the full range of Internet outlets to get their music heard for free. While access to listeners is cheap, finding audiences will always be a problem. Getting them to pay is another challenge. There are music sites dedicated to independent music that require a dedicated audience. But the achievement of broad appeal still requires marketing and promotion, as it generally has since the heyday of pop music in the 1930s and 1940s. This is why most musicians have sought to sign deals with labels with the capital to produce, distribute, and promote them. Indie labels and DIYers have added more musical content to the scene, but much of it results in multiplicity rather than genuine diversity. There often is an inherent tension between artistic success and artistic creativity. Success generally follows imitation. Producing music that challenges the dominant genres and provides a critique of the existing political-economic order is work for both the artist and the listener. Music has proven to be a site of resistance and has played a role in promoting social change, domestically and globally. However, the global reach of the major labels mostly leads to homogenization of music as global pop spreads. There is also a process of hybridization of music—for example, mixing imported music in with indigenous influences. This makes maintaining a purely indigenous sound extremely difficult, as local labels must compete with global subsidiaries of the Big Four.

Will digital distribution of music make the major labels any less powerful? Not if one's desire is to sell a million copies or more. According to data from the International Federation of Phonographic Industries (IFPI), the industry global trade association, the idea that artists no longer need record labels thanks to the Internet is "the biggest myth."[56] The average investment in a pop act costs around $1 million, including an advance of $200,000 to the band; $200,000 to produce the recording; $200,000 for three videos; $100,000 for tour support; and $300,000 for promotion—the greatest expense.[57] These expenses are then left to the band to recoup through royalties earned on music sales, touring, merchandise, endorsements, and fan-club fees. Previously, touring was a loss leader for the band, an expense intended to sell albums. Often a band would find itself owing the record companies seeking to recoup their investments. Another risk is that the band will not be promoted and sufficiently branded to become successful. Major labels do not have to release the music if they see no market potential. In cases such as these, a band may be able to buy its music back from the label; otherwise it will never be heard. A label contract is no guarantee of success. According to the IFPI, estimates of commercial major label success vary between one in five and one in ten.[58]

MUSIC FOR MONEY

Retail: The Song Remains the Same

It is important to examine changes in the music industry in the retail, concert, and radio sectors since the beginning of the new century. Since the early 1980s, concentration in the music recording industry was matched by concentration at the retail level. Chain music stores accounted for 53 percent of total U.S. album sales in 2001. Mass merchants, including department stores such as Wal-Mart, Kmart, and Target, in addition to consumer electronics outlets such as Best Buy and Circuit City, accounted for another 30.2 percent of 2001 album sales. Independent retailers continued to see their share of record sales decline in 2001 to 13.4 percent. Concert, television, and online outlets accounted for another 3 percent of record sales in 2001.[59] The decline of independent retailers was part of a larger trend that included the demise of independent video outlets and bookstores. The loss of independent music stores had its price. They often guaranteed an eclectic stock, as well as impassioned and knowledgeable personal service. Chains and mass marketers relied on central buyers and employees who had little influence over what appeared on their store shelves.

Music, video, and bookstore chains and mass merchants relied on heavy sales of blockbuster titles and rapid turnover of inventory. A CD, video, or book that sits on the shelf represents unsold product and costly space. This results in the massive hype of best sellers, which take up most of the shelf space. The large discount electronics retailers have used CDs and DVDs as a loss leader, selling them below cost to draw customers into their stores and tempt them with more expensive items. The large retail chains, department stores, and video dealers such as Wal-Mart, Kmart, and Blockbuster took it upon themselves to monitor the content of the products they sold. Wal-Mart alone accounted for somewhere between 7 and 10 percent of annual record sales in the late 1990s. The monster retailer therefore had the power to require record labels and bands to change album design covers and inserts, delete songs from albums, electronically alter objectionable words, and even change lyrics.[60]

For example, Wal-Mart rejected a 1996 Sheryl Crow recording due to lyrics suggesting that the company sold guns to children. Wal-Mart asked Crow and her label, A&M Records, to change the lyrics on all copies of the album, not just those meant for its own retail outlets. Crow refused, forgoing 10 percent of her potential record sales. For Crow fans in Murphy, North Carolina, Wal-Mart was the only record outlet around at the time. The nearest record stores were 50 to 150 miles away in Atlanta and Gainesville, Georgia.[61] The effects of the concentrated structure of music production, distribution, and retail made many music fans and musicians hopeful that the Internet would break up the music oligopoly. That assumption remained dubious with regard to music production and distribution. The retail sector also evolved as a result of Internet technology but remained highly concentrated. In 2010, iTunes was the largest music retailer, with 28 percent of all music—both physical and digital—purchased in the United States. Amazon finished in a tie for second with Wal-Mart at 12 percent.[62] This meant that 80 percent of the digital downloads were accounted for by just two companies, with the remainder split among a number of smaller services. The top three retailers of CDs were Wal-Mart (17 percent), Best Buy (14 percent), and Amazon (11 percent). Both of the brick-and-mortar stores reduced their overall inventory to sell nothing but blockbusters.

One victim of the shift in the retail market was the decline of music retail chains. One of the most historic chains, Tower Records, filed for bankruptcy and was liquidated in 2006. Two other important chains, Wherehouse Records and Virgin Megastores, also closed. Although chain stores also relied on sales of blockbusters, they offered more variety than the big box stores in terms of back catalogs. In 2011 there were four thousand record stores with revenues of $3 billion. The top three chains were Trans World Entertainment, Hastings Entertainment, and CD Warehouse. Out of the four thousand retail outlets, just fifty controlled 80 percent of the total business.[63] There were only about fourteen hundred independent record stores nationwide. The independents created Record Store Day in 2007 to highlight their existence, after their number dropped 40 percent between 2004 and 2010.[64] To attract customers, they offered exclusive vinyl records and limited-edition CDs. A small but loyal group of music fans, especially those of rock music, still enjoy the tangibility of a record, its artwork, lyrics, and liner notes, as opposed to music reduced to zeros and ones.

The few music chains remaining, such as Trans World (986 stores in 2000 declining to 565 by 2010), have diversified their line of products while narrowing the pipeline for CD sales. At Trans World, only 37 percent of sales were generated by music in 2010.[65] Chains were forced to cut prices on CDs in order to combat predatory pricing (that is, pricing below wholesale) by the big boxes. The decline of the CD was not caused solely by the rise of digital delivery systems. The wholesale prices of CDs were kept artificially high even as the costs of manufacturing them declined. For years, music buyers complained about the high price of CDs. At the same time, the performing artist or band often never saw a dime from CD sales unless it sold a million or more, after the record labels first recouped their expenses first. Traditionally, recording artists have not received royalties when their music is used in a public performance—on the radio, TV, at bars and restaurants, or anywhere else the music is used. This was based on the notion that public performances generated record sales from which artists would ultimately benefit according to their contract with the labels, generally set at 8 percent or higher for big name acts, minus 25 percent for a packaging fee. The Digital Performance Rights in Sound Recordings Act of 1995 gave recording artists their first performance right to directly receive royalties for digital performances via non-interactive Webcasts and satellite radio.

Mechanical royalties for the use of a song are paid to songwriters and publishers, not the artist. Mechanical rights were not extended to digital downloads, ringtones, and other services until 2008, based on a ruling by the Copyright Royalty Board that set rates for permanent digital downloads at 9.1 cents for each track, the same as for physical recordings. Music download stores, like brick-and-mortar stores, pay the record label, which in turn pays the recording artist a royalty based on the contract between the two parties. However, by treating music downloads as so-called new media/ technology, the record companies paid artists a lower royalty rate than for physical music while still charging a packaging fee. Still, the industrialization of legal digital music downloading did not slow the decline in overall music revenues. This is what inspired labels to come up with 360-degree deals, through which they could generate revenues from ancillary outlets including publishing rights, concert receipts, merchandising, and other income streams flowing to performing artists. The practice was still in its infancy at the time of this writing, and the jury was still out as to whether the deals would be productive. One effect is that record companies would no longer focus just on music sales. Through exploitation of ancillary rights, they could now focus on branding bands, giving them greater control over recording artists while reducing deals with performers that did not lend themselves to becoming brands.

Live Music Nation

Concerts provide music fans direct contact with performing artists. Touring is an essential part of building a fan base. Some tours can be highly profitable for big name acts; other times bands end up losing money from touring once all expenses are paid. In 2010 live music concerts generated $9.3 billion in the United States.[66] However, concert revenues declined that year, as total ticket sales dropped 12 percent from 2009 to 26.9 million (7 percent worldwide).[67] In 2009, just two promotion companies, Live Nation and the Anschutz Entertainment Group (AEG), accounted for two-thirds of all live music tickets sold in the United States. In January 2010, the concert industry became even more highly concentrated, with the Justice Department's approval of the merger of Ticketmaster and Live Nation. Ticketmaster had already conquered the live-event ticket sales market with 70 percent, and Live Nation, after being spun off from the Clear Channel radio chain in 2005, had gained control of concert venues. In 2010, Live Nation was the largest live entertainment company in the world, connecting roughly

200 million fans at 100,000 events in forty countries. Within this range, Live Nation was the largest producer of live music events in 2010, bringing in 47 million fans to more than 21,000 events for over 2,300 artists. Globally, Live Nation owned, operated, obtained booking rights for, and/ or had an equity interest in 128 venues, including House of Blues chain of music venues and other notable venues such as the Fillmore in San Francisco and the Hollywood Palladium.[68] Ticketmaster was the world's leading live entertainment ticketing sales and marketing company, based on tickets sold. Since its establishment in 1976, it grew to serve clients worldwide for leading arenas, stadiums, professional sports franchises and leagues, college sports teams, performing arts venues, museums, and theaters. This vertically integrated company was also one of the world's leading artist management companies, based on the number of artists represented across music genres. Its Front Line division had about 250 artists on its rosters and over ninety managers providing services to performers including Miley Syrus, Willie Nelson, Van Halen, Neil Diamond, Christine Aguilera, Kid Rock, Marroon 5, and the Kings of Leon. Finally, it was the world's largest music marketing network for corporations to integrate their advertising into the concert experience and generate additional revenue.[69] It also partnered with Bacardi on its mobile website in 2011 and was seeking deals with other major brands.

Live Nation concerts were the company's largest source of revenue in 2010 at 67 percent, $3.4 billion of the company's total revenues of just over $5 billion.[70] This money was earned with the company as promoter, with revenue coming primarily from ticket sales that are used to pay performers, either a fixed amount and/or a percentage of ticket sales or event profits. As a venue operator, Live Nation generated revenue primarily from the sale of food and beverages, parking, premium seating rental income, venue sponsorships, and service charges on tickets sold at the company's venues or by third parties under ticketing agreements. Its ticketing segment, Ticketmaster, sold tickets for events on behalf of Live Nation clients and retained a convenience charge and order processing fee for its services. In 2010, the ticketing business generated approximately $1 billion, or 20.5 percent of the company's total revenue.[71]

Irving Azoff became chairman of the board of the newly merged Live Nation after chairing Ticketmaster since 2008. Azoff had a long history as a music mogul and was one of the most powerful individuals in the music industry. He played a large role in the rise of the professional stadium-tour era. Then he became "as close to a commissioner for live music as this country has ever had."[72] Indeed, under his guidance, income shifted for performing artists from music sales to live music. More leading artists began to make the bulk of their money from touring and merchandise sales. They decided they would rather deal through Ticketmaster and earn money from ticket sales. The price of tours and merchandise began to skyrocket much faster than the rate of inflation. Ticketmaster tacked on more fees to increase its cut: A Lady Gaga ticket included a $2.50 facility charge, a $15.45 convenience charge, and $2.50 to print out the ticket at home.[73] Some of this money traditionally went back to promoters in the form of rebates, but under Live Nation it became an in-house transaction. To gain federal government approval of the deal, however, the two sides were barred from sharing data. Other conditions included the sale of Paciolan to Comcast, and rights granted to AEG to use Ticketmaster's technology for five years.

AEG's Live Events division was Live Nation's biggest rival for concert venue ownership or exclusive booking arrangements, with thirty-five top venues. Its touring roster included artists such as Taylor Swift, the Black Eyed Peas, Bon Jovi, Usher, Carrie Underwood, Daughtry, Justin Bieber, Leonard Cohen, Kenny Chesney, Pink Floyd, and Paul McCartney. Its fifteen worldwide regional offices produced over 4,500 concerts a year, while its Goldenvoice division operated several music festivals.[74] Although the live music division was much smaller than that of Live Nation, the Anschutz Company (see chapter 3) had much deeper pockets and was more diversified in terms of its range of operations. A much smaller player was MSG Entertainment, a division of the Madison Square Garden Company. MSG presented or hosted over one thousand concerts, along with family shows and special events reaching more than 5 million people. Its venues included Madison Square Garden, Radio City Music Hall, The Theater at Madison Square Garden, The Beacon Theatre, The Chicago Theatre, and The Wang Theatre in Boston.[75] Still, it was not a formidable competitor with Live Nation.

The industry was structured such that audiences were never a primary consideration. Instead, Ticketmaster's most important clients other than Live Nation were unaffiliated venues. Its structural role was to expand the number of affiliated venues to sell more tickets. Promoters such as Live Nation kept raising prices on merchandise, including concessions and parking, and increasing advertising sponsorship of its concerts. Again, any system that depends on advertising is prone to give advertisers what they want, not necessarily what the audience wants. Furthermore, tours sponsored by beer or liquor companies exclude dry venues found on many college campuses. VIP pricing also became part of the ticketing sales structure, as more artists sought to maximize their gross and get a share of the market value for the best seats on resale sites such as StubHub. Top acts could make as much money on 10 percent of VIP seats as the other 90 percent of seats in the house. VIP sales for a Jon Bon Jovi concert in 2010 sold for $1,878, which included a takeaway chain, a leather bag, and a catered meal.[76] The worldwide tour brought in the highest gross that year, with revenue of $201 million. His North American take was $103.2 million, the lowest total in the recent years leading up to 2010. The other top tours in 2010 in North America ranked by earnings were Pink Floyd's *The Wall* tour ($89.5 million), Dave Matthews Band ($72.9 million), Canadian pop crooner Michael Bublé ($65.7 million), and the Eagles ($64.5 million). The record haul for a concert tour was generated by U2's 360° Tour, which grossed $624 million between 2009 and 2011 with a total attendance of 6.1 million.[77] The highest average ticket price in 2009 was $173.89 for Van Morrison's Astral Weeks Live; in 2010 it was the Pink Floyd tour, which charged $126.14 per ticket.[78] To be able to charge such prices, concerts turned increasingly into spectacles, diverting attention from the music itself. The special effects were seen as necessary to keep ticket prices high and to attract audiences to concert venues. Concentration in the concert industry leads to monopoly pricing, which is why prices kept rising. The barriers to entry into the live music industry remained high, as in the music industry as a whole.

Radio: A Sad Situation

Radio continued to play a major role in shaping audience listening preferences. In 2010, revenues in the radio business totaled $17.3 billion, levels not seen since 2006.[79] The industry was helped by politicians buying ads during election season that year. But overall, the industry was hit hard by the Great Recession, as advertisers cut the purchase of radio airtime. Advertising, both local and national, accounted for 90 percent of a radio station's revenue.[80] The largest spenders on advertising were communications/cellular services, auto dealers/manufacturers, television/networks/cable providers, restaurants, and financial services. The largest spot advertisers at the beginning of 2011 were AT&T, McDonald's, and Comcast.[81] The health of any advertiser-supported medium is at the mercy of advertisers. Cuts in radio or magazine advertising spending reduces revenues and the chances of survival. Listenership is also tied to employment; the higher the employment rate the more time people spend in cars commuting to work. Radio is most listened to in cars. At the same time, there were fewer radio listeners with the increased uses of personal electronic devices, podcasts, and webcasts. Video never really killed the radio star. In fact, the two created a symbiotic relationship so that what gets played the most is what gets bought or downloaded (legally or illegally). Concentration in the radio industry once again violates the normative goal of a democratic media system, which should provide genuine diversity—in this case, a rich variety of music.

The company with the largest share of the radio station market was not terrestrial, but satellite. In 2010, Sirius XM Radio led with 17.4 percent of the radio industry market. Sirius and XM merged in 2008, after both faced bankruptcy at the peak of the Great Recession. Both claimed they could not survive unless they merged. The merger, however, left just one company with the dominant position in the satellite radio industry and was opposed by media reformers for that reason. It allowed the company, whose programming could only be accessed through the company's own satellite radios, to integrate with manufacturers of autos that come with the radios. For out-of-car use, listeners needed a Sirius radio. In 2010, its subscriber base increased to 20.1 million, with each subscriber paying between $6.99 and $18.99 per month.[81] All music channels were ad-free, but the temptation of tapping the advertising market moved the company to put ads on nonmusic channels, producing a dual revenue stream from subscriptions and advertising. Sirius XM further cut costs through more thorough integration of the two separate companies, eliminating redundant operations and cutting employees. Its primary competition came from iPods and High Definition radio stations, as well as the largest terrestrial radio chains. The largest of these was CC Media Holdings, with 15.9 percent of the radio industry's market share, which operated the Clear Channel radio chain.[83] By 2011, Sirius XM started to sound more like its main terrestrial competitor.

At first, satellite radio Sirius and XM looked like they would provide an alternative to the homogenized and ad-supported radio industry. Both were not only ad-free but also more diverse, providing not just the mainstream hits but second-, third-, and fourth-tier music not available elsewhere. But due to mechanical royalty fees paid to music publishers and songwriters, these less popular channels did not justify the expense, even though they had dedicated fans. The companies also began spending large amounts of money on nonmusic content, such as the National Football League, Major League Baseball, Oprah Winfrey, and Howard Stern. The high cost for these deals drove the companies to begin cutting channels with less mainstream attractions, such as jazz, blues, and punk. After the merger, Sirius XM came out with Satellite Radio 2.0, with the potential to increase the number of channels the company could provide and bring back lost listeners. The more Sirius XM, and the radio industry in general, move toward nonmusic programming such as talk radio, the less focus there is on music itself. When satellite radio was dedicated to music, it served as a unique niche in reaching out to music fans.

When the Telecommunications Act of 1996—a backroom, communications-industry-written act—became law, the effects of deregulation in the radio industry were immediately felt. The law eliminated restrictions on the number of radio stations one company could own, and hence the overriding logic of capitalism toward economic concentration kicked in. Clear Channel Communications emerged as a dominant force during this period of expanding radio chains. Clear Channel went on a $30 billion spending spree to acquire more than twelve hundred radio stations. In the end, it controlled as many as seven stations in a single market; 60 percent of the rock radio stations in the United States; concert venues closely synergized

Chapter 4

with its radio stations (which refused to promote artists playing in venues not affiliated with Clear Channel); equity stakes in 240 international radio stations; outdoor advertising companies with 910,000 display locations worldwide; fifty television stations; and spot advertising reaching more than three thousand radio and TV stations. Clear Channel dubbed itself a specialist in so-called gone-from-home entertainment and information services for local communities, when in fact its radio stations were largely programmed from network headquarters in San Antonio, Texas. Its total audience reach was 145 million, roughly 75 percent of the U.S. adult population.[84]

In late 2006 Bain Capital Partners and Thomas H. Lee Partners began negotiations to take Clear Channel private. Bain and Lee offered $19.5 billion, including the assumption of $8 billion in debt, in a deal that originally was to close by the end of 2007. It was the largest private equity deal involving the media at the time. Clear Channel postponed shareholder votes twice during 2007 to stave off stockholder resistance. Then it began selling off assets to reduce debt, halt decline of share prices and profits, and keep Bain and Lee interested. Assets sold included live entertainment venues, 448 smaller-market radio stations, and 42 TV stations in twenty-four markets. In May 2007, Providence Equity Partners bought radio and TV stations from Clear Channel for $1.2 billion, less than 10 percent of the company's 2005 revenue, as it remained a behemoth in the radio industry.[85] The sale of the venues produced capital losses that were offset by spinning off broadcasting properties, resulting in "very efficient after-tax proceeds," according to Mark Mays, Clear Channel's CEO at the time.[86] Clear Channel then partnered with Google, guaranteeing the popular search engine a portion of thirty-second spots on Clear Channel stations.

Shaky credit markets led to an extension of the purchase date during which either party could have terminated the deal. At the same time, the five banks providing debt capital to Bain and Lee tried to back out as the credit market tightened. Bain and Lee, as well as Clear Channel, sued the banks for breach of contract, and the banks backed down. When Bain and Lee took over Clear Channel, it explicitly announced its intention to remain the nation's largest radio company while scaling down operations to only focus on the profitable stations. By 2010, it controlled 894 radio stations: 264 AM and 630 FM stations, earning revenues of $2.6 billion with net profits of $843 million.[87] The company also has decreased diversity throughout the industry. Clear Channel had already built a reputation for having an overt, conservative political orientation and shunning artists with any type of radical edge. Of course, Bain and Lee and the banks from which they borrowed did not care about the music at all. For private equity firms, the central goal is to recoup enough to pay off debts and hope to turn profits.

Advertisers love large media chains because they lower the transaction costs of buying ad time. Instead of dealing with thousands of individual radio stations, a newspaper or radio chain gives advertisers a bigger bang for their buck. In turn, as the dominant ad-supported radio company, CC Media Holdings could charge advertisers monopoly prices and earn monopoly profits—again, above a normal profit in a competitive industry. But the economies of scale still make dealing with chains a logical choice under capitalism. Basically, advertisers need the media as much as ad-supported media needs them, but sponsorship can also be pulled at any time if advertisers are uncomfortable with the radio station's content. So the relationship is not equal. Economies of scale are also achieved through the use of syndicated material and centralized programming, so much so that if one drives a long distance, passing through a number of listening areas, everything sounds the same. Radio, a medium highly suited for local programming, has become increasingly nationalized and homogenized. There once was a time when listeners could actually call up a disc jockey and request a song. This practice does not fit with pre-programmed, centralized broadcasting.

CBS Radio ranked first among terrestrial radio broadcasters, with 8.9 percent of the industry's market share in 2010.[88] The company was a division of CBS that in turn was controlled by Sumner Redstone's National Amusements (see chapter 2). Viacom acquired Infinity Broadcasting in 1999 from Westinghouse Electric Corporation, which acquired CBS Inc. in 1995 and Infinity Broadcasting in 1997. Under Viacom, Infinity Radio was reorganized to become CBS Radio. CBS owned 130 radio stations; all but one was located in the nation's top fifty markets and 75 percent were in the top twenty-five markets.[89] The stations offered news, sports, talk, rock, country, Top 40, classic hits, Spanish, urban formats, and more, for a total of twenty different formats.[90] CBS Radio also owned the CBS Radio Network, providing networked radio programming and traffic and weather information to CBS stations and competitors. The company was also the largest sports broadcaster, with play-by-play coverage of more than two dozen of the leading sports franchises in the United States. Among them were Major League Baseball, the National Football League, the National Basketball Association, the Women's National Basketball League, and the National Hockey League. Among the teams for which it provided radio coverage were the New York Yankees, New York Mets, St. Louis Cardinals, New England Patriots, New York Giants, Chicago Bears, and Detroit Red Wings. CBS Radio was among many media companies trying to gain leadership in digital outlets and bring about the convergence of new and traditional content with advanced delivery systems. Two hundred of its radio stations and some custom channels were available online. Another outlet for these stations was applications for a variety of mobile devices, including iPhone, iPod touch, iPad, Android, and Zune. Ten percent of its listenership used such devices.[91]

CBS Radio's corporate parent, CBS Corp., was made up of five divisions in 2010. Its Entertainment division was composed of the CBS Television Network, CBS Television Studios, CBS Studios International, CBS Television Distribution, CBS Films, and CBS Interactive. This division generated the largest portion of the company's revenue, with 53 percent. Its Cable Networks division was composed of Showtime Networks, CBS College Sports Network, and a joint venture with Smithsonian Networks to operate the Smithsonian Channel on cable. Cable networks accounted for 10 percent of the company's revenues. Its Publishing unit was made up of one of the nation's largest book publishers, Simon & Schuster, which included imprints such as Pocket Books, Scribner, and Free Press. Publishing accounted for 6 percent of revenues. Radio stations were located in its fourth division, called the Local Broadcasting segment. Local Broadcasting was composed of sixteen CBS broadcast television stations and the CBS Radio unit. Together this segment brought in 20 percent of total revenues. Its fifth segment, Outdoor, was responsible for the unavoidable advertising around us, such as plastered billboards, transit shelters, buses, rail systems, mall kiosks, retail stores, and stadium signage. This segment earned CBS 13 percent of its gross.[92]

CBS Radio used its diverse formats to help advertisers reach both mass and niche audiences. In those markets where it held multiple stations it did the same, formatting according to the needs of advertisers. Advertising produced the majority of the segment's revenues. Its strategies included employing popular on-air talent on its own stations and licensed to others; acquiring rights to non-CBS programming for its stations; acquiring the rights to broadcast sports play-by-play; and producing and acquiring news content for its radio stations. The major categories of advertisers included automobile, retail, health care, telecommunications, fast food, beverages, movies, and entertainment. It used its reach to create unique division-wide marketing and promotional initiatives for major national advertisers. CBS radio managed to attract the participation of major artists in these national campaigns. In the digital realm, nearly all of its radio stations operated websites, many of which were combined with the websites of the company's television stations in co-located markets, creating synergies. CBS operated music radio station websites, and its division Radio.com streamed the broadcast of its stations. Radio.com also powered custom channels for AOL and Yahoo! Together their apps had been downloaded 15 million times. Finally, it operated Last.fm, a music discovery and social networking site, mp3.com, and TheStreetDate.com. All of these websites earned most of their revenues from advertising, another sign of the continued commercialization of the Internet.

CBS faced competition not only from other terrestrial radio chains such as Clear Channel and Cumulus Media Inc. but from Sirius XM as well. Its

Internet operations faced competition from Internet radio services such as Pandora, Live 365, and Rhapsody. While CBS had a broad range of operations, as described above, radio also had to compete with other media, such as broadcast, cable and satellite television, newspapers, magazines, and direct mail. Its concern was that audiences would become increasingly alienated by ad-supported commercial radio and choose noncommercial sites for a monthly fee instead. For this reason, CBS radio stations implemented high-definition radio to increase the quality of its broadcasts. Over one hundred of its stations were broadcasting in high definition in 2010 and several others in HD2, HD3, and the first HD4 channel. But in its annual 10-K report filed with the Securities and Exchange Commission, the company expressed uncertainty about the impact of digital broadcasts and what effect they would have on CBS Radio or its ability to compete generally.[93] CBS Radio had a better chance of survival with its deep pockets and brand than most other companies in the industry.

In 2010, IBIS*World* estimated Citadel Broadcasting took in 3.5 percent of the radio industry share.[94] It was the second-largest terrestrial radio group in the United States, with a national footprint reaching fifty markets. It controlled 166 FM stations and 59 AM stations in the top markets. Citadel brands included WJA, NBC Blue, ABC Radio, and ESPN Radio Network. It also had more than 4,400 affiliate radio stations, which purchased and aired Citadel's programming, as well as more than 180 streaming websites and podcasts. Citadel acquired a majority of its debt from its 2007 acquisition of ABC's radio stations and network from Disney, leading to bankruptcy in 2009. After exiting bankruptcy proceedings in May 2010, the company's shares ended up in the hands of debtholders, private equity firm TPG Capital, JPMorgan Chase & Co., and hedge fund R2 Investments. In June 2011 the radio oligopoly became smaller, when Cumulus Media bought Citadel in a deal worth $2.4 billion in cash and stock.

Cumulus Media Inc. was once the second-largest radio broadcaster in the United States, with 350 stations in sixty-seven markets back in 2006. It also was involved in joint ventures with 34 stations in eight markets. Ninety percent of its revenues came from local, regional, and national advertising.[95] Cumulus focused on middle-range markets, with a few larger stations in larger markets. Forty percent of the company's stock was owned by chair and CEO Lewis Dickey and his family. In July 2007, Dickey agreed to merge with Merrill Lynch Global Private Equity, while Merrill Lynch Capital Corp. agreed to assume Cumulus's debt, bringing the total value of the deal to $1.3 billion. Then in September of that year, Bank of America said it would step in to provide the debt financing, since Merrill Lynch had been hit hard with the onset of the Great Recession (Bank of America eventually bought Merrill Lynch in 2009). The deal was set to close in early 2008, with Lewis Dickey remaining as CEO and chair along with brother John as co-chief operating officer. Cumulus had planned to take over smaller so-called distressed radio operations and promised listeners higher-quality programming as it took over small local independent radio stations or chains. Its strategy was to take advantage of the growth of big box stores as a means of increasing advertising revenue. Here homogenized consumer goods met with homogenized radio programming.[96]

Cumulus's venture into the private equity market was dashed in May 2009; the $1.3-billion deal was too rich for Merrill Lynch, as the economy became increasingly sour and radio advertiser and consumer spending began to decline. The company continued to be traded on the NASDAQ, but control remained in the hands of Lewis Dickey and his family with 33.8 percent of its shares. Bank of America acquired roughly 5 percent of the company's stock through its private equity division and insisted on the right to appoint a member of the board.[97] The continuing dramatic decline in the company's stock price signaled that the family and its investors needed to trim costs, combine operations, and outsource. The commitment to quality radio was, at best, an afterthought. The next year it began to expand coverage and cut costs, leading to the merger with Citadel in 2011.

Cumulus became the fourth-largest broadcaster with the takeover, including Sirius XM. It ranked third after Clear Channel and CBS Radio among the top terrestrial radio chains. The merged company, Cumulus, controlled 572 radio stations across 120 markets. The primary goal of the deal was to cut operating costs by eliminating redundant units and synergizing the programming controlled by the two companies. It also meant the elimination of jobs. Cumulus, with a market value in 2011 of $212 million, bought out Citadel with a value of $2.4 billion. It raised the funds for consummating the deal with a commitment for as much as $500 million in financing from private equity groups Crestview Partners and Macquarie Group and up to $3.03 billion in debt financing from banks. The Federal Communications Commission (FCC) reviewed the deal and approved it based on Cumulus's argument had been that only consolidation could help terrestrial radio survive.[98]

Behind these leading companies were a handful of smaller chains including Entercom Communications Corporation, with 2.5 percent of the radio industry's market share in 2010. It operated more than one hundred stations in twenty-three markets nationwide. The company, headquartered in Pennsylvania, focused on local programming, talent, and audience participation. It also had ties with several sports teams. Next came Cox Enterprises, with 2.3 percent of the radio market share. In 2009 Cox purchased Cox Radio Inc. from shareholders to take it private. In 2010, it controlled eighty-six stations (seventy-one FM and fifteen AM) in nineteen U.S. markets. Its holdings were concentrated in the Southeast region, but it had stations in five other states as well.[99] Cox Radio was part of Cox Communications Inc., the ninth-largest media company in 2010[100] and ranked third behind Comcast and Time Warner Cable, in broadband cable television, telephone, wireless, and Internet connections serving more than 6 million residences and businesses. The Cox Media Group was an integrated broadcast, publishing, and digital media company. Along with eighty-six radio stations, it operated fifteen television stations, one local cable channel, four metro newspapers, more than a dozen nondaily publications, and one hundred digital services. The division also controlled Valpak, one of the leading direct mail services in the United States. Cox's Internet unit and Cox Digital Solutions helped bring together advertisers and online services serving more than seven thousand specialty content and thirteen hundred local websites. Its other Internet service was Kudzu.com, which helped homeowners plan projects, solve problems, and find contractors. Cox was also in the automotive business through Manheim, the world's leader in automobile remarketing services. This vast conglomerate helped the company maintain steady growth with total revenues of $15 billion in 2010.[101]

The top four radio companies—Sirius XM, Clear Channel, CBS, and Cumulus—controlled almost 50 percent of the market by the end of 2011. The rest of the industry, made up of six thousand stations and 2,800 companies, was comprised mainly of regional chains or independently owned stations with little market power. These were the most affected by the drop in advertising revenues during the Great Recession. Given that the radio market is not expected to grow, the trend toward concentration will be the primary means of survival, which will mean fewer radio companies that stick to existing formulas that best serve advertisers, rather than listeners. Radio has great potential as a local medium, as so many decisions about our daily lives are made at the local level, such as education, zoning, infrastructure maintenance, police and fire operations, garbage and recycling, and so on. But being local does not fill the need to keep the community informed for the purposes of self-governance with the necessary local news and public affairs coverage required. Most stations rely on cheaper syndicated programming rather than producing their own. Syndicated programming means more of the same, whether it is listened to in the car or digitally.

In a *Rolling Stone* article aptly title "Why Radio Sucks," Jenny Eliscu listed five ways that giant corporations were ruining the airwaves.[102] The first problem was that big companies were getting bigger, with the lifting of station ownership limits due to the Telecommunications Act of 1996. Deregulation, meaning self-regulation by the industry, was therefore a main culprit. In 2007, ownership restrictions on cross-media ownership—radio, television, and newspapers—were loosened by the FCC. This led to a long and continuing judicial challenge to the FCC led by the Prometheus Radio

Project. In July 2011 the Third Court of Appeals remanded the case to the FCC, deciding that the 2007 deregulation was not properly conducted to allow ninety days for public comment. The FCC was required to reexamine the rules at the same time and find a way to increase radio ownership by women and minorities. Cross-ownership is deadly to diversity, especially with 99 percent of cities and towns served by one newspaper and when linked to television and radio stations.

The second problem with radio was so-called legal payola. This pay-for-play system has a long history in the industry. In the late 1950s and early 1960s, record labels regularly paid disc jockeys to play their music. This was outlawed. To get around the law, the industry came up with what appeared to be legal payola, since the payments to radio stations by record companies became so-called consulting fees. At the time, record label insiders admitted that they had paid as much as $300,000 to get airplay for one song. Action against this sort of payola was taken by the New York attorney general's office. In 2005 WMG paid $5 million and Sony BMG $10 million for pay-for-play practices. In 2006, UMG agreed to pay $12 million to settle accusations that executives paid radio programmers to play songs. UMG was accused of using a broad range of tactics to achieve this, including bribing programmers with laptop computers, tickets to sporting events, and luxury hotel stays. Other activities included deception by record label representatives by inflating songs on the charts and hiring outside consultants to manipulate call-in request lines to inquire about hearing new songs.[103] The purpose of banning payola is that it gives the record majors greater power over independent labels and artists.

A third reason the airwaves were being ruined was the bullying of artists, particularly by Clear Channel, which owned concert venues at the time. If artists did not use one of its venues, their music would not get airplay on the company's radio stations. Clear Channel of course denied the charges, but once again artists privately admitted that in order to get airplay they were pressured to perform radio festivals sponsored by Clear Channel stations. Artists feared alienating the giant radio company and were afraid to speak up. As noted above, the situation continued, just had a change in hands with the rise of Live Nation and its massive control over concert and festival venues, as well as ticket sales. Performing artists became more dependent on making money on tours with the decline of CD sales, and access to venues became a key issue, especially to those in the top tier.

The fourth reason the radio industry was failing was the disappearance of local DJs. This was the industry's way of cutting costs and keeping playlists consistent. The airing of prerecorded DJ chatter across the United States reduced the variety of music available at the local level. If not under the influence of payola, DJs once had a certain level of autonomy in what they played. There were also stations that promoted local artists through airplay.

Centralized DJs began customizing shows for other radio stations, where they inserted local news to give the illusion of local coverage.

All of these factors were compounded by the fifth reason: There was not enough new music being played on radio. Although radio companies touted their diverse formats, there was still a large overlap in playlists between formats. Furthermore, within each format only thirty to fifty songs got significant airplay each week. The overlap between different formats reduced variety by playing the biggest hits on even more stations. Don Henley, testifying at a Senate hearing in January of 2003, insisted at that time that "getting your record on the radio is the lifeblood of our business. The playlists keep shrinking, and people don't get a chance to discover new things. Music and culture suffer for it, and it's all done in the name of giving the people what they want."[104] In 2011, the industry was saying the same thing.

THE ELEPHANT IN THE ROOM: MUSIC PIRACY

I Want My MP3 . . .

The history of new media technologies is colored by a spectrum of hopes and fears concerning their impact on society. From the early days of the printing press, new communications technologies have been greeted with some suspicion, but those who develop and deploy them always promise that new media technologies will bring new opportunities for improving the human condition. The technological inventions and innovations that made possible the telegraph, wireless radio, motion picture, telephone, television, cable, VCR, personal computer, and Internet have all been heralded as revolutionary, as if the very fact of their existence guaranteed a better quality of life for all. The pervasive notion that progress might be realized through the development of new technologies themselves—with little or no regard for who controls them or even who has access to them—is problematic, to say the least. The latest manifestation of this utopian technological determinism can be seen in the widespread belief that the Internet would set music makers and music lovers free from the major players in the radio industry that controlled the world's recorded music at the turn of the twenty-first century.

In the late 1990s, the major record labels suddenly became very nervous about MP3, a digital compression format enabling audio files to be stored and exchanged from one computer to another. With its introduction, it seemed that the new technology actually *threatened* to enhance diversity in the music industry while nibbling at a tiny slice of the then five majors' share of the pie. As *Rolling Stone* reported after surfing the Web: "It has never been easier to find free music on the Web. And thanks to MP3, there were literally millions of near-CD quality songs that music fans could download in a matter of minutes."[105] Accordingly, one *New York Times* report claimed in 1999 that MP3 had "spawned an explosion of web sites" and "frightened the nation's $13.5 billion recording industry with the specter of mass distribution of pirated music over the Internet."[106] Another stated that "frustrated record companies have watched helplessly as millions of illegally copied songs circulate on the Internet."[107]

Of course, there were doubts about how helpless the industry really was and how seriously the MP3 format would affect its record sales, not to mention how much it would benefit music makers and record consumers. As these fears and hopes played out in the press, four common myths surrounding MP3 emerged: that it would liberate established recording artists; that it would usher in a renaissance for independent musicians; that its primary beneficiaries would be music consumers; and that it posed a serious threat to the existing oligopolistic structure of the music industry.

The first myth was that MP3 would liberate established musicians from the artistic and commercial constraints imposed by their record labels. This myth is perhaps best expressed by a somewhat dubious *Rolling Stone* reporter who wrote: "Flag wavers of the MP3 revolution, such as Ken Hertz, a powerful music industry lawyer whose clients include Alanis Morissette and Will Smith, will tell you that we are about to see the beginning of a new era in which artists will seize control of their careers once again and reconnect with fans, while the moguls who have dominated the industry for so long will finally get their comeuppance."[108] Actually, Morissette probably did feel liberated, given the deal she cut with MP3.com to sponsor her 1999 tour. Morissette signed a three-year promotional contract in exchange for 658,653 shares of MP3.com stock at 33 cents per share. The payoff looked good as the company went public and its stock hit $63 per share on the first day of trading, raising Morissette's stake in MP3.com to $42 million. As *Spin* magazine mused, "The singer would have to sell nearly 30 million copies of *Supposed Former Infatuation Junkie* to get the profit she netted in one afternoon. Maybe Internet entrepreneurs really are the new rock stars. Why dodge bottles at Woodstock when you can simply sit at home, think, and grow rich?"[109] Of course, after MP3.com's court battles ended and the dot-com bubble burst, Morissette was faced with the prospect of once again actually performing in front of her audiences.

Then there is the case of Tom Petty, who had the temerity to post his new single, "Free Girl Now," on MP3.com in March 1999 as a goodwill gesture toward fans and a way to boost the buzz on his upcoming album release. "It was a bold move," according to *Rolling Stone*, "considering the unspoken agreement among major labels not to allow acts to post MP3 files, particularly for new songs, until there is a way to contain the technology."[110] Just two days after "Free Girl Now" was offered online—and 150,000 people had downloaded it—the song was abruptly yanked from the site. Representatives for Petty and Warner Music refused to comment, but *Rolling Stone* surmised that "Petty and his camp realized that the time to antagonize your label is not weeks before it releases one of your albums."[111] In 2007, Petty recorded his album titled *The Last DJ*, a searing indictment of the industry's focus on money over music. The Beastie Boys initially fought the demands of its label, Capitol Records, to remove MP3 files of its music from its own website. The Beastie Boys and the label finally reached a compromise: EMI's Capitol artists were allowed to post certain songs on the Capitol website, provided they obtained prior approval from the label. The band went on to sign a new deal with Capitol with an estimated $30 to $40 million advance rather than find another label or go independent. As Hilary Rosen, president and chief executive of the Recording Industry Association of America, commented, "They found that the existing system had a lot of advantages for them."[112] Not only does "the existing system" pay up front, but it also provides the marketing power that is essential for making a musical group visible.

The second myth was that MP3 would bring about a renaissance for garage bands and independent musicians by enabling them to distribute their own music and establish their own fan bases. It was such a hopeful moment that it was painful to call this myth into question, and here Tom Petty's upstart idealism and implicit pitch for MP3 in *Rolling Stone* was particularly poignant: "There's a whole lot of artists that exist beyond the periphery of the corporate music business who suddenly have the power to make this stuff available. It gives these artists a huge outlet—you can have a little band and just get on the computer and sell your stuff and build all these fan bases for things that are completely outside the music industry. I love the fear it strikes into the hearts of these moguls who have shit on us all."[113] Despite the MP3 hype, garage bands remained anonymous on the service, and MP3.com had yet to find a way to support them in their efforts. The works of most musicians who posted their works remained lost in cyberspace.

The third myth was the one that did indeed strike fear in the hearts of the moguls in the industry: the idea that music should and would be free (that is, more easily shared than sold). This myth was based on actual practice and held revolutionary potential to the extent that it challenged the very structure of intellectual property rights. The music industry's counterattack required putting MP3.com, along with Napster, out of business and turning back the ease with which music could be copied and downloaded. The Big Five soon began offering their own "pirate-proof" versions of online music and joined the Secure Digital Music Initiative (SDMI), an antipiracy organization backed by the consumer electronics and technology industries. The record companies also worked the media to counter the growing sentiment that music should be free. Accordingly, the *New York Times* announced in October 1999 that "a crackdown on digital piracy that will have a wide-ranging impact on consumers is about to begin" and warned consumers that some CD burners already added a digital serial number to every CD so that copyright owners could trace any recording to the machine that made it. The industry also announced new software for digitally watermarking CDs that would prevent SDMI-compliant devices from playing ripped disks. Even if a disk was legitimate, the watermark only allowed its owner to make four copies, each of which contained information that allowed it to be played on only one machine. So to listen to music on a home stereo, office PC, and car stereo would require separate copies for each, with all the time, inconvenience, and expense involved.[114]

The fourth myth, that online music distribution posed a serious threat to the major record labels, is probably the biggest myth of all. As *Rolling Stone* noted, "While the record industry has always been good at profiting from anthems of revolution, it has never undergone a revolution itself."[115] The point, of course, is that although new technologies may be used for revolutionary purposes, technology itself is never revolutionary. In a music industry driven by the logic of capitalism, he who pays the piper still calls the tune. Within a couple of years of the predicted revolutionary restructuring of the music industry, free sites like MP3.com and Napster had been effectively shut down.

But You Can't Always Get What You Want

After losing its battles in court, MP3.com agreed in late fall 2000 to settle its legal disputes with the last of the Big Five, Universal Music Group. MP3.com gave Universal Music a stake in the company as part of the settlement. Universal officials knew that the large settlement claims imposed by the courts would bankrupt MP3.com anyway and that the company had no choice but to settle. Napster found itself in the same boat. After several legal setbacks, the company began final settlements with the Big Five in early 2002, since it was about to run out of money. MP3.com and Napster were victims of both the deep pockets the music oligopoly used to finance the pursuit of litigation and legislation to stifle the threat to their control of the industry. The two upstarts also were doomed by the logic of capitalism. Under capitalism, music compositions and performances belong to the copyright owners, the publishing companies and the composers. The role of the government is to protect these rights and their market value. Laws passed by the legislature and enforced by the courts must, out of structural necessity, consistently uphold the rights of intellectual property owners. New means of distributing intellectual and artistic works have inevitably been integrated into the existing market structure since they enter an economic system in which private property rights prevail. The state simply cannot undermine these rights for the sheer convenience of consumers, and any attempts to argue for access to information and entertainment on the basis of the public good cannot hold weight against property claims.

After vanquishing MP3.com and Napster, the major record labels still faced competition from a number of services using peer-to-peer computer networks, such as Morpheus, Kazaa, and Aimster. While pursuing the new predators through litigation, the record companies launched their own online music services to undermine them. These services promised to be more convenient for the casual computer user, but of course would not be free. In April 2001, three of the then Big Five—Warner, BMG, and EMI— announced a new online music subscription platform called MusicNet. Shortly thereafter, Universal and Sony announced their joint online digital subscription service, called Pressplay. Like the film industry, the majors also began hedging their bets on the online music business by licensing their music catalogs to upstarts. By July 2002, Listen.com had secured rights to music from all five of the major labels for its subscription-based streaming service. In another deal, Warner Music sold rights to 25,000 songs, a small fraction of its music library, to Full Audio. Full Audio intended to charge consumers 99 cents for the right to download and burn a copy of any of the 25,000 tracks.

Throughout the first decade of the twenty-first century, the industry battled illegal sharing of music in a whack-a-mole game, while trying to turn digital uses of music into so-called legitimate markets. Many of the deals resulting in the rise of legal music sites were discussed above. The most common form of online copyright infringement in 2011 was still file-sharing networks that permitted illegal downloads using either peer-to-peer sharing or central servers that were not legally licensed to distribute digital music. By 2011, the IFPI announced in its Digital Music Report that it had enlisted Internet service providers (ISPs) in its efforts to stop mass piracy by providing user identification numbers to seek out those publicly disseminating copyright-infringing material—a major win in the battle against illegal copying. It also filed suit against Limewire, the biggest source of infringing downloads in the United States, and the service was found to be illegal. Minova, a major BitTorrent site, also shut down its illegal operations. Visa and Mastercard promised they would not provide credit services to illegal sites. The report also pointed out that North American digital revenues were up 6 percent to $4.6 billion in 2010, with more than four hundred licensed services.

Additionally, music services such as VEVO and MTV built audiences for ad-supported content on line. YouTube remained the most popular platform for viewing music videos online in 2010, accounting for around

40 percent of online videos watched in major markets, again with ads. The report concluded that legal digital music services was a sector with tremendous growth potential but still inhibited by piracy. In 2010 only 16.5 percent of online users in the United States and 14 percent in the U.K. purchased music online. [116] An entire generation grew up with free music, and it has been hard to change their habits and convince them to actually buy from or subscribe to legal sites. The industry says these people must be reeducated. One system deployed in the United States was the voluntary Copyright Alert System. This allowed ISPs to send up to six e-mails to subscribers notifying them that their account may have been misused for online content of film, TV shows, or music. [117] Participants in the system included the Motion Picture Association of America and its members Disney, Paramount, Sony, Twentieth Century Fox, Universal, and Warner Bros.; the RIAA and its members UMG, WMG, SME, and EMI; the ISPs AT&T, Cablevision, Comcast, Time Warner Cable, and Verizon; the IFTA, representative of independent producers of film and television program; and A2IM, which represented 283 small and mid-size music labels. The system also put in place so-called mitigation measures intended to stop online theft on those accounts that appeared to persistently fail to respond to copyright alerts, but it did not include termination of service or sharing subscribers' names with copyright owners. Backed by legislation and the courts, the industry filed infringement suits against individuals, largely for publicity purposes, some of which backfired when the defendant could not possibly pay the fine. Another tactic was to blame digital piracy for massive lay-offs in the industry, while ignoring the fact that it had been downsizing for a decade to maintain profits.

For years, the music industry had been fighting piracy at the global level, from audiocassettes to CDs to the Internet. The U.S. Trade Representative (USTR) issued its annual *Special 301* report for 2011, highlighting intellectual property theft in foreign countries. The report became mandatory after the copyright industries managed to push through trade legislation putting other nations on a priority-watch list with the ultimate threat of trade retaliation by the United States. Countries on the 2011 list included China and Russia. Theft levels in China were above 90 percent. This helped contribute to the trade imbalance between China and the United States. Russia saw a similar trend as in China; first, physical digital works, such as videocassettes, DVDs, and CDs were heavily pirated. Digital music simply shifted the source of obtaining infringing works. Canada made the watch list for being virtually alone in the developed world in failing to bring its copyright standards into line with accepted international standards in the digital age, making it a hotbed for illegal digital services. The report also highlighted Spain and Italy. Spain had seen its local music market decline significantly due to piracy. The USTR pointed to the Spanish government for failing to implement policies to make meaningful enforcement possible. Italy also had a severe piracy problem, and the USTR was closely watching new legislation that aimed to curb the practice.[118] Besides bilateral efforts, the copyright industries undertook multilateral efforts to control their property through the World Trade Organization (WTO). An agreement was made to ensure that intellectual property trade disputes be handled like any other trade dispute and that unfair practices such as infringement could be brought to the WTO to seek relief.

What we are seeing here is the inherent nature of information and culture as public goods that want to be free, but under capitalism are made scarce for the purposes of turning them into commodities. Copyright emerged in the 1700s to protect book publishers from pirate printers. The first laws provided exclusive rights to artistic and intellectual creators for a limited period of time. Generally, though, actual creators did not have the capital to bring their work to the market and so began an exploitative system by which they gave up their rights to those who did. Matthew David argued that file-sharing is a way of challenging this system from below: "an economic restructuring and an informational opening up that challenge capitalist relations of intellectual property rather than merely updating productive forces to boost existing social relations, as was the initial application." He continued, "As virtual property becomes central to the profitability of global capitalism so its scope for global sharing becomes increasingly dangerous to a system based on scarcity [or] the contradiction between profitability and potential suspension of scarcity."[119] This challenging of the system from below does indeed pose a threat to capitalists who own intellectual property; while efforts to curb practices such as online music sharing have generally been ineffectual, it is not undermining the oligopolistic structure of the music industry, merely creating new oligopolies to take charge of the latest technological developments.

The Internet has been a huge financial success for some. It has become concentrated, commoditized via e-commerce, and commercialized with the increasing encroachment of advertising. The music industry will continue to change its practices, but structurally it will remain the same until capitalism itself is overthrown. In a postcapitalist society, music would remain essential to enhancing our human potential but be free from commerce. Artistic and intellectual creators will no longer need to alienate their labor to the capitalist owners of the means of communication. Instead of making music for profit it would be made for pleasure, as well as a struggle with oneself and society. It requires accepting the fact that everyone is a creator of artistic and intellectual works, and hence the abolition of the division of labor that is based on the idea that only some creators are worthy of our attention. This will require genuine equality and a system that meets our genuine human needs, including music.

5

The News and Advertising
Industries: All the News That Fits

The motto of the newspaper of record in the United States, the *New York Times*, is "All the news that's fit to print." When Adolph Ochs purchased this "failing and demoralized" operation in 1896, he spoke of "a sincere desire to conduct a high standard newspaper, clean, dignified and trustworthy, [with] honesty, watchfulness, earnestness, industry and practical knowledge applied with common sense."[1] Ochs spoke of his readers as "thoughtful, pure-minded people" and promised that the *Times* would "not soil the breakfast cloth" with sensationalism or scandal as its "esteemed freak contemporaries" were wont to do.[2] "To be seen reading the *New York Times*," an early self-advertisement aimed at schoolteachers and college professors proclaimed, "is a stamp of respectability."[3] In 1897, the *Journalist* praised the *Times*, taking special note of the economic incentives for distinguishing a paper on the basis of its propriety in an age of yellow journalism: "It has lived up to its motto of 'All the news that's fit to print,' and the great cultivated well-to-do class do not want anything beyond that. As an advertising medium for good goods it is steadily growing in value. It may not have so large a number of readers as some of its less conservative contemporaries, but its readers represent more dollars, which, after all, is what the advertiser is after."[4] Early advertisers in the *New York Times* included makers of designer fashions and fine musical instruments, in addition to manufacturers of dry goods and patent medicines.[5]

Nearly three-quarters of a century later, *Rolling Stone* announced its arrival on the San Francisco music scene with a roguish play on the famous appeal of the *New York Times* to decency and decorum, declaring its motto to be: "All the news that fits."[6] As aware of the sensibilities of his intended readership as Ochs, founding editor Jann Wenner set out to produce "sort of a newspaper and sort of a magazine . . . for the artists and the industry, and every person who 'believes in the magic that can set you free.'"[7] The first issue of *Rolling Stone* featured an interview with Donovan Leitch (the Scottish folksinger who pioneered psychedelic pop), an article about Jimi Hendrix (the legendary American guitarist), and a "photographic look at a rock and roll group after a drug bust" (the Grateful Dead on the front porch of their Haight-Ashbury home brandishing clenched fists and rifles).[8] Early issues openly invited submissions from amateur music reviewers: "We'll read it; maybe we'll print it; maybe we'll pay you."[9] In 1969, author Tom Wolfe praised the young *Rolling Stone* for capturing the impudence, gaudiness, and "slightly mad freedom" of a time when "the notion of glamour began to involve a calculated disdain for propriety."[10] Wolfe didn't comment on the magazine's calculated appeals to advertisers, but early issues of *Rolling Stone* featured ads for psychedelic posters, alternative theater productions, rock concerts, record labels, and stereo equipment. Early subscription drives offered marijuana paraphernalia as an enticement.

Rolling Stone's parody of the *New York Times* motto hinges on two different meanings of the word *fit* in relation to news coverage: *fit* as in having enough pages or column inches to squeeze in the necessary material, and *fit* as in being suitable or appropriate for a particular audience. Both definitions, we argue, are equally important to the business of selling news as a commodity: the practice of gathering and packaging information as a product for distribution to readers and viewers, whose attention (and presumably patronage) is then sold to advertisers for profit. First, the news industry's reliance on advertising is such that the space left over after a newspaper has filled its pages with ads is known as "the news hole." The issues and events of the day, it seems, must finally be shoveled in. In the magazine industry, noncommercial material is referred to as "the editorial well," suggesting that it must be drawn out in small amounts as needed. Second, the advertising industry's concern not only for audience size but also for demographics necessitates that information be selected and shaped so as to attract the most desirable clientele, be it the "great cultivated well-to-do class" of the 1890s or the counterculture youth market of the 1960s. All of this, of course, raises the question of news that either does not fit or is not fit to print. The emergence of the Internet as a major source of news and information in the twenty-first century has complicated the question of "fit" in some ways: Column inches are not rationed in cyberspace, and appropriateness is in the eye of the user or subscriber. But the economic relationship between news and advertising has remained essentially the same, and the threat this relationship poses to democratic communications has gone largely unchallenged.

We begin this chapter with a brief history of news as a commodity: its emergence as a service for merchant capitalists in the late fifteenth century, its transformation into a mass industry in the late nineteenth century, and its consolidation into a multibillion-dollar sector of commerce controlled by a handful of media conglomerates today. Our review of these milestones in journalism history is not meant to be exhaustive, but rather to lay the groundwork for an examination of the intricate links between the news and advertising industries in all media as they have evolved under capitalism. We then turn to advertising and journalism as ideological institutions, which function to perpetuate or negate certain ways of thinking. We examine a number of widely held beliefs about the functions and effects of both enterprises in a democratic society. Finally, we offer specific examples of advertising as an economic institution that has direct and indirect influence on both the structure and content of the news. We question the widespread belief that new communications technologies have produced better-informed citizens. We argue that the symbiotic relationship between journalism and advertising frequently renders them functionally equivalent, despite the best intentions of reporters and the dubious claims of advertisers to inform and educate the public.

YOU SAW IT HERE FIRST: A BRIEF HISTORY OF NEWS AS A COMMODITY

The news business first emerged in the Italian city-states of the late fifteenth century, with the rise of capitalism and the development of the modern printing press. At that time, Venice was a center of commerce, banking, finance, and textile production. It was also the first city in Italy, and practically the first in Europe, in which the business of printing and publishing became important. The Venetian city government sought to encourage the importation of new industrial techniques and stimulate the growth of local commerce by granting certain printers exclusive publishing rights, laying the foundation for later copyright laws.[11] Early printers found that there were tidy profits to be made in providing merchant capitalists with current information about markets and political conditions. The news business thus developed throughout Europe and in many countries around the world as a business aimed primarily at political and mercantile elites.

The Information Industry

The industrialization of the news business in the nineteenth century resulted in the transformation of news into a mass-produced commodity. The extension of the circulation of newspapers beyond the realm of an educated elite or business class is a familiar feature of press histories in many countries. In the United States, as Michael Schudson notes, this shift is reflected in significant changes in newspaper names and prices, as well as advertising and editorial content. In the 1830s, conservative names such as the *Chronicle, Patriot, Republican,* and *Telegraph* gave way to more flamboyant ones such as the *Sun, Star, Herald,* and *Tribune.* Penny papers hawked by newsboys on street corners replaced six-cent papers sold exclusively through annual subscriptions. Advertising, "which heretofore addressed the reader only insofar as he was a businessman interested in shipping and public sales or a lawyer interested in legal notices, increasingly addressed the newspaper reader as a human being with mortal needs."[12] With this development, the range and scope of news content expanded to cover a wider terrain of human events and social behaviors. Human interest stories and dramatic descriptions of sordid events replaced political argument and analysis. As Calvin F. Exoo aptly summarized: "Stories of rapes, robberies, suicides, abandoned children left in baskets and the brawling of drunken sailors were the common fare of most penny papers."[13]

Ironically, in retrospect, most newspapers were hostile to advertisers at this time, believing that "large ads wasted space and were 'unfair' to the small advertisers who were the foundation of advertising revenue."[14] According to Schudson, many early editors felt that advertising should command only a limited amount of column inches, and often confined ads to agate-size type. James Gordon Bennett, who founded the *New York Herald* in 1835 and remained its editor until his death in 1872, is a good example. Bennett believed that "the advertiser should gain advantage from what he said, but not from how the advertisement was printed or displayed."[15] Advertisers would not have to put up with such dictates for long.

In 1848, a group of New York newspapers took advantage of the newly invented telegraph and organized the Associated Press (AP). The AP was designed to gather news for a variety of different papers with widely different political allegiances. It could only succeed by making its reporting "objective" enough to be acceptable to its motley crew of subscribers. Here we see the seeds of the journalistic norm of objectivity—the belief that one can and should separate facts from values—which took root in the 1920s and remains prevalent today. The journalistic norm of objectivity was actually invented to help sell wire service stories across the land: to keep reporters in check so as to ease owners' fears of alienating audiences and, increasingly, advertisers. By the late nineteenth century, as Schudson notes, AP dispatches were markedly more free from editorial comment than most stories written for local newspapers.[16]

The relationship between newspapers and advertisers changed dramatically in the 1880s and 1890s. Advertising textbooks like to naturalize the history of advertising by tracing its roots to prehistoric times ("Some of the earliest cave drawings refer to the makers of primitive objects"[17]), but most rather grudgingly admit that advertising as we know it today emerged in the late nineteenth century along with transportation, urbanization, and industrialization.[18] Thanks in part to the growth of department stores and the development of brand names and trademarks by national manufacturing concerns, business demand for advertising space accelerated. The ratio of editorial matter to advertising changed significantly at this time, from about 70:30 to 50:50. Advertising revenues rose from 44 percent of total newspaper income in 1880 to 55 percent by 1900.[19] At the beginning of the twenty-first century, one could read newspapers from the *New York Times* to the *State College (Pa.) Centre Daily Times* free online, increasing the dependence of news reporting on advertising even further.

In the first few decades of the twentieth century, big-brand advertisers began to use national magazines to spread the virtues of consumption, not only through the ads themselves but also through editorial content. Entrepreneurs like William Randolph Hearst (*New York Journal*) and Joseph Pulitzer (*New York World*) seized the day with "lurid, multi-column headlines; seductive portraits of the lives of the rich and famous; 'women's' pages displaying the allure of being a fashionable consumer; and especially, sensational, often prevaricated 'news' of crimes, accidents, scandals, and bizarre or sentimental 'human interest.'"[20] Pulitzer initiated the practice of selling advertising space on the basis of actual circulation and selling it at fixed prices. He also abandoned the traditional penalties for advertisers who used illustrations or broke column rules. Pulitzer's most enduring legacy—far more profound and wide-reaching than the prestigious prize bearing his name—is to have helped rationalize newspaper business practices, especially the relationship between newspapers and advertisers.

Media Monopoly

Today, the shift from "telling the people to selling the people" is a given.[21] Newspapers have been bought and sold by multinational corporations, "mammoth entities that answer to stockholders who expect big profits and constant growth."[22] In 2010, the major broadcast and cable television news operations were all owned by international conglomerates as well. CNN was owned by Time Warner, ABC News by the Walt Disney Company, CBS News by Viacom (National Amusements Inc.), NBC News and MSNBC by General Electric, and the Fox News Channel by News Corp. Even the "fake news" shows aired on Comedy Central were controlled by Viacom. As a 2006 editorial in *The Nation* reminded us, "while we might hate the rigid recitation of conservative talking points on Fox News programs and love the Internet frontier reached by MySpace.com, both Fox and MySpace are owned by Rupert Murdoch's News Corporation." Moreover, "it is important to keep in mind that NBC's primary owner at the time, General Electric, had more than a passing interest in the development and operation of nuclear power plants."²³ The cards may change hands even as this book goes to press, but the concentration of the news industry nationally, and its domination of news coverage internationally, is indisputable.

A century after Adolph Ochs scooped up the "failing and demoralized" *New York Times*, the business of the news has flourished. In the early 1980s, Ben H. Bagdikian reported that the U.S. newspaper industry was "fabulously profitable," with a 17 percent return on stockholders' equity.²⁴ In 2000, Benjamin M. Compaine noted that the "rapid rate with which newspapers have been bought at increasingly higher multiples of dollars per reader or earnings is a sign of a prosperous industry."²⁵ According to Compaine, the U.S. newspaper industry was worth $37.225 billion in 1996, accounting for 0.5 percent of the gross domestic product (GDP). Daily circulation of newspapers in 1998 was 56.2 million. In 1997, revenues for Gannett alone were $4.73 billion, and profits were $713 million, representing a 15.1 percent return on revenue.²⁶ In 2007, according to Hoovers Inc., the U.S. newspaper industry included about two thousand companies with a combined annual revenue of $50 billion. Large companies included Gannett, McClatchey, Advance Publications, the Tribune Company, the Washington Post Company, and the New York Times Company. Hoovers reported that the industry was highly concentrated: The top fifty companies controlled almost 80 percent of the market. Many of the larger companies also owned and operated TV stations.²⁷

At the turn of the twenty-first century, the *New York Times* had evolved into the New York Times Co., described by Standard & Poor's as a "diversified media company including newspapers, television and radio stations, magazines, electronic information and publishing, Internet businesses, and forest products investments [logging and paper mills]."²⁸ The company was ranked number 468 on the *Fortune 500* list of "America's Largest Corporations" when we wrote the first edition of this book in 2001; it was holding its own at number 583 on the *Fortune 1000* with revenues reported at $3.2 billion in 2007.²⁹ By 2010 it ranked twenty-eighth among leading media companies.³⁰ The company's core purpose, as reported in a 2006 press release, was "to enhance society by creating, collecting and distributing high-quality news, information and entertainment."³¹ Adolph Ochs—whose heirs still run the business—would undoubtedly be pleased to know that the *New York Times* has won more Pulitzer Prizes than any other newspaper, and the New York Times Co. is routinely ranked among *Fortune*'s "Most Admired Companies" in the publishing category.³²

Meanwhile, *Rolling Stone*, the would-be antithesis of the *Times*, evolved into a glossy music industry magazine filled with ads for expensive cars, top-shelf booze, high-tech gadgets, and designer fragrances. In 2008, *Rolling Stone* was owned by Wenner Media LLC, which also published the gossipy *US Weekly* and slick *Men's Journal*. In 2001, Jann Wenner and then Walt Disney Company CEO Michael Eisner (number 359 on the *Forbes 400* at the time, with $720 million) announced a partnership "to make *US Weekly* a mainstay in the celebrity journalism business."[33] Eisner said he "appreciated the soft-shoe approach that *US* takes in its celebrity coverage"[34] (a bit of a far cry from Jimi Hendrix and the Grateful Dead). Industry analysts noted that "*US Weekly* provides Disney a chance to control a media outlet catering to consumers hungry for news about celebrities and entertainment."[35] Wenner originally envisioned *Men's Journal* as competing with *Esquire* and *GQ*, but eventually brought in editors from *Playboy* and British "lad mags" like *Maxim* to attract an even younger male readership. In 2005, *Rolling Stone* ranked number 69 in paid circulation at 1.3 million. In 2006, *Rolling Stone* published its one thousandth issue, and in 2007 it celebrated its fortieth year in print, amid criticism that it had sold out to advertisers and music industry moguls, pandered to rock fogies, and never really connected with grunge, hip hop, or new heavy metal artists and their fans.[36] Ads in *Rolling Stone* came to include a tattoo removal system (for youthful mistakes), Alka-Seltzer (for hangovers), Valtrex (for genital herpes) and classic collector's editions of *Rolling Stone* (for fogies). To invoke the Stones themselves, "What a drag it is getting old."

News in New Media

The *New York Times* and *Rolling Stone*, though different in many ways, had both become established U.S. publications with storied histories and unusually explicit agendas, audiences, and appeals to advertisers. In 2010, the McClatchy-owned *State College (Pa.) Centre Daily Times* noted that President Barack Obama gave many interviews to the *New York Times*, "which the White House uses to deliver its message to the nation's cultural and economic elite, starting with network and cable television news producers."[37] Both publications have weathered many changes and faced unique challenges at the turn of the twenty-first century, with the proliferation of new sources of information, including twenty-four-hour cable news outlets such as CNN, MSNBC, and Fox News Channel; fake news shows such as *The Daily Show* and *The Colbert Report*; and online outlets including the websites of other newspapers and magazines, search engines such as Yahoo! and Google, and innumerable websites and blogs devoted to delivering news and entertainment. This explosion of information outlets has not, however, made readers better informed. According to a 2007 report titled "Young People and the News," based on a study of eighteen hundred young Americans, "most teenagers and adults 30 and younger are not following the news closely at all." This study was conducted by researchers at the Joan Shorenstein Center on the Press, Politics, and Public Policy at the John F. Kennedy School of Government at Harvard. "Despite the popular notion that young people are flocking to the Internet," the survey found, "teenagers and young adults were twice as likely to get daily news from television than from the web."[38]

A nationwide survey conducted by the Pew Research Center for the People and the Press in 2007 found that "the coaxial and digital revolutions and attendant changes in news audience behaviors have had little impact on how much Americans know about national and international affairs."[39] In 2007, asking questions identical or roughly comparable to those in a 1989 survey, the Pew researchers found that somewhat fewer respondents were able to name their governor, the vice president of the United States, or the president of Russia. Knowledge levels were highest among those who regularly visited the websites of major newspapers and watched fake news shows such as *The Daily Show* and *The Colbert Report*; they were lowest for those who relied on local TV news, network morning shows, online news discussion blogs, and the Fox News Channel.[40]

In *The Greatest Story Ever Sold* (2006), Frank Rich notes:

> It was in the mid 1990s that the American electronic news media jumped the shark. That's when CNN was joined by even more boisterous rival 24/7 cable networks, when the Internet became a mass medium, and when television news operations, by far the main source of news for Americans, were gobbled up by entertainment giants such as Disney, Viacom and Time Warner.

This led to the emergence of what Rich calls a "new mediathon environment" in which "once-definable distinctions between truth and fiction were blurred more than ever before, as 'reality' was redefined in news and prime-time entertainment alike." According to Rich, "The very idea of truth is an afterthought and an irrelevancy in a culture where the best story wins."[41]

Which brings us back to advertising. Although some media have traditionally relied on direct consumer sales (e.g., the purchase of a record album, novel, or movie ticket), the newspaper, magazine, broadcast, and Internet industries are dependent upon advertisers. The news media derive significant revenues from advertising: around 50–60 percent for magazines, 80 percent for newspapers, and 100 percent for radio and television broadcasters. Cable news channels get a double dip, from subscription fees and advertising. The point is that the sources from which we gain much of our knowledge about the world around us are beholden to companies with a vested interest in how that world is (or is not) represented. The United States is home to the largest advertising market and the largest advertising industry in the world. According to *Advertising Age*, U.S. businesses spent $285 billion on advertising in 2006—nearly $1,000 for every man, woman and child in the nation.[42] Newspapers accounted for about 20 percent of advertising expenditures, and magazines for another 20 percent. Network and cable television accounted for about 45 percent. Radio and outdoor ads added 8 percent. Although Internet advertising rose dramatically at this time, it still represented a relatively small slice of the pie (about 7 percent of total advertising expenditures in 2006).[43] By 2010, net revenue by media sector for newspapers stood at nearly $18.7 billion with 5.7 percent, magazines at nearly $13 billion with 4 percent, broadcast and cable television networks at $80 billion with 25 percent, radio at $9.4 billion with 2.9 percent, and digital at $23 billion with 7.2 percent of the total $322.5 billion net revenues earned by the top 100 media companies.[44] These revenues include both advertising and other sources of revenue such as subscription income.

It is worth noting in this light that in 1999, the leading national advertisers had fifteen directors sitting comfortably on the boards of six major media companies. Cigarette manufacturer Philip Morris, the third-leading advertiser and number 11 on the 2001 *Fortune 500* list, had two directors on the board of News Corp. Pharmaceutical giant Pfizer, fourth among U.S. advertisers and number 53 on the *Fortune 500*, had directors on the boards of Viacom, AOL-Time Warner, and Dow Jones. DaimlerChrysler had a director on the board of Viacom, and Ford Motor Co. had one with the New York Times Co. and another with Dow Jones. Sears, Roebuck & Co. had representatives on the boards of AOL-Time Warner, the Tribune Co., and the New York Times Co. PepsiCo had directors on the boards of the New York Times Co. and AOL-Time Warner. The continuing symbiotic relationship between the news, advertisers, and advertising—regardless of the medium through which information is delivered—should now be apparent from the tables on interlocking boards of directors in chapters 2 and 3. It is therefore worth digging a little deeper to examine the ideologies underpinning each institution.

THE IDEOLOGY OF ADVERTISING

Before it could be an industry, career, or college major, advertising was an ideology. That is, advertising is not only an economic institution operating for the benefit of a few major corporations and their owners, it is also an ideological institution that supports and negates certain ways of thinking. The purpose of a particular ad might be to convince us that life is richer for those whose teeth are whiter or whose hips are slimmer, or to assure us that "buying a Bud" is the same thing as making a friend. But the overarching purpose of advertising as an institution is to promote capitalism itself.

Selling Capitalism

The values and practices associated with capitalism include private ownership of the means of production, the pursuit of profit by self-interested entrepreneurs, and the right to unlimited gain through individual economic effort. According to Exoo,

> In its 'ideal' formulation, capitalism also stresses competition among producers, a substantial measure of laissez-faire, and market determination of

production, distribution, and economic reward. Certain notions from indi-
vidualist doctrine and the so-called Protestant ethic, such as an emphasis on
achievement and hard work, are also widely held as part of the capitalist creed.[45]

Studies have shown an overwhelming support for capitalist ideology in
the United States.[46] For example, 68 percent of Americans believe that the
most important factor in determining who gets ahead is hard work (over
luck and family background), and 70 percent believe that America is the
land of opportunity where everyone who works hard gets ahead. Eighty-
five percent of Americans believe that incomes cannot be made more equal
since people's abilities and talents are unequal, and 95 percent agree with
the statement, "There is nothing wrong with a man trying to make as much
money as he honestly can." Eighty-seven percent of Americans believe that
private ownership of property is as important to a good society as freedom.[47] It is worth noting here that a common criticism of President Barack
Obama in 2010 was that his proposed health care plan was "socialist," even
though it was passed by the U.S. Congress.

But the studies mentioned above, like the ideology of capitalism itself,
are fraught with contradictions. Americans also tell pollsters that, in their
opinion, "Some have too little, others too much." They agree that "life's
road is harder for some—for women, for blacks, for working- and lower-
class people—than for others." And they feel that government is run on
behalf of "a few big interests."[48] Finally, however, it seems that most Americans have come to associate the ideal of freedom with free enterprise, free
markets, and free trade. Advertisers have sold them on the idea.

If capitalism is our national religion, consumerism is its ritual sacra-
ment. The Center for the Study of Commercialism defines consumerism
as "ubiquitous product marketing that leads to a preoccupation with individual consumption to the detriment of oneself and society."[49] Conspicuous consumption is not so much the accumulation of wealth (which is
really not an option for most Americans) as the acquisition of stuff. The
American ideal of consumerism is epitomized in a 1998 ad for Levi's jeans
in which an androgynous adolescent waif declares: "If you work hard, you
should have nice clothes." Other familiar advertising slogans associate
brand names with self-worth ("L'Oreal—because I'm worth it") or measure
romantic love along product lines ("He went to Jared"). In 2010, the *New
York Times* reported a proliferation of "Don't Steal My Prom Dress" Facebook groups, which focused on designer labels and encouraged competition and (ironically) individualism among teenage girls.[50]

One problem suggested by the Levi's ad is that lots of folks who work
hard do not have nice clothes, and lots of those who do not work hard do.
The connection between being a worthwhile person and deserving a certain
brand of hair dye, receiving a particular cut of jewelry, or laying claim to
a designer dress seems even more absurd. But in this worldview, success,

happiness, and even love are measured by one's ability and inclination to consume. The good life means a good lifestyle. Goals are material rather than spiritual, sensual, social, or political. Advertising is designed to make people ascribe to such a worldview and to promote respect, admiration, and envy for those who have achieved success according to the doctrines of the members of the ruling capitalist class.

It is important to remember that consumerism did not become the American way of life without a struggle.[51] Other normative values once stood in its way, "like Indians on the frontiers of . . . development," as Stuart Ewen reminds us in *Captains of Consciousness*.[52] One need only consider the negative connotations associated with the pursuit of fortune and the trappings of wealth in U.S. popular culture. Classic Hollywood films, for example, rarely attempt to glamorize bankers, industrialists, or stock speculators. After the stock market crash of 1929, as John Belton notes, capitalist figures tended to be identified with the fiscal misman- agement that brought about the Great Depression—"but their villainy is more often seen in terms of individual greed than of class oppression."[53] Common sayings such as "Money isn't everything," "You can't take it with you," "Money can't buy happiness (or love)," and "Money is the root of all evil" attest to the resonance of the Protestant work ethic and the Cath- olic vow of poverty in U.S. society. The Bible tells us that it is easier for a camel to pass through the eye of a needle than for a rich man to enter the kingdom of heaven. "All of this asceticism and humility," as Exoo quips, "was, of course, bad for business."[54]

So advertisers had to work hard to combat negative images of con- sumption and to perpetuate popular myths of classlessness or at least positive images of upward mobility. The hero of the Horatio Alger stories is "Ragged Dick," an honest lad of cheerful perseverance who, with luck and pluck, achieves his just reward (in most versions of the tale, a middle management position rather than fabulous wealth). Dick is a self-made man who pulls himself up by his own bootstraps. Since, however, "the key to great wealth in America is still choosing wealthy parents,"[55] luck remains a powerful element of the equation. Contests, lotteries, and chances to win free prizes (often with the hollow disclaimer "no purchase necessary") lure shoppers, and game shows such as *Who Wants to Be a Millionaire?* attract viewers. Consuming (rather than, say, saving or shar- ing) is widely regarded as the appropriate reward for hard work. Indeed, to do otherwise is often depicted as downright un-American. The business pages of the newspapers constantly remind us that consumer spending makes up 70 percent of U.S. economic activity. Recent U.S. presidents have done everything from making a media event out of buying a pair of socks to urging Americans to take a trip to Disney World in the name of patriotism. In the economic recession beginning in 2007, working

Americans struggling to make it through the month were routinely chas-
tised for lacking "consumer confidence," thereby causing "sluggish sales"
at retail outlets such as Wal-Mart, Target, and Sears (numbers 1, 33, and
38 on the 2007 *Fortune 500* list with revenues of $151 billion, $59 billion,
and $53 billion, respectively).[56]

Manufacturing Demand

If the overarching purpose of advertising is the promotion of consumption, its immediate goal is the creation of needs. Newspaper owners often
justify the number of column inches devoted to ads by insisting that advertising informs consumers. In fact, it is inherently against the interests of
advertisers to make us truly informed consumers, since then they would
have to meet genuine needs rather than those they attempt to create—and
to warn us of the dangers their products may hold. For example, the Food
and Drug Administration (FDA) legalized direct-to-consumer advertising of
prescription drugs in 1997, but mandated that drug makers who advertise
the benefits of their remedies also warn consumers of potential risks. In
2007, Pfizer, the world's largest drug company, ran an ad campaign featuring middle-aged men and women talking in a made-up language, save for
one word: "Viagra." According to the *New York Times*, dialogue in one ad included: "Viagra spanglecheff?" "Minky Viagra noni noni boo-boo plats!"[57]
The same year, McDonald's introduced two-second ads (also known as
"nano ads" or "blinks") which began popping up on stations owned by
Clear Channel Communications, the radio behemoth that developed the
concept and began selling it to marketers in 2006.[58] One would be hard-
pressed to argue that there is anything informative about such ads.

Ironically, as Exoo argues, much advertising prescribes the products
created by capitalism as therapy for the injuries wrought by capitalism:
consumption as a remedy for the loss of community, autonomy, craftsmanship, and nature.[59] A credit card promises to buy intimacy with family,
friends, and lovers: "There are some things money can't buy. For everything
else, there's MasterCard." Ads for mass-produced goods stress individual
craftsmanship, and ads for processed foods stress homemade flavor. Food
and beverage factories are depicted as cozy country kitchens and brewer-
ies. Actors portraying workers in cereal factories are shown taking personal
pride in the contents of every box, although most real factory workers are
struggling to keep their jobs and feed their families.

In the latter half of the twentieth century (a period that advertising
textbooks euphemistically refer to as "the research era"[60]), the advertising
industry entered into what *Business Week* referred to as a "torrid love affair" with the psychology profession.[61] Since then, one ad industry strategy
has been to focus less on the strengths of the product and more on the
weaknesses of the consumer.[62] Increasingly, advertisers have suggested that

social and personal relations can be improved by purchasing products such as deodorants and mouthwashes. It is easy enough to ridicule ads from the 1960s and 1970s in which a homemaker's worth (or lack thereof) is measured by a ring around the collar of her husband's shirt or the yellowing wax on her kitchen floor, but it is also worthwhile to consider the extent to which advertising appeals can come to seem natural or commonsensical in our culture. Having a dry scalp is seen as repulsive, thanks to the makers of dandruff shampoos. Natural body odors are offensive, thanks to manufacturers of antiperspirants and feminine hygiene products. People with straight hair are seen as lacking chemical curls, and people with curly hair are seen as lacking chemical straighteners. As comedian George Carlin commented wryly, "[We're] all being trained to be part of this big circle of goods being pumped out and everyone buying them and everyone going to work to help make more of them for other people to buy." Carlin claimed to have given up on the whole human species, even suggesting we let insects have a go at world power. "You know, I don't think they'll come up with sneakers with lights on them, or Dust Busters, or salad shooters, or snot candy."[63]

People have real needs, of course, in addition to those created for them by capitalism or manufactured for them by advertisers. One of the primary goals of advertising is to differentiate between the scores of virtually indistinguishable products that promise to fulfill our needs, to persuade consumers that products manufactured by large, national companies with famous brands are superior to those made at home or in town. As a 2001 advertising textbook unabashedly explains, "One important function of advertising is to create, or enhance, the gap between the price of a product and the subjective value given it by individual consumers." And the greater this "value gap," the better.[64] Keeping consumers uninformed or misinformed makes it easier for advertisers to persuade consumers to make decisions based on emotional bonds with their products. One of the most cynical examples of these emotional appeals, as Naomi Klein notes, is to associate high-end lifestyle product lines with risqué art and progressive politics.[65] We call this tactic "marketing diversity."

Marketing Diversity

Benetton's sportswear ad campaigns of the late 1980s and early 1990s are perhaps the most notorious examples of this ploy. Writing for *Advertising Age*, Bob Garfield called these "supposedly socially conscious" ads featuring kids of all colors wearing overpriced knits nothing less than "cynical, trite garbage."[66] Later Benetton ads eliminated the clothes altogether, attempting to associate the brand with "provocative" images including mating horses, dying AIDS victims, and teeming refugees.[67] "Flattering itself as courageous, this shockvertising was actually a cowardly assault on the sensibilities of unsuspecting readers, who have no expectation of being confronted with human tragedy by the ready-to-wear industry," as Garfield wrote.[68] A 2000 "Death Row" campaign finally proved disastrous, when Sears threatened to remove all Benetton products from its 400 stores. In 2001, the company sought to polish its tarnished image with a return to a kinder, gentler marketing of diversity: "colourful photographs of young black or white people positioned against a white background wearing Benetton T-shirts, jumpers or swimwear."[69] It is not that Benetton executives felt remorseful for the offensive ads; it is just that they did not work. Ultimately, advertisers will do whatever it takes to sell stuff.

A number of other corporations, including Denny's and TCI (the multi-system cable operator bought by Comcast in 2001), have also been known to exploit images of racial, ethnic, and sexual diversity to sell their products and services. In January of 1999, Denny's was hailed as "perhaps the first national advertiser to focus a TV campaign on race."[70] According to the *Atlanta Journal and Constitution*, "The spots feature a young minority spokesperson and end with the words 'Diversity. It's about all of us.' Only the Denny's logo identifies the sponsor."[71] Denny's sought to portray itself as a leading advocate of the golden rule—"do unto others" with an emphasis on "others." In fact, the ads were mandated as part of the $54.4 million settlement of two class-action suits against Denny's brought by thousands of African American customers who claimed that restaurants in the chain persistently refused to seat or serve them. Despite this slap on the wrist, Denny's remained "a corporate poster child for racial discrimination," a restaurant chain "known as much for bias as for breakfasts."[72] Indeed, the very same day in 1999 that Denny's announced its $2 million diversity ad campaign, a group of South Bay Latino customers filed yet another discrimination lawsuit against the chain.[73] This raised serious doubts about the company's sudden "redemption" in 2000, when Denny's was ranked number 1 on *Fortune*'s list of the nation's "Best 50 Companies for Minorities."[74]

In one more example, a 1999 ad for TCI celebrated rabid individualism masquerading as multiculturalism by parading a rainbow of racial and ethnic minorities on the TV screen, each proclaiming "I will be the one" or "It will be me." The ad reaffirmed the myth of the individual rising above the collective, rather than the collective enabling and empowering the individual. It closed with an image of a black man standing at the seashore and a voiceover narrator suggesting that if it were not for diverse sources of information like those brought to us by TCI, we might still think the world was flat. The unintentional irony, of course, is that the Age of Exploration ushered in colonialism, genocide, and the slave trade.

This ad was part of the company's larger campaign to promote product loyalty to cable television as a superior option to satellite. It aired just as TCI was merging with AT&T in a deal worth nearly $50 billion. The combined company hoped to become a one-stop information store, providing local and long-distance telephone service, cable TV, and Internet access, as Comcast and Verizon eventually did. Wall Street analysts and economists hailed the deal as bringing about a new age of competition in local telecommunications markets. They ignored the threat it posed to information diversity, as the combination involved control over both the information pipelines and programming. TCI already had a reputation for using its list of 19 million subscribers to promote cable networks in which it held an equity stake, while rejecting others on the grounds of limited channel capacity. Media activists blamed TCI's cancellation of The 90s Channel—a one-hour news magazine show with a radical take on political, economic, and social issues—in part on the conservative politics of its owner, John Malone (number 90 on the 2001 *Forbes 400* list, with $2.1 billion).[75]

Corporate sponsors of media programs are pleased to promote diversity, but media concentration squashes it and media moguls are happy to exploit it for a buck. Cable television has increased the number of channels and fractured the television audience into niches of race, age, and gender, as in the former Fox Boyz and Girlz channels. A 1999 *New York Times* editorial lamented the increasing fragmentation and marginalization of audiences, the emergence of what one producer called "a chitlin' circuit on TV." The column nonetheless concluded with the suggestion that anyone worried about losing a sense of national community as television grapples with its recombinant future should "get a life."[76] The truth is that the capitalist marketplace, in which the advertising industry plays so central a part, cannot deliver diversity. Even the *New York Times* was forced to recognize the unlikelihood of media concentration leading to a broader spectrum of programming: "Established networks and cable channels have an enormous advantage, even as they clone themselves, because they already control a stockpile of paid-up shows. That is why when digital channels begin to multiply we will be watching a lot of leftovers. Luckily, Americans are used to that."[77] The Comcast/NBC Universal Combination in 2011 became the penultimate example.

Multiplicity doesn't equal diversity any more than concentration equals community, and celebrations of identity and difference often spiral into debates about whether "my oppression is worse than yours." Such fragmentation invites defeat, for it prevents the type of unified struggle against dominant forms of oppression and exploitation that are necessary to produce significant social change, especially when it is really all about selling designer clothing, fast food, and finally, in the case of TCI, media concentration itself.

THE IDEOLOGY OF JOURNALISM

Like advertising, journalism is an ideological institution that functions to support and negate certain ways of thinking. Among the most important values and practices associated with journalism in the United States are (1) the journalistic norm of maintaining apparent objectivity, or at least fairness and balance, in reporting; (2) the storied tradition of "muckraking" to discover the truth, as in investigative journalism; and (3) the responsibility of a free press to act as a watchdog for society, protecting citizens from government, as well as Big Business. These three journalistic values and practices are closely related to one another and reflect deeply held beliefs about the functions and effects of the news media in a democratic society. It is therefore worthwhile to take a closer look at each.

Both Sides Now

The notion that journalists can and should separate facts from values has long been cultivated by the U.S. news media and is so pervasive in our culture as to risk being thought of as a "given." As noted above, the norm of objectivity was originally invented to help sell wire service stories, but in professional journalism it evolved into a kind of moral philosophy, a declaration about "what kind of thinking and writing one should engage in."[78] Given the obviously subjective nature of journalistic practice—determining what stories are reported, how they are treated, where they are placed—contemporary newsmakers have backed off from claims of objectivity, and more typically purport to seek "fairness and balance" by covering "both sides" of an issue. This, too, is a problematic concept, as it obscures the broad spectrum of ideas and opinions that might be held on any given issue, not to mention the many different issues that might emerge in a less rigid media format and a truly democratic communications system.

Nonetheless, in journalistic practice, the ideal of objectivity has become a simple rule of thumb: there are two sides to every story and good reporters should represent each of them. The "both sides" premise was epitomized in the 1970s by debate shows like the "Point-Counterpoint" segment of *60 Minutes*, which pitted left- and right-wing pundits against each other on an issue of the week. The format was gleefully parodied on *Saturday Night Live*'s fake news show "Weekend Update," in which a liberal viewpoint presented by Jane Curtin was rebutted with a reactionary rant delivered by Dan Aykroyd (one that invariably began, "Jane, you ignorant slut"). This simplistic and bombastic formula was nonetheless adopted (apparently without irony) by CNN with *Crossfire* (1982–2005) and by Fox News Channel with *Hannity & Colmes* (1996–2009).

The belief that there are two sides to every story is still embraced by many journalists and can be seen embedded in the basic structure of many news reports. For example, a 1998 AP story published in the *State College (Pa.) Centre Daily Times* speculated on voter turnout in light of "fallout from the Lewinsky affair." The reporter was careful to quote opposing sides. The first source cited was described as a Democratic construction worker from Louisville, "wearing a blue hard hat with a stubby pencil over one ear": "I'm so bitter at Republicans, it makes my support of Democrats even stronger." The second source was identified as a Republican pollster who cited his "detailed survey" of voter intensity as evidence: "The Democrats are not as likely to be interested in the election, they are less intense about voting and about supporting their candidate."[79]

This example is an interesting one in terms of the practice of "balanced reporting." A careful reader might note that the passion of the Democrat appears to undermine the calculations of the Republican, even though a "detailed survey" undoubtedly carries more weight than a "stubby pencil" when it comes to the credibility of sources. But such an analysis ignores the broader spectrum of ideas the report might have included: the thoughts of a Green Party member, a conscientious nonvoter, or someone who thought the question was stupid in the first place. In a true media democracy—in which the subjects of public debate and journalistic inquiry are determined by the people whose lives are actually affected by them—"fallout from the Lewinsky affair" would probably not have been on the political agenda at all.

Subjects like this are routinely rendered newsworthy by reporters' "professional" treatment of them. (The very term "Monicagate" drew an absurd parallel between President Richard Nixon's orchestration and cover-up of a break-in at the Democratic National Headquarters in the 1970s and President Bill Clinton's consensual fling with a White House aide in the 1990s.) At the same time, vital policy issues involving health care, the environment, education, and war are rendered neutral by the same journalistic practices. A classic example dates from the 1950s and 1960s: As evidence mounted that cigarettes had devastating effects on the health of smokers, the press continued to present the tobacco industry's claims that the practice was harmless. More recently, as an overwhelming majority of scientists worldwide became convinced of the dangers of global warming, the belief of a few that it was simply "nature's way of adjusting" was given equal emphasis. The journalistic norm of objectivity compelled reporters to balance news of violence, devastation, and chaos in Iraq with the George W. Bush administration's claims that the war was going well, that the surge was working, that the lives of Iraqi citizens had been improved. The "two sides" premise then found its way into the classroom, when creationists insisted that the theory of evolution taught in science classes be "balanced" by literal interpretations of the Bible. In most of these examples, journalists did not have to work hard to seek out the balancing opinions; they were supplied by "experts" in positions of power and authority.

Working the Beat

Even journalists who are truly committed to "beating the bushes" are routinely relegated to "working the beat." The difference, as noted in chapter 1, is crucial. Searching out stories that are not advertised or announced requires time, effort, and crucially, money. Relying on a golden Rolodex to cover the courthouse, police station, city hall, or Wall Street ensures stories on a predictable timetable and at low cost. The result is that news and public affairs are often defined by authority figures such as politicians, corporate spokespersons, and readily available experts from think tanks and research institutes. Such officials are prone to beating around the bushes—to withholding information, spreading half-truths, or just plain lying.

Meet the Press, the NBC Sunday morning news show to which the title of chapter 1 alludes, is a good example, although there is no need to single out one network here. CBS's *Face the Nation*, ABC's *This Week*, CNN's *Late Edition*, the former NBC/PBS *The McLaughlin Group*, and the Fox network's *Fox News Sunday* all serve the same function. They are the sites where Washington's elite meet to set government and media agendas for the week. According to *Extra!* these programs are watched every week by White House staff and congressional aides "to determine the 'hot' issues confronting the public."[80] No one knows how many other folks tune in, because only Washington, D.C., ratings are measured. Nonetheless, the topics discussed on these Sunday shows invariably become the subjects of national newspaper reports and analyses on Monday. The media thereby becomes the means by which officials define public issues and set the parameters of policy debates.

Those in power also use the media to determine what is *not* news and what therefore will not be debated. Important arguments are often left unspoken, and significant news is unreported or banished to the last paragraph of a column or the final minutes of a broadcast. George Farah and Justin Elga conducted an exhaustive analysis of the transcripts of four Sunday morning news talk shows and concluded decisively that issues of corporate power are not on the mainstream media agenda. None of the four shows surveyed (*Meet the Press, Face the Nation, This Week,* and *The McLaughlin Group*) even once mentioned the World Bank, the International Monetary Fund (IMF), or foreign trade during the last seven months of 1999. This is astonishing, considering that massive protests at the World Trade Organization (WTO) meeting in Seattle in late November and early December of 1999 were major news stories (see chapter 7). As Farah and Elga put it: "Instead of addressing consumer issues, environmental matters, corporate crime, the IMF, the WTO, labor rights or the minimum wage, the 1999 shows devoted time to topics like the Women's World Cup soccer victory, a moon landing tribute, Jerry Springer's possible senatorial campaign, Father's Day, a heat wave and Tina Brown's kick-off party for *Talk Magazine*."[81]

As this study suggested, the celebrity beat often takes precedence over substantive news. According to the Pew Research Center, in the two days following the death of former *Playboy* model Anna Nicole Smith (due to an accidental drug overdose in February 2007), nearly a quarter of the news from all sectors (24 percent) was devoted to this story, and fully half of all cable news. So is this just Big Media just giving the people what they want? No. When asked about which issues, if any, were given too much attention from the news media, fully 40 percent of respondents to the Pew survey cited celebrity news—more than three times the number citing any other subject. As the researchers observed,

> The belief that the news media pays too much attention to celebrity news—including Hollywood gossip and stories about individual celebrities such as Britney Spears and Paris Hilton—is widely shared. Comparable numbers of Republicans, Democrats and independents—and men and women—cite celebrity news as receiving too much news media attention. Young people are among the most likely to say there is too much celebrity coverage.[82]

Although their avowed purpose is to entertain rather than inform, and although they sometimes fawn over celebrity guests, fake news programs such as *The Daily Show with Jon Stewart* and *The Colbert Report* have made Big Media itself their beat—and ruffled some feathers in the process. When asked at a *New York Times* luncheon how *The Daily Show* managed to dig up such damning clips catching the president and other administration officials contradicting themselves, Stewart reportedly shot back, "A clerk and a video machine."[83] In October 2004, Stewart appeared on *Crossfire*, where he was taken to task by Tucker Carlson and Paul Begala for throwing softball questions to then Democratic presidential candidate John Kerry. Stewart reminded the CNN "debaters" that he was merely a comedian, and insisted it was *their* job as journalists to ask the hard questions. "The problem is that news organizations look to Comedy Central for their cues on integrity," he observed. When the pundits persisted, Stewart exclaimed, "You're on CNN! The show that leads into me is puppets making crank phone calls! What is wrong with you?" He pleaded with them to "stop hurting America." *Crossfire* was canceled in January 2005 (by some accounts, in direct response to Stewart's criticism), in favor of a "gentler" segment of *Inside Politics*—precisely *not* what Stewart was arguing for.[84]

Watchdog on a Leash

There are two popular views of the relationship between the media and the government in the United States; both are comforting in the sense of living in a bad neighborhood but having a good security system. The first is that the media function as a watchdog for society, protecting citizens from government graft, greed, and the general abuse of political power. This view is reflected in the notoriety of investigative reporters such as Bob Woodward and Carl Bernstein, who uncovered the Watergate scandal, and in the popularity of ethical (if fictional) newspaper editors like television's Lou Grant (the *Lou Grant Show*, MTM Productions, 1977–1982). The second is that the government serves as a watchdog for society, guarding citizens against economic concentration and market manipulation. This view is bolstered by news coverage of the antitrust suit brought by the U.S. Department of Justice against the Microsoft Corporation in the late 1990s. When Judge Thomas Penfield Jackson handed down his "stinging ruling"[85] finding Microsoft guilty in April 2000, the press could barely conceal its glee. The lead of the top story on the front page of the *New York Times* read: "The Microsoft Corporation violated the nation's antitrust laws through predatory and anticompetitive behavior and kept 'an oppressive thumb on the scale of competitive fortune,' a federal judge ruled today."[86]

Of course, Microsoft's egregious abuse of market power made the company an easy target for the press. More importantly, the Microsoft case exemplifies an enduring value Herbert Gans found in the news, which he called "responsible capitalism."[87] Journalists hold "an optimistic faith that in the good society, businessmen and women will compete with each other in order to create increased prosperity for all." Therefore, Gans explained, "While monopoly is clearly evil, there is little explicit or implicit criticism of the oligopolistic nature of much of today's economy." Journalists expect both government and business officials to be honest and efficient and to see corruption and bureaucratic misbehavior in either as undesirable. They are nonetheless somewhat more tolerant when these norms are violated by business than when they are transgressed by government.[88]

Webster defines "watchdog" singly and specifically as "a dog kept to guard property."[89] Technically, then, both the media and the government are doing their jobs. The essential connection between the government and the capitalist class is that they both seek to protect private property. Since the U.S. media are private property controlled by the capitalist class, an essential contradiction emerges: The goals of amassing great profits and informing ordinary citizens are distinctly at odds with one another. So both the media and the government tend to act more like lapdogs for each other than as watchdogs for the people. Comedian Stephen Colbert made this point when he was (inexplicably) invited to be the keynote entertainer at the 2006 annual White House Correspondents' Association Dinner. Performing in character as a right-wing ideologue modeled after Fox News Channel's Bill O'Reilly, Colbert carefully explained the job of the press corps to the members of the press corps:

> The president makes decisions; he's the decider. The press secretary announces those decisions, and you people of the press type those decisions down. Make,

announce, type. Put them through spell check and go home. Get to know your family again. Make love to your wife. Write that novel you got kicking around in your head. You know, the one about the intrepid Washington reporter with the courage to stand up to the administration. You know—fiction.

The president and his prestigious guests were reportedly not amused. "Americans watching the performance at home got the joke," according to *Extra!* "but the journalists in the room mostly acted as if someone had released a foul odor."[90]

The ideal of a free press protected by the First Amendment ignores the role government officials play in setting media agendas, not to mention more direct forms of intervention such as laws and regulations regarding libel and obscenity, allocations of radio and satellite frequencies, and protecting national security. More importantly, it ignores what Edward Herman calls "market system constraints on freedom of expression,"[91] or the ways in which profit-making goals result in the suppression of diversity. If indeed the marketplace of ideas is prone to failure, then the assumption that "the truth" will prevail becomes problematic.

The reporting of "money matters" in the *State College (Pa.) Centre Daily Times* (*CDT*) provides a good example. A 1998 story, prominently placed in the first section under the heading "Local and State" news, announced that a regional chain, Uni-Marts Inc., had hired the Kaiser Group, a marketing firm "with a proven track record in the convenience store industry." Kaiser was reported to specialize in merchandizing, store design, and point-of-sale programs. This business story, compiled from staff reports and presented as local news, highlights the pro-corporate bias of the media, celebrating the efforts of a locally based company to rescue its falling stock prices by selling more Twinkies. If this is news rather than advertising—that is, pertinent information gathered for readers to consider rather than a public relations release reprinted to spur consumption—there ought to be other sides to the story.

A little history would have helped readers put the story into context. A marketing historian, for example, might point out that convenience store chains are filling the retail gap left by the disappearance of neighborhood mom-and-pop grocers. Locally owned stores have been driven out of business by large supermarket and Big Box chains, which lure consumers with lower prices and the appearance of variety reinforced through large advertising expenditures. A psychologist might note that convenience stores capitalize on impulse buying, allowing them to charge high prices on a limited stock of brand-name snack foods and drinks. Since consumers are primed for an impulse buy, point-of-sale displays strengthen the stimulation to consume. A nutritionist might suggest that the Kaiser Group is aiding and abetting Uni-Marts in increasing consumption of nutritionally bereft products. (The *CDT* would never have referred to them as "junk food pushers," although two weeks earlier it did run a Knight Ridder story headlined "Food Police: Teens Consume

Too Much Soda," dismissing a study conducted by the Center for Science in the Public Interest as "unfounded consumer alarm." See chapter 6.) Even a person on the street might have pointed out the downside to the fact that Uni-Marts Inc., newly armed with "the best marketing team in the country," also operated twenty-one Choice Cigarette Discount Outlets. Providing this kind of context would have been bad for business.

ALL THE NEWS THAT SELLS:
THE EFFECTS OF ADVERTISING ON NEWS

Advertisers exert two main influences over the information programming they sponsor. First, they influence the context in which news as a commodity is produced, the structure of the entire media industry of which news reporting is only one small part. Second, they influence the text of news as it is reported, the actual form and content of information as it is presented to consumers. In this section, we examine some specific examples of direct and indirect influence of advertising on the structure and content of the news.

Advertising and News Structure

Advertisers determine the structure of media industries simply by choosing where to spend their money. They support media outlets that reach the right demographic groups, audiences that consume the most. Media producers seeking to serve "undesirable" audiences cannot count on advertising revenues to finance their operations and therefore remain marginalized. Casualties of advertiser indifference or disdain for unprofitable media markets include the working-class press, competitive newspapers, African American radio stations, and independent magazines.

The Working-Class Press

At the turn of the twentieth century, the U.S. labor movement published hundreds of newspapers in dozens of languages. According to Jon Bekken, "These newspapers practiced a journalism very different from that of the capitalist newspapers (produced and sold as commodities by publishers closely tied to social and economic elites), which, they contended, were poisoning the minds of the public."[92] Advertisers had little interest in the vibrant working-class press, not only because working-class audiences had little to spend on manufactured goods, but also because the anticapitalist sentiments these newspapers expressed were obviously contradictory to their goals. Advertisers therefore shunned publications that challenged consumerism as a lifestyle, especially as it became more essential to sustaining the capitalist industrial system. Hearst and Pulitzer, meanwhile, responded to the "New Woman" movement of the period by addressing women as consumers. Thus, although advertisers had no vested interest in women's suffrage, as Schudson remarks, "They must have been favorably impressed by the growing coverage of fashion, etiquette, recipes, beauty culture, and interior decorating" in the mainstream papers.[93]

In England, as Curran and Seaton explain,

> Radical newspapers could survive in the new economic environment only if they moved upmarket to attract an audience desired by advertisers or remained in a small working-class ghetto with manageable losses that could be met from donations. Once they moved out of that ghetto and acquired a large working-class audience, they courted disaster.[94]

Even nonsocialist newspapers found that controversial editorial policies led to the loss of commercial advertising. As one early advertising handbook warned, "You cannot afford to place your advertisements in a paper which is read by the down-at-heels who buy it to see the 'Situations Vacant' column." Another advised, "A journal that circulates a thousand among the upper or middle classes is a better medium than would be one circulating a hundred thousand among the lower classes."[95]

The Only Game in Town

Mainstream newspapers with moderate politics and wide circulation are not immune to the effects of advertising. Bagdikian charts the dramatic decline of towns in the United States with competing newspapers over the last century, and offers Washington, D.C., as a compelling case study of "the process by which competitive papers have been eliminated from the United States for the last three generations."[96] When the *Washington Post* was founded in 1877, the city had a population of 130,000 and five daily newspapers. By 1970, the number of dailies had shrunk to three, even though the metropolitan population had grown to 2.8 million. At that time, the *Post* had a circulation of 500,000, and the other two dailies, the *Star* and the *Daily News*, had about 300,000 and 200,000, respectively. The costs of producing and distributing each paper were roughly the same, but the *Post*, with the highest circulation and lowest cost per unit, could deliver its half-million papers more cheaply than the others. The *Post* could also charge the most for advertising, which it did. If an advertiser could afford the larger investment in a *Post* ad and could use the same ad for the whole geographic area, the *Post* ad actually cost far less per household.

Big advertisers took advantage of the opportunity. "The *Post*, with ever-increasing revenues and profits, could spend more on salespeople, on editorial vigor, and on circulation promotion. The *Star* and the *News*, their revenues and profits shrinking, had less to spend while they were under growing pressure from the *Post*."[97] The rest of the story has become all too

familiar. The *News* suspended operations in 1972, and the *Star* followed
in 1981, leaving only one newspaper in the nation's capital. In 1920, according to Bagdikian, there were 700 cities with competing dailies.[98] Compaine's research shows that just three years later, in 1923, the number of
cities with competing dailies was down to 502. By 1953 it had shrunk to
91. In 1996, only 19 cities, or 1.3 percent of all cities and towns with daily
newspapers, had head-to-head newspaper competition.[99] The "only game
in town" newspaper is likely to be owned by a large chain. In 1996, the
three largest chains (Gannett, Knight Ridder, and Newhouse) accounted for
22.5 percent of total daily circulation.[100] By 2007 the four largest newspaper
firms controlled 29.4 percent of the newspaper industry, and the eight largest had 45 percent of the market.[101]

The effects of newspaper concentration due to mass advertising are far
reaching. For example, monopoly newspapers have hurt small businesses,
which do not need mass circulation and cannot afford monopoly advertising rates. Chain newspapers go hand-in-hand with big box chain retail outlets and with the demise of mom-and-pop stores. Of even greater concern
is the fact that the concentrated structure of the news media is completely
out of sync with the nation's political system. In the United States, most
public policy is set at the local level. Local officials govern schools, courts,
zoning, water, fire, police, and other vital functions. However, as a smaller
number of newspapers grew larger in size, fewer communities had local
papers to help them make informed decisions about issues that affect their
daily lives. In 1920, there were 2,722 urban places and 2,400 daily papers
in the country. By 1980 there were 8,765 urban places and only 1,745
dailies, leaving more than 7,000 American cities with no daily newspaper
of their own.[102] As Bagdikian writes, "The inappropriate fit between the
country's major media and the country's political system has starved voters
of relevant information. . . . It has eroded the central requirement of a democracy that those who are governed give not only their consent but their
informed consent."[103]

Advertising and Minority Media

Much as early advertisers shunned the working-class press, later advertisers avoided radio stations with largely African American or Latino
audiences. In 1999, the Federal Communications Commission (FCC)
released a study conducted by the Civil Rights Forum on Communication Policy investigating practices in the advertising industry that posed
potential barriers to competition in the broadcast marketplace. The study
focused on two business practices: "no urban/Spanish dictates," the
practice of not advertising on stations that target programming at racial
and ethnic minorities; and "minority discounts," the practice of paying

minority-formatted radio stations less than general market stations with comparable audience size.

An analysis of the data, drawn from 3,745 radio stations in 1996, concluded that advertisers regularly discriminate against minority-owned stations and stations with large African American or Latino audiences, either excluding them altogether or paying them less. Ninety-one percent of minority broadcasters indicated that they had been subject to no-urban dictates. Survey respondents estimated that 61 percent of the ads purchased on their stations had been discounted by an average of 59 percent. The dictates and discounts were attributed to a variety of factors, including advertisers' assessments of listener income and spending patterns, and racial and ethnic stereotypes that influence the media buying process.[104] "This report's findings are bleak and shameful," as Congresswoman Carolyn C. Kilpatrick (D-MI) said in a press release. "However, they come as no surprise."[105]

When advertisers do choose minority media, they often ghettoize. The magazine industry is a good example. Cigarette advertising in most magazines surged in the 1970s, when tobacco companies withdrew from radio and television in order to terminate the FCC-mandated Fairness Doctrine messages of the American Cancer Society and others.[106] By the early 1990s, according to the *Wall Street Journal*, cigarette companies were "turning away from the educated, upscale readers that so many magazines court and targeting their efforts to lower-income women and minorities."[107] The trend may have resulted in a windfall in advertising revenues for some minority magazines, but it was certainly not in the best interests of the health of these communities. When the no-urban dictates study was released, FCC Chairman William Kennard stated, "Minority broadcasters should have a fair opportunity to compete for ad dollars."[108] The problem with this is that advertisers who once shunned minority audiences have proven themselves all too willing to exploit them. Advertising has contributed to the perpetuation of racial and ethnic inequality in the United States by suppressing media diversity and exploiting minority markets, not to mention by perpetuating stereotypes in the ads themselves.

Magazines without Umbrellas

Like working-class newspapers and minority radio stations, companies that exist to publish a single magazine lend diversity to an increasingly concentrated and homogenous media environment. They are also, however, vulnerable to the whims of advertisers. The benefits of single-title publishing can include not being bogged down by conflicting agendas, not having to answer to shareholders, and simply not being distracted from the mission of putting out a magazine. Solo publications have been rated as some of the best in quality. *Nylon*, founded in 1998 as "an old-fashioned mom-and-pop operation," was a finalist for a National Magazine Award for general excellence and was named Magazine of the Year by the Society of Publication Designers in 2001. *Outside*, an outdoor lifestyle magazine, had a circulation of 665,000 and was one of only a handful of independently owned magazines among the top moneymakers. In December of 2001, it was feeling the pain of going it alone in an advertising recession. "Unlike magazines owned by media conglomerates like Gruner & Jahr [a subsidiary of Bertelsman, Germany's largest publisher and a giant in U.S. book publishing and music recording], Hearst, or AOL Time Warner, *Outside* does not have any corporate parent to absorb the losses or cash-cow sibling publications to tide it over."[109]

The biggest drawback to solo publication, from a business standpoint, is not being able to sell ads in discounted packages with other media. "It's harder for the independents," Mark Gleason, publisher of *Book Magazine*, told the *New York Times*. In an economic downturn, a car manufacturer is more likely to spend its resources on "a multiplatform deal with one of the big guys, with TV, Internet and print. We have to wait and see what budgets are left over."[110] Mass advertising has driven the concentration of the media. Media companies have merged with the express purpose of attracting advertisers. Indeed, according to the *Wall Street Journal*, major advertising packages were precisely the kind of deals that Time Warner executives envisioned when the two media giants, Time Inc. and Warner Inc., joined forces in 1990. Advertisers could not have been more pleased. In 1991, Time Warner signed an $80 million cross-media advertising deal with General Motors (GM) and announced a $100 million deal with Mazda. As the *Wall Street Journal* reported, "GM executives have said their arrangement will allow the company to market different car models with targeted media. One model, for instance, could be promoted in selected magazines, brochures and videos sent to prospective customers' homes, and ads on cable TV."[111]

While solo magazines struggled to stay alive, Big Media magazines began striking deals with Big Advertisers for solo sponsorship. In 1999, Ford Motor Company marketing executive David Roper told the American Magazine Conference, "We still need ad pages, but we need more creative ways to use your pages."[112] The year before, Ford was the lone sponsor of *Time* magazine's "Heroes of the Planet" series, focusing on environmental issues. According to *Extra!* the coverage explicitly excluded any criticism of automobile pollution.[113] With this in mind, we turn to the effects of advertising on news content.

Advertising and News Content

Advertisers exert direct and indirect influence over news media content. There are many documented cases, and surely many more undocumented ones, of advertisers canceling or threatening to cancel their accounts because of critical reporting. GM, the company that salivated over the cross-media marketing possibilities of the Time Warner merger, has become infamous for withholding advertising dollars as punishment for unfavorable coverage and as warning against future bad publicity. In 1990, for example, GM ordered its advertising agencies not to place commercials on television programs that featured documentary filmmaker Michael Moore.[114] Moore's film *Roger & Me* (1989) is a scathing indictment of GM's cavalier closing of its truck plant in Flint, Michigan, which put 30,000 employees out of work and devastated the city. In 1992, GM sentenced *Automobile Magazine* to three months without advertising after the magazine's editor, David E. Davis, criticized the company in a speech at the Washington Automotive Press Association's annual black-tie gala.[115] Expressing dismay at GM's announcement of twenty-one more plant closings eliminating 74,000 more jobs, Davis likened the company's management to "piano players in whorehouses" who knew what was going on upstairs but did not get personally involved. Davis later told the *New York Times* that since *Automobile* sold only about nine hundred pages of advertising annually, "the 50 or 60 from GM could well be the difference between a profit and a loss for the magazine."[116] Such tales of corporate censorship are damning, but the indirect influence of advertising on news content is more ubiquitous and insidious. It affects the quality and quantity of news reporting on vital topics such as war and health care.

"Not an Upbeat Environment"

In 1991, the *New York Times* reported that national advertisers were "extremely reluctant" to buy commercial time on special network news programs about the war in the Persian Gulf. Executives at the three major networks said that advertisers' skittishness about war coverage was costing them millions of dollars. Howard Stringer, president of the CBS Broadcast Group, said the news division would be forced to scale back plans for prime-time war specials, despite the fact that they had received high ratings, several attracting more viewers than entertainment programs competing with them on other channels. The specials sold only 20 percent of available commercial time, making them economically unfeasible for the network.[117] Richard Dale, an executive at Deutsch Advertising, explained the ad industry's rationale for not running ads on war news programs: "I just think it's wasted money. Commercials need to be seen in the right environment. A war is just not an upbeat environment."[118]

The projected effects of the news media's dependence on advertising during the Gulf War included the following: First, there would be fewer prime-time news specials on CBS. As Peter Lund, executive vice president of the CBS Broadcast Group, told the *New York Times* in 1991: "In fairness to our shareholders, we can't lose $1 million every time we do one of them, and we are losing an easy million between what we lose in ad revenue and the production costs."[119] Second, there would be less war coverage even on regularly scheduled news programs such as *60 Minutes* and *48 Hours*. An anonymous NBC executive could almost be heard heaving a sigh of relief as he told the *Times*, "*The Today Show* got back to more normal programming, and the advertisers were happy with that. A lot of them said they wanted us to get back to Gene Shalit's movie reviews and the other light stuff."[120] Finally, war coverage would be "tailored" to provide a better context for commercials. CBS executives admitted that they courted advertisers with assurances that commercials could be inserted into "segments that were specially produced with upbeat images or messages about the war, like patriotic views from the home front."[121] They seemed to have taken heed of another rationale offered by Dale from the Deutsch ad firm: "After a segment about a chemical attack that includes a shot of a disfigured face, it might not be the best time to talk about Oil of Olay skin care."[122]

Ten years later, in 2001, the *New York Times* lamented, "There is never a good time for a war, but for big media and news companies, the timing of the current crisis is especially poor."[123] The *Times* reported that the networks lost $500 million in advertising revenues in the days immediately following the September 11, 2001, attacks on New York's World Trade Center and the Pentagon in Washington, as they went on twenty-four-hour news. In October, Wall Street analysts estimated that ABC, NBC, and CBS were each incurring $1 million a day in extra costs covering the aftermath. "Most say they are trying to look beyond the short-term financial impact to see the long-term value that extensive coverage can bring to their news 'brands.' They remember that when CNN distinguished itself during the Persian Gulf War, the cable network's halo lasted for years."[124] Like CNN, the major broadcast television news operations are owned by international conglomerates with deep pockets. Because news is just one small part of what these companies do, they can better afford to wait and see how long a crisis drags on before deciding whether to let news spending hurt their overall financial results. By contrast, news is the main operation for companies like the *Washington Post* and the *New York Times*. As the *New York Times* admitted, "There may be less leeway for trimming costs—and so less ability to avoid financial pain,"[125] not to mention less information for readers.

Health and Beauty Aids

When it comes to the sale of products that affect people's health in one way or another, advertisers usually have one of two missions. The first is to assure consumers that a product rumored to be bad for them really is not (or at least to suggest that those who consume the product will feel so hip and happy that it does not matter if they are healthy). The second is to convince consumers that a product that has not been proven to be good for them really is (or at least to imply that those who use the product will look so young and lovely that everyone else will think they are). The tobacco industry has taken on the first challenge, and the pharmaceutical and cosmetics industries have taken the second. Advertisers for these industries have affected news coverage of health issues related to the products they sell.

In 1988, a California company named Advantage/Quik-Fit attempted to launch a national magazine advertising campaign for its new smoking cessation system, Cigarrest. Donald L. Danks, vice president of sales and marketing, was reportedly stymied by the refusal of *Time, Newsweek, Sports Illustrated, Life,* and *US* magazines to carry the company's ad. Perhaps he should not have been. Earlier the same year, RJR Nabisco removed more than $70 million worth of food advertising from Saatchi & Saatchi after the agency created ads that heralded Northwest Airlines' ban on smoking.[126] In 1992, the *New England Journal of Medicine* published a study proving that magazines that relied heavily on cigarette advertising were far less likely than others to write about the dangers of smoking. The study surveyed nearly one hundred magazines over a period of twenty-five years and found that those carrying tobacco ads were 38 percent less likely to discuss smoking risks than those that did not.[127] Women's magazines were the worst offenders; they were 50 percent less likely to cover the health dangers of smoking.[128]

Time and *Newsweek* magazines—known for sniping at each other over issues of journalistic integrity—provide textbook examples of the *New England Journal's* findings. In 1985, *Time* carried a special section devoted to health. The American Academy of Family Physicians supplied the informational copy. *Time* provided the editorial expertise that deleted all references to the hazards of smoking—a decision that undoubtedly delighted the tobacco companies, which bought seven pages of ads in the same edition. In 1988, *Newsweek* published a cover story titled "What You Should Know about Heart Attacks." The back cover featured an ad for Malibu cigarettes, while on the inside, editors deleted any suggestion that smoking contributes to heart attacks.[129]

In 1998, ten years after Cigarrest ads were shunned by mainstream magazines, smoking cessation programs had become far more fashionable, as the tobacco industry ended a slew of state-initiated, health-related lawsuits by agreeing to make annual payments to the states worth $246 billion. The following year, according to the Federal Trade Commission (FTC), the five largest cigarette manufacturers spent $8.24 billion on advertising and promotions—a 22 percent increase from 1998.[130] Backed by Big Advertising, the tobacco industry made it clear that it would not go down without a fight.

The pharmaceutical and cosmetics industries are known less for strong-arm tactics than for exploiting the fears and weaknesses of consumers to sell their wares. As a prosperous generation of baby boomers matured in the 1990s, both industries actively promoted products associated with aging. Both industries also significantly affected the ways in which issues of aging were treated as news. A March 2000 issue of *Parade* magazine featured supermodel Lauren Hutton on the cover, promising that she and other celebrities would "share their secrets for looking good—and feeling good too—near or past 50."[131] A small picture of Hutton appears on page 10, at the top of the cover story. She attributes her good health to losing a few pounds and briefly outlines her diet and exercise regimen. "But my No. 1 secret is estrogen," she declares. "It's good for your moods, it's good for your skin. If I had to choose between all my creams and make-up for feeling and looking good, I'd take the estrogen."[132]

A third picture of Hutton, this one full-body and nearly full-page, is featured on page 15, in an ad sponsored by Wyeth-Ayerst Laboratories warning of "the consequences of estrogen loss at menopause."[133] The ad blends perfectly with the celebrity bias and "editorial" content of the magazine. It also perfectly illustrates the findings of a 2000 study conducted by researchers at the University of California, Davis, and published in the *Journal of Family Practice*: "In addition to failing to educate, most [prescription drug ads] don't explain the basics and some cleverly obscure facts about the products they promote."[134] There is no mention of debates among health-care professionals about the benefits and risks of taking estrogen supplements in this issue of *Parade*.[135]

Meanwhile, newsmakers routinely treat cosmetic matters typically associated with aging as news. In September 1998, the *State College (Pa.) Centre Daily Times* reported that as "baby boomers fight the war on wrinkles," remedies for "visible signs of aging" rank among the "top ten unmet needs" of contemporary consumers. This "news" was provided by product development managers at Oil of Olay, Mary Kay, Q-Tips, and Vaseline.[136] In March 2000, New York's WCBS-TV carried a news report about a Web ad for laser surgery that featured live video of an elective operation. "Advertisements are not generally considered news," as media watchdogs at *Extra!* pointed out, "but the station seemed to think that the fact that it was placed on WCBS's own website made it more newsworthy." Station managers ordered that the ad be treated as news, angering journalists. The eye center, which paid more than $300,000 for the ad, was delighted. "The funny thing about it," a representative was quoted as saying, was that CBS decided to do a news story on the surgery right after the paid webcast. "That was a bonus. That was free."[137]

A Real Estate Advertising Disaster

News content also includes form, which is the way in which information is reported or presented. Although the classified advertising section of a paper is not presented as news in the manner of war coverage or health-care reports, it can certainly be used for information purposes, especially if one is looking to sublet an apartment or buy a used car. In 1990, the *Boca Raton News*, a Knight Ridder paper, began organizing such notices in a grid that allowed readers to compare what was offered more easily. For example, all the Mazda 323s were listed together in descending order by model year and then by price. This innovation was extremely popular with subscribers: A *News* survey showed that 87 percent of readers loved the grids. Unfortunately, however, many advertisers did not. "The grids were a real reader benefit, but a real estate advertising disaster," according to Thomas P. O'Donnell, publisher of the rival *Fort Lauderdale Sun-Sentinel*. O'Donnell reported that advertising in the South Palm Beach edition of the *Sun-Sentinel* had increased 82 percent since the *News* began running the grids. He credited advertiser animosity toward the *News* for his own paper's gains.[138] The *New York Times* reported that the Boca Raton case became the "subject of intense interest throughout the newspaper industry" as the *Boca Raton News* struggled to "resolve whether advertisers or readers have a higher priority."[139] James Gordon Bennett, who argued in the early 1800s that advertisers should gain advantage from the substance of their ads rather than appearance or placement,[140] would surely have been dismayed.

Covering the Capitalist Class

The biggest void in news content is not caused by the direct or indirect influence of any individual advertiser on any particular newspaper or media company. The real hole in the news is a by-product of advertising as an institution. The primary effect of the ideology of advertising on the practice of news reporting is the coverage (or cover-up) of the capitalist class as a class. Most mainstream newspapers have "business" sections, but few devote space to labor and fewer still even acknowledge the existence of capitalism. As noted in chapter 3, snippets of news on media moguls can sometimes be found in syndicated gossip columns such as "People Watch," produced by the Associated Press and featured daily in newspapers around the country. Because so many members of the capitalist class have either made their fortunes in media enterprises or invested their fortunes in media companies, this is a good place to begin searching for news about them.

"The Sundance Kid doesn't have a monopoly on the name," a 1998 "People Watch" story begins, rather gleefully reporting that Robert Redford had lost a trademark battle with Ed Bass over the right to establish a chain of Sundance Theaters in Texas, where Bass and his brothers already held a chain by that name. Redford is duly identified as the actor "who played the outlaw in *Butch Cassidy and the Sundance Kid*" and as a businessman who founded Sundance Enterprises, the Sundance Institute, and the Sundance Film Festival. A file photo of Redford accompanies the item, for readers who may have forgotten what he looks like. The Bass brothers are identified only as brothers, and come off like mom-and-pop theater owners thumbing their noses at a Hollywood movie star in defense of their right to use a common word.

Here is the hole in the news. Robert Redford may be rich and famous, but the Bass brothers are superrich. Ed was the least so, ranked at number 236 on the 2001 *Forbes 400* list, with $1 billion. Brother Lee was number 55, with $3.3 billion. Brothers Sid and Robert were numbers 60 and 70, with $3 billion and $2.6 billion, respectively, while father Perry came in at 172, with $1.3 billion. The Bass brothers and their father thus had a combined net worth of $11.2 billion. In this context, which "People Watch" of course fails to provide, it seems less surprising that Redford lost his trademark battle. By taking great pains to identify one of the most visible figures in the entertainment industry, and none at all to identify a family that quietly invested its oil wealth in the media to expand an already great fortune, this story serves to perpetuate a myth of equal opportunity and classlessness in the United States, obscuring who the real controllers of wealth, power, and information are.

As it turned out, Ed Bass was allowed to keep operating his Sundance theater chain throughout Texas, and Redford got permission to use the name anywhere else on the planet he might decide to put up theaters. The issue of whether anyone should be entitled to claim the term "sun dance" (which, according to Webster, denotes "a ceremonial dance of North and South American Indians in honor of the sun at the summer solstice"[141]) as private property was never called into question. Texas moviegoers were more likely to see Disney animations than Sundance productions at Ed's theaters in 1998, and not just due to fallout over the trademark rivalry. The entire Bass family—including Perry, who inherited the oil empire, and Sid's ex-wife Anne, described by Forbes as "poster dame for the First Wives Club"—held 18 percent in Disney stock at the time.

CONCLUSION

Perhaps a celebrity gossip column cannot be expected to raise issues of class structure in the United States. The editors of *Forbes*, who proudly wear the badge of "capitalist tool" and openly fawn over the superrich, can only be expected to celebrate it. But news coverage of the business dealings of members of the capitalist class should at the very least attempt to escape the ideology of advertising and embrace the values of journalism. Their mergers and acquisitions affect the quality of our information and culture.

The editors of *Forbes* regularly come up with tortured interpretations of their list of "The 400 Richest People in America" to perpetuate a myth of classlessness. The introduction to their 1996 survey, for example, instructed readers to "Forget America's 50 families. Forget old money. Forget silver spoons. Great fortunes are being created almost monthly in the U.S. today by young entrepreneurs who hadn't a dime when we created this list 14 years ago."[142] Even if that were true, at least half of those on the list started out with $50 million or more—the equivalent of a good leadoff from third base. The editors of *Forbes* bristle at the suggestion, but the key to great wealth in America is still "choosing wealthy parents."[143]

The AP's ritual coverage of the *Forbes 400* list often makes front-page news. In September of 1998, for example, it was featured on page 1 of the *State College (Pa.) Centre Daily Times*. The bold headline read "Market Woes Lessen Ranks of Billionaires."[144] Apparently, a stock market dive that summer "left empty chairs at the billionaires' club." Bill Gates remained sitting, with $58.4 billion, despite the fact that the Microsoft chief's net worth "plunged" $9 billion that year. Others, like David Filo of Yahoo! and Roy Disney of Walt Disney, "missed the cut to remain mere megamillionaires." A letter to the editor of the *Centre Daily Times* "applauded" the paper for "reprinting the most inane, incomprehensible piece of 'news' in recent memory," noting that it would take him 464 years to clap once for each of Bill Gates's dollars. The editor responded that the paper had also published six stories since April on poverty and homelessness in Centre County.[145]

Buried at the bottom of the column (and cast as a "disturbing trend for parents and teachers"), was the news that fifty-eight members of that year's *Forbes 400* never finished college and yet had amassed an average fortune of $4.8 billion. The message is clear: "Parents, don't bother sacrificing to send your kids to Ivy League schools. Graduates of these prestigious colleges averaged only $2.3 billion." The column suggests that one need not have a good education or even connections to become superrich; all it takes is "smarts." Bill Gates, perennially number one on the list, is often cited as an example. In fact, Gates started on first base. Son of a professional couple, he attended Harvard, where he met Paul Allen (number 3 on the 2001 list, with $28.2 billion) before dropping out. His big break came in 1980 when IBM contracted him to develop the operating software system for its first PC. Gates and Allen did not develop that software—they merely bought QDOS for $50,000, renamed it MS-DOS, and rode to fortune on the backs of Big Blue. With MS-DOS in more than 90 percent of the world's PCs, Microsoft used its market power to stifle competition. Contrary to popular belief, much of Gates's $54 billion fortune was based on questionable business practices rather than "smarts." Most of it, moreover, is the result of contributions to computer technology produced by scholars and researchers and funded by taxpayer money.

The 2007 *Forbes 400* celebrates "Cash Countesses," the record thirty-nine women who made the list of richest Americans (all billionaires) that year. *Forbes* rather grudgingly admits that the majority of these women (already less than 10 percent of the club) inherited their wealth. But it singles out eight women (a whopping 2 percent) as "dollar divas" who "built their fortunes from the ground up or have an active role running their family empires." Put the emphasis on "or." A closer look at the list reveals that seven of the eight "dollar divas" actually inherited businesses from their fathers or dead husbands. It's no surprise to us that a woman (especially one privileged with a business education from Princeton or Harvard) can a run a company when it's dropped in her lap. But *Forbes* seems to be implying that the playing field is equal and the glass ceiling is a myth. So all women, especially poor black women, can look to Oprah Winfrey (number 167 on the 2007 list, at $2.5 billion) as evidence of class, gender, and racial equity under capitalism.[146] On March 7, 2008, *the Philadelphia Inquirer* reported a "shake-up" on the *Forbes 400* list: Warren Buffett displaced Bill Gates as the world's richest man (yawn.) Only two women appear on this *Forbes* list of "most important people alive": Oprah ($2.5 billion) and onetime starving writer J. K. Rowling, author of the Harry Potter books ($1 billion).[147]

The *Forbes 400* reinforces false notions of upward mobility in what is actually a very rigid U.S. class structure. Again, perhaps we should expect nothing more from the self-proclaimed capitalist tool. In a sense, *Forbes* does us a service by publishing its annual list so that we can see how obscenely wealthy the superrich are—but readers should expect that rather than simply repeating the *Forbes* line, our "watchdog" media would take the ritual report as an opportunity to put the list into context.

The unequal distribution of wealth and income in the United States is beginning to resemble that of many Third World societies. In 2001, according to the Institute for Policy Studies and United for a Fair Economy, the average chief executive officer of a major American corporation made 531 times as much in pay, bonuses, and stock options as the average factory worker.[148] Wealth is even more concentrated. According to Federal Reserve data from 1996, the richest 500,000 U.S. households (out of 100 million) owned one-third of the total wealth in the United States (minus home equity, the main repository of most household wealth). The richest 10 percent of the population owned a whopping 77.5 percent of the total wealth (again, minus home equity), and they owned 84 percent of the stock as well as 90 percent of the bonds.[149]

The wealth gap increased through the first decade of the twenty-first century, inspring the Occupy Wall Street movement to use "We are the 99 percent" as its motto. The movement forced the media to examine the distribution of wealth in the United States. However, media coverage soon shifted to police breaking up the Occupy camps. Attention to wealth and income distribution in the media ironically returned during the Republican presidential primaries in 2012 as opponents to Mitt Romney raised the issue. Suddenly, private equity and capital gains moved from the business section to the news pages. At the same time, economic realities began to shatter the myths of Horatio Alger and the American Dream, and leaks emerged in the hegemonic consent of the dominated. Hence the increasing use of force.

The absurdly unequal distribution of wealth and income within the United States is magnified globally. More than 1 billion of the world's 6.2 billion people go to bed hungry every night. At the turn of the twenty-first century, 900 million people existed on less than $1 a day in Asia alone.[150] This state of affairs and the discontent it fosters require the rich to use more coercion to protect their fortunes, fueling conditions for increased social conflict internationally. With the global spread of Occupy movements inspired by the 2011 Arab Spring uprisings, it became more apparent that the concentration of the world's wealth in the hands of a few poses a serious threat to democracy, since great wealth gives those who own it inordinate power to dictate public policy and mold public opinion through the media. The media reluctantly began filling the hole in the news—and could no longer provide just a handful of features about what a shame it is to be poor, or what a drag it is to be a little less rich.

6

Ad Creep: The Commercialization of Culture

"Ad creep" is a relatively new term used to describe the gradual expansion of advertising into nontraditional spaces such as public playgrounds, school buses, sidewalks, and beaches.[1] The term has a decidedly negative connotation, and indeed, is specifically defined by Wikipedia as advertising that is "*invasive and coercive,* like ads in schools, doctor's offices and hospitals, restrooms, elevators, on ATM's, on garbage cans, and on restaurant menus."[2] According to one online source, "commercial creep" is epitomized by "the annoying addition of multiple ads prior to movies shown in theaters"[3]—something to which filmgoers once objected but have since grown accustomed. Others point to the kaleidoscope of corporate logos swirling behind batters in televised baseball games (not to mention "commercial time-outs") as evidence of ad creep.

The advertising industry has a number of upbeat euphemisms for marketing strategies that result in ad creep—"integrated," "embedded," "ambient," and "organic" advertising, to name a few. Critics have coined less flattering terms, including "brandalism," "street spam," and "corporate masturbation." The British refer to it as advertising of the "pavement and urinal" variety. Those who produce it are sometimes called "ad creeps." Meanwhile, media consumers have been likened to everything from robots to roaches. As a senior ad executive in the Omnicom Group observed, "You spray them and spray them and they get immune after a while." As Robert McChesney noted, "So, you spray them some more."[4]

Slogans and slurs aside, the basic definition of ad creep as "gradual" and "nontraditional" becomes problematic when one considers the rapidly changing meaning of such words in a wired world. Speed is a relative thing, and novelty fades fast. The expansion of advertising has become less gradual, and the exploitation of venues once considered nontraditional is now commonplace. Not long ago, it was unthinkable to advertise a soft drink on a baby bottle. Now, as one critic noted, your child's first visual experience can be "a huge Coke or 7Up logo with a nipple on it."[5] Airsickness bags bear commercial messages, and pregnant women's bellies are leased for temporary tattoos. One advertiser is said to have bought space on the bottom of a prizefighter's shoes in the event that he might be knocked out during a televised bout. He was.[6]

In this chapter, we focus primarily (though not exclusively) on product placement and integration as two particularly invasive yet increasingly accepted forms of ad creep. First, we examine the expansion of product placement, from its once sporadic to now pervasive presence in popular cultural forms such as movies, television, and music. Next, we examine the encroachment of advertising and marketing into traditionally "higher" art forms such as literature and theater. We turn then to a critique of ad creep into children's culture, from virtual playgrounds to slumber parties. We conclude with an examination of advertising in new media, from cell phones and search engines to social networks and virtual worlds. We argue that the once gradual creep of advertising into virtually every aspect of daily life functions to make the conspicuous consumption of branded goods and services seem vital to any meaningful participation in contemporary society. But at what cost?

PRODUCT PLACEMENT IN POPULAR CULTURE

Product placement in popular culture has become so pervasive as to risk being thought of as natural or commonsensical. As McChesney notes, "Corporate power is woven so deeply into the culture that it becomes invisible, unquestionable."[7] Indeed, it is sometimes difficult for an entire generation of media consumers to imagine things otherwise. (Why do you think they call it "creep"?) A brief survey of product placement in Hollywood movies, network and cable TV shows, and rock and rap music suggests that the hypercommercialization of culture is a fairly recent phenomenon, one that functions to place the accumulation of stuff at the very center of our lived and shared experiences, from the cradle to the grave.

Movies

Hollywood has always promoted acquisitive or "aspirational" lifestyles, though not usually with brand names attached. Happy endings on the silver screen often celebrated heterosexual romantic love combined with socioeconomic class rise (however rare such serendipity may be in real life).

Storylines sometimes revolved around breakfasts at Tiffany's or diamonds by De Beers, but systematic product placement in classical Hollywood cinema was relatively rare. Product placement in postclassical Hollywood is usually traced back to the 1970s and 1980s. The .44 Magnum brandished by Clint Eastwood in *Dirty Harry* (1971), the Reese's Pieces nibbled by the cuddly alien in *E.T.* (1982), and the Ray Ban sunglasses sported by Tom Cruise in *Risky Business* (1983) all resulted in dramatic increases in sales of these products. Advertisers and marketers took notice.

Movie product placement proliferated in 1990s with the rise of agencies brokering deals between advertisers and film studios, offering sliding scales for background appearances, hands-on use, and insertion into dialogue. One example is *Home Alone* (1990), in which there are forty-two mentions of thirty-one products, including Budget Rent-A-Truck, American Airlines, Nestles' Juicy Juice, and Pepsi. The seasonal turkey TV dinner originally written into the script for Macaulay Culkin's solo Christmas meal was changed by marketers to the more brand-friendly Kraft Macaroni & Cheese and justified by producers as more obviously "comfort food" for the unwittingly abandoned young boy.

In the early 2000s, product placement became more central to Hollywood production and promotion budgets. The producers of *Minority Report* (2002) purported to mount a cinematic critique of branding in the future—but made lucrative deals with dozens of advertisers, including Lexus, Reebok, Nokia, Guinness, Bulgari, American Express, Ben & Jerry's, Burger King, and Aquafina. The James Bond franchise became notorious for its flagrant promotion of luxury cars, high-tech gadgets, designer fashions, and top-shelf booze. *Die Another Day* (2002) reportedly had at least half of its $240 million production and promotion budget supplied by advertisers, earning it the nickname "Buy Another Day" in the movie industry.

There have been negative product placements as well. Pepsi was associated with bad guys and sad circumstances in films such as *Missing* (1982) and *Murphy's Romance* (1985) after Coca-Cola bought Columbia Pictures. Product placement was parodied in *Wayne's World* (1992) and *Josie and the Pussycats* (2001)—but as many critics have noted, such plugs may be even more effective when viewers feel like they're in on the joke. In a remarkable example of reverse product placement (or life imitating art), a dozen 7-Eleven stores were renamed "Kwik-E Marts" as part of a promotion for *The Simpsons Movie* in the summer of 2007. For a "limited time only," thousands of 7-Eleven stores in the United States and Canada sold "Buzz Cola," "Krusty-Os Cereal," and "WooHoo! Squishees," all inspired by the popular TV show and designed to sell tickets to the spin-off film.

As Janet Wasko notes, "Products have moved into important narrative roles with entire movies revolving around specific products, as in the case of *Cast Away* [2000] and *You've Got Mail* [1998]. Branded products and services played major roles in these two films, with narrative elements structured around the products."[8] This shift has had a profound impact on both the kinds of stories that are told and the ways in which they are told. Genres that lend themselves well to product placement (e.g., action adventure films that spotlight technology and speed) abound. And the conventions of classical Hollywood genres such as romantic comedy have been tweaked to serve the needs of contemporary sponsors, sometimes with unsettling results. *You've Got Mail* provides a good example of the latter.

Case Study: You've Got Mail

You've Got Mail is a romantic comedy written and directed by Nora Ephron, distributed by Warner Bros., and "collaborated upon" by America Online (AOL). The film stars Meg Ryan as Kathleen, the perky proprietor of a small children's bookstore bequeathed to her by her mother, and Tom Hanks as Joe, the cocky heir to a big box bookstore chain that routinely and ruthlessly puts independents like Kathleen out of business. Unbeknownst to both, they are engaged in an anonymous online relationship, one that grows increasingly intimate and romantic even as their public battle grows more hostile and Kathleen's prospects grow more dismal. Viewers familiar with the conventions of the genre anticipate that Joe will undergo a transformation upon realizing that the woman he is crushing in real life is the pen pal he has grown to cherish in cyberspace, paving the way for a happy ending. But he just doesn't. Rather, he uses the information to manipulate her both personally and professionally. In the end, the bookstore baron gets the shop girl, after systematically destroying her family business. And she melts into his arms at the end, telling him "I wanted it to be you so badly" to the strains of "Somewhere over the Rainbow."

AOL and Warner Bros. declined to describe the details of their arrangement, but people involved with the film said that Ephron and AOL worked closely together. Some sources claim that no money changed hands; other say the deal was worth $1 million to $3 million. In any case, AOL was effectively a "partner" in the filmmaking. Company executives reviewed Ephron's script and suggested changes to make the e-mail correspondence seem more "realistic." The company persuaded Ephron to change the film's original title from *You Have Mail* so that it matched the AOL phrase exactly. "We really don't think of it as a promotion," insisted Wendy Goldberg, an AOL spokeswoman. "It's a love story, not a technology story."

But the real love affair in *You've Got Mail* is between the film and big business. It is essentially a two-hour ad for AOL, with equal time given to Macs and PCs, to be swallowed with tall cups of Starbucks. In this film's world, the heroine's boyfriend is coded as "the wrong one" due to his Luddite tendencies (he's a writer who cherishes his typewriters) and progressive politics (he's named Frank Navasky, an apparent reference to the founding editor of *The Nation*). The film doesn't merely promote a conspicuously consumptive and technology-driven lifestyle but actively condemns alternatives. Frank is coded as "annoying" because he is disconcerted that the "cute quirk" about Kathleen's lovable accountant, Birdie (Jean Stapleton), is that she is living off a fortune left to her by a former lover, one Francisco Franco. To get rid of Frank, who is passionate about politics, Kathleen tells him that she once opted to get a manicure instead of voting. And to win Kathleen over, Joe buys her a bouquet of daisies, providing a convenient product tie-in. 1-800-flowers offered a specially designed *You've Got Mail* bouquet and placed promotional posters and giveaways at the company's 2,650 owned and affiliated floral shops around the country.

The perversity of these remarkably unromantic but advertiser-friendly plot twists was not lost on reviewers. As one critic wrote simply: "Why audiences didn't riot at the end is completely beyond me."[9] Even the "Manly Men's Movie Reviews" website (which one might have expected to approve of Hanks' uncharacteristically macho character) expressed disbelief and disappointment that Ryan's character "recovers from her loss almost instantly and forgives her suitor almost magically."[10] Nonetheless, *You've Got Mail* took in $116 million at the box office in the United States and $251 million worldwide. It continues to be aired on TV and sold on DVD. In 2006, the film was packaged as a Mother's Day present, complete with gift bag and card, to be sold at Rite-Aid stores across the nation for $9.99. "It has major stars and a warm and fuzzy story," explained Norm Marshall, head of a product placement firm in Sun Valley, California. "It's absolutely priceless."[11]

Television

Television has always been sponsored by advertisers, of course, but the prominent placement of products on sitcom sets and the integration of branded merchandise into TV dramas is a relatively new trend. From an advertising industry perspective, product placement and integration were made "necessary" by the development of technologies designed to capture television programming for later viewing, from the Betamax VCR in the 1970s to TiVo in the 1990s. Such recording or time-shifting devices, however different in design and format, equipped viewers with the tools to zip, zap, and otherwise dodge commercials.

Unlike the film industry, which is largely self-regulated, the broadcast and cable industries are overseen by a number of government agencies. The Federal Communications Commission (FCC) requires full disclosure of paid advertisements. The Federal Trade Commission (FTC) is charged with battling deceptive marketing practices. The Food and Drug Administration

(FDA) monitors packaging and advertising of food, prescription medicines, over-the-counter drugs, medical devices, and cosmetics. Media watchdogs such as Commercial Alert and Campaign for a Commercial-Free Childhood have repeatedly petitioned all three agencies for stricter guidelines and tighter enforcement. But product placement on TV has thus far flown smoothly under the radar of regulators.

In the early 2000s, TV viewers were seduced by sexy Buicks on Disney/ABC's *Desperate Houswives*, where the ladies of Wisteria Lane wore Halston gowns in kitchens furnished by Thermador and Bosch. Campbell's Tomato Soup was served up lovingly in NBC's *American Dreams*, and Coke was displayed prominently on Fox's *American Idol*. The young doctors of NBC's *Scrubs* played Hasbro's *Operation* board game, while two gal pals in WB's *What I Like about You* competed against each other to be Clairol's "Herbal Essence Girl." Lee jeans were featured in a photo shoot in one episode of UPN's *America's Next Top Model*, which then became the basis for a print ad in *People* magazine.

Theoretically, product placement of pharmaceutical drugs would raise far more complex concerns than the fetishization of luxury cars and designer frocks on prime-time television. The FDA legalized direct-to-consumer advertising of prescription drugs in 1997, resulting in a deluge of TV ads urging viewers to "Ask your doctor about . . ." and a dramatic increase in demand for certain pharmaceuticals. As noted in chapter 5, drug makers who advertise the benefits of their products are required to warn consumers of potential risks. The first TV drug ads, according to *Fortune* magazine, invariably featured "dancing geriatrics celebrating newfound health, followed by a lengthy voice-over of dizzying side effects." Such spots, as *Fortune* further noted, were "considered ineffective."[12] Product placement seemed an irresistible alternative.

Perhaps it is no coincidence that medically themed TV shows enjoyed a resurgence in popularity around the same time. The painkiller Vicodin, the erectile dysfunction drug Viagra, and the cosmetic treatment Botox all found their way into prime-time shows such as *Scrubs*, *House*, and *Grey's Anatomy* in the early 2000s. The contraceptive Nuvaring was prominently displayed on clipboards and posters on *Scrubs* and *Grey's Anatomy*, and mentioned in dialogue on *King of Queens*. An entire episode of *Boston Legal* revolved around a teacher accused of wrongful death after one of her students suffered a fatal allergic reaction to peanuts. The drug she allegedly failed to inject in a timely fashion is referred to throughout the show by its brand name. As the boy's father testifies, "If the Epipen isn't administered, it can be fatal." Such placements are undoubtedly more effective in appealing to viewers' emotions than cumbersome thirty-second spots, but they certainly don't inform consumers about the potential risks and side effects of prescription medications.

The practice of making branded products central to television narratives, as in the *Boston Legal* case, has become increasingly common. The legendary sixtieth episode of *Seinfeld* was written around the candy Junior Mints, with popular characters such as Kramer reciting lines like "Who's gonna turn down a Junior Mint? It's chocolate, it's peppermint—it's delicious!" In 2003, an episode of *Sex and the City* revolved around a fictional ad campaign for Absolut Spirits. In another noteworthy case of reverse product placement (or life imitating art), the "Absolut Hunk Cocktail" introduced on the show became all the rage at New York nightspots (prompting the actor featured in the fictional-turned-actual ad campaign to sue the show's producers).

Case Study: Friends

The eleventh episode of the sixth season of *Friends* is aptly titled "The One with the Apothecary Table," as the plot revolves around a piece of furniture. Produced by Time Warner, the episode aired on NBC in January 2000, and has since been syndicated on TBS and sold in DVD collections. The story involves Rachel ordering an apothecary table from a Pottery Barn catalogue, although Monica warns her that Phoebe will hate it because it is mass manufactured. So Rachel tells Phoebe that she stumbled on the table at a flea market, and Phoebe loves the idea of its having a unique history. Phoebe suspects the truth when Ross orders the exact same table, although he attempts to conceal it with Pottery Barn linens. Rachel insists that the chain store replicated and mass marketed their original, and proceeds to furnish their entire apartment with Pottery Barn products. When Phoebe finally recognizes the merchandise in a showroom window, Rachel begs her not to be mad. Phoebe replies, "I *am* mad. I *am* mad because this stuff is everything that's wrong with the world and it's all in my living room and all I can think about is . . . I don't have that lamp."

It should be noted that Phoebe's initial rejection of mass-produced merchandise is entirely in keeping with her constructed character. Although decidedly ditzy and frequently used to provide comic relief, Phoebe is viewed by many fans as the moral center of the ensemble cast. She is the least materialistic of the group, the one who fails at jobs in advertising and telemarketing. In one episode, she reminds her professional friends that there are economic class disparities between members of the group. In another, she performs "Jingle Bitch Screwed Me Over," written for a former singing partner who sold out to the advertising industry. But in "The One with the Apothecary Table," Phoebe's resistance to mass production and conspicuous consumption is mocked, sometimes callously. ("How can anybody hate Pottery Barn?" Ross asks incredulously. "It's because she's a twin. Twins are weird.") Phoebe is ultimately (and inevitably) seduced by the charms of Pottery Barn collectibles. As in *You've Got Mail*, the Big Box retailer triumphs over the ideals of a sympathetic character, and viewers are encouraged to join the shopping spree.

When questioned about the episode, Peter Roth of Warner Bros. downplayed criticism by stating simply that the deal struck with Pottery Barn helped to "offset the high cost of production."[13] In a 2004 feature marking the end of *Friends*, *Entertainment Weekly* ranked "The One with the Apothecary Table" first on its list of "Best Product Placements" on the long-running show. Patrick Connolly, executive vice president and chief marketing officer of Pottery Barn's parent company Williams-Sonoma, called the episode a "gift that keeps on giving," adding that the "phones light up with catalogue requests every time it airs in syndication."[14]

So what of the aforementioned federal regulators of sponsors on broadcast and cable television? In 2003, Commercial Alert challenged the FTC to require TV producers to fully disclose product placements as paid advertisements, perhaps with pop-up labels. A number of powerful industry organizations formed a coalition to lobby against such a move, calling the proposal "radical and misguided." In 2005, the FTC officially declined to pursue the matter further, claiming that "the existing statutory and regulatory framework provides sufficient tools for challenging" deceptive practices. The National Association of Broadcasters "applauded the decision," as the *New York Times* reported. In September 2007, two U.S. representatives, Henry Waxman (D-CA) and Ed Markey (D-MA), wrote a letter to FCC Chairman Kevin Martin similarly urging the FCC to regulate product placement more vigilantly. "In our view, the blurring of the line between advertising and content represented by product placement and integration is unfair and deceptive if it occurs without adequate disclosures to the viewing public."[15] But as of this writing, the FCC had taken no significant action to address the issue. The FDA had expressed no explicit position on product placement of prescription medicines. And the United States remained the only industrialized nation in the world to permit ads for pharmaceutical drugs on television.[16]

Music

The history of popular music lyrics is punctuated with brand name references. In keeping with rock's emphasis on speed, sex, and instant gratification, fast cars, hot fashions, and fast food are especially prevalent. Think "Hot Rod Lincoln," "Mustang Sally," and "Little Red Corvette," along with all the Maseratis, El Dorados, and pink Cadillacs strewn along the highway. Bruce Springsteen serenaded small-time hoods meeting "outside the 7-Eleven store" and John Mellencamp sang of "sucking on a chili dog outside the Tasty Freeze" (with a girl wearing Bobbie Brooks jeans), while Jimmy Buffet recalled promising to "pay the Mini-Mart back" for shoplifted groceries. But it's safe to say that Springsteen's stark images of a "barefoot girl sitting on the hood of a Dodge" under the glow of "that giant Exxon sign that brings this fair city light" did not have the intent or effect of selling cars or gas.

Some brand-name references in rock lyrics are clearly meant to be derisive, from the escapist Learjet in Carly Simon's "You're So Vain" and Pink Floyd's "Money," to the infectious "Mercedes Bends" in the Eagles' "Hotel California." As noted in chapter 4, Sheryl Crow's reference to the ease of buying guns at Wal-Mart in "Love is a Good Thing" got her album banned by the retail giant. In "Eat the Rich," Aerosmith's Steven Tyler tells mustard connoisseurs in no uncertain terms what they can do with their Grey Poupon. However disdainful, such lyrics are not likely to harm brands. Indeed, an online search for the lyrics to Green Day's "409 in Your Coffee Maker" yielded ads for a variety of coffee brewers, mugs, and beans (if not spray disinfectants).

Our concern here is with brand names intentionally inserted into lyrics, songs specifically written to promote products (though not labeled as such), and popular recordings licensed to advertisers to create emotional associations with their products. Such practices were unthinkable in rock music until fairly recently. The term "jingle" once connoted a song that played on in one's head for all the wrong reasons, and those who wrote them were derided as hacks or shills. But song licensing and product placement are increasingly common practices in the contemporary music industry. In rock, existing songs are laid over seductive commercials; in rap, brands are inserted or integrated into the songs themselves. Both practices have been gradually accepted and, in some cases, passionately defended by music artists and listeners alike. As such, they provide a particularly salient example of ad creep.

Rock

In the early 2000s, advertisers focused mainly on "classic rock" hits to pitch products, tapping into the nostalgia of baby boomers and, some argue, creating a new generation of fans for the music of the 1960s and 1970s. Randy Bachman, front man for Bachman Turner Overdrive, retained publishing rights to the group's catalogue, and licensed their 1973 hit "Takin' Care of Business" to Office Depot some thirty years later. Bachman called the partnership a "perfect marriage" between song and product—although it must be noted that this claim is debatable. Lyrics not used in the ads include: "If your train's on time you can get to work by nine / And start your slaving job to get your pay / If you ever get annoyed, look at me I'm self employed / I love to work at nothing all day." Other Office Depot ads with superficial lyrical tie-ins included the Spinners' "Rubber Band Man" and Alice Cooper's "School's Out." Bachman declined to disclose how much money he made on the deal, but he admitted, "You make more in one year with that commercial than you do in your entire lifetime of your band in the '70s with that song."[17]

As the practice of raiding rock archives became more widespread, some advertisers earned notoriety for the sheer number of musical vaults they managed to pilfer. Cingular commercials featured songs by AC/DC, Peter Gabriel, the Allman Brothers, Tommy Tutone, Etta James, and The Band. Fidelity Investments used works by David Bowie, Billy Preston, King Harvest, Blondie, and Paul McCartney & Wings. Hewlett-Packard licensed music by Deep Purple, The Cure, The Kinks, and the Bobbettes. Other advertisers were taken to task for using songs about world peace and political protest to sell fast food and gas-guzzling SUVs. Nike was castigated for using the Beatles' "Revolution" to plug sneakers in 1987, leading to a lawsuit by the band's surviving members. Pete Townsend was criticized for licensing The Who's "Happy Jack" to sell Hummers and the theme from *Tommy* to plug Clariton—at the same time refusing to let documentary filmmaker Michael Moore use "Won't Get Fooled Again" in *Fahrenheit 911.*[18]

As the last example suggests, individual musicians became targets of criticism from fans who felt betrayed. A website devoted to "The Ten Cheesiest Rock Commercials" included a "Sellout Quotient" for each artist listed. The quotient was understandably low for John Fogherty of Creedence Clearwater Revival, who didn't own the rights to "Fortunate Son" (a song about the privilege and hypocrisy of the ruling class under the Nixon administration during the Vietnam War) and was reportedly angry that the song was eventually used to sell Wrangler jeans. The quotient was low as well for the Ramones, who "can't really do much to stop this, being that most of them are dead."[19] (The authors of the site did, however, suggest that the ghosts of the punk band should haunt the ad execs responsible for using their first single, "Blitzkrieg Bop," to hawk Diet Pepsi.) The sellout quotient was higher for Iggy Pop, who owned the master recording of his 1977 album *Lust for Life* and licensed the title track to Royal Caribbean Cruise Lines (whose ads conveniently omitted the song's references to alcohol, heroin, and "flesh machines"). It was highest for Devo, who rerecorded their 1980 hit "Whip It" (by most accounts, a song about sado-masochistic sex) with new lyrics suitable for a floor mop commercial ("When you've got a dirty floor / You need Swiffer"). Bob Dylan didn't appear on this list, but he took a lot of flak from fans for licensing a 2004 remix of his 1997 song "Love Sick" to Victoria's Secret and appearing in TV ads with a model clad only in a bra, panties, and Victoria's Secret's signature angel wings. Editorials criticizing the campaign came under headlines such as "The Undies They Are A-Changin'" and "Tangled Up in Boobs."[20]

Case Study: John Mellencamp

John Mellencamp emerged in the 1980s as a singer/songwriter who developed a folk/rock style of music associated with the U.S. heartland and was often compared with the works of Bob Seger, Bruce Springsteen, and Tom Petty. Mellencamp had a number of hit singles in the 1980s, including "Jack and Diane," "Hurts So Good," "Pink Houses," and "Small Town." He continued to record and tour throughout the 1990s but virtually disappeared in the 2000s—that is, until he agreed to license a single from his 2006 album to Chevrolet. "People say I sold out," he told a reporter for the *New York Times*. "No, I got sold out. Sometime during the '90s record companies made the decision that us guys who had been around for a long time and had sold millions of records and were household names just weren't as interesting as girls in stretch dresses."[21]

In 2006, Mellencamp signed the rights to "This Is Our Country" to General Motors to replace Bob Seger's longstanding "Like a Rock" as the anthem for Chevy's Silverado truck. The song was laid over a number of video montages, and the ads played in very heavy rotation, especially during high-profile sporting events. Mellencamp performed the song live at the second game of the 2006 World Series. The ads generated a fair amount of controversy. Some fans complained about Mellencamp selling his music to an advertiser in the first place, especially since he was known to have criticized others for doing so in the past. Others objected to the accompanying visuals, a mixture of patriotic landmarks, homeland vistas, and historical touchstones. "It's not OK to use images of Rosa Parks, MLK, the Vietnam War, the Katrina disaster, and 9/11 to sell pickup trucks," wrote one blogger. "It's wrong."[22] Most music lovers and sports fans were simply annoyed by the overexposure.

Mellencamp's defense of his decision in a *Rolling Stone* interview was passionate and poignant. He admitted to being adamant, in the past, that artists should not license their songs. "I was outspoken about it. But times have changed. Dylan's selling his songs." He also spoke highly of Tom Petty's latest work, a "beautiful" album called *Highway Companion* with an "unbelievable" single titled "Saving Grace." Mellencamp claimed he never once heard any of this on the radio ("If nobody's playing Petty's record, why the fuck would they play mine?").[23] Finally, he said, "I don't want to spend a year and a half making a record for no one to hear. I'm a songwriter and I want to get my message out, but I didn't feel like there was an avenue to do that." In the contemporary music industry (profiled in chapter 4), that avenue was apparently left for General Motors to provide. As Mellencamp told the *New York Times*: "Sometimes I get sad about it really. I still don't think that people should sell their songs for advertising."[24]

Rap and Hip Hop

As in rock, there is a rich history of product references in rap lyrics. According to hip hop historian Jeff Chang, "As far back as the Sugar Hill Gang [1979], the braggadocio included brand-name dropping and talk of having 'more money than a sucker could ever spend'; there was always an aspirational aspect to this poetry born of poverty."[25] Systematic product placement in rap music is usually traced back to 1986, when Run-D.M.C. scored a huge hit with "My Adidas." Although not intended as a promotion for sneakers, the title hinted at the commodity fetishization that would become a hallmark of hip hop culture ("bling"). The song and its popular music video were played in heavy rotation on radio and MTV, and led to a $1.5 million sponsorship deal between the recording artists and the footwear manufacturers.

That deal, as McChesney notes wryly, "appears quaint by today's standards."[26] Since then, rap artist Sean "P. Diddy" Combs has converted his successful music career into a massive marketing empire. In 2003, Diddy's Blue Flame Marketing and Advertising Company announced its plan to "build brands that are targeted to trend-setting consumers." Clients included Versace, Bacardi, Bentley, Nike, and Foot Locker. "The line between the entertainment and marketing and advertising world has virtually disappeared, and we have created this partnership division to further solidify the relationships between the corporate and music worlds," said Jameel Spencer, president/principal of Blue Flame.[27] "It used to be cool to not have money when Run-DMC rapped about 'Calvin Klein is no friend of mine,' but now hip-hop is more entrepreneurial."[28]

Other rap artists have created their own product lines and plugged them in their own songs. Shawn "Jay-Z" Carter joined with Damon Dash and Kareem "Biggs" Burke to form Rocawear, a line of clothing reflecting an "urban aesthetic" and promoting a "borderless global lifestyle."[29] According to Rocawear's website, the trio realized that "their ability to create culture far transcended the realm of music." In 2007, Jay-Z sold the rights to the Rocawear brand to the Iconix Brand Group for $204 million. Jay-Z retained his share and stake in the company, and continued to manage the marketing, licensing, and product development for the line.

Meanwhile, outside advertisers began targeting rap artists more aggressively for paid placements. In 2002, Busta Rhymes' "Pass the Courvoisier" (like "My Adidas," reportedly a purely artistic choice) was credited with fueling a double-digit spike in U.S. sales of Courvoisier brandy, and a promotional deal was cut.[30] The same year, Hewlett-Packard pursued a deal through which its products would be prominently featured in songs by Def Jam artists in exchange for extensive play in Hewlett-Packard ad campaigns. In 2004, Seagram's Gin arranged for placement in Petey Pablo's smash hit "Freak-A-Leek" through an agency. In 2005, McDonald's worked with the same agency to solicit hip hop artists to plug Big Macs. McDonald's retained final approval of lyrics and minimized risk by arranging to pay artists according to radio rotation.

The cooptation and corporatization of rap music and hip hop culture was a particularly bitter pill to swallow for some believers, especially given the deep roots of these forms of cultural expression in political protest and social activism. As Chang commented, "Once a cacophony of diverse voices, the genre now looks like a monoculture whose product, like high-fructose corn syrup, is designed not to nourish us but to get us hooked on other products, from McDonald's to Courvoisier."[31]

PRODUCT PLACEMENT IN "HIGH ART"

The fine arts have always been patronized by wealthy individuals and subsidized by public and private endowments, but until recently they managed to maintain the appearance of being above the crass commercialism of advertising and marketing. Some advertisers assumed that the *literati* who buy theater tickets and hardcover books would be offended by the bastardization of canonical texts for promotional purposes. Playwrights and novelists were generally thought to have a higher calling, and ticket prices on Broadway were already steep. Nonetheless, advertising crept into traditionally high art forms such as theater and literature less stealthily than one might imagine.

Theater

In 1992, Chrysler Corp. brought "splashy, sports-style promotions to the stage" in a product placement deal with the producers of the Broadway hit *Will Rogers Follies.* Chrysler's Jeep Grand Cherokee was written into dialogue recited by the show's Oscar- and Golden Globe Award–winning star, Keith Carradine. Actual Jeep Cherokees with life-size cutouts of the show's Ziegfeld chorus girls were parked outside (and, where space permitted, inside) the lobbies of all fifty theaters where the touring show was booked nationwide. According to the *Wall Street Journal,* "This tie-in makes the Super Bowl look practically commercial-free."[32] Although some reviewers complained about the aggressive promotional campaign, the hypercommercialism surrounding the production did not adversely affect its critical or commercial reception. *Will Rogers Follies* ran for 981 performances and was nominated for eleven Tony Awards, winning six. The promotional angle behind the sponsorship was that Will Rogers had Cherokee ancestry.

By 2005, Broadway product placements had evolved into elaborate marketing campaigns. With the blessing of playwright Neil Simon, Jose Cuervo International brokered a deal to have the dialogue in a revival of

Simon's acclaimed play *Sweet Charity* altered to include "Gran Centenario" tequila. Cuervo logos were incorporated into sets and advertised on the playbill. Cuervo specialty drinks were served in the lobby and at parties for cast members and critics.[33] Although not as successful as *Will Rogers Follies*, the show ran for 369 performances and was nominated for three Tony Awards, including Best Revival of a Musical, Best Performance by a Leading Actress in a Musical, and Best Choreography, winning the award for Best Revival.

Theater critics and patrons generally accepted and even embraced product placements as long as they appeared "natural." In the musical *City of Angels*, for example, a generic liquor bottle sitting on a desk was replaced with Johnny Walker Black with little fanfare. But some recent Broadway product placements seem painfully ironic. In a 2003 production of *Les Misérables*, the sets featured billboard-style ads for Piper-Heidsieck champagne at $90 a bottle, and a Montblanc fountain pen with diamonds encrusted in 18-karat gold. Recently, community theaters (which should, theoretically, be supported by communities) began turning to product placement as well. According to Steven C. Helsel, operations manager for the Altoona (Pa.) Community Theatre, "Now that *Cats* has reached community theater, there are many possibilities with all the trash on the set."[34] It remains to be seen whether multinational corporations will pay community theaters to incorporate the refuse of their packaging as garbage on stage sets. But it wouldn't surprise us.

Literature

Kurt Vonnegut's great American novel *Breakfast of Champions* (1973) famously includes the following disclaimer:

> The expression 'Breakfast of Champions' is a registered trademark of General Mills, Inc., for use on a breakfast cereal product. The use of the identical expression as the title of this book as well as throughout the book is not intended to indicate an association with or sponsorship by General Mills, nor is it intended to disparage their fine products.[35]

Readers familiar with the novel know that the title alludes, in part, to an affable cocktail waitress in a small town pub who utters the Wheaties slogan every time she serves a martini. As a slice of Americana in the 1950s, Vonnegut's novel is scattered with references to cars (Plymouth Fury and Buick Le Sabre), hotel accommodations (Holiday Inn and Magic Fingers), and fast-food chains (Burger Chef and Kentucky Fried Chicken). With savage wit and economy, Vonnegut mocks name brands, advertising slogans, and copyright laws—along with the American obsession with them. Such is not the case with contemporary branded literature.

In 2001, the Italian jewelry company Bulgari commissioned noted British author Fay Weldon to write a novel that would feature Bulgari products. *The Bulgari Connection* was printed in a limited edition of 750 copies, which were richly bound and presented to an elite group of the company's clientele. The original deal specified a dozen specific mentions of the brand in exchange for an undisclosed amount of cash. But Weldon reportedly got carried away; Bulgari became central to the plot and is mentioned at least three dozen times. In one scene set in the Bulgari store in London, a mogul buys his wife an £18,000 necklace, duly described as "a sleek modern piece" with "stripes of white and yellow gold, but encasing three ancient coins, the mount following the irregular contours of the thin worn bronze." When HarperCollins negotiated a deal to publish the book in paperback, Bulgari readily agreed to help with promotion.

As Weldon told the *New York Times*, "When the approach came through I thought, oh no, dear me, I am a literary author. You can't do this kind of thing; my name will be mud forever. But after a while I thought, I don't care. Let it be mud. They never give me the Booker prize anyway." Weldon's agent, Giles Gordon, was less reserved in expressing his delight. "The door is open and now the sky is the limit," he told the *Times*. "I've suggested that in her next book she includes a whole string of top companies, Disney, Levis, McDonald's, the lot, and we write to all of them and say 'Ms. Weldon is including a mention of your fine company in her next book, what do you reckon?'"[36] Such a pitch no longer seems facetious.

A recent trend in literary product placement is to construct characters that develop extraordinarily intimate relationships with their automobiles. British chick lit author Carol Matthews changed the vehicle of choice for the heroine of her 2004 novel *The Sweetest Taboo* from a Volkswagon Beetle to a Ford Fiesta, when Ford offered her an (again) undisclosed amount of cash to do so. Ford later commissioned Matthews to write "short stories" for its website. A characteristic one reads:

I look out of the window of the shop and eye my lovely Ford Fiesta Roxanne with something approaching misery. Last year was a different story. Business was booming and I splashed out on my first-ever new car. Brand spanking new—complete with enough gadgets to keep even Alex amused. She's red, raunchy and drives like a dream and now, she's got to go. Believe me, it will be like cutting off one of my own arms.[37]

James Patterson, author of a popular series of crime thrillers featuring a widowed sleuth named Alex Cross, appears to have jumped on the bandwagon. An excerpt from a chapter of *Cross* (2007), is illustrative: "So we stopped at the Mercedes dealer. . . . Jannie and Damon ogled a silver CLK500 Cabriolet convertible, while Ali and I tested out the spacious front seat of an R350. I was thinking family car—safety, beauty, resale value.

Intellect and emotion." One reader complained that the entire chapter was devoted to such deliberations. Alex Cross ends up buying the R350 and describing it in detail each time he drives. "I liked the vehicle's zip and also the dual-dash zone climate control, which would keep everybody happy, even Nana Mama."[38]

In light of such trends, it seems entirely possible that first-time readers of *Breakfast of Champions* might not recognize the sarcasm in Vonnegut's recounting of a car dealer scolding one of his salesmen for dressing like a mortician: "Perhaps you haven't noticed, Harry, but the Pontiac has now become a glamorous, youthful adventure for people who want a *kick* out of life!"[39] Fictional characters are simply more inclined to spout advertising slogans these days. "Novelists who sell their characters to financial sponsors are like teacher's pets," according to author Jane Smiley. "Instinctively we know that their allegiance is divided. They say they want only to please us, the readers, but really . . . it's pretty clear that we aren't first on the list at all."[40]

Smiley's reference to "teacher's pets" seems prescient, now that advertisers have discovered teen chick lit. *Cathy's Book: If Found Call (650) 266-8233* was written by Jordan Weisman and Susan Stewart, both of whom have backgrounds in marketing. Promoted as an innovative and interactive reading experience for teens, *Cathy's Book* was designed to look like a high school student's journal, complete with drawings and manufactured mementos. Also sprinkled throughout the book are functioning phone numbers and websites that readers can call or visit. Doodles on one page include "UnderCover Girl," "Waterproof Mascara in Very Black" and "Eyecolor in Midnight Metal." These are actual products manufactured by Proctor & Gamble's Cover Girl division, which signed an unusual marketing partnership with Running Press, the unit of Perseus Books Group that published the novel in 2006. Reportedly, Cover Girl neither paid the publisher nor the book's authors for the privilege of having its makeup showcased in the novel. But P&G did actively promote the book on Beinggirl.com, a website directed at adolescent girls that features games, advice on handling puberty, and yes, makeup tips.[41]

In 2007, a marketing professor at Sacred Heart University in Connecticut proudly posted his latest class project online: "Using Teen Chick Lit Novels to Teach Marketing." He offered *Cathy's Book* as a good example. Of particular note was the professor's admitted surprise that his students raised concerns regarding "ethical issues involving marketing high end products to what they considered to be an overly impressionable demographic" including "pressure placed on single parents to purchase these goods" and "peer-pressure on students to have them." "This," the researcher reported, "was a result I had not expected."[42] It is heartening that college students expressed concerns about the youth and vulnerability of their own "target audience," if troubling that their professor did not. But why should he? The industry they are preparing to enter rarely rewards such scruples.

The consumer advocacy group Commercial Alert urged book reviewers to boycott *Cathy's Book,* and both the *New York Times* and *Los Angeles Times* published editorials critical of the promotional deal. Coauthor Weisman admitted that conversations about the book tended to focus on the product placements instead of the other "innovative things we did with that book." David Steinberger, president of Perseus, said such criticisms did not affect sales, and noted that the book had sold 43,000 copies in hardcover, hitting best-seller lists in many countries. Nonetheless, when *Cathy's Book* was released in paperback in February 2008, all references to Cover Girl products had been removed. Weiss said simply that there was "no expectation that the cross-promotion would extend beyond the hardcover launch."[43]

AD CREEP AND CHILDREN'S CULTURE

Young children are the most lucrative demographic for advertisers seeking to instill brand recognition and loyalty in future consumers. According to Juliet B. Schor, "Contemporary American tweens and teens have emerged as the most brand-oriented, consumer-involved, and materialistic generations in history."[44] Schor cites research showing that children can recognize logos as early as eighteen months, and before reaching their second birthday, they're asking for products by brand name. By three and a half, kids start to believe that brands communicate their personal qualities (for example, that they're cool, strong, or smart). Even before starting school, the likelihood of having a television in their bedroom is 25 percent, and their viewing time is just over two hours a day. Upon arrival at the schoolhouse steps, Schor reports, the typical first grader can evoke two hundred discrete brands.[45]

While acknowledging other factors, Schor places the bulk of the blame for the commercialization of childhood on a "marketing juggernaut characterized by growing reach, effectiveness, and audacity."[46] Evidence to support this claim is overwhelming. To give just one example, a study published in the *Archives of Pediatrics and Adolescent Medicine* in 2007 found that children aged three to five consistently reported that identical food samples—including not only hamburgers and fries, but also baby carrots and milk—"tasted better" when they were served in McDonald's wrappers. The correlation was highest among children with multiple TVs in their homes.[47]

Remember the baby bottles with soft drink logos mentioned at the beginning of this chapter? Dentists estimate that infants and toddlers are four times likelier to be fed soda out of those bottles than out of regular baby bottles.[48] This didn't stop the American Academy of Pediatric Dentistry from accepting a $1 million grant from the Coca-Cola Company in 2003.

Nor did a similar conflict of interest deter the National Parent Teacher Association from offering the Coca-Cola Company a position on its board of directors the same year. Everyone, it seems, has a price.

Family Fun

Many people remember picture books and board games as an integral part of early childhood. Parents and caretakers can engage, educate, and socialize kids by reading to them and playing with them. Extended family and friends often join in. Increasingly, however, advertisers are crashing the play dates, and consumption is the object of the game.

Children's Books

Just in time for the 2005 holiday season, HarperCollins teamed up with Saks Fifth Avenue to publish a children's book titled *Cashmere If You Can*. As the *New York Times* reported, this lavishly illustrated book chronicles the misadventures of Wawa Hohot and her family of Mongolian cashmere goats, who just happen to live on the roof of Saks's midtown Manhattan store. A promotional blurb exclaims, "Haute hijinks ensue as these colorful characters clamber to the top of the fashion world and to the roof of Saks' flagship store in New York City." The book features references to designers such as Roberto Cavalli, Giorgio Armani, and Paul Gaultier for the benefit of fashion-conscious toddlers and their shopper moms. The success of *Cashmere If You Can* inspired HarperCollins (a unit of News Corporation) "to make a business out of these sorts of collaborations."[49]

Susan Katz, publisher of HarperCollins Children's Books, said she was not concerned about a possible backlash against corporate sponsorship of books aimed at such a young audience. "If you look at Web sites, general media or television, corporate sponsorship or some sort of advertising is totally embedded in the world that tweens live in," she said. *McKenzie Blue*, a HarperCollins series aimed at eight-to-twelve-year-old girls, was planned to be full of references to brands. An author of the series, Tina Wells, also happens to be chief executive of Buzz Marketing Group. Wells said that she wouldn't change the fact that McKenzie loves Converse sneakers, whether the company was interested in partnering or not. But, she added, "Maybe another character could become a Nike girl."[50]

For parents more concerned that their children learn about fractions than fashions, advertisers have sponsored a number of "learning books" for readers aged four to eight. Titles include *Skittles Riddles Math*, *The Hershey's Kisses Addition Book*, *The M&M's Brand Counting Book*, *Twizzlers Percentages Book*, and *Kellogg's Fruit Loops Counting Fun Book*. A promotional blurb for *The Oreo Cookie Counting Book* exclaims: "Children will love to count down as ten little Oreos are dunked, nibbled, and stacked one by one . . . until there are none!" Oreo cookies are featured prominently on every page.[51] These books were featured prominently on Amazon.com, despite mounting concerns about childhood obesity in the United States. Parents pay for the privilege of marketing candy and cookies to their children. It's not hard to imagine fun books for kids using healthy snacks to teach math skills; calculating the calories in carrots and blueberries, or using percentages to construct a nutrition pyramid come to mind. Such primers might prove popular with kids, but they're not likely to be sponsored by Hershey or Mars.

Board Games

Old-fashioned family board games with storied histories have succumbed to ad creep as well. In 2006, Hasbro released a new "Twists and Turns" version of its classic *Game of Life*, originally created in 1860 by Milton Bradley. In the modern version, players are issued Visa credit cards instead of play money. In anticipation of criticism from concerned parents and children's advocates, Visa included money management booklets with the game. But it's not hard to imagine young children learning that living on credit is natural and developing brand loyalty to the sponsor.

The same year, Parker Brothers (a subsidiary of Hasbro) released a new "Here and Now" edition of *Monopoly*, a game the company claims has been played by more than one billion people around the world since it was copyrighted in 1935. (Ironically, *Monopoly* is said to have been modeled after *The Landlord's Game*, first published in England by Elizabeth Magie, a Quaker political activist who hoped to educate players about how monopolies end up bankrupting the many while giving extraordinary wealth to one or few individuals.) New tokens in the "Here and Now" version included a Toyota Prius, a New Balance shoe, McDonald's French fries, and a RAZR mobile headset (replacing an old shoe, sewing thimble, Scottie dog, and top hat from the original version). New landmarks include Nashville's Grand Ole Opry and the Mall of America in Minneapolis. In most new versions of *Monopoly*, as in *Game of Life*, Visa replaces the play money.[52] The "classic" versions of both games, of course, always endorsed the logic of capital (although some critics complained that succeeding in *Life* was left more to luck than pluck). But branding both the means and ends of winning is yet another example of ad creep.

Movies and Television

Between 1929 and 1949, according to John Belton, roughly 80 million to 90 million Americans—that is, virtually every American between the ages of six and sixty—went to the movies every week.[53] While most classical films weren't specifically aimed at children, they were deemed suitable for all ages under the dictates of the Motion Picture Production Code. Some stars (Shirley Temple and Mickey Rooney) and certain genres (animal stories and westerns) were particularly popular with young viewers, and matinee times and ticket prices made them more accessible. In television, children's programming has always been popular. Indeed, some of the earliest TV shows for kids spanned generations. *Captain Kangaroo* debuted in the mid-1950s and ran for twenty-nine seasons (1955–1984), while *Mister Rogers' Neighborhood* began in the late 1960s and ran for thirty-three seasons (1968–2001). Although it's almost unthinkable now, children's movies and TV shows didn't always revolve around promotional tie-ins. Today, children's media and merchandising are inextricably intertwined.

Children's Movies

Disney was one of the first companies to connect watching movies with selling toys. Successfully combining the consumption of media and merchandise, Disney's animated films have long provided a "marketplace of culture," a launching pad for products including videos, DVDs, sound track albums, clothing, furniture, plush toys, fast food, and theme park rides. As Henry Giroux wrote in *The Mouse That Roared* (1999): "Disney constructs a culture of joy and innocence for children out of the intersection of entertainment, advocacy, pleasure, and consumption."[54]

Janet Wasko's analysis of "Disney synergy" using its thirty-fifth animated feature, *Hercules,* is exemplary. Promotion for the film and licensing for related merchandise began long before the movie's release in June 1997. Trailers were shown before theatrical screenings of other Disney films such as the 1996 remake of *101 Dalmatians* and included on videocassettes such as *Toy Story* during the 1996 Christmas season. In February 1997, five months before the film's premiere, a twenty-city MegaMall Tour featuring Hercules attractions began, and a traveling *Hercules on Ice* show opened in 1999. Nearly a hundred manufacturers were licensed to produce six to seven thousand Hercules-themed products. The film and merchandise were promoted on ABC and the Disney Channel, in Disney Stores and catalogues, and on the Disney website. Promotional tie-ins were established with McDonald's, Nestlé, Quaker Oats, and General Motors. "Even though the film may not have been the predicted box-office or merchandising success expected by the Disney Company," Wasko notes, "the characters from the film were added to Disney's stable of 'classic' characters and continue to be promoted across the company's different media."[55]

"Packaging" classic characters into product lines has since proven to be one of Disney's most profitable business ventures. In 2001, eight Disney heroines were combined to create the "Princess Line," described by *Variety* as "a global marketing machine shrewdly designed to accessorize young girls with all the sparkly merchandise their little hearts desire."[56] The original cast of princesses included Snow White, Cinderella, Aurora (*Sleeping Beauty*), Jasmine (*Aladdin*), Belle (*Beauty and the Beast*), and Ariel (*The Little Mermaid*). Pocahontas and Mulan were quickly added, and Tiana, Disney's first African American princess, joined her sisters in 2009. There are now about 25,000 different princess dolls, sticker books, pajamas, sleeping bags, toothbrushes, vanity tables, digital cameras, cell phones, and multilevel Nintendo videogames. Global sales of Disney consumer products reportedly jumped from $300 million in 2001 to $3 billion in 2006.[57]

Packaging the Disney heroines as a line of contemporary princesses entailed extricating the characters from their individual stories. It is worth noting that these stories often involved severe hardship, which Disney's scrappy heroines managed to overcome: abject servitude in *Cinderella*, domestic violence in *Beauty and the Beast*, threatened dismemberment in *Aladdin*, and attempted homicide in *Sleeping Beauty* (not to mention sexism, racism, genocide, and war in *Mulan* and *Pocahontas*). All but one of the princesses are motherless, and their fathers are either tyrannical or ineffectual (which seems odd since the parents of young girls shell out most of the cash for Disney princess merchandise). But orphans in rags and cinders don't sell costumes and accessories; princesses in tiaras and glass slippers do. One mother who took her young daughter to a live performance of *Cinderella* reported that the child was reduced to tears when she discovered that Cinderella was a servant for most of the story. So much for the stories and their morals, however debatable the merits of these may be.

Children's Television

Sesame Street, first broadcast in 1969, is now the longest-running kids' show on television. The program is produced by the nonprofit Sesame Workshop (formerly the Children's Television Workshop) and broadcast on PBS. Although loved by children, acclaimed by critics and approved by parents, it is worth noting that *Sesame Street* lent itself well to merchandising from the first. The furry muppets were always, to borrow Wasko's term, "toyetic," and their images have sold millions of dolls and puppets, backpacks and lunch boxes, bed sheets, and even chess sets. In 1996, a scarcity of "Tickle Me Elmo" dolls during the Christmas shopping season caused a frenzy. In February 2012, a Google search for "*Sesame Street* merchandise" yielded 382,000 links.

One of the major players in today's commercialized children's programming is Nickelodeon. Launched by Viacom in 1979, Nickelodeon had big hits in the 1990s with shows such as *Blue's Clues* and *Rugrats*. In 2006, Nickelodeon boasted the top ten most-watched animated series for children, notably *SpongeBob SquarePants* and *Dora the Explorer*. These two shows have generated millions of dollars in advertising revenue for Nickelodeon, but much more in merchandising: $4.5 billion in product sales as of 2006. Future prospects for *Hey Arnold!* and *The Fairly OddParents*, two other popular Nickelodeon shows, were not as bright. According to Cyma Zarghami, then president of Nickelodeon, they "were some of the highest rated animated shows for years, but we couldn't sell a T-shirt."[58] (*Arnold* ran from 1996 to 2004; *OddParents* went on "hiatus" in 2006.) In 2006, the *New York Times* reported that Nickelodeon was "looking over its shoulder at Disney" in the increasingly competitive market of children's television.[59] As media analyst Michael Nathanson observed, Nickelodeon needed some new hit shows "to lure advertisers and create consumer products."[60]

Competition from Disney in the children's TV market was due in large part to two Disney productions that became pop culture crazes in 2006: the made-for-TV movie *High School Musical* and the TV series *Hannah Montana*. *High School Musical*, produced by Disney Channel Original Movies (DCOM), has been described as a modern-day *Romeo and Juliet*. It premiered in January 2006 to an audience of 7.7 million viewers. The sound track became the best-selling album of the year and was certified quadruple platinum by the Recording Industry Association of America (RIAA). The film grew into a franchise, with a concert tour, stage musical, and ice show, in addition to books, magazines, and video games. *High School Musical 2* aired in August 2007, and *High School Musical 3: Senior Year* in October 2008. Licensed products included backpacks and bookmarks as well as pennants, pajamas, and pillows. A number of sites listed "party supplies" as one of the most popular categories, in keeping with a growing industry trend of promoting theme parties hosted by young girls as a peer-to-peer marketing strategy.

Case Study: Hannah Montana

The Disney Channel launched *Hannah Montana* in March 2006. The series centered on an "ordinary" high school girl played by Miley Cyrus (daughter of popular country singer Billy Ray Cyrus), who leads a secret second life as a pop singer and teen idol. Predictably enough, Miley Cyrus became a real star, and CDs, DVDs and an actual concert tour followed in 2007. The sixty-nine-city tour was enormously popular, especially with young girls, and tickets invariably sold out instantly. They were scalped on eBay for hundreds of times their face value, and there was even a much-publicized scandal involving a mom who lied about her husband dying in Iraq to win a Hannah Montana concert prize package for her daughter.

In 2008, Disney followed up on the franchise with the release of a 3-D concert film, *Hannah Montana/Miley Cyrus Best of Both Worlds Concert Tour*. Promotion for the film consistently highlighted Disney's desire to make Hannah Montana accessible to fans who either couldn't score or couldn't afford tickets to the live shows. A theater spokesman in Witchita, Kansas (echoing a line spoken by many others), said, "In addition to giving disappointed children an opportunity to see the concert, the movie will be a first of its kind: It will present a full concert in Dolby digital 3-D technology, giving viewers the effect of actually being in the crowd."[61] But there were a few hitches. *Hannah* was scheduled to run for just one week (February 1–7, 2008). It was initially screened in only 683 theaters (as compared to Disney's *Pirates of the Caribean: At World's End*, which opened in 4,362, or Warner Bros. *Spiderman 3*, which opened in 4,253). Ticket prices, even for preteens attending matinees, were set at $15. Disney representatives declined to explain the limited engagement or to say whether the film would be distributed on DVD (though there was little doubt about either). Feature stories about Girl Scout troops who couldn't attend screenings together were widely circulated. As one reporter wrote, "Some parents worry it could be disappointment all over again for their children."[62]

Not to worry. Days before the film's premiere, Disney announced a partnership with Wal-Mart to offer Hannah Montana merchandise at affordable prices. Nationwide, 750 Wal-Marts set up "Hannah Montana Shops," featuring 140 unique items, including apparel and footwear, handbags and cosmetics, bedding, room decor, games, music, and blond wigs. The new line was designed to "appeal to tweens looking for on-trend casual and athletic-inspired styles as well as accessories and décor."[63] Janet Bareis, marketing vice president for Wal-Mart, reiterated the accessibility theme: "The concert tickets were really hard to get, and really expensive. What we're trying to do is give more access." Wal-Mart's licensed goods were targeted— but not limited—to the "marketing sweet spot" of girls aged six to fourteen. As Bareis noted gleefully, "We see 4-year-olds who are dancing around and want Hannah Montana merchandise."[64]

Since most fans couldn't get either concert or film tickets, purchasing *Hannah Montana* merchandise became an event in itself, with both Disney and Wal-Mart promoting theme parties to encourage young girls to "share the experience" with their friends. "Extreme Party Packs," including Hannah Montana invitations, tableware, balloons, tattoos, cake decorations, and thank-you notes, ran upwards of $250 (as did those of *High School Musical*). Extras like Hannah Montana cell phone gum dispensers, compact mirrors, nail polish, charm bracelets, microphones, guitars, tambourines, yard signs, and pink feather boas were not included.

Hannah Montanna brought in $31.3 million in box office over its premiere weekend, the biggest debut ever for a Super Bowl weekend release.

The Disney Company immediately announced that it would extend the film's run for another week (and admitted that it had quietly promised theater owners as much). Critics noted that the limited-time offer is "one of the oldest tricks in the marketing book" and that "no one is a good at this as Disney." Jeremy Herron of the Associated Press wondered, "Were parents duped into rushing their kids to the theater? Or was it just another case of Disney's marketing mastery?"[65] These choices are not, of course, mutually exclusive (see chapter 3). But Disney insisted that it wasn't trying to manufacture scarcity to drum up demand. Mark Zoradi, president of the Motion Picture Group at Walt Disney Studios, sounded almost as diabolical as a Disney villain when he told reporters, "If we were trying to make it scarce, we would have had a *more* limited release."[66] At the end of its second week, *Hannah Montana* had brought in nearly $58 million in U.S. box office alone. Of the 8,275 IMDb user ratings, the weighted average was a mere 2.7 on a 10-point scale, with 52.4 percent giving it a rating of one.[67] The Disney Channel further extended the franchise with the world cable television premiere on July 26, 2008, attracting 5.8 million viewers.[68]

Virtual and Actual Playmates

Slumber Parties

Disney is just one of many companies that have enlisted the aid of a marketing firm called Girls Intelligence Agency (GIA) to collect information about the buying habits of young girls. The signature product of GIA is a "Slumber Party in a Box" that the company uses to market new products and conduct research. GIA recruits girls, secret-agent style, to host sleepovers where they open a box full of movie and TV previews, branded T-shirts, and cosmetic samples aimed at the tween market. The company collects girls' reactions from thousands of slumber parties and reports back to clients, including Disney, Fox, and Neutrogena.[69]

The aggressive marketing and overt militarism (not to mention the lingering lasciviousness) of the language on GIA's website is disturbing:

- 40,000 GIA Secret Agents are on call nationwide, ready to invite you into their bedrooms, to hang out with their closest friends and give you candid feedback on your concept, product or brand.
- Espionage you can trust: Specifically designed in-room hangouts and slumber parties give you the authentic insight you need to move ahead.
- Girl Ammo: Stay on top of emerging trends and understand how to leverage BFF friendship networks controlled by influencers.
- Spy Cam: Track the motivations behind critical spending patterns across all categories from fashion to wireless and toys and autos.

- Behind Enemy Lines: See what is inside her bedroom, closets, drawers, backpacks and bathroom. What is she buying and why? Who is successfully marketing to her and how?[70]

In this business venture, the adolescent hostesses are exploited as both marketresearchers and stealth advertisers, and their guests are transformed into commodities whose affinities and aspirations are then sold to (and shaped by) advertisers. As Schor notes, marketers such as GIA ultimately teach kids "to view their friends as a lucrative source they can exploit to gain products or money," resulting in the corruption of friendship itself.[71] According to Susan Linn, a psychologist at the Judge Baker Children's Center, "In this value system, what gets crowded out is creativity, sharing, kindness, altruism, and compassion."[72] Simply put, the goal is not to share your toys with others; it's to get them to buy their own.

Virtual Playgrounds

As children grow computer literate at increasingly younger ages, companies have created products linking real-world toys and dolls with the Web; among the most popular are Mattel's Barbie Website, Disney's Club Penguin, and Hasbro's Littlest Pet Shop.[73] One of the most successful of these ventures is Webkinz, a line of small stuffed animals developed by the privately owned Canadian toy and gift company Ganz. Marketed to kids aged six to thirteen, each plush little creature comes with a code that can be entered into the Webkinz website to create a computer-animated version of it. Children who purchase Webkinz are issued KinzCash, virtual currency they can use to buy food, furniture, apparel, and accessories for their pets. Attending to and providing for the virtual pet keeps it happy and healthy, so children are given a strong incentive to return to the site frequently. Buying more real-world toys, playing games, and entering quizzes earns users more KinzCash to lavish upon their virtual pets. The account lapses after a year, so if kids want to keep up the relationship with their virtual pets they have to buy another real toy (at about $12 each). In 2007, there were fifty-one Webkinz and twenty-nine Lil'Kinz toys to collect, and Ganz had sold more than 2 million of them. The Webkinz website attracted 7.3 million unique users in November 2007 alone.[74]

Dr. Sonia Livingstone, a professor in the Department of Media and Communications at the London School of Economics, warned that an overreliance on such virtual entertainment could be detrimental to a child's imaginative development. "Educational theory is clear that play which demands imaginative input from the child is far more beneficial than play in which all the pieces are provided and the scope for imaginative responses is extremely limited," she said.[75] As with the Slumber Party in a Box, the focus of play becomes the acquisition of stuff. And like other virtual playgrounds, Webzinz prepares children to enter online "communities" rooted in commercialism and consumption.

ADVERTISING AND NEW MEDIA

The road to hell, according to an old adage, is paved with good intentions. Even this cannot be said of the "information superhighway," which was for the most part developed to wage war. Nonetheless, as noted in chapter 2, new communications technologies are invariably introduced with the promise of increasing diversity and fostering democracy. New media are promoted as more innovative, interactive, convenient, and creative than those before them. It is well worth remembering that citizens band radio and motion pictures were hailed as harbingers of media democracy long before the emergence of the World Wide Web. But existing economic and political forces invariably work to undermine such possibilities. Thus, as Ken Boetcher noted, for any "real student of the media it should come as no surprise that new media are being commercialized just like older means of communication."[76] What follows is a snapshot of the ad-littered landscape of the wired world, focusing on ad creep in new media including search engines, cell phones, social networks, and virtual worlds. These products and services are inextricably intertwined and overwhelmingly dominated by commercial interests that harness their economic, social, and political potential.

Search Engines

Search engines were first developed in the early 1990s to enable Internet users to navigate billions of Web pages, largely through the use of keywords and links. A number of sophisticated systems, including Yahoo! and Google, as well as search engines developed by America Online and Microsoft, rose to prominence in the early 2000s. Advertisers quickly recognized the potential for profits in using search engines to "guide" users to links featuring ads for their products (or, more intrusively, to have their ads literally pop up, forcing users to attend to them, if only to clear the screen). In 2011, Google was the most popular search engine in the United States, accounting for over 80 percent of Internet searches.[77] Yahoo!, Microsoft's Bing, Ask, and America Online ranked well behind Google in searches. Because it had the most searches, Google could direct the largest number of consumers to the ads on its search pages. Google's AdWords and AdSense services enabled advertisers to target consumers through the same logic of keywords and links. Its total advertising revenue in 2011 amounted to nearly $38 billion.[78]

The role advertisers play in determining the results of online searches became a contentious issue early on. According to *Consumer Reports,*

> Many online consumers think of search engines as online tools that help them to quickly find Web sites most relevant to their keyword queries, particularly when they are unsure of where to surf next. This trust in search engines may make them vulnerable while online, as they are largely unaware such navigation sites often accept fees in exchange for giving advertiser Web pages prominent placement on their search results pages.[79]

In 2001, Commercial Alert filed a complaint with the FTC charging that many of the most popular search engines did not provide clear disclosures about how their results could be influenced by advertisers (paid placement), and even fewer explained how companies paid to increase the likelihood their websites would appear in searches (paid inclusion). "Without clear and conspicuous disclosure that the ads are ads," such "concealment may mislead search engine users to believe that search results are based on relevancy alone, not marketing ploys."[80]

One year later, in 2002, the FTC replied: "After careful review, the staff of the Bureau of Consumer Protection has determined not to recommend that the Commission take formal action against the search engine companies listed in your complaint at this time." Rather, the FTC offered "encouragement" to corporations to consider a handful of "suggestions" for full disclosure. The FTC recommendations included the following: that paid ranking search results should be distinguished from non-paid results with clear and conspicuous disclosures; that the use of paid inclusion should be clearly and conspicuously explained and disclosed; and that no affirmative statement should be made that might mislead consumers as to the basis on which a search result is generated.[81]

Another year later, in 2003, a Consumer Reports WebWatch study found that most users still could not determine the difference between a paid search versus a "pure" or "algorithmic" search on America's most popular search engines. Compliance with FTC recommendations for disclosure varied widely. Even the report's testers, information professionals by trade, found disclosure and transparency practices among many search engines confusing and confounding.[82] In a follow-up study published in 2005, researchers noted: "Despite many changes among the sites in the study, *WebWatch* found that nearly half the sites stayed the same, a third got worse, and only three of the 15 sites improved. Key areas considered were prominence of disclosure headings, along with clarity and accessibility of disclosure statements."[83] As with product placement in television, the FTC adopted a hands-off approach to questionable practices in online advertising. That left the major search engine providers to battle among themselves for the biggest slice of the pie.

And battle they did. Google bought YouTube in 2006 and announced plans to allow advertisers to use material from YouTube videos in 2007. The same year, Microsoft helped delay Google's $3.1 billion bid for the online advertising company DoubleClick. In 2008, in turn, Google laid the groundwork to delay, and possibly derail, Microsoft's $45 billion bid to buy Yahoo! In the meantime, the first order of business for all search engines, selling users to advertisers, proceeded apace. The growing practice of exploiting user-produced content in ads flourished. For example, in 2008, Google entered into a partnership with 1-800-flowers.com, a lucrative venture given that the online floral and gift sales industry accounted for $2 billion in sales in 2007.[84] Their first joint promotion was a "Will You Marry Me?" contest, inviting love-smitten users to submit their marriage proposal videos to a special YouTube channel in hopes of winning a wedding hosted by Sandals Resorts, with transportation provided by American Airlines, and an engagement ring from the Internet jeweler Blue Nile.[85]

Cell Phones

The speed with which the mobile telephone went from being a relatively exotic and expensive gadget (suitable for stockbrokers and spies) to a ubiquitous virtual appendage (indispensable for ordinary citizens) is astonishing. In 1987, according to CTIA-Wireless Association, there were 1,230,855 cell phone service subscribers in the United States, representing about 2 percent of the population. In 2007, that figure had leaped to 250,000,000, approaching an 83 percent penetration rate.[86] By June 2011, the number of wireless subscriber connections in the United States and its territories totaled 324 million with a 102 percent population rate.[87] Cellular worldwide subscriptions reached 6 billion by January 2012, equal to the world population.[88] Less a telephone today than a multipurpose computer, cell phones function as game consoles, still cameras, e-mail systems, text messengers, carriers of entertainment and business data, nodes of commerce. As a researcher at an MIT consortium observed, "The cell phone has become a laboratory—some would say an asylum—for testing the limits of technological convergence."[89]

Apart from the convenience and connectedness they purport to provide, and the unintended consequences they have unleashed, cell phone services have presented advertisers with new opportunities to exploit intimate, 24/7 access to consumers. Mobile advertising doubled between 2010 and 2011, totaling $2.1 billion, of which 77 percent was earned by Google.[90] In January 2007, Google executives had predicted that phone service "will one day be free and supported by advertisers."[91] To invoke another old adage, there is no such thing as a free lunch.

In 2003, Americans clamored to get their phone numbers added to a national "Do Not Call" list, a registry that prohibited telemarketers from calling residences. Originally slated to expire after five years, the program was extended in 2008 "to avoid the wrath of millions of angry constituents" (150 million numbers were listed).[92] Over the same period of time, ironically enough, many Americans made themselves more accessible to advertisers through cell phones with Internet capabilities.[93] In 2007, Internet giants began creating advertising networks tailored for mobile phones. Google announced that it would begin selling ads on Web pages to be viewed on cell phones (AdSense for Mobile), and Yahoo! and AOL launched similar plans. Microsoft made a deal with Sprint to enable Sprint customers to use Microsoft's service to search the Web on their cell phones. The *New York Times* reported that "customers will be able to choose to have Sprint track their whereabouts, so that when they search for local content, they will not have to type in their location."[94]

In September 2007, a company called Pudding Media announced a new service offering calls without any toll charges—in exchange for permission to eavesdrop on conversations in order to display targeted ads on the user's computer screen. So, for example, a conversation about movies might elicit reviews and ads for new films that the caller would receive during the conversation. Pudding worked on ways to send ads via e-mail and have them appear on the cell phone screen of the caller as well as the person on the other end of the line. In a truly Orwellian development, Pudding chief executive Ariel Maislos observed that the advertising content had a tendency to determine the direction of conversations. "The conversation was actually changing based on what was on the screen," he said. "Our ability to influence the conversation was remarkable."[95] Privacy concerns eventually led Pudding to shut down the service in 2010.

Social Networks

Like cell phones, online social networks offered a kind of mediated communication with the promise of intimacy within a community, one that was quickly invaded by advertisers. Websites such as Myspace and Facebook provided an interactive, user-submitted network of friends, personal profiles, blogs, groups, photos, music, and videos. Ads on social networks were expected to garner $1.2 billion worldwide in 2007, and $1.9 billion in 2008.[96] Myspace, which was bought by News Corp. in 2005, was the largest Internet social network in 2007, with 110 million monthly active users. Both sites were available "free" to users, generating revenue from advertising, including banner ads and sponsored groups. By 2009, Facebook became the dominant social network and the number of MySpace users quickly declined. By 2012, Facebook had hundreds of millions of users. In 2011, its sales of advertising and virtual goods generated $371 billion, producing a $1 billion profit.[97]

Online social networkers create profiles that contain photos and lists of personal interests, exchange private or public messages, and join groups of friends. The viewing of detailed profile data is restricted to users from the same network or confirmed friends. In a 2006 study conducted by Student Monitor, a New Jersey-based limited liability company specializing in research concerning the college student market, Facebook was named as the second most "in" thing among undergraduates, tied with beer and sex and losing only to the iPod.[98] But the illusion of an intimate, private online community proved to be just that. In this case, the headlines really do say it all. On November 7, 2007, the *State College (Pa.) Centre Daily Times* reported: "Facebook opens doors to advertisers: Companies will be able to target based on behavior of users, friends." The protests from Facebook users was immediate and loud. One month later, on December 6, 2007, the *Centre Daily Times* reported, "Facebook pulls online about-face: Users can now opt out of advertising feature that shows Internet activities."

Virtual Worlds

Virtual worlds are computer-based simulated environments that users can "inhabit" via avatars (cyber alter egos). In virtual worlds, avatars can interact with other virtual residents and procure goods and services with virtual money that can sometimes be converted into real world rewards. If this sounds familiar, it's because the virtual playgrounds for children discussed above are merely kid-friendly versions of such sites—the main difference being that adult users are more inclined to manipulate fanciful versions of themselves than to play with precocious penguins. Virtual worlds meld elements of chat rooms, video games, and online stores with user-generated content sites such as Google's YouTube, Myspace, and Facebook. Most virtual worlds allow for multiple inhabitants to interact in a persistent online world that is active and available 24/7. Therefore, like search engines, cell phones, and social networks, they are extremely attractive to advertisers.

According to Richard Siklos,

The sudden rush of real companies into so-called virtual worlds mirrors the evolution of the Internet itself, which moved beyond an educational and research network in the 1990's to become a commercial proposition. . . . Already, the Internet is the fastest-growing advertising medium, as traditional forms of marketing like television commercials and print advertising slow. For businesses, these early forays into virtual worlds could be the next frontier in the blurring of advertising and entertainment.[99]

Second Life was an online service with one of the most popular virtual worlds. In October 2007 alone, 573,000 users visited *Second Life*. According to Siklos, *Second Life* online was fast becoming a three-dimensional test bed for corporate marketers, including Sony BMG Music Entertainment, Sun Microsystems, Nissan, Adidas/Reebok, Toyota, and Starwood Hotels. "In *Second Life*, retailers like Reebok, Nike, Amazon and American Apparel have all set up shops to sell digital as well as real world versions of their products. Last week, Sun Microsystems unveiled a new pavilion promoting its products, and I.B.M. alumni held a virtual world reunion."[100]

It wasn't long before advertisers sought exclusive rights to their own virtual worlds. A service called there.com, operated by Makena Technologies, offered advertisers the option of creating their own islands on its site. Visitors to Coca-Cola's island, "CC Metro," created alter egos (avatars) that could dance at the Coca-Cola diner and shop for clothing and accessories using reward points culled from (actual) Coke bottle caps. In 2007, the most popular rewards were digital goodies like virtual patio furniture, couches, and lamps. "Creating a good use of virtual worlds takes a bit of creativity," said Michael Wilson, chief executive for Makena Technologies, noting that people couldn't actually taste Coke when their avatars take a gulp. Approached by Proctor & Gamble about an ad for Secret deodorant on MTV's Virtual Laguna Beach, Wilson assured them that "my avatars don't sweat." Unwilling to relinquish access to a lucrative demographic, P&G resorted to a promotion on the site in which users shared their "secrets."[101]

CONCLUSION: GETTING THE CREEPS

While researching and writing this chapter, we frequently felt inclined to invoke humorist Dave Marsh: "I swear I'm not making this up." But if advertisers are successful, consumers will not be concerned or alarmed about any of the marketing trends discussed herein. We hope that's not the case. We know *why* advertisers do it: to make billions of dollars by selling the attention of media consumers (in the theater, at home, or online) as well as unsuspecting citizens (in school, at the beach, or on the bus) to multinational corporations. We've seen *how* they do it: by creating and exploiting brand loyalties that seemingly compel individuals to consume vast quantities of goods and services, often based on appeals to community, freedom, and romance (ironically, by promising to fulfill the dreams dashed by capitalism itself). And we've seen *how they get away with it*, even when their methods are deceptive or their targets very young: by counting on federal regulators to favor corporate interests over public welfare.

But how and why do citizens in a democracy accept, dismiss, rationalize, and even embrace the encroachment of commercialism into virtually every aspect of daily life? In our examination of ad creep as exemplified by product placement in contemporary culture, a number of recurrent themes emerged: that it's okay because it's realistic, entrepreneurial, and educational, and/or because it makes stuff free. We would like to conclude this chapter by briefly addressing each of these claims.

The idea that ad creep is "realistic" is best exemplified by rationalizations for product placements in narrative art forms such as movies, television, literature, and theater. Age-old debates about the virtues of verisimilitude in art aside, the plausibility argument is perhaps most problematic in the case of action adventure films like *Die Another Day*, in which we suspend disbelief to watch athletes (who we know to be body doubles) pretend to be actors (who we know aren't really super spies) defy the laws of gravity and relativity (with the help of branded technologies and special effects) all in the name of realism(?!). It's perhaps most troubling in the case of romantic comedies such as *You've Got Mail*, in which communications technologies instantly dissolve fundamental personal, political, and philosophical differences with the click of a mouse. As humorist Cynthia Heimel quipped, "In movies, they call it romance. In real life, call 911."[102]

The defense of ad creep as entrepreneurial, especially in "aspirational" forms of cultural expression such as rock and rap music, is closely linked with the claim that advertising dollars provide artists with access to audiences and the incentive to create. Here we must point out that humans were creative and productive long before their practical or fanciful inventions were harnessed by capitalism, copyright laws, or advertising. And we have to ask, to what do we really aspire and why? What kind of lives do we envision for our children, and at what cost? If we truly value the contributions that artists make to society, can't we find another way to compensate them for their efforts?

The claim that advertiser-supported media are educational is best exemplified by the widespread acceptance of commercialism in children's culture and new media. Discounting the considerable discoveries and inventions made before the creation of mass media, we know that children once thrived on noncommercial programming such as *Mister Rogers' Neighborhood* and that college students once conducted fruitful academic inquiries without the help of Wikipedia. But the larger point is that if our society values education and our democracy depends on access to information, shouldn't they be free of commercial constraints and available to all? (The commercialization of education is the subject of chapter 7.)

The illusion that corporate-supported media is free remains remarkably widespread, although everybody knows that the high cost of TV and Internet advertising is passed on to consumers in the inflated prices of brand name products. And the costs that we as a democratic society pay for "free" TV programming, online searches, and cell phone minutes are incalculable. As sociologist Sherry Turkle writes:

People are connecting one on one—they have their online social networks or their cell phones with 250 people on speed dial—but do they feel part of a community? Do they feel responsibility to a shared set of political commitments? Do they feel a need to take responsibility for issues that would require that they act in concert rather than just connect? Recently, connectivity and statements of identity on places such as Facebook or Myspace have themselves become values. It is a concern when self-expression becomes more important than social action.[103]

To those who justify ad creep on the grounds that it's realistic, aspirational, educational, or free, we argue that, in fact, it's insidious, ubiquitous, invasive, and often absurd. It's a disincentive to those who would write love songs from the heart or pursue news stories from the gut. It limits the imagination of children, channels the curiosity of students, and censors the research of scholars. It's costly to the economy, the environment, the ideals of democracy, and indeed, to the human condition. The belief that "there is no alternative" is most disheartening when expressed by our students, who are the scriptwriters, filmmakers, journalists, TV producers, and advertisers of the future. It is up to us to help them envision a better world.

7

The Commercialization of Education: Students for Sale

Advertising aimed at children, teens, and young adults reached a new high in sophistication—and sank to a new low in scruples—when corporations began to invade public schools and universities. Although it is well known that the media are in the business of selling audiences to advertisers, most of us like to believe that the classroom is a place for exploration and inspiration rather than exploitation and consumption. Even the American Beverage Association claims to believe that schools are "sacred places to teach children how to have healthy behavior."[1] (More on that later.) Most folks would probably rather not think of our children as commodities whose brand loyalties are sold to the highest bidder from the moment they get on the bus. Increasingly, however, this is the case. Elementary education is compulsory in the United States; for kids up to age sixteen, going to school is not just a right but a responsibility. And it is the obligation of a democratic society to provide equal educational opportunities for all children. In recent years, however, more and more struggling school districts have found it difficult to resist corporate sponsorship, and more universities have adopted corporate models. So it is in the once-sacred realm of public education that advertisers have found a most lucrative captive audience.

In this chapter, we examine the commercialization and privatization of education in the United States, focusing on developments in the last ten years. We start with a look at the marketing of "educational" and "developmental" products for infants and toddlers, as well as the increasingly aggressive advertising of brand name school supplies for elementary, middle, and high school students. We turn then to corporate sponsorship and control of school materials and activities in K–12, including the subjection of students to advertising in classrooms, hallways, gymnasiums, and cafeterias.

227

We consider the ramifications of the 2002 No Child Left Behind Act for elementary and secondary education in the United States. We go on to examine the increasing commercialization of colleges and universities, focusing on sponsored research, exclusive contracts, and the private appropriation of public space. We pay special attention to the corporate world's exploitation of academia's fascination with new information technologies. Finally, we look at some of the conditions that have made it seem necessary for public schools and land-grant universities to seek private funding, and have made it easier for corporations to exploit this perceived need.

READING, WRITING, AND RETAIL

In chapter 6, we cited baby bottles emblazoned with soft drink logos as a particularly insidious example of "ad creep." Of course, many parents wouldn't dream of purchasing such products for their infant children any more than they would buy their toddlers candy cigarettes (chalky confections complete with red tips that were once quite popular and are still readily available online). But as the brisk sales of math primers using products such as Twizzlers and Trix suggest, consumers can be persuaded to buy almost anything labeled as "educational" for their children. Back-to-school "must have" lists have expanded from pencils, notebooks, and protractors to include day planners, calculators, computers, iPods, and iPads. And students who purchase branded school supplies are transformed into walking advertisements for everything from movies and TV shows to fast food and designer fashions.

Getting a Head Start

The motto of the BabyPlus Company is "Your womb . . . the perfect classroom." BabyPlus is a "prenatal education system" with a battery-operated sonar device that moms-to-be are instructed to strap on for one hour twice a day, beginning at eighteen weeks. For $150, the company promises that the rhythmic sounds passing through the woman's abdomen will produce infants who are "better relaxed at birth" and have "increased ability to self soothe." Later in life, BabyPlus kids are purportedly destined to exhibit "enhanced intellectual abilities," "greater creativity and independence," and "improved school readiness."[2]

Once the gifted child has arrived, parents can sell the used BabyPlus device on eBay and turn to Brainy Baby, a company that produces educational videos encouraging toddlers to imitate sounds they hear. "And what," the company's website asks, "is more satisfying than asking, 'What does a doggie say?' and hearing a proud little 'Woof, woof!'" A set of four DVDs runs around $55. It's not clear exactly what is educational about Brainy Baby's long line of plush toys, but a smartly stuffed frog can be had for about $30.[3]

The Baby Prodigy Company vows to help parents and caretakers "raise smarter, happier babies" with "captivating" educational videos. The captivation factor seems significant, since the company's founder admits she was inspired to create the product line by a colicky daughter who "would scream for hours" until mommy got her glued to the tube. In 2004, Baby Prodigy announced a promotional partnership with Nestlé to market baby formula along with its videos internationally.[4] This despite the fact that an international boycott of Nestlé products, particularly breast milk substitutes, had been in effect since 1977. As of 2008, the boycott was coordinated by the International Nestlé Boycott Committee, and company practices were monitored by the International Baby Food Action Network, consisting of more than two hundred groups in over a hundred countries.[5]

The BBC show *Teletubbies*, which aired on PBS from 1997 to 2001, was marketed as an educational program for children as young as one year old, although there was no evidence to support this assertion. Indeed, the American Academy of Pediatrics has recommended that children under two years of age watch no television at all. Nonetheless, *Teletubbies* gift packs were distributed to newborns in hospital maternity wards, and the show's producers entered into toy promotion deals with Burger King and McDonald's. In 1999, evangelical pastor Jerry Falwell managed to create an international Teletubby controversy by alleging that one of the fanciful cartoon creatures, "Tinky Winky," was a "hidden homosexual symbol" (because he was purple and sported a triangular antenna). There was, however, little public debate over the show's dubious claims to educate infants or its promotional partnerships with toy manufacturers and fast-food chains.

Disney's *Baby Einstein* product line, including CDs, DVDs, toys, and books for infants and toddlers, proved to be one of the company's most lucrative ventures. In 2004, Susan Linn, associate director of the Media Center of the Judge Baker Children's Center and an instructor in psychiatry at Harvard Medical School, reported that 27 percent of U.S. infants had viewed a *Baby Einstein* video. In 2005, estimated revenues for the product line reached $400 million. In 2007, the *Journal of Pediatrics* published a study conducted by researchers at the University of Washington who found that children aged eight to sixteen months who regularly viewed videos including *Baby Einstein* scored significantly lower on standard language development tests than those who did not. "There is no clear evidence of a benefit coming from baby DVDs and videos and there is some suggestion of harm," said lead author Frederick Zimmerman. "We don't know for sure that baby DVDs and videos are harmful, but the best policy is safety first. Parents should limit their exposure as much as possible." Disney merely disputed the findings and continued to reap the revenues.[6]

We found most of this information by searching for "educational toys" online. But as noted in chapter 5, the mainstream media often serve as unpaid advertisers for big business, with uncritical reporting of press releases, promotional events, and trade shows. So, for example, in February 2008, the *State College (Pa.) Centre Daily Times* ran a *Philadelphia Daily News* article on the American International Toy Fair in New York City. It was the equivalent of a full-page color ad for Fischer-Price, Intellitoys and LeapFrog: "So, you want to buy your children an electronics learning toy but don't have time to supervise them? LeapFrog's got the answer." The reporter admitted being "staggered by the 'smarts' and improved educational value in the many microprocessor-based and increasingly internet-connected toys [he] encountered" at the show. He swooned over a "Learn Smart Bounce & Spin Pony" marketed to "tykes as young as 12 months old" that is designed to be "positioned in front of a television, with a separate piece of electronic hardware plugged into the TV set to communicate with the pony via wireless, infrared signals."[7] (Yikes!)

All of this amounts to what Alissa Quart has referred to as the nation's "Baby Genius Edutainment Complex," an industry that preys on the status anxiety of neurotic parents. In an essay published in the *Atlantic Monthly* in 2006, Quart argues convincingly that "parents who press their children to succeed do so in hopes of preparing them for an adulthood of high achievement. Economically anxious, many parents see their children's accomplishments as a sort of insurance against the financial challenges of old age."[8] In 2006, Warren E. Buffett (number 2 on the 2007 *Forbes 400* list, at $52 billion) announced that he would star as a cartoon version of himself in "The Secret Millionaires Club," a thirteen-title DVD series for children aged five to twelve produced by DIC Entertainment.[9] We have to give Buffett credit for admitting that his line of videos was designed to make kids richer, not smarter or happier.

Back to School with the Right Stuff

One way corporations have wormed their way into public classrooms is by suggesting that students will perform better at school (and eventually succeed better in business) if they purchase designer school supplies. An example of this ploy can be seen in a 1998 Office Depot commercial featuring characters from the popular comic strip *Dilbert*. One of the strip's recurring characters is Dogbert, an evil and cynical business consultant (who is, in a tribute to the military-industrial complex, costumed as General Patton in this ad). Dogbert informs elementary school children: "Some students will shop at other stores. They will grow up to be your feeble-minded servants." Parents are then assured that Office Depot has the National Parent Teacher Association's official seal of approval, sanctioning the company's conflation of consumerism, power, and greed as "smarts." Children whose families can afford to purchase "the right stuff" (i.e., expensive school supplies sold at places such as Office Depot) are given license to belittle their less privileged classmates as geeky underlings. All because they have loose-leaf binders in shades like eggplant, ebony, and teal rather than purple, black, and blue.

Actually, it's not all that surprising that Office Depot would attempt to boost sales of brand-name calculators and kiddie day planners by threatening students with the prospect of being treated like dimwitted servants by their peers if they don't buy them. Discount retail chains like Kmart and Wal-Mart routinely appeal to tweens' and teens' desire to be popular (or at least not unpopular) at school in their efforts to promote sales of logo-laden school supplies. The more Bratz stickers, Hannah Montana gum dispensers, Spiderman backpacks, and Transformers lunch boxes retailers sell, the more self-confident students will be, or so the logic goes. Actually, students might feel more confident if their families were financially secure. In August 2005, the National Education Association joined with the American Federation of Teachers and the United Food and Commercial Workers in calling for a boycott of back-to-school shopping at Wal-Mart, on the grounds that Wal-Mart employees were forced to seek government subsidized health-care benefits, drawing billions away from public money that could be used to support public education.[10]

Although advertisers' claims that children can attain an intellectual advantage or a positive self-image through consumption is troubling, our larger concern here is the extent to which public schools themselves are being infiltrated and even dominated by corporate interests. As noted in chapter 5, big businesses are eager to create brand loyalty in the 78 million young people born in the United States between 1978 and 1998, 48 million of whom were enrolled in elementary and high schools by 1999.[11] So where better for corporate America to teach children to be good consumers than in the classroom? We thought the pressure on kids to go back to school with "the right stuff" was bad enough. A generation of "baby boomerangs" is going back to school with the Fortune 500 as well.

BRANDED FOR LIFE: THE COMMERCIALIZATION OF K–12

Although corporate influence in the classroom has increased dramatically in recent years, it is not a new phenomenon. In *The Media Monopoly*, a classic text now in its sixth edition and further revised in 2004 as *The New Media Monopoly*, Ben Bagdikian argued that corporate materials have long been prominent in our public schools. In the first edition, published in 1983, Bagdikian cited evidence that only 1 percent of already tight public school budgets was being used for instructional materials. He noted that industry had rushed in to fill the gap with largely self-serving publications. Even then, "complimentary" classroom materials were being produced by 64 percent of the five hundred largest American corporations, 90 percent of utility companies, and 90 percent of industrial trade associations. Most of these materials concentrated on nutrition, economics, energy, and the environment—and almost all were supplied by industries with a significant stake in their own solutions to the problems posed.[12]

Bagdikian rightly predicted that commercialism in the classroom would grow—and, we might add, grow increasingly aggressive and manipulative. For example, in 1998, a public relations consultant advised members of the Independent Petroleum Association of America to develop "a more grassroots approach to telling industry's story in the nation's public schools" in an effort to "assuage the guilt of Americans concerned about global warming or the dangers of petro-chemicals." The consultant recommended that in addition to supplying schools with free course materials, energy companies should host workshops for teachers "in resorts or campuses in pleasant surroundings."[13]

The 1990s saw a widespread selling out of U.S. public schools to big business. According to the Center for the Analysis of Commercialism in Education (CACE), "Commercial activities now shape the structure of the school day, influence the content of the school curriculum, and determine whether children have access to a variety of technologies."[14] A CACE study showed significant increases in a number of corporate activities in the classroom between 1990 and 1999, including the following: a 1,875 percent increase in industry sponsorship of educational materials, a 231 percent increase in corporate contests and other incentive programs, a 384 percent increase in exclusive agreements between businesses and schools, and a 539 percent increase in the private appropriation of public school space. The figures themselves are staggering; the actual practices are worth examining.

Sponsored Educational Materials

Sponsored educational materials are products or services purporting to have instructional content that are supplied directly to schools by corporations or trade associations. Although no educational resource is value-neutral, promotional materials produced by corporations with specific agendas, disguised as "straight" history, science, or math, are cause for concern. Younger students may not have the ability to read such materials with a critical eye; older students who know they will be tested may have no incentive to do so; and teachers with scarce resources may feel that they have no choice but to use them.

Channel One

Perhaps the most notorious example of a sponsored educational service is Channel One, a twelve-minute news program launched by Primedia Inc. in 1990 and broadcast daily to 10 million students in 320,000 U.S. classrooms at its peak in 2002. Here's how it worked: Primedia installed about $25,000 worth of TVs and VCRs in participating schools, and in return the schools agreed to require 80 percent of their students to watch Channel One programs on 90 percent of all school days. The catch? Channel One programs were peppered with ads for Fortune 500 companies. Firms such as Reebok and Nintendo paid about $200,000 for each half-minute commercial, and peer pressure to purchase their upscale products was undoubtedly heightened in such a setting. Channel One also tempted impulse snackers with ads for M&Ms, Snickers, Twix, Hostess Cakes, Milky Way, Doritos, Mountain Dew, Nestlé Crunch, and Skittles.[15]

In 2000, CACE calculated that Channel One was costing taxpayers and their kids $1.8 billion a year in classroom time, including $300 million for the commercials. In 2002, Channel One reaped $50.2 million in ad revenues. Former Channel One president Joel Babbit boasted, "The biggest selling point to advertisers [is that] we are forcing kids to watch two minutes of commercials" (a remark so unabashedly blunt, as one critic noted, that it explains why Babbit soon became a *former* president).[16] A *Washington Post* reporter who sat in on a Channel One screening in 2000 observed that only three of the fifteen seventh graders in the class he visited appeared to be paying attention to anything but the ads.[17] And indeed, in 2006, the American Academy of Pediatrics reported that children who watched Channel One tended to remember the commercials more than the news.[18]

Channel One became the target of much criticism, and by 2007 the number of students forced to watch it was down to 6 million in 270,000 classrooms. The company stopped accepting commercials for nonnutritious foods such as candy, soda, and snacks and lost most of its ad revenues. In 2007, Primedia sold Channel One to Alloy Media & Marketing for $10 million. According to *Advertising Age*, "Channel One could emerge as even more controversial due to its connection to Alloy, particularly given the company's association with the books that inspired the sex-infused *Gossip Girl*, now airing on the CW, and social-networking sites such as *Sugar Loot*, where scantily clad teens often post photos to be voted as 'hottest girl' or 'hottest guy.'"[19] To attract advertisers, Alloy brought in a new head of sales, Andrew Knopf from World Wrestling Entertainment. Gatorade agreed to sponsor a "news" segment entitled "Player of the Week." In 2008, Channel One advertisers included film studios such as Warner Brothers and Sony Pictures, video game marketers including Nexon and Activision, and military recruiters from the U.S. Army, Navy, and Marines.

ChannelOne.com is the official online partner to Channel One News, and in 2010 was produced in partnership with CBS News. A representative edition from May 2010 featured two brief news stories (1.5 minutes on the Gulf oil spill and 4.5 minutes on immigration debates); soft spots ("Sports Play of the Week"); a multiple choice pop quiz on music "administered" by singer/actress Selena Gomez (students were given 10 seconds to choose between (a) soprano, (b) alto, (c) bass, and (d) tenor as the highest vocal range); and ads for Canon, Old Spice, ABC Family, Alloy TV, and Facebook. Transitions between segments plugged the musical group of the day (the Lee Roessler Band) and announced a vote-in Artist of the Year competition.

The onscreen space devoted to the news was markedly less than that devoted to ads *throughout* the program. A banner ad dominated the top of the screen consistently, and a montage of ads faded in and out of a space parallel to and precisely the same size as the "news hole." Competing for visitors' attention to oil spills and immigrants, at the bottom of the page were invitations to check your horoscope, "primp your prom," or review the "Week in Rap." An unintended consequence of Channel One may be that students *expect* their education to be entertaining, with sound bytes of information and ideas squeezed between layers of fluff.

The New Math

Textbooks can also be seen as sponsored educational materials, although publishers bristle at the suggestion. One example is a glossy mathematics primer published by McGraw-Hill. The book is graced with what appear to be advertisements for products like Cocoa Frosted Flakes, Gatorade, and M&Ms, as well as Sega and Sony video games. We say "appear" because McGraw-Hill insists that the inclusion of color photos of brand-name products in the textbook cannot be considered advertising since the corporations don't pay for it. A spokesperson for McGraw-Hill claimed that the brand names are used only to give junior high school students some examples they can appreciate. In one story problem, budding mathematicians are asked how long a child will need to save his allowance in order to purchase a pair of Nikes.[20]

It is difficult to imagine the same textbook asking students to calculate the profit Nike makes on each $120 pair of sneakers produced by a southeast Asian girl working in a sweatshop for pennies per hour, or to figure out how long it would take Nike CEO Philip Knight (number 30 on the *Forbes 400* list of the richest people in America in 2007 and up to number 24 during the economic recession in 2009) to deplete his $9.8 billion fortune if he spent, say, $100,000 a day on Cocoa Frosted Flakes. Rather than encouraging consumption, such exercises would invite students to contemplate the unequal distribution of wealth in the United States and worldwide.

Incentive Programs

Incentive programs are arrangements whereby corporations provide awards, goods, or services to students, schools, or school districts in return for their participation in specified activities. Such programs often appear altruistic, but they inevitably benefit the corporations far more than the schools. Students who participate get trinkets splattered with corporate logos, token cash awards, or certificates good toward the purchase of the company's products. Corporations get good publicity, cheap advertising, and easy access to an attractive demographic group. Although these programs often purport to be incentives to learning, many students find that their intellectual curiosity and creativity are limited by corporate dictates.

Sponsored Science Projects

A 1999 article in the *State College (Pa.) Centre Daily Times* celebrated "the gadgetry of young inventors," putting a hometown spin on a contest administered by the National Science Teachers Association (NSTA). We were delighted to see that two local students were finalists, and we were especially impressed by a fourteen-year-old's ingenious "Anti-Squirrel Birdfeeder Defense System." But creative students who envisioned gadgets that didn't run on batteries weren't eligible to enter. Why? Because although the contest was administered by NSTA, it was sponsored by Duracell. All inventions were required to "educate, entertain, make life easier or perform a practical function"—and, crucially, to "be powered by Duracell batteries."[21] Such sponsorships are one of the many ways in which Proctor & Gamble (number 1 on *Advertising Age*'s list of Leading National Advertisers, with expenditures of $4.9 billion in 2006) manages to create brand recognition and loyalty for something as seemingly standard as a battery.

The veneer of the educational value of incentive programs in schools is fading ever thinner. For example, Cape Cod Potato Chips sponsored a contest in which New England middle school students were required to build model ships in honor of the Sail Boston 2000 festival using Cape Cod Potato Chips.[22] Campbell's offered schools a science experiment designed to prove that its own Prego spaghetti sauce was thicker than Ragu.[23] It seems clear that such incentive programs are utilizing public education to cultivate brand loyalty and foster consumption rather than inspire exploration.

Ronald McDonald Report Cards

In 2007, a promotional partnership between McDonald's restaurants and the Seminole County School Board in Florida drew national attention, thanks to the actions of a concerned parent and support from the Campaign for a Commercial-Free Childhood (CCFC). In the "report card incentive program," as it was called, McDonald's provided report card jackets for students from kindergarten through fifth grade (at a total cost of about $1,500), and promised kids free food for good grades. Susan Pagan, the mother of a fourth grader at Red Bug Elementary in Winter Springs, Florida, was sufficiently disconcerted to find her daughter's report card surrounded by a cartoon of Ronald McDonald, the Golden Arches logo, and photographs of Happy Meals, to file a protest with the school board. "I thought it was appalling," she said. "You get a reward for good grades by eating—and eating fast food." Susan Linn, director of CCFC, agreed. "Turning report cards into ads for McDonald's undermines parents' efforts to encourage healthy eating."[24] Linn urged McDonald's to stop the practice—and, crucially, informed reporters of her efforts.

Spokespersons for both McDonald's and the Seminole County School Board were decidedly dismissive of Pagan's complaint and CCFC's intervention when the story was first reported in the *New York Times* in December 2007. One month and lots of bad publicity later, however, McDonald's USA offered to reprint the report card jackets without the ads, and the Seminole County School District immediately accepted. The case gained further notoriety when both Pagan and Linn appeared on *The Colbert Report* in February 2008. As Linn concluded, "In the absence of needed government regulation to protect schoolchildren from predatory companies like McDonald's, the burden is on parents to be vigilant about exploitative marketing aimed at children."[25]

Exclusive Agreements

Exclusive agreements are contracts drawn up between school districts and businesses whereby the schools agree to sell and advertise one company's products and, of course, not to sell or advertise any competing brands. The schools get much-needed cash upon signing, and the corporations get a chance to hook young consumers on their products for life. Some sponsor companies are very protective of what "their" students are exposed to. Schools that made deals with Pepsi or Coke in the early 2000s were required to remove juice and bottled water machines from their hallways.[26] Schools that entered into deals with McDonald's agreed not to sell ordinary beef patties in their cafeterias, even though students on the federal lunch program could not use their vouchers to buy Big Macs. The *New York Times* reported that in 2008, "two-tier" lunch programs had stigmatized poor students so much that only 40 percent of eligible high school students in New York City and only 37 percent in San Francisco participated in subsidized meal programs.[27] As one student wrote in a letter to the editors of *Adbusters*: "What ever happened to the good, old-fashioned lunch lady who would slop some mystery meat on your tray and a carton of 2% milk?"[28]

Cola Wars

The giant soda manufacturers fought some of the fiercest battles for exclusive contracts with schools in the late 1990s. By 2000, according to CACE, about 175 districts around the nation had arrangements with either Coca-Cola or PepsiCo.[29] The deals varied according to the number of students the schools had to offer and how much brand loyalty they were willing to pledge. Some schools agreed to purchase all cups, carbon dioxide, and related materials from the same vendor. Coke and Pepsi made it hard to resist. One of the biggest payouts went to a Colorado Springs school district: $8.1 million from a Coke bottler for a ten-year deal.

At first, soda manufacturers didn't feel the need to pretend that their products were good for kids. As a spokesman for the National Soft Drink Association put it, "Soft drinks make no nutritious claims."[30] How could they? Studies show that a significant increase in soda consumption among teenagers, along with a decrease in their intake of milk and fruit juices, has left them deprived of calcium and Vitamin C and made them overweight. From 1990 to 1994, the number of clinically obese children aged six to eleven in the United States nearly doubled from 6.5 percent to 11.4 percent. A study published in the medical journal *Lancet* in 2000 found that "an extra soft drink a day gives a child a 60 percent greater chance of becoming obese." The study involved tracking 548 children aged eleven to twelve from public schools across Massachusetts for two years. The soft drink–obesity link was found to be independent of the food children ate, how much television or videos they watched, and the amount of exercise they got.[31] By 2008, 20 percent of children aged 6–11 and 18 percent of adolescents aged 12–19 were obese (defined as having excess fat).[32]

Nonetheless, the news media often derided those who objected to sodas being advertised, sold, or given away in public schools. For example, Knight Ridder distributed a story about a congressional bill designed to prohibit the sale of foods of minimal nutritional value during federally funded meals. The story cites a study conducted by the Center for Science in the Public Interest (CSPI), which highlights the negative nutritional effects of soda on young people. The headline reads "Food Police: Teens Consume Too Much Soda" and the sarcastic lead disparages the CSPI: "They warned you about Chinese food, oil-soaked popcorn and cinnamon buns. . . . Now the nation's food police have taken on a new scourge. Soda pop." The report celebrates the fact that soda is often "a free treat" for students provided by soft drink companies and emphasizes that many of the lawmakers supporting the bill "hail from dairy states," suggesting that their motives are purely economic. Concerns raised by the CSPI study in this news story were ultimately dismissed as "unfounded consumer alarm."[33]

Mainstream coverage of the cola controversy reflects the probusiness bias of the media, even when the health and welfare of children are at stake.

Nonetheless, protests by physicians, dieticians, parents, teachers, and other activists continued. In the summer of 2001, Coca-Cola announced that it would end its exclusive beverage contracts with schools, include juice and milk in its vending machines, and "tone down" its advertising aimed at kids. Pepsi promised to follow suit. The announcements came one month after the U.S. Department of Agriculture announced that all food sold in schools should meet nutrition standards. The strategy of the cola companies, as a number of critics noted in 2001, was to "give the teacher an apple" so they wouldn't be expelled for good.[34]

The critics were right. In 2006, soda manufacturers and bottlers once again pledged to make "diligent efforts" to abide by "voluntary guidelines" to "limit sugary beverages" sold in schools. But by 2007, 75 percent of U.S. high schools, 65 percent of middle schools, and 30 percent of elementary schools had entered into contracts with Big Fizz. And they weren't easy to get out of. School administrators in Portland, Oregon, and Racine, Wisconsin, who attempted to abort long-term contracts were slapped with bills for $200,000 to $600,000—fines they said their school districts simply couldn't afford to pay. According to Portland attorney Deborah Pinkas (who, along with Nicola Pinson, wrote a study on beverage contracts), "Many school districts are stuck with a deal with the devil."[35]

Kevin W. Keane, a spokesman for the American Beverage Association, argued that bottlers should not be expected to "take a financial hit" to implement the new guidelines. "Schools ask for money upfront," Keane explained. "So companies have made an investment. If you're going to alter that dramatically, the one side is going to bear the brunt of the financial pain, which isn't fair."[36] We don't know what the typical operating budget for a public school in Racine, Wisconsin, looks like, but we do know that PepsiCo and Coca-Cola were numbers 63 and 118 on the 2007 *Fortune 500* list of America's largest corporations, reporting revenues of $20 to $35 billion. Yet the terms of the debate, as set by Big Beverage and reported by Big Media, became whether or not struggling schools owed soft drink companies "fair" compensation for their trouble. The idea that soda manufacturers and bottlers might be penalized for predatory tactics wasn't even raised. And the larger issue of why public schools were forced to seek corporate funding in the first place was barely broached.

In March 2010, threatened by proposed sugar taxes in several states, the American Beverage Association announced that its voluntary guidelines limiting sales of soft drinks in elementary, middle, and high schools had resulted in "unqualified success." In an article titled "Soda Makers Claim War on Sugary Drinks Is Won," Sarah Gilbert of *Daily Finance* notes that this was only after Coke's CEO had likened President Barack Obama's pledged support of a soda tax to communism.[37] Under the banner of the Alliance for a Healthier Generation, Big Beverage began running print and television ads touting a joint initiative to remove full-calorie soft drinks from schools nationwide. Or, as *Advertising Age* put it, "Ad Collaboration between Coca-Cola, Pepsi, Dr. Pepper Hopes to Show Industry in Positive Light."[38] Gilbert put it more bluntly: "Is Pepsi's Removal of Sodas from Schools Just a Publicity Stunt?"[39]

The soft drink industry *needed* some good PR in 2010, especially given First Lady Michelle Obama's campaign against childhood obesity. And although revenues decreased a smidgeon with the industry's self-regulation of sodas in school, they were way up from 2004 to 2009 for both Coca-Cola and PepsiCo (a whopping 47 percent).[40] Kids had already developed brand loyalties, and they were simply getting their soft drinks elsewhere. The response of the beverage industry to consumer outcry was welcome, and the school ban had no long-term effects on sugar consumption and childhood obesity, as rates kept climbing. But the initiative was finally less about children's waistlines and more about corporate bottom lines.

Private Appropriation of Public Space

Private appropriation of public space refers to any allocation of public school facilities for corporations to display logos, advertisements, or products. Also included under this heading is the use of classroom time or school facilities for commercial activities, such as recruiting students for product testing or market research. In exchange for granting such privileges, the schools are rewarded with cash or supplies, and the students are often given free samples. The corporations get rapt audiences and invaluable marketing profiles to inform future ad campaigns. Corporate logos and ads are plastered on scoreboards, basketball backboards, bulletin boards, display cases, and buses. They are commonly placed on school calendars, book covers, assignment books, and sports schedules. They are ubiquitous on computer screens.

Some product displays are school-related, as in the case of school pictures, yearbooks, or class rings, but even these promotions are based on exclusive contracts and designed to create peer pressure to consume. Other examples of commercial use of class time and school facilities are decidedly less justifiable. Hershey, the number one chocolate manufacturer in the United States, gave schools cash for every Peppermint Pattie or Almond Joy wrapper kids brought in. General Mills rewarded young students who collected cereal box tops from Lucky Charms and Frosted Cheerios with a classroom visit from the Trix Bunny. McDonald's gave students cookies, juice, and coupons in exchange for watching a recruitment video and filling out job applications. Clairol gave high school girls shampoo samples for completing a survey with questions like "Was this a good hair day or a bad hair day?"

As a representative for the Citizens Campaign for Commercial-Free Schools said simply, "If there is a national problem with funding our schools, then selling off the school environment to corporate interests surely isn't the answer to it."[41] Yet freedom from corporate sponsorship is fast becoming the exception rather than the rule in elementary and secondary education, although some students, parents, teachers, and administrators have resisted it. School boards in State College, Hershey, and Pittsburgh, Pennsylvania, for example, were reported to "weigh," "ponder," "question," and "raise concerns" over exclusive drink contracts.[42] The school district of Madison, Wisconsin, which signed a three-year contract with Coke in 1997, declined to renew it in 2000.[43] In 1998, Berkeley High School turned down lucrative offers from both Pepsi and Nike in response to student protests. In 1999, the San Francisco School Board approved the Commercial-Free Schools Act, which prohibits the district from signing exclusive beverage contracts or adopting educational materials that contain brand names.[44]

Increasingly, however, public and private school teachers and administrators are defending corporate sponsorships with explanations that sound, well, defensive. For example, when students at Our Lady of Assumption Elementary School in Lynnfield, Massachusetts, spent two days testing cereals and answering opinion polls, their principal, Martha Marie Pooler, compared the exercise to a science experiment: "It's a learning experience," she said. "They had to read, they had to look, they had to compare." The school got $600 for its part in the lucrative market research project.[45] As Lisa Seed, an English teacher at Harrison High School in Colorado Springs said of the ZapMe company, which offered schools thousands of dollars' worth of computers, all of which displayed a constant stream of onscreen ads: "They are absolutely using the kids—and I don't like it when my kids are used. On the other hand, I'm happy to be sitting in a room with fifteen computers."[46]

No Child Left Untrained

On January 28, 2008, President George W. Bush delivered his final State of the Union address. Faced with the lowest approval ratings of any president in U.S. history, Bush was forced to acknowledge concerns about a looming economic recession, environmental catastrophes, and the devastating wars in Afghanistan and Iraq. He nonetheless touted his No Child Left Behind Act (NCLB) as an unmitigated success:

> Six years ago, we came together to pass the No Child Left Behind Act, and today no one can deny its results. . . . Members of Congress, the No Child Left Behind Act is a bipartisan achievement. It is succeeding. And we owe it to America's children, their parents and their teachers to strengthen this good law. We must also do more to help children when their schools do not measure up.[47]

"Measuring up" was crucial, since NCLB tied federal funding for public education to mandatory standardized tests derived from "scientifically based research." The tests were required to be uniform within each state, and to emphasize reading and math. Most states adopted the least expensive exam format, multiple choice, despite its obvious limitations.[48]

Although Bush chose to ignore all criticism, NCLB has been the subject of heated debates since it was signed into law in 2002. Critics contended that it put pressure on educators to "teach the test" (e.g., to drill students with formulas and equations rather than engage them in story problems that might help them apply their knowledge to a wide range of situations); it created incentives for states to improve test scores by lowering standards, and caused an increase in "gaming," or the "creative reclassification" of dropouts; it led to drastic cuts in resources allotted to music, art, social studies, foreign languages, and physical education; and it was used as a tool for military recruitment.[49]

After blithely declaring the success of NCLB in his State of the Union address, Bush renewed a proposal to spend $300 million for a "grants for kids" program to "liberate poor children trapped in failing public schools." The plan was to pluck good students out of bad schools so that they might find "new hope at faith-based or other nonpublic schools," which Bush claimed were "disappearing at an alarming rate in many of America's inner cities." Presumably, the struggling schools whose students failed to meet competency requirements would lose federal funding, virtually ensuring a further downward spiral. Many students, it seemed, would indeed be "left behind."[50]

In February 2008, one month after the State of the Union address, the *Centre Daily Times* ran a *Pittsburgh Post-Gazette* article celebrating the implementation of corporate management strategies in K–12. The article reported that Total Quality Management, the "management model that made Toyota the world's top-selling automobile company," was being utilized at schools such as Washington Elementary in Mount Lebanon, Pennsylvania, where the "workers" were actually "pint-sized pupils," and the "products" were better spelling, reading, and math scores. The article focused on the use of mission statements, balanced scorecards, class graphs, and individual data binders to chart performance. There was no mention of inspiring intellectual curiosity, encouraging exploration, or instilling a love of learning. The emphasis seemed to be on producing a barely skilled workforce, and a bored and battered one at that.

One six-year-old was reduced to tears when her less-than-perfect score on a "sight words" reading test was displayed for the class to see. Her teacher interpreted this as a sign of the power of continuous improvement as a motivational tool. "Guaranteed, she'll have them all right next week," she said. The only other criticism of the corporate model, buried near the bottom of the lengthy (twenty-nine-paragraph) article, came from a professor emeritus of education at Stanford University. "Programs like [this] are cosmetic," he said "It's like Botox to wrinkles." The management model was said to be especially effective in schools that had not made adequate yearly progress under the No Child Left Behind Act.[51]

In February 2010, the Obama administration pledged to revisit and revise NCLB. In its 2010 budget request, according to the *New York Times*, the White House said it "hoped to replace the law's much-criticized school rating system, known as adequate yearly progress, with a new accountability system."[52] The Bush law had required states to adopt "challenging academic standards" in math and reading to be eligible to receive federal funding for poor students—but left it up to the states to determine what constitutes "challenging." The result was that individual states set standards at wildly varied levels. The Obama revision stressed nationally shared standards. A White House statement declared:

> Because economic progress and educational achievement go hand in hand, educating every American student to graduate prepared for college and success in a new work force is a national imperative. Meeting this challenge requires that state standards reflect a level of teaching and learning needed for students to graduate ready for success in college and careers.[53]

In a sharply divided nation, forty-eight states began collaborating to write common standards in math and reading in 2010. Only Texas and Alaska declined.

This is noteworthy in part because the Texas Board of Education has become notorious for rewriting state standards that textbook publishers must follow to get lucrative contracts for providing teaching materials for every student in the state, from first grade through high school. As Jim Hightower wrote in *The Progressive*, "They're hell-bent on supplanting classroom education with their own brand of ideological indoctrination."[54] Examples include removing Thomas Jefferson, the prime author of the Declaration of Independence, from a list of revolutionary political thinkers because he coined the term "separation between church and state," and insisting that the "positives" of Joseph McCarthy's crusade against communists in the 1950s, commonly thought of as a witch hunt, be acknowledged. As Hightower argues, "Any concepts that might spur progressive thoughts in young minds were expunged."[55] Textbook publishers in the big state of Texas were only too happy to oblige.

ACADEMIA, INC.: THE
CORPORATIZATION OF THE UNIVERSITY

The notion that institutions of higher learning might be impervious to the encroachment of the corporate sphere is, perhaps, naive. Yet the culture of academia has been likened "more to the ideals of communism than to capitalism," with the supposedly free exchange of artistic and intellectual discoveries.[56] In many ways, as Naomi Klein argues, schools and universities remain our culture's most tangible embodiment of public space and collective responsibility. "University campuses in particular—with their residences, libraries, green spaces and common standards for open and respectful discourse—play a crucial, if now largely symbolic, role: they are the one place left where young people can see a genuine public life being lived."[57] Klein's observations are particularly poignant in light of the tendency—both inside and outside of the academy—to refer to the private, corporate sphere as "the real world" and the university as an "ivory tower." Increasingly, often in the name of preparing students for the so-called real world, institutions of higher learning are emulating big business.

Major universities and even smaller, alternative colleges are selling campus facilities and curriculum decisions off to the highest bidder. According to Stanley Aronowitz,

> As long as they get the cash, desperate administrators are eager to have their university reflect the whims of individuals and the interests of corporations. They will train corporate America's workers and conduct its research. Small private colleges like Hampshire hire a veritable army of consultants, marketing staff, and fundraisers to attract students, beef up their endowments and organize partnerships with industry.[58]

Indeed, corporate spending on academia has risen dramatically in recent years, surging from $850 million in 1985 to $4.25 billion less than a decade later.[59]

As in grades K–12, university partnerships with corporations sometimes involve sponsored materials. Corporations routinely supply universities with books, films, and videos; computers, software, and Internet access; classrooms, labs, and even entire buildings. But university professors are less directly dependent on corporate-sponsored educational materials than many of their colleagues teaching K–12. College students pay tuition, lab dues, and activity fees. They are required to buy textbooks or course packs assigned by professors. Often, they come with their own computers and are issued e-mail accounts. University classrooms are well equipped, and libraries and archives are richly stocked. Academic freedom, though constantly under attack, is still fiercely defended. The very notion of being required to screen a college-level version of Channel One in class is unthinkable to most university professors.

Nonetheless, the corporatization of the American academy is palpable and in some ways more profound than in K–12. Corporate incentive programs, exclusive agreements, and the private leasing of public space have become central to the structure of many universities. Moreover, the stakes are higher and the profits bigger at the college level. Incentive programs give professors and graduate students huge research grants to test experimental drugs, develop alternative energy sources, and create weapons of war. Exclusive agreements bring in millions of dollars in cash and merchandise for universities—and billions of dollars worth of brand recognition and sales for corporations. The corporate appropriation of campus space for advertising and sales has transformed student unions into shopping malls and profoundly altered the very nature of the university experience.

Corporate Incentive Programs

Chairs, Centers, and Think Tanks

One marked trend in this area is an increase in industry-endowed chairs, centers, and think tanks, many of which come with strings attached. For example, Kmart endowed a chair in the management school at West Virginia University that required its holder to spend up to thirty days a year training assistant store managers. Other endowed chairs are rather obvious attempts at damage control: Freeport-McMoRan, a mining company embroiled in allegations of environmental misconduct in Indonesia, created a chair in environmental studies at Tulane University. Among the more promotional academic titles are the Yahoo! Chair of Information Systems Technology at Stanford University, the Lego Professorship of Learning Research at the Massachusetts Institute of Technology, and the Taco Bell Distinguished Professor of Hotel and Restaurant Administration at Washington State University.[60]

Why settle for a chair when you can have a whole center? Many universities have sought to attract corporate sponsors by creating research centers bearing their names or serving their interests. The Pennsylvania State University established an AT&T Center for Service Leadership in 1994 and an MBNA Career Services Center in 1999. In 2000, General Electric awarded Penn State $475,000 to bring the schools of engineering and business together in a Center for Product Realization. However euphemistic its name, the purpose of this center is avowedly to "foster entrepreneurship."[61] In 2000 also, six communications companies—IBM, Xerox, AT&T Wireless, Delphi Ventures, SAP, and Unisys Corp.—pledged $1.85 million to create the Penn State eBusiness Research Center, with faculty and graduate students providing a corporate "think tank." According to a representative for Xerox, "The advantage here at Penn State is knowledge to identify and test new areas that we can consider taking advantage of." Her thoughts were echoed by a representative for Unisys: "If we can get input on where the world is moving, we'll have a greater chance one of our initiatives will be a winner."[62]

In each case, the advantages to big business are obvious and those to academia only apparently so. Corporate sponsorship of educational materials and facilities allows industry to influence the kinds of research projects that are conducted and the kinds of findings that will be rewarded. The mission of the university to advance knowledge is superseded by that of big business to increase profits while promoting corporate images.

Partnerships and Alliances

Corporate incentive programs, which are often administered through endowed chairs and centers like those described above, have spawned what Eyal Press and Jennifer Washburn have called "The Kept University."[63] To wit, Penn State's Center for Product Realization is charged with developing "a new four-course sequence for engineering students on the principles and practices of entrepreneurship."[64] Faculty and students who study engineering for more altruistic reasons need not apply. As Aronowitz puts it, "Those who choose to remain aloof from the new regime risk extermination or marginality."[65]

The six companies that pledged nearly $2 million to Penn State's eBusiness Research Center were unabashed about the profit-making impetus for their donation. The *Centre Daily Times* quoted the vice president of worldwide e-business marketing and strategy for Unisys Corp. as saying, "We're going to the university as a corporation and saying we want to tap its ideas early on." Later in the article, it was revealed that Unisys did product development in-house and was looking to the Penn State center (merely) to test its own e-business ideas. Unisys promised to "submit a number of research proposals to the center." It seemed unlikely that these proposals were scrutinized, criticized, revised, or rejected by faculty and graduate students newly beholden to Unisys and partners, especially since the center was headed by a new faculty member who just happened to be a former IBM executive.[66]

In a deal heralded by the *Centre Daily Times* as "a unique partnership between business and academia," the Shaner Hotel Group and the University of Delaware announced plans to collaborate in the development and management of an upscale "branded" hotel catering to business and leisure travelers. According to Plato Ginos, the Shaner Group's vice president of development, a member of the university faculty would manage the hotel, and students in the department of hotel, restaurant, and institutional management would "be able to utilize the facility as an active learning environment"[67] (i.e., they'd work there). This partnership is not nearly so unique as the *Centre Daily Times* would have it. A number of universities have made similar arrangements with the Walt Disney World College Program, billed as "an intensive yet fun internship program that provides students with a chance to live and learn, while becoming a member of the Disney crew." Job categories include park greeting, food service, and custodial work, and the pay is $6.00 per hour. What used to be called a summer job is now referred to as an internship, and students can earn up to eighteen college credits for participating.[68] The internships include "classes" promoting the Disney business philosophy.

In 1998, the University of California at Berkeley entered into a partnership that made these deals seem benign by comparison. The corporate sponsor was Novartis, a Swiss pharmaceutical giant and producer of genetically engineered crops. Under the terms of the agreement, Novartis promised to give Berkeley $25 million to fund basic research in the Department of Plant and Microbial Biology, one of four departments within the College of Natural Resources. In exchange for the cash, Berkeley granted Novartis first rights to negotiate licenses on roughly a third of the department's discoveries—including not only the results of research funded by Novartis but also by state and federal sources. It also granted the company unprecedented representation (two of five seats) on the department's research committee, which determined how the money was to be spent, and allowed the company to postpone the publication of the university's research findings for up to four months.[69]

The National Institutes of Health recommended that universities allow corporate sponsors to prohibit publication for no more than one or two months, the amount of time ordinarily necessary to apply for a patent. Yet studies showed that a majority of life-science companies require delays of more than six months. Such delays allow not only for exclusive rights, but also for damage control. Not that it is often necessary: A 1996 study published in the *Annals of Internal Medicine* found that 98 percent of papers based on industry-sponsored research reflected favorably on the drugs being examined.[70] Occasionally, however, researchers tell corporate sponsors things they don't want consumers to hear.

For example, four researchers working on a study of calcium channel blockers (used to treat high blood pressure) quit the project in protest when their sponsor, Sandoz, deleted passages from a draft of their report that highlighted the potential dangers of the drugs (including stroke and heart failure). More than a year before the appetite suppressant Fen-Phen was pulled off the shelves, a group of researchers published a study in the *New England Journal of Medicine* warning that drugs like it could have potentially fatal side effects. The same issue contained a commentary written by two academic researchers downplaying the dangers of the drugs. It turned out that the "balance" here was provided by two authors who had served as paid consultants to the manufacturers and distributors of similar drugs— connections that were not mentioned.[71]

As Mildred Cho, a senior research scholar at Stanford's Center for Biomedical Ethics, contends: "When you have so many scientists on boards of companies or doing sponsored research, you start to wonder, How are these studies being designed? What kinds of research questions are being raised? What kinds aren't being raised?" One thing seems clear: The answers have more to do with corporate profits than public health or welfare. And yet sponsored research programs are almost universally celebrated in the press as "win-win" situations.

Such was the case in 2007, when Penn State and Chevron Corporation announced a five-year "alliance" to "collaborate on coal-related research." The announcement made the front pages of both the *Centre Daily Times* and the *Daily Collegian*, and understandably so; it involved a commitment of $17.5 million from Chevron and a promise of twenty-four new faculty positions by Penn State. The deal was announced at a ceremony on campus, and sound bytes were provided by former Penn State President Graham Spanier, former Senior Vice President for Research Eva Pell, Dean in the College of Earth and Mineral Sciences Bill Easterling, and Director of Industrial Research Tanna Pugh. For Chevron, Vice President Donald L. Paul and Communications Manager Tommy Lyles pitched in. The *Collegian* reported that the alliance would "allow for Penn State Faculty to visit Chevron" and "weave real world research into the classroom."[72] The *Centre Daily Times* reported that Chevron Vice President Paul "was struck by the university's emphasis on integrating its research with business applications."[73]

Both papers highlighted Chevron's commitment of $17.5 million to Penn State over the next five years. Neither mentioned that Chevron CEO David J. O'Reilly had earned compensation of $52.6 million over the previous five years; that Chevron (number 4 on the *Fortune 500* list in 2006 and 2007) reported $14 billion in profits in 2006; or that profits of the five biggest international oil companies had tripled since 2002 while prices at the pump rose dramatically.[74] There was not a whisper of concern about Chevron's egregious record of environmental abuses. This record, had reporters sought to examine it, would have revealed numerous accidents, illegal additives, oil spills, cover-ups, dumping of toxic wastes, and violations of the Clean Air Act.[75]

We don't believe that reporters for either paper consciously engaged in damage control for Chevron when they filed their stories (although Chevron's avowed emphasis on how best to convert fossil fuels for "cleaner future uses" might have raised an eyebrow or two). We hope that follow-up stories on the credentials of the faculty who were hired, the parameters of the projects that were funded, and the recommendations of the research that was published will be the subject of future inquiry. But as noted in chapter 5, the economics of the contemporary news industry discourage investigative and follow-up reporting of this sort.

Corporate Consultation

The increasingly corporate culture of academia need not be legitimized by sponsored centers or chairs. Faculty mentors who serve as "consultants" to big business also serve as role models for young scholars. In 2008, students of biostatistics and nutrition at the University of Alabama got a glimpse (if not a dollar figure) of what their professional opinion might some day be worth to the food industry. New York City's Board of Health was set to implement new rules for menu labels at chain restaurants operating in the city. Restaurants with fifteen or more restaurants nationally would be required to list calories alongside menu items (e.g., a Double Whopper with cheese has 990 calories). Supporters of the new rules included consumer groups such as Center for Science in the Public Interest and Public Citizen, as well as professional organizations such as the American Medical Association, the American Academy of Pediatrics, the American Diabetes Association, and the American Heart Association.

Dr. David B. Allison, a professor of biostatistics and nutrition at the University of Alabama, was scheduled to begin a one-year term as president of the Obesity Society in October 2008. He nonetheless agreed to write an affidavit on behalf of the New York State Restaurant Association, which was suing to block the new rules. Dr. Allison, who had previously served in advisory roles for Coca-Cola, Kraft Foods, and Frito-Lay, submitted an opinion that was filed with the United States District Court for the Southern District of New York. In it, he argued that informing customers about calories might (1) tempt them to eat even more junk food (the "forbidden fruit" factor) or (2) lead them to eat less junk food at the restaurant, only to gorge themselves at home later (the "so few calories, so not full" factor). Better to keep consumers ignorant, he concluded. We assume Dr. Allison was well paid for this opinion, although he declined to say how much.[76]

Fortunately, future health-care researchers and practitioners can still find principled role models in academia. Dr. Barry M. Popkin, director of the Interdisciplinary Obesity Center at the University of North Carolina, told the *New York Times* that many of the Obesity Society's 1,800 members were outraged that the president-elect of "an organization that cares about obesity and cares about healthy eating, wants to hold back information from people that helps them make healthy choices." In a statement released in February 2008, the Obesity Society declared its belief that "more information on the caloric content of restaurant servings, not less, is in the interests of consumers." The controversy led Dr. Kelly D. Brownell, director of the Rudd Center for Food Policy and Obesity at Yale University, to conclude, "The field is incapable of policing itself."[77]

Exclusive Agreements

Collegiate Cola Wars

Like elementary and high school cafeterias, university campuses have become battlegrounds as the major soft drink companies compete for exclusive access to college students. According to a Coca-Cola spokesperson, campus deals are important because "they help 'brand' students at a point in their lives when they have a lot of years of consuming left to do."[78] Coke and Pepsi pay millions of dollars for sole rights to soda advertising and sales on all university properties—including classrooms, libraries, dorms, cafeterias, offices, sports arenas, performance centers, restaurants, and even golf courses. They also demand benefits such as secrecy clauses and antidisparagement rules that put a lid on cola critics.

Pepsi won out at Penn State, and the university has taken its vow of fidelity to this brand of brown-colored bubbly sugar water quite seriously. In the summer of 2001, a local distributor offered to continue its tradition of donating money and bottled spring water to the Second Mile Golf Classic, a charity event that was held annually at Penn State. The cash was accepted but the water was not. It seems that a strict interpretation of the university's exclusive agreement with Pepsi prohibited even the donation of "not-for-sale" beverages to private charities using Penn State properties.[79]

School Spirit

Following their leaders in business, many universities have in turn forced manufacturers and retailers big and small to enter into exclusive arrangements with the academy. They use their own registered trademarks, patents, and copyrights to generate revenues. The most obvious example of this is the licensing of athletic logos and mascots to manufacturers. With so many teams named after lions and tigers and bears (not to mention gophers and ducks), the granting of exclusive rights to cartoon animals can become absurd in practice (although it has worked well for Disney). Few Penn State fans probably know that the five-toed Nittany Lion paw print—which manufacturers pay the university lavishly to emblazon on everything from sweat pants to dog collars—is "anatomically incorrect." South Carolina's Clemson Tigers own the trademark for a proper four-toe/one-pad paw print, so no other school in the nation is allowed to use it. Penn State's coordinator for licensing programs has instructed all licensees to use either a three-toed or five-toed design.[80]

Although Penn State was forced to defer to Clemson on the paw-print issue, the university has valiantly defended the integrity of its brand against formidable opponents such as . . . Conway Elementary School in Fredericksburg, Virginia. In an incident uncomfortably reminiscent of the Disney Company threatening to sue Florida day-care centers for unauthorized use of Mickey Mouse in murals in 1989[81] or Warner Bros. threatening legal action against the Marx Brothers for a spoof titled *A Night in Casablanca* in 1946,[82] the Collegiate Licensing Council (CLC) ordered Conway to change its new Cougar logo in 2006 on the grounds that it was "confusingly similar" to Penn State's Nittany Lion.[83] Like Groucho Marx, who insisted that "the average movie fan could in time learn to distinguish between Ingrid Bergman and Harpo,"[84] we're pretty sure students enrolled at Conway Elementary know they're not attending Penn State. We were pleased, however, to learn that Conway was given permission to keep the offending logo on a time capsule to be opened in 2010, and to use floor mats with the logo already printed on them until they wore out. In 2012, the litigious university filed a trademark infringement suit against Double Domer Properties and Rent Like a Champion, both of South Bend, Indiana, for using the phrase "PSU Football House Rentals" in their ads for rental housing for Penn State football weekends, on the grounds that it caused "confusion." The defendants responded that use of the ad "in no way competes with the uses of the university [and that] there is little likelihood of confusion."[85] These types of suits become revenue generators for the university.

University of Tennessee fans can at least get the color of their house paint right. The school has lent its name to a particular shade of orange paint being sold at Home Depot stores in Knoxville. A gallon of Tennessee Orange semigloss sold for $25, about twice the cost of regular orange. A shopper at Nebraska's Husker Authentic minimalls could pick up an Adidas sports bra for $26 and a red Cornhuskers football jersey for $200.[86] The really big money, however, is not in schools selling their logos to businesses; profits from such licensing arrangements are generally limited to the purchases of students, alumni, and loyal locals. More and more universities are cashing in by selling their playing fields and student athletes themselves to be used as advertising billboards for corporate sponsors.

Nationally, more than a dozen schools have sold naming rights to new athletic facilities for fees ranging from $300,000 at Wichita State University to $25 million at the University of Maryland. The University of Nebraska touts its scoreboard in the north end zone of Memorial Stadium as an ideal vehicle for corporate messages (a five-year package included one fifteen-second electronic message per quarter, at a rate of $40,000 per year). The University of Texas signed deals with American Airlines, Budweiser, and Southwestern Bell. Its annual football game against the University of Oklahoma has been sponsored by Miller Beer, Mercedes Benz, Bank of America, and Dr. Pepper.[87]

In return for millions of dollars in cash and merchandise from Nike, Reebok, or Adidas, college teams have put their names, logos, and storied traditions on the block. Under the terms of its five-year contract with Nike, for example, the University of Florida received more than $1.2 million a year in cash, $400,000 worth of Nike products, and an additional $150,000 in cash and products. Nike, for its part, gained prized marketing opportunities and access to Florida's coaches and facilities. (Coaches were required "to exercise best efforts to wear Nike products while appearing on any television broadcast, show, or special relating to their activities.") A deal between the University of Texas and Nike provided the school with $850,000 in cash annually and more than $1 million in jackets, jerseys, shoes, and other gear.[88] Even Penn State's austere uniforms—with no player, team, or university name—sport the Nike swoosh.

Nike executive Chris Bevilacqua explained the company's strategy like this: "College sports was essential to Nike. It really hits in the sweet spot of the Nike consumer. It gets them at a time in their lives when they are starting to get their disposable income and they start spending money on these kinds of products." Nike is careful not to include the word "advertising" in its contracts, so schools don't have to pay taxes on the revenue. Nonetheless, the company's intent is clear, as this clause from University of Florida's contract illustrates: "UNIVERSITY acknowledges that one of the principal inducements for NIKE's entrance into this agreement is: the accompanying brand exposure . . . and that such continued exposure is of the essence of this agreement." The contract goes on to say that Nike may slash its payment if the size, color, or location of its logo on team uniforms is changed in any way. If an athlete tapes over the Nike logo on his shoes, it could result in a 10 percent cut of the total base compensation (about $120,000) for the first offense and a 15 percent reduction ($180,000) for the second.[89]

With the ramifications of such exclusive agreements under increasing scrutiny, the National Collegiate Athletic Association (NCAA) commissioned an investigation into the commercialization of college sports.[90] The Knight Commission's report, released in 2001, advocated sweeping changes in the structure of college athletics. If the proposed changes were to be adopted, corporate logos would be eliminated from team uniforms, games would be scheduled independently of the wishes of television networks, and programs that fail to graduate at least 50 percent of their student-athletes would be ineligible for postseason competition.[91]

"I think departments will resist [limiting commercialization] because there's big money involved," said former Penn State president Bryce Jordan, a member of the Knight Commission. "But the position of the Commission was simply, we don't think student-athletes ought to be an advertising medium." If Penn State's response to the report is any indication, then Jordan was right to expect resistance to change. Asked by the *Centre Daily Times* to comment, former head football coach Joe Paterno could not be reached, former men's basketball coach Jerry Dunn declined to comment, and former women's basketball coach Rene Portland fretted that she would have to spend "a big chunk of change" on shoes and uniforms without support from Nike. In a masterful dodge, Penn State President Graham Spanier remarked, "I think the report is very principled, and I support the principles and the spirit, and the motivation for it is worthy. The actual specifics and the implementations, I think you could have a pretty good discussion about." Spanier reminded readers that he has "religiously defended the NCAA's right to limit the size of the logos." As Jordan accurately predicted, "You're not going to see an explosive change."[92] Indeed, the Knight Commission's recommendations were ignored while the hypercommercialism of college sports accelerated.

Private Appropriation of Public Space

Campus Life

Perhaps the most visible evidence of the corporatization of the university is the increasing allocation of university space for businesses to display advertisements, logos, and branded products. Sometimes products are sold or given away, often with strings attached. Sponsored student activities, whether fun or philanthropic, become grand-scale advertising productions and quickly find their way online. Posters appear in dormitories, cafeterias, auditoriums, stadiums, and even lavatories.

When students at Ontario's Trent University went back to school in the fall of 2000, they found their previously ad-free environment covered with Zoom Media posters. Over the summer break, Trent had granted Zoom exclusive advertising rights on campus in exchange for $18,000. The ads were concentrated in hallways, dining areas, and, predominantly, washrooms. According to a company representative, students would enjoy the idea of ads in washrooms, especially since Zoom ads were "funky, trendy and fun."[93] As it turned out, Trent students were not amused. An imaginative group of culture jammers struck back, retouching and covering Zoom ads. They even pasted thirty-five of them on Trent President Bonnie Patterson's large office windows. The university's security force was ordered to patrol restrooms, and for two consecutive weeks the local Crime Stoppers unit featured Zoom vandalism at Trent as the county's "crime of the week."[94]

In another invasive action, Tommy Hilfiger made an appearance at one of Penn State's most hallowed traditions, the Intrafraternity Council–Panhellenic Dance Marathon. The annual THON, now into its fourth decade, raises money for children with cancer through the Four Diamonds Fund. Just before the spring 2000 event, Hilfiger representatives conducted a "student casting call" at a local mall. The company's "stylist extraordinaire" and a group of professional dancers worked with the chosen ones to produce a fashion show designed to lift the spirits of the participants, and of course, to sell designer jeans. The *Centre Daily Times* reported that Tommy Hilfiger himself would deliver a video address to dancers and spectators and "offer the THON experience to supporters outside University Park via his Web site, Tommy.com."[95] The THON has relied on corporate sponsors for donations, but few ask for more than an acknowledgment in the program or a banner on the wall in return.

Hilfiger used the charity event as background for an online advertisement. The students raised more than $3.5 million for cancer that year, a fraction of what Hilfiger spends on guerrilla ad campaigns notorious for packaging popular youth culture, branding it as a lifestyle, and licensing the name to manufacturers of upscale lifestyle goods.

Student Credit

Students are able to buy such products because they have credit cards. Another striking example of the corporate appropriation of university space in the early 2000s was the proliferation of booths, tables, and tents from which vendors could hawk credit cards. Most offered free gifts such as T-shirts, phone cards, and water bottles to students who signed up. First USA offered credit cards to University of Tennessee students at the 2000 opening football game, part of a $14 million deal between the bank and the school. According to Robert Manning, a sociologist at the Rochester Institute of Technology, credit card issuers are hungry to hook college students, who often stay with their first card long after graduation. Two studies—a joint survey by the Education Resources Institution and Institute for Higher Education Policy, and a survey by the firm Student Monitor—found that nearly two-thirds of all college students have at least one credit card. Between 6 and 13 percent have four or more. Almost half of those students got their first credit card during their freshman year. According to a study conducted by Nellie Mae, the student loan provider, the average undergraduate student credit card debt in 2000 was $2,478. Thirteen percent of the students surveyed had balances between $3,000 and $7,000, and 9 percent had even higher ones. The figures for graduate students are even more alarming, with the average debt near $5,000. Twenty percent of graduate students owed between $6,000 and $15,000.[96] Some students used credit cards to make tuition payments, although the maximum interest rate for most federal government–backed student loans at the time was 8.25 percent, less than half that for most credit cards.[97] In Manning's view, "The unrestricted marketing of credit cards on college campuses is so aggressive that it now poses a greater threat than alcohol or sexually transmitted diseases."[98]

MBNA, the largest independent credit card lender in the world, with $62 billion in managed loans, committed $10 million to Penn State to extend and expand its role as exclusive provider of the university's official credit card. Forty percent of the gift was earmarked for an MBNA Career Services Center (which was renamed the Bank of America Career Services Center after BofA acquired MBNA in 2006). The arrangement serves a dual purpose for the bank. First, students become indebted to MBNA, then the career center helps them find jobs so they can make their credit card payments. Students are largely unaware of the high interest rates that come with consumer credit. In a survey conducted by the Public Interest Research Group, students were asked how long it would take to pay off a $1,000 debt at 18 percent interest by making the minimum 3 percent monthly payments. Only 20 percent guessed the correct answer: six years.[99] Credit card companies are no longer permitted to issue cards to applicants younger than twenty-one without an adult cosigner or proof of adequate income, and the tables offering applications and goodies were banned at Penn State. But we don't know many students who don't have a wallet full of them.

Although students may not be fully cognizant of the inflated amount of money they will eventually owe, they are nonetheless aware of their looming credit card and student loan debts. In 2010, the average student loan debt was $25,250 and the unemployment rate for college graduates was 9.1 percent.[100] Along with pressure from parents and peers, these debts increase pressure on students to pursue majors that promise to prepare them for high-paying jobs, regardless of their genuine interests and aspirations. The gravitation of students to corporate vocational prep programs diminishes the vitality of liberal arts and humanities programs. The loss for individual students here is also a loss for the university community and society as a whole.

NO MORE PENCILS, NO MORE BOOKS: HI-TECH/VO-TECH

Manufacturers of new information technologies have been particularly successful at infiltrating public schools and universities. "There's a fervor among educators to embrace the Internet," according to Jeffrey Chester, executive director of the Center for Media Education. "Companies know this, and they've tried to seize control of the technology."[101] The corporate world has skillfully exploited not only the nation's fascination with new technology but also its fear of being without it. A popular metaphor at Penn State likens modern technology to a train. Faculty members are expected to get on the train whether or not it's going their way. This can mean anything from substituting chat rooms for class discussions to offering entire courses online. Those who don't get on the train will be left at the station, and if they try to stand in its way, they'll get run over.

Advertisers have responded to objections to corporate-sponsored technology in the classroom with grim metaphors of their own. In his book *Adbashing: Surviving the Attacks on Advertising*, for example, marketing executive Jack Myers compares schools without state-of-the-art technology to juvenile detention centers:

> The choice we have in this country is for our educational system to join the electronic age and communicate to students in ways they can understand and

to which they can relate. Or our schools can continue to use outmoded forms of communications and become the daytime prisons for millions of young people, as they have become in our inner cities.[102]

But Can He Type?

Such reasoning, as Klein points out, baldly equates corporate access to schools with access to modern technology—and, by extension, to the future itself. New information technologies lent a new urgency to problems caused by the chronic underfunding of public education. Just as schools were facing ever-deeper budget cuts, the costs of delivering a modern education were rising steeply, forcing educators to look to alternative sources for help. Swept up by info-tech hype, schools that could barely afford new textbooks were suddenly expected to provide students with audiovisual equipment, classroom computers, and Internet access. In this context, corporate partnerships and sponsorships came to seem not just attractive but essential, especially in poorer school districts.[103]

This is despite the fact that, as many education experts have pointed out, the pedagogical benefits of technology are dubious at best. Indeed, there is mounting evidence that study habits have suffered since pupils began preferring "the chaos of the web to the drudgery of the library."[104] In the fall of 2000, an organization called the Alliance for Childhood issued a statement calling for a moratorium on the further introduction of computers into elementary schools until their effects on young children have been assessed more carefully. The statement was signed by more than eighty-five experts in fields as varied as psychiatry, education, philosophy, neurology, and nutrition. One of the signers, educational psychologist Jane M. Healy, said she was appalled at the flood of money being allocated to computers in schools at the expense of other programs. "For the sake of technology, schools have cut reading and math specialists, arts, music, phys ed, all the things we have clear evidence that prepare kids for the real world."[105] Even some classroom technology advocates have qualified their claims. John Bosco, a professor at Western Michigan University and chairman of the Consortium for School Networking (a nonprofit group that promotes technology in schools), admitted: "We're beginning to see that it is not magic, and that there are things done in the name of information technology which are either foolish or wasteful."[106]

Teachers and administrators have nonetheless been pressured into believing that they need wireless bells and whistles, and the technology giants have been only too willing to oblige. For example, the *Centre Daily Times* reported, "Students in the Governor's School for Information Technology at Penn State this summer [2000] are experimenting with the newest handheld computers, thanks to donations by two corporations." Palm Inc. and

3Com donated one hundred handheld computers for a group of high-achieving high school juniors to play with during the month-long program, probably just long enough for most of them to want one of their own—at $450 a shot—when the school reclaimed them to lend to the next batch of students.[107] The following year, Palm awarded eighty similar grants nationwide, awards that included a week for teachers at the company's technology training center in San Francisco.[108]

Such corporate donations, endowments, and awards are almost always uncritically reported by local news media. "Penn Staters Tinker with Computers" and "State High Teacher Awarded Palm Grant" were headlines of the articles just mentioned. The unqualified celebration of corporate gifts of technology to schools often leads to sins of omission in the press. For example, a *Centre Daily Times* article titled "Raytheon Grant Helps Endow State High Award" reported that the Raytheon Company's Matching Gifts for Education program awarded $10,000 to the State College Area School District to endow the Superintendent's Award for Educational Innovation. The recipient of the first grant was Bill Hughes, who teaches a technology education class in which sixth graders design, build, and engineer air-power rockets. "The grant was for a timer so we could accurately time the speeds of these [rockets] and take the information and add math lessons to calculate velocity and acceleration," explained Hughes.[109] No mention is made of the fact that Raytheon is a major U.S. defense contractor, or that the goals of the class project parallel those of the National Missile Defense System.

New Information Technologies and the New Global Economy

The symbiotic relationship between the government and big business in creating and serving the technological needs of education is exemplified by the ninety-second annual meeting of the National Governors Association, held in State College in the summer of 2000. The official theme of the conference was "Strengthening the American States in a New Global Economy," and the focus was on new information technologies. Pennsylvania was touted as one of the top eight "cyberstates" in the nation, an honor bestowed by the American Electronics Association. Penn State used the opportunity to introduce its new $41 million School of Information Sciences and Technology.

Town and gown rolled out the red carpet for the governors and their entourages with a gala reception showcasing interactive displays of Pennsylvania's technology initiatives, including the distinction of being the first state to put its World Wide Web address on its license plates. The life of the party was a robotic poodle named Aibo ("pal" in Japanese). The *Centre Daily Times* noted that the $3,000 pet "has its own personality and can be trained like a real dog" thanks to "advanced chip technology." The story was accompanied by a photo of a pretty young representative of the Sony Corporation presenting the "mechanical mutt" to a beaming then governor Tom Ridge.[110]

The focus of the National Governors Association conference on the "New Global Economy," along with the host committee's emphasis on new technologies, points up two poignant ironies. First, the new information technologies that serve as the nerve system of the new global economy have been primarily developed and deployed to serve the needs of big business. Global telecommunications systems have allowed multinational corporations to extend their access to cheaper raw materials and labor, while maintaining centralized control over production and distribution. These same technologies distribute entertainment programming and advertising designed to promote the consumption of mass-produced, brand-name goods—in short, the same old stuff.

Second, although the vendors of new information technologies often purport to be "freeing" us, we are, in fact, increasingly enslaved by their machines. As *Boston Globe* columnist Ellen Goodman writes: "The ability to work anywhere means that you work everywhere. The cell phone that allows you to connect makes it impossible to disconnect. The equipment that makes it possible to do the job at home turns home life into moonlighting."[111] An ad in a United Airlines on-flight magazine even suggests that a good time to check your e-mail might be while sitting on the toilet. It is no surprise that manufacturers of new information technologies have fueled the fear that not being hooked up or plugged in means missing out. Their advertising campaigns seek to cultivate this fear and to establish brand loyalty to the products that assuage it.

In his speech at the National Governors Association meeting, former Federal Reserve Chairman Alan Greenspan challenged the nation's governors to "develop an American work force with lifelong conceptual skills as well as technical expertise and to devise public-private partnerships to meaningfully integrate technology into schools."[112] According to the *Centre Daily Times*, Greenspan's message was simple: Those who commit to training workers, supporting innovation, and having a flexible labor market will be prime locations for firms at the cutting edge of technology. In other words, the successful twenty-first-century university will attend to the business of producing information technologists at the behest of global capitalists, with little or no concern for the nature of the information they are processing.

Technology, Teaching, and Taxes

Both the government and big business have worked to foster the high-tech aspirations of school administrators, teachers, students, and parents—and both have fueled their fears of being left at the virtual station or locked behind bars in the unwired classroom. In the 1990s, a growing number of politicians made "a computer on every desk" a rallying cry. Toward the end of his presidency, Bill Clinton trumpeted his goal of "connecting every classroom in America to the Internet by the year 2000."[113] However, technology in the classroom is meaningless if schools don't have the human resources to utilize it effectively. First and foremost, this means the ability to hire teachers who are trained not only to operate new information technologies but also to think with them. The difference is crucial. Most often students in poorer school districts are taught data processing, while their peers in richer school districts are taught data programming.

Education funding shortages have long been a problem in the United States due to the unequal distribution of tax money for school systems and the contradictory way the public thinks about taxes. The largest portion of public school revenues is generated from local property and income taxes. This naturally creates large gaps between rich and poor school districts that are based on where the students live. Although everyone wants their children to have access to new technologies and the skills to work creatively with them, those living in poor neighborhoods cannot afford it and those living in richer neighborhoods don't want to pay for it. Both groups tend to view taxes as an infringement upon their right to consume rather than as a way of sharing resources to provide services and build communities.

The broader issue here is whether the tax system is fair and just in its collection and redistribution of tax revenues. This requires informed citizens who can see beyond the bottom line on their checkbooks and credit card statements each month. How we allocate our tax dollars has long-term ramifications. In the late 1970s, few Californians probably realized that they were setting into motion the decline of the best state university system in the country when they voted to cap annual increases in property taxes with the passage of Proposition 13. Voters in Colorado Springs stopped approving tax increases for education in the mid-1970s. By 1989, the school district was $12 million in debt, and in 1993, it became the first in the nation to "sell for cash something we always had, but never knew we had," as Superintendent Kenneth Burnley put it: access to students.[114] Voters in the state of Washington failed to pass a tax increase for Seattle's schools in 1999—just months after the approval of $336 million for a new baseball stadium for the Mariners. Seattle education funding advocates argued that "continued public spending on stadiums—combined with populist-styled initiatives to roll back car registration fees and other state taxes—could have a ripple effect on education."[115] In Pennsylvania in 2002, both the Republican and Democratic gubernatorial candidates advocated the installation of slot machines at the state's racetracks to fund education. In 2007, Pennsylvania's first stand-alone casino opened.

In a democracy, the education of all children is the responsibility of all citizens, but tax dollars earmarked for education need not be spent on new information technologies. Indeed, they might better be used to revive devastated music and art programs. In a 1995 essay, Neil Postman marveled at our blind worship of technology. He likened it to a religion in that we believe in it, rely on it, feel bereft when denied access to it, and alter our lifestyles, schedules, habits, and relationships to accommodate it—even though, for most people, it works in mysterious ways. "It is strange," Postman wrote, "indeed shocking—that with the twenty-first century so close, we can still talk of new technologies as if they were unmixed blessings—gifts, as it were, from the gods."[116]

Steven Manning has likened sponsored technology to a "digital Trojan horse," a beguiling gift that brings with it a corporate invasion.[117] Educators and administrators in beleaguered public schools, as well as those in wealthier districts, accept such gifts from information technology firms all too readily. In exchange, school officials offer up captive students to corporations seeking to develop lifelong loyalties to expensive and instantly outmoded products in a new group of consumers. At the same time, they give corporations the right to determine what kinds of intellectual and creative endeavors are encouraged and rewarded in the classroom.

CONCLUSION

At the turn of the twentieth century, institutional economist Thorstein Veblen argued that far from engaging in disinterested higher learning, American universities were constituted to serve corporations and other vested interests. The claim seemed heretical at the time. At the turn of the twenty-first century, what was once a hidden curriculum, the subordination of higher education to the needs of capital, has become an open, frank policy of public and private education. Today, as Aronowitz writes, "Leaders of higher education wear the badge of corporate servants proudly."[118]

In 1952, historian Richard Hofstadter wrote: "It has been the fate of American higher education to develop in a pre-eminently businesslike culture. . . . Education is justified apologetically as a useful instrument in attaining other ends: it is good for business or professional careers. Rarely, however, does anyone presume to say that it is good for man."[119] Half a century later, Hofstadter's observations seem truer than ever. Successful business dealings have become not only the means with which education is provided, but the end as well. The idea that the ultimate goal of education is to train students to serve and succeed in business was taken to its logical extreme in the form of elementary charter business schools designed to turn out junior MBAs. In these proposed schools, according to the *Utne Reader*, kids would wear office attire and sport business-style haircuts. Reading material would consist of resumes, memos, and business reports. Students would be encouraged to carry briefcases rather than backpacks.

These critics focus on the crucial role education plays in reproducing the labor force by giving students the skills necessary to become good workers. Now, with the commercialization of schools and the commodification of students as audiences, the educational system itself has been transformed into a profit-making industry. This makes it necessary for school administrators to choose between the fundamental principles of education and the logic of business. Some have already made that choice. As University of Florida President John V. Lombardi declared, "We have taken the great leap forward. . . . 'Let's pretend we're a corporation.'"[120] Rather than a makeover, Wall Street would prefer a takeover. Writing for the *New York Times*, Arthur Levine, president of Teachers College at Columbia University, recounts the following warning, issued to him by a corporate entrepreneur: "You know, you're in an industry which is worth hundreds of billions of dollars, and you have a reputation for low productivity, high cost, bad management and no use of technology. You're going to be the next health care: a poorly managed nonprofit industry which was overtaken by the profit-making sector."[121] One could argue that education need only be seen as a failed industry if educators insist on seeing it as an industry in the first place. Perhaps the point is that under capitalism, it can be nothing else. The barbarians have already crashed the gates of the ivory tower.

8

Media and Democracy: Taking It to the Streets

In this book, we have raised serious concerns about the problematic—indeed antithetical—nature of the relationship between democracy and capitalism, particularly with regard to corporate media. When we began writing the first edition of *Big Media, Big Money* at the turn of the twenty-first century, we were inspired by an extraordinary wave of impassioned protests against global capitalism—demonstrations that were staged and struggled and sometimes squashed but never silenced at meetings of the rich and powerful around the world. There is a long history of such struggles, of course, but this round began with massive protests at the World Trade Organization (WTO) meeting in Seattle in the early winter of 1999. An estimated fifty to seventy thousand people marched through the streets of the city, protesting the WTO's attempts to advance global capitalism by "lowering trade barriers." The protesters came under a number of different organizational umbrellas but were unified in their conviction that the policies of the WTO enabled the superrich and powerful to exploit workers, trample human rights, squeeze Third World countries, and destroy the environment—all in pursuit of obscene profits. Over the next two years, scores of protests against global capital were mounted at similar meetings in the United States and abroad. Many participants credited Seattle with tapping into a widely held and deeply felt sense of outrage at "a grotesque and dangerous polarization and inequality around the world."[1]

By the time we went to press with the first edition in early 2002, the Twin Towers had fallen, the United States had invaded Afghanistan, and the Bush administration seemed to have risen from the ashes. In his 2002 State of the Union address, Bush declared that "our war against terror is only beginning" and vowed to take on "regimes that sponsor terror," including an "axis of evil" comprised of Iraq, Iran, and North Korea (none of which had anything to do with 9/11). In his 2003 State of the Union address, Bush raised the issue of weapons of mass destruction (WMDs) and claimed there was evidence of Iraq attempting to obtain uranium from Africa. The United States staged a preemptive attack on Iraq in March 2003, without the support of the United Nations, and declared its mission accomplished the following May. There were no WMDs, no Al Qaeda, and certainly no Osama bin Laden (wrong country). The media, notably the *New York Times* and Fox News, are now widely seen as complicit in the rush for vengeance. By 2011, public opinion polls in the U.S. had shifted against the military intervention in Afghanistan, prompting President Obama to announce that most troops would be withdrawn by 2014.

On January 28, 2008, President Bush delivered his final State of the Union address, beginning a countdown, as a popular bumper sticker proclaimed, to "the end of an error." (Calendars and clocks promising to take Bush-weary citizens "through 2008 to the glorious end" were also abundant on Amazon.com at the time.) In the last years of his presidency, Bush's approval ratings sank first to personal and then to historic lows. Standing before what AP correspondent Terence Hunt described as "a hostile, Democratic-led Congress eager for the end of his term," Bush urged the nation "to persevere against gnawing fears of recession and stay patient with the long, grinding war in Iraq."[2] With his approval rating near its all-time low, Hunt wrote, "Bush lacked the political clout to push bold ideas and he didn't try." Finally, "a major challenge for Bush in his address was simply being heard when many Americans already are looking beyond him to the next president."[3]

The 2008 U.S. presidential election was a historic one by any standard. For the first time, the Democratic candidates for president included a woman, New York Senator Hillary Rodham Clinton, and an African American, Illinois Senator Barack Obama. (The Republican candidate, Arizona Senator John McCain, was not generally seen as a traditional representative of the GOP, either.) Obama sailed to victory on a wave of "hope" for "change" and was sworn into office in January 2009. But by 2010, Obama's approval ratings had also dropped sharply. Despite his obvious intelligence, acknowledged eloquence, and apparent integrity, Obama failed to achieve many of his lofty goals early on. To many, he seemed shackled by a sharply divided legislature beholden to special interests. In 2010, the president of the United States was said to be "the world's most powerful prisoner." And protests by the people continued.

In this chapter, we offer a flashback to the protests of the early 2000s, with particular attention to their coverage in (and containment by) the mainstream media. We then flash forward to snapshots of more recent demonstrations, again examining the ways in which they were reported by the media. President Obama is said to have brushed off protests against the G20 summit in Pittsburgh in 2009, noting that they were mild compared with some in the past at international gatherings. "I fundamentally disagree with their view that the free market is the source of all ills," he said. "Many of the protests are just directed generically at capitalism."[4] Writing in the midst of the worst economic recession since the Great Depression of the 1930s, he never reconsidered his stance.

FLASHBACK: LIKE IT'S 1999

Protests against the WTO meeting in Seattle in 1999 effectively shut down the talks, as thousands of police and National Guard troops arrested hundreds of protesters amid vague reports of black-masked anarchist provocateurs. Peaceful protesters were showered with pepper spray and pummeled with rubber bullets. Seattle's chief of police resigned amid charges of incompetence and brutality.[5] The mainstream media quickly christened the events the Battle of Seattle. The lead story in the *New York Times* the following day cynically reported that "what was planned as the biggest American demonstration yet against global trade . . . turned into a burst of window-breaking and looting," a "surge of violence that ended in a civil emergency. . . . It died out with the image of a grinning young man in a Gap sweatshirt trying to cart off a satellite dish from a Radio Shack store."[6] Meanwhile, alternative news sources denounced the mainstream media's "prattle on Seattle." As one participant observer told *Z Magazine*, "Most of what has been written is so inaccurate that I can't decide if the reporters in question should be charged with conspiracy or simply incompetence. . . . The police, in defending their 'mishandling' of the situation, have said they were 'not prepared for the violence.' In reality, they were unprepared for the nonviolence."[7]

Over the next two years, scores of protests against global capitalism were mounted at similar meetings in the United States and abroad, including Washington, D.C., New York, Philadelphia, London, and Paris, as well as Porto Alegre (Brazil), Madrid and Barcelona (Spain), Genoa (Italy), Salzburg (Austria), Davos (Switzerland), and Göteborg (Sweden). In 2001, the *Irish Times* reported, "Ever since antiglobalization groups staged protests at a meeting of the World Trade Organization in Seattle in 1999, major gatherings of world leaders have become targets for increasingly violent demonstrations."[8] In "previews" of a gathering of the "Group of Eight" (G8) in Genoa that summer, the Italian media routinely referred to the expected protesters as "Il Popolo di Seattle" (Seattle People).[9] As a protester at the 2002 World Economic Forum (WEF) in New York said, "Seattle was definitely a wake-up call."[10] Indeed, by that time, the *New York Times* had its protest coverage down to a neat formula: The Meeting, The Streets, The Protestors, The Police.[11]

WHEN THE ELITE MEET

The mainstream media tend to refer to global trade meetings variously (and sometimes euphemistically) as gatherings, conferences, summits, conventions, forums, and retreats. (The retreat tag was most appropriate to the 2001 G8 Summit, where delegates were scuttled off to boats moored in the Port of Genoa to avoid protesters.) News coverage of most of the meetings tended to focus on eruptions of violence in the demonstrations outside, rather than on the policies debated within. When the media did discuss the meetings, they often treated them as celebrity events or personality parades, focusing on who was invited and who was not, who accepted and who declined. For example, "34 heads of state from the Americas (all except Fidel Castro) declared their commitment to democracy" at the Summit of the Americas in Quebec.[12] They also tended to reduce profound political and economic differences to the level of individual quarrels or conflicting personalities: "The 'BB' (Berlusconi/Bush) factor suggests Genoa is likely to be anything but peaceful."[13] An abbreviated listing of some of the most notable meetings, all of which drew significant protests, attests to our characterization of antiglobalization and indeed anticapitalism as a movement.

Several took place in the United States within months of the aborted WTO meeting in Seattle. In April 2000, representatives of the International Monetary Fund (IMF) and the World Bank met in Washington, D.C. Tens of thousands of peaceful protesters gathered to greet them. Four hundred people were arrested, mostly on charges of creating a nuisance, disturbing the peace, or parading without a permit. In July 2000, President Bill Clinton and Federal Reserve Chairman Alan Greenspan addressed a meeting of the National Governors Association in State College, Pennsylvania. Hundreds of students at Penn State University, citizens of the surrounding county, and supporters from across the state protested. Fifteen people were arrested, including a handful of students who hung an anti–global capital banner from a classroom building balcony across the street from a Penn State venue where the governors gathered. Many participants said they planned to continue on to Philadelphia the following August for demonstrations at the Republican National Convention. There, tens of thousands of protesters were met by heavily armed police, some of whom had infiltrated protest coalitions by posing as activists in the weeks before. More than three hundred people were arrested.

In April 2001, President Bush attended the Summit of the Americas to negotiate the proposed Free Trade Area of the Americas (FTAA). Delegates convened high on the hill of old walled Quebec, which was further buttressed by a 2.5-mile chain-link fence and six thousand police officers. The FTAA was designed to follow the North American Free Trade Agreement (NAFTA) in giving corporations the power to overturn laws and collect damages from governments if they believe a government policy threatens future profits. According to David Moberg of *In These Times*, "It is also likely to give corporations new power to attack public services, forcing deregulation, privatization and marketization of the public sphere." Tens of thousands of people protested, successfully bringing down the chain-link "wall of shame" but failing to disrupt the meetings.[14]

Bush embarked on a European tour the following summer, where thousands gathered to protest his policies on missile defense, global warming, and capital punishment. Many top European Union (EU) officials supported them.[15] In June 2001, the EU held a summit in Göteborg, Sweden, in an effort to keep their plans for expansion on track despite Irish opposition. (Earlier that month, Ireland was the only EU member to reject the Treaty of Nice, a complex document designed to open the door for a dozen new members. Ireland was also the only member nation that allowed its citizens to vote on the issue.[16]) The summit drew an estimated 25,000 protesters, including environmentalists and antiglobalization activists. Clashes with police left forty-three people hospitalized, including three with gunshot wounds after police opened fire. The Associated Press reported, "The mayhem forced the EU leaders to change their dinner plans from a posh restaurant to the conference center where the summit was held behind police barricades."[17] Later that month, thirty-two protesters were injured at an anti–World Bank rally in Barcelona.

In July 2001, in Salzburg, Austria, hundreds of protesters marched on the European Economic Summit, sponsored by the World Economic Forum (WEF) and chaired by billionaire financier George Soros (one of those who "slid" from number 23 on the *Forbes 400* list of the richest people in America in 2001 with $6.9 billion, to number 33 in 2007 with $8.8 billion[18]). The protesters gathered at the local Communist Party headquarters, carried communist hammer-and-sickle flags, and chanted, "Our world is not for sale, put the bankers into jail!" They were turned away by five thousand police "on duty to make sure mayhem doesn't erupt in Salzburg, the hometown of Wolfgang Amadeus Mozart."[19] Later that month, the G8 convened in Genoa, Italy. Leaders of the world's eight richest nations (the United States, Canada, Germany, Japan, Russia, France, Italy, and Britain) gathered behind a steel cordon "beset by political and economic worries and ringed by protesters determined to drown out their annual summit."[20] Estimates of the number of police officers ranged from 15,000 to 60,000. Navy frogmen, army sharpshooters, twelve air force helicopters, and specialists in nuclear, germ, and chemical warfare were reportedly deployed. The two thousand delegates and six thousand journalists huddled in boats on the harbor, where, as an Irish reporter noted, "we can all sleep easy, safe in the knowledge that U.S. aircraft carrier *Enterprise*, not to mention various Italian navy boats," will be on patrol nearby.[21] There were 200,000 protesters.

Finally, the World Economic Forum, which had for thirty years convened annually at a ski resort in Davos, Switzerland, was moved to New York City in February 2002. Founder Klaus Schwab made a highly publicized pretense of supporting the city in the wake of attacks on the World Trade Center, but in fact the Swiss government had balked at the cost of providing security for the event, which had begun to draw increasing numbers of protesters. United Nations Secretary General Kofi Annan, Bishop Desmond Tutu, and U2's Bono joined elite leaders of Big Business at the meetings. Serge Schmemann, who covered the meeting for the *New York Times*, charged that the annual event had been "portrayed by outsiders as a gathering of the world's richest and most powerful men shaping a global agenda from which the weak and poor were excluded." As an insider, Schmemann got the impression "of an elite struggling to comprehend the increasingly threatening forces of antiglobalization, militant Islam, terrorism and poverty, forces that gained an immediacy in the inferno of Sept. 11."[22] Police estimated that 7,000 people protested, while demonstration organizers said the number was closer to 25,000. Two hundred people were arrested. Perhaps the most organized protest against the World Economic Forum in New York City was a larger parallel gathering in Porto Alegre, Brazil.

Annan, who addressed both gatherings, reminded those in New York that the title of the Brazilian conference, "World Social Forum," was intended as a criticism of theirs. They are "implying that you are interested only in economics, or in profit, and that you do not care about the social effects of your economic activities," he said. Annan cited a number of channels through which corporations could contribute, including the Global Health Initiative and the United Nations Development Program. In attendance at the forum, Microsoft Chairman Bill Gates (number 1 on the 2001 *Forbes 400*, with $54 billion) agreed that the question of "whether the rich world is giving back what it should in the developing world" was a "legitimate" one. David H. Komansky, chairman of Merrill Lynch (number 25 on the 2001 *Fortune 500* list of America's largest corporations, with revenues of $44.8 billion), remarked, "We're trained as businessmen, but we're being asked to pass judgment on the moral and ethical value of these [development] projects."[23]

As the protests of the people in the streets grew louder, global capitalists were continually forced to defend themselves. As David Moberg predicted, it would become "difficult for any politician to talk about global economics without addressing links to labor rights, human rights, food supplies, and the protection of both consumers and the environment."[24] The protests themselves were acts of communication, of course, but since most people learned about them through news reports, our focus will be on how the issues that inspired them and the events surrounding them were reported by corporate media and countered by independent media.

THE ISSUES: WHAT ARE WE FIGHTING FOR?

When thousands of protesters marched on Washington to protest the 2000 meeting of the IMF, the mainstream media—always happy to denounce communism and, more recently, socialism—had trouble even coughing up the word "capitalism," preferring the related but far more vague and euphemistic "globalization." When journalists did feel the need to offer some explanation for the protests, they did so in decidedly dismissive tones: "Parading under an anti-globalization banner, the protesters believe that the operating rules of the WTO, IMF and World Bank are rigged in favor of wealthy multinational corporations at the expense of poor people, labor unions and the environment."[25] All evidence supports these claims. Predictably, however, the news media either blurred or simply buried the issues at stake—the "beliefs" that compelled hundreds of thousands of people to "parade" for causes in which most of them had no personal stake.

The Associated Press crowed when animal rights activists protested the Washington IMF meeting in a peaceful but pungent act of civil disobedience, and the *State College (Pa.) Centre Daily Times* reprinted the story. The headline read, "PETA Dumps Four Tons of Manure near World Bank," and the article beneath it described how the "Department of Public Works carried away the pile in a city vehicle escorted by a police van with siren blaring and lights flashing."[26] The full name of the activist group and a vague reference to their criticisms of the IMF were banished to the last paragraph of the column and topped off with their punishment: "The driver and passenger in the manure truck were from People for the Ethical Treatment of Animals, which is protesting World Bank Agricultural Policies. One was charged with crossing a police line, the other with illegal dumping."[27] The article did not bother to explain that PETA objects to the raising of animals for food—to be processed and packaged for the likes of McDonald's and Taco Bell—not only on the grounds that it is unethical to eat meat, but also because it is destructive to the environment.

The IMF and the World Bank aren't regularly the subjects of top news stories, and these and other protesters helped make them front-page news. Lacking, however, was any history to help readers put things in perspective. The IMF and the World Bank were formed in the late 1940s and presented as a means of achieving modest financial safeguards in a world reeling from war. They came into the spotlight of international economic policy planning in the 1980s, when they stepped in to stave off global financial collapse by lending money to Third World countries that had borrowed heavily during the 1970s. By utilizing their influence over international lending practices, these organizations imposed a blueprint for economic and social policies to be followed by debtor countries around the world. The basic goal of international finance capital has been to make neoliberalism the economic policy of necessity at the level of the nation-state, which includes market liberalization, export-oriented production, and massive privatization of state-owned industries. At the same time, the austerity plans promoted by the World Bank and the IMF ravaged the social welfare state with the effect of pulling the floor out from under the poorest segments of a nation's people. Consequently, the gaps between the rich and poor widened significantly as the gains of popular social movements of the 1960s and 1970s were reversed.[28]

Furthermore, the internationalist sectors of domestic capital have become increasingly integrated into the global capitalist economy, leading them to identify more and more with the interests of international capitalists and less and less with those of their own national populations. Free trade agreements such as NAFTA and FTAA; global organizations such as the WTO, IMF, and World Bank; congregations of global business and government elites such as the G8 and WEF; and an increasingly interventionist United Nations and increasingly militaristic United States acting as a global police force all serve as pillars of the "New World Order" in which capital reigns supreme.[29] As Moberg explains,

> The long-standing issues posed by capital's easy mobility—such as job loss, environmental damage, economic insecurity and inequality, sweatshops, 'structural adjustment' squeezes, and threats to farmers and food consumers from agribusiness—have not disappeared, but they are increasingly being consolidated within a broader framework of debate.

The issues are as much political as economic: the human rights of individuals against unfettered freedom of capital, democracy against corporate power and privilege, values of solidarity and justice against a totally marketized society.[30]

MEDIA COVERAGE: STORMY WEATHER

Media coverage of protests at most of the global trade meetings followed an all-too-familiar pattern, with the initial focus on disruption followed by an emphasis on the restoration of order. Conflict, of course, is an essential news value, and the media could not ignore the street battles and larger challenges to the existing economic and political order that the various protest participants represented. The specter of violence haunted journalists even before the street fighting broke out at the WTO meeting in Seattle, because journalists tend to assume that whenever people get together for a political cause or set up a picket line, mob behavior will ensue. This assumption is not without cause, considering the history of massacres of strikers by company guards, the shooting of students by the National Guard at Kent State and Jackson State universities, or the clubbing of protestors by police at the 1968 Democratic Convention in Chicago.[31] Violence also helps sell newspapers and boost broadcast ratings, and often, as in the case of media coverage of Seattle, it becomes a dominant theme.

Media owners and workers themselves, from publishers down to reporters, are deeply integrated into the existing order and therefore have a profound stake in the status quo. Media owners want to amass wealth and exert influence; journalists need to pay off mortgages and car loans. The owners know for sure that they will benefit from the policies of organizations such as the IMF and WTO; most journalists probably assume they will, too. Hence, like the National Guard in Seattle, the media help to restore order after a disturbance of the peace. Journalistic practices that serve this function include symbolically dividing and conquering protesters by casting them as fractious and quarrelsome, and either vilifying demonstrators as violent or dismissing them as failures. Police officers and officials, on the other hand, are generally cast as highly trained professionals doing a difficult and dangerous job or as benign father figures protecting the people. They are also unapologetically celebrated as valiant protectors of private property, which is, of course, the central role of the state under capitalism.

Disturbing the Peace

A Motley Crew

One way the media sought to symbolically contain the many protests from Seattle in 1999 to New York in 2002 was by depicting antiglobalization activists as a fractious and disparate lot with too many different causes and internal conflicts to sustain a unified movement. Writing in the *New York Times*, for example, Thomas L. Friedman described the WTO protesters as "a Noah's Ark of flat-earth advocates, protectionist trade unions and yuppies looking for their 1960s fix."[32] The *Philadelphia Inquirer* claimed the protesters had "a stew of grievances so confusing that they drowned any hope of broad public support," while *U.S. News* dismissed them as "all-purpose agitators."[33] When the WTO meeting was shut down, ABC's Peter Jennings remarked that "the thousands of demonstrators will go home, or on to some other venue where they'll try to generate attention for whatever cause that moves them."[34]

Such divisive descriptions and predictions may have begun with Seattle, but they persisted in press coverage of antiglobalization protests even as the movement gained momentum and solidarity in the following years. As organizers prepared for protests at the GOP Convention in Philadelphia, for example, the Associated Press reported, "With so many issues apparently vying for attention, there is concern that the demonstrations either will be misconstrued by journalists or will not have enough participants for the message to be heard at all."[35] As the WEF in New York was wind-ing down, the *New York Times* reported, "The collection of causes and protesters was wide: groups as disparate as Save the Redwoods/Boycott the Gap Campaign, the Anti-Capitalist Convergence, Queers for Racial and Economic Justice, the Pagan Cluster and even the Earth and Animal Liberation Coalition attended."[36] The *Irish Times* characterized G8 protest-ers in Genoa as follows: "Coming from all over Europe, Africa, Australia, India and South America, the ill-defined 'Seattle People' range from hard-line Marxists to Catholic Church groups, passing through anarchist centres along the way."[37] Only occasionally were such descriptions followed by an admission that the protesters "seemed unified by opposition to what they viewed as Bush's American imperialism"[38] or that they "seemed united by a sense that many world problems can be traced to a profit-hungry corporate elite."[39]

The Specter of Violence

Even before the WTO meeting in Seattle began, the *New York Times* was reporting that police officials in the city feared "some violence." In one reporter's words, "The meeting has become ground zero for anyone with a complaint about the world economy."[40] The day after the meeting con-vened, the *State College (Pa.) Centre Daily Times* printed a small Associated Press item on page A4 reporting that the opening activities had been de-layed due to a bomb search. The remainder of the article focused on various protest actions and a small number of arrests.[41] The *New York Times* buried news of the meeting on page A14 in a short article headlined "Trade Talks Start in Seattle Despite a Few Disruptions."[42] The next day, 1 December 1999, the *Centre Daily Times* front-page headline read "WTO Protests Turn Violent." The story was accompanied by three color AP photos of police spraying pepper gas on groups of protesters, a longhaired man rubbing his teary eyes, and a woman with blood running down her face.[43]

The *New York Times* front-page headline that day declared, "National Guard Is Called to Quell Trade-Talk Protests." The story appeared above a photo of police in Darth Vader–like riot gear drowning protesters in a haze of tear gas.[44] Network television news programs that evening showed video footage of a protester being clubbed and then shot with a rubber bul-let at close range. The images belied the text, which spoke little of police misconduct until it officially became "news" when Seattle's chief of police resigned the following week. The larger point here is that the WTO talks themselves—at which a handful of rich and powerful individuals gathered to set government and business trade policies affecting the lives of billions of people throughout the world—weren't front-page news until the protests against them turned violent.

Early media coverage of the protests against the meetings of the IMF in Washington, D.C., was also haunted by the specter of violence. Indeed, the media's pre-rally coverage seemed to serve as a justification for police brutality. "Washington Braces for IMF Protesters," a typical Associated Press story carried by the *Centre Daily Times* announced. Charles Ramsey, chief of Washington's Metropolitan Police Department, was widely quoted: "They ain't burning our city like they did Seattle. They didn't know what to expect in Seattle."[45] Ten days before the IMF meetings, an Associated Press story warned: "The protest groups on the streets as the World Trade Organization meetings collapsed in a cloud of tear gas in Seattle are taking aim at an even bigger target: the April 16–17 meetings of the world's largest multinational lending agencies."[46]

When the meetings convened and the marches set forth, a large, boldface headline read: "Trade Protest Roils Capital."[47] The choice of words here is rich. According to Webster, *roil* is a verb meaning "to stir up, make turbid, irritate or vex." Capital can be used as a noun to denote either "a city serving as a seat of government" or "the owners of wealth," or as an adjective meaning "forfeiture of life." The firearm metaphor (protesters "taking aim") was apparently seen by the media as an appropriate way to describe the goals of opponents of global capital—a far cry from news coverage of the Million Mom March for gun control the following May, which was described as a "personal statement" for which protesters "sold muffins for bus fare."[48] Unlike the moms, protesters against the IMF and the World Bank were described as "swarms" who "raged" and "clogged" the streets of the capital.[49] As an *In These Times* commentator put it, "The news media, frustrated at the lack of images of violence and destruction, took vengeance in the only way they know how: They declared the event a victory for police."[50]

Related to the media's focus on violence as a strategy for containing protests is their emphasis on failure when violence doesn't occur. As the mainstream media reported, when protesters in Seattle shut down the WTO meetings, they failed to remain peaceful, and when protesters in Washington, D.C., remained peaceful, they failed to shut down the IMF meetings. The headline of a Knight Ridder story on the IMF meeting carried by the *Centre Daily Times*, for example, announced: "Protesters March, Fail to Block World Finance Meeting."[51] An Associated Press report the next day appeared under the banner: "IMF Protesters Try—and Fail—to Shut Down Meetings."[52]

The *Centre Daily Times*, which was owned by Knight-Ridder at the time, adopted the failure theme in its coverage of the IMF meeting, publishing a color Associated Press photo of Washington cops in riot gear captioned, "Thousands of marchers failed to stop world finance leaders from meeting." The failure theme was then repeated in the *Centre Daily Times* local coverage of protests against the U.S. National Governors Association meeting in State College the following July. For example, a front-page article about an organizational meeting held by a local activist group, Redirection2000, was headlined, "Protest Preparation Fails to Draw Crowd."[53] As Yale anthropology professor David Graeber wrote for *In These Times*, "If the police manage not to run amok, but are calculating in their application of brutality in repressing constitutional rights, they win, and the newspapers will praise them; if the protesters fail to run amok, they lose."[54]

Restoring Order

Highly Trained Professionals

One media strategy for restoring order is to focus on the police as highly trained and disciplined professionals whose difficult job is to keep the peace and protect the people by outwitting protesters. This strategy figured heavily in coverage of security at the IMF talks in Washington, D.C., in the wake of the police debacle in Seattle,[55] and it continued in coverage of the WEF meeting in New York. The journalists covering the police beat for the *New York Times*, William K. Rashbaum and Al Baker, had high praise for the strategic planning of the force: "Using a combination of intelligence, a large deployment of police officers and careful planning, the department seemed to be everywhere at all times—and, much to the chagrin of the protesters, seemed to be able to anticipate their every move."[56] Rashbaum and Baker commended the cops for claiming the streets first, flooding the area around the Waldorf-Astoria Hotel with thousands of officers, surrounding demonstrators with police motorcycles, and monitoring protesters with television cameras mounted high above the Waldorf and on a police helicopter.[57]

When the media departed from their representation of police as security strategists, it was usually to grace the long arm of the law with a firm but gentle father's hand. The police were often depicted in the press as benign parental figures, protecting citizens from protesters and protesters from themselves. For example, the Associated Press reported that Terry Gainer, executive assistant chief of police in Washington, D.C., told demonstrators to "give yourselves a hand" as his heavily armed force "orchestrated a good-natured arrest of some 400 demonstrators" who had "failed to shut down the two days of meetings of the World Bank and International Monetary Fund."[58] Gainer reportedly gave protest organizer Mary Bull flowers before placing her under arrest.[59] Washington, D.C., Police Chief Charles Ramsey, quoted before the IMF meeting as warning, "They ain't burning our city like they did Seattle," was quoted afterward as saying that most of the demonstrators were "just kids with a cause."[60] According to the *New York Times*, "As the demonstrations ended, both sides claimed a kind of victory and even a certain grudging mutual respect." Police Chief Ramsey declared it "a win-win for everybody."[61]

Coverage of New York police at the World Economic Forum meeting sometimes took on softer tones as well. (New York police officers, after all, had become heroes after September 11.) Even Rashbaum and Baker, fond of military metaphors, opted for allusions to baseball and dance to describe their performance: "Like a fastball pitcher brushing back a batter, the Police Department staked out a claim to its home plate—the streets of New York City—before the World Economic Forum even began, with a carefully choreographed strategy that officials say helped keep the peace by keeping protesters off balance." Rashbaum admitted that the police "were not without critics" and quoted Leslie Brody, a protest volunteer from the National Lawyers Guild, for journalistic balance. Brody criticized the police as if they were overly stern parents scolding mischievous children too harshly: "These are kids who wanted to act out in a creative way, and I think early on they were tagged for dressing or looking differently."[62]

Protecting Private Property

Another media strategy for restoring order is to shift the focus away from political and economic issues, and even from human pain and suffering, to destruction and protection of property. The *New York Times* coverage of the Seattle protests centered on "anarchists" and "vandals" who ran "uninterrupted . . . smashing windows, spray-painting walls and tossing newspaper boxes and garbage cans into the streets."[63] In fact, the map of "Seattle's Violent Scene" published in the *New York Times* belies U.S. government and Big Media claims that the attacks on property were committed by vandals or anarchists in wanton acts of looting and destruction.[64] The actions of the "Black Bloc" in Seattle were anything but random, as David Graeber of *In These Times* points out.[65] Their targets were carefully selected and represented an attack on the central icons being protected and promoted by what has been referred to as the "World Trademark Organization."

The targets included the storefronts of such brand-name operations as Old Navy, Gap, Nordstrom, Banana Republic, Niketown, Levi's, McDonald's, Starbucks, Warner Brothers, and (the aptly named) Planet Hollywood. Rather than exploring whether there may have been a method behind this "anarchy," the media restored order by signaling customers that all was clear and encouraging them to come back downtown to finish their Christmas shopping. Retailers offered free coffee and free parking along with the usual generous "discounts." With the "anarchists" contained, the National Guard went home while the media continued to restore order.[66]

A week after the protests, the *Centre Daily Times* ran an Associated Press story on the resignation of Seattle's chief of police, referring to him as the "first casualty" of the Battle of Seattle. Civic leaders argued that the police department had not prepared sufficient force and merchants claimed they had suffered nearly $20 million in property damage and lost sales. So Seattle's police chief, who was planning to retire anyway, was offered up as a sacrifice to the media, this time shifting blame from a rogue group to an incompetent individual but still with no significant discussion of the essential systemic issues prompting the protesters' passion.

FLASH FORWARD: HERE WE GO AGAIN

Disturbing the Peace

In September 2009, a decade after the Battle in Seattle, the Group of Twenty (G20) gathered in Pittsburgh, Pennsylvania, to discuss global economics. The "packed agenda" included proposals to "raise capital requirements for financial institutions, rein in executive compensation and reduce imbalances between shop-till-you-drop countries like the United States and export behemoths like China, Germany and Japan."[67] Critics complained that it was unclear whether the Obama administration supported free trade or protectionism. The effects of globalization on the environment, as well as concerns over the proliferation of nuclear weapons, were debated. So it's no surprise that the summit attracted a diverse group of demonstrators. "To a certain degree," according to Mac Lojowsky, "some of the protesters and activists played into their mainstream media assigned roles."[68] It is nonetheless disappointing that the media once again chose to focus on skirmishes between protesters and police, rather than the issues they came to debate.

A Motley Crew

Although there were far fewer protesters at the G20 meeting in Pittsburgh than at the WTO in Seattle or the IMF in Washington, D.C., a decade earlier, those who participated were a remarkably motley crew. Representatives of United Steelworkers of America, Iraq Veterans Against the War, Bail Out the People, Women's Peace Initiative, Three Rivers Climate Convergence, G20 Fight AIDS, Free Tibet, Free Palestine, Greenpeace, Poets on the Loose, the Raging Grannies, and CODEPINK were among them. This meeting of minds was celebrated in the alternative press; as Lojowsky wrote for *Z Magazine*, "Even in the face of extreme police presence, the march was a well-organized display of the diverse components of the global justice movement."[69] But there was far less emphasis in the mainstream media on the diversity (or flamboyance) of demonstrators this time around. A reporter for the *Pittsburgh Post-Gazette* referred to one contingent of protesters as consisting of "many students and several other journalists."[70] The *New York Times* noticed that demonstrators were mostly dressed in black. Because protesters were *expected* to show up this time, the mainstream media focused primarily and almost excitedly on the potential for violence.

The Specter of Violence

As noted above, one media strategy for restoring order is to focus on the police as highly trained and disciplined professionals whose difficult job it is to keep the peace and protect people and property by outwitting protesters. Echoing reports that Washington, D.C., had "braced itself" for the IMF meeting in 2000, the *Wall Street Journal* proclaimed, "Pittsburgh Steels Itself for G-20 Protests."[71] Other presummit headlines included "G-20 Protest Plans Raise Alarm in City" (*Pittsburgh Tribune Review*)[72] and "Hospital Coordinator Anticipates Unknown during G-20 Summit" (*Pittsburgh Post-Gazette*).[73] The *New York Times* reported that Pittsburgh city officials announced that they had made one thousand jail cells available, after county officials freed up additional space the week before by releasing three hundred people who had been arrested on minor probation violations.[74]

A day after the summit convened, the *New York Times* published a full-color, under the masthead, above the fold, photo of Pittsburgh police looking a bit like Ninja turtles in full riot gear. The issues on the "packed agenda" were relegated to pages 4 and 10. The front-page photo caption reads: "Group of 20 protesters in Pittsburgh were met by the police and tear gas. At least a dozen people were arrested."[75] One young protester's explanation for his participation in the demonstration did appear on page 10, albeit alongside images of tear gas, riot police, and broken windows: "The fact that 20 or so individuals right now are determining economic trade policies for four to five billion people just isn't right. That's why we're here."[76]

Restoring Order

The mainstream media's emphasis on restoring order, seen in coverage of the WTO Battle in Seattle, the IMF meeting in D.C., and the WEF gathering in New York a decade earlier, was echoed in reports of the 2009 G20 meeting in Pittsburgh. We noticed particularly Big Media's celebration of the strategies employed by police officers in their efforts to subdue protesters and protect private property.

Highly Trained Professionals

The *New York Times* article mentioned above (photo on page A1 but context buried on A10) is worth quoting at length here:

> As the two day Group of 20 meeting brought leaders of the world's industrialized nations here Thursday, the police were out in force, patrolling on bicycles, foot and horseback, by river and by air. In the afternoon, protesters trying to march toward the convention center where the gathering is being held encountered roaming squads of police officers carrying plastic shields and batons. After firing a sound canon that emitted shrill beeps, causing demonstrators to cover their ears and back up, the police threw tear gas canisters that released billowing clouds of white smoke and stun grenades that exploded with sharp flashes of light.[77]

The *Times* further described the event as "a cat and mouse game in which protesters, many in all black, evaded large forces of heavily armed police officers in the streets near Liberty Avenue." The police eventually won the game, of course, with the use of "riot control agents" and "less lethal munitions" including tear gas and "concussion grenades."[78] The *Pittsburgh Post Gazette* reported that the G20 summit "was largely successful, and leaders earned accolades because the level of disruption did not mirror the destructive experiences of other cities that hosted it."[79] Still, destruction of private property became a key theme in mainstream media coverage of the 2010 G20 summit.

Protecting Private Property

As with their coverage of the Battle in Seattle and other meetings in 1999–2000, the media tended to shift the focus away from political and economic issues, and even from human pain and suffering, to destruction of property at the G20 summit in Pittsburgh. Unlike the protesters in Seattle—who targeted brand-name operations including Starbucks, Niketown, Gap, and Banana Republic—the Pittsburgh protesters made the mistake of hitting up mom-and-pop shops, eliciting sympathy for the proprietors and animosity toward activists in the popular press.

The *New York Times*, noting that the protesters did not have a permit to march, reported that a large metal trash container was rolled down Thirty-seventh Street, stopping short of several police vehicles and in front of a women's clothing boutique. "It was scary," the *Times* quoted Alissa Martin, the shop's owner, as saying. "You feel like you're living in a war zone."[80] A Penn State student, writing as part of a community journalism initiative, covered a similar incident for the *Center Daily Times*, citing an eyewitness account by a University of Pittsburgh student, Samantha Larsen: "Pamela's Diner, a local business owned and operated by Tim Blosat, 45, and Michelle Mazzella, 48, was one of the businesses Larsen saw being targeted by protesters." Blosat and Mazzella reportedly spent the night erecting plywood over broken windows—and hanging up "Open" signs. "A police officer stopped in to see how everything was going, and to make sure they weren't protesters breaking in."[81] The next morning, the streets were "eerily quiet." Order had been restored.

SHAPING NEWS COVERAGE OF PROTEST

In an article entitled "Mostly Pleased, but Knowing Few Heard Their Message," reporter Andrew Jacobs covered the protesters' beat of the 2002 World Economic Forum for the *New York Times*. As the headline suggests, the story perpetuates the failure motif that characterizes so much mainstream media coverage of anti–global capital protests. Unlike most reports, however, this one acknowledges the protesters' criticism of the media's sensational coverage of their demonstrations and its failure to analyze the issues that inspired them: "While the marches and rallies drew plenty of attention from journalists, the organizers said the attention was the wrong kind. Most press accounts focused on security concerns and the potential for violence, they said, leaving little room for explanations of why people were protesting in the first place."[82] Jacobs then quotes Antonia Juhasz, an organizer with the San Francisco–based International Forum on Globalization: "The news is not the protesters or the police. The news should have been what issues brought us to the streets. The coverage was just appalling."[83]

Such criticism could hardly have surprised the *New York Times* reporter, but it does appear to have stung him. After dutifully noting the protesters' dissatisfaction, he adds, "But they acknowledged that for many reporters on deadline, the panoply and complexity of issues was too much for a simple sound bite."[84] The image of an elite journalist attempting to persuade a group of grassroots organizers to agree on principle that reporters cannot possibly explain the issues that motivate protesters to the people who read newspapers is a chilling one indeed. It exemplifies an assumption held by many news media reporters and owners that readers are unwilling or unable to grasp anything beyond "a simple sound bite." It is a far cry from the journalistic ideal of beating the bushes to discover and reveal the truth.

Whether because or in spite of the "appalling" media coverage of their actions, protesters did crash the gates of the global capitalist party at the turn of the twenty-first century. In the wake of Seattle, the *New York Times* conceded that labor, environmental, and human rights groups had a legitimate complaint against the WTO as an exclusive businessman's club, and that they deserved a seat at the table.[85] The message was also clear that only those accepting the inevitability of global capitalism were invited. Those who questioned such a future were not welcome.

CONCLUSION

In 2011 the struggle for a seat at the table moved back to a struggle in the streets and town squares as the expansionary processes of global capitalism continued unabated. The cheerleading by the Big Media became exposed as oppressed people around the world found ways to communicate directly with one another face-to-face and through alternative media, especially social media networks. Such was the case when, on September 17, 2011, five thousand protesters answered a call by *Adbusters*, a Canadian alternative publication, and descended on Lower Manhattan's financial district, setting off the "Occupy Wall Street" (OWS) movement that attacked bank bailouts, corporate greed, and economic inequality. At first, the New York media treated the occupation as a local news story while the Big Media remained largely silent, unlike its love fest for Tea Party demonstrations.[86] It was not until police used brutal force against peaceful protesters that OWS began making the headlines.[87] However, beyond press coverage of police violence, the Big Media struggled to frame the movement because of the broad range of issues it addressed and diverse perspectives of its participants.

Furthermore, the OWS movement deliberately refused to anoint anyone as a leader. A Associated Press (AP) headline on the front page of the *State College (Pa.) Centre Daily Times* on October 16, 2011, read, "Protesters Push Ahead Even without Leaders." The dateline from New York was followed by the lead: "They were out to change the world, overthrow the establishment and liberate the poor. But first somebody would have to do something about those bongo drums."[88] Neighbors had complained about the noise, and although protestors had tried to put a time limit on the drumming, the "drummers refused to obey" the rule, apparently due to the lack of leadership. Acknowledging that the movement had gone national, it was derided as "stubbornly decentralized," complicating the news media's efforts to define it. The lack of leaders led the reporters to focus on sanitation, or rather the lack thereof, which later became a primary justification to break up OWS camps around the nation (other excuses were safety issues, illegal camping on public and private property, drug use, and so on).

The AP report then moved its focus to violence by protesters in Rome, where a "peaceful demonstration against corporate greed" was "hijacked" by a small group that began "smashing windows, torching cars and hurling bottles," leading "Italian riot police" to fire tear gas and water cannons against the protesters. This incident was *exceptional* as the article continued that "hundreds of thousands nicknamed 'the indignant' marched without incident in cities across Europe" in response to governments' austerity measures. The report again suggested that the lack of leadership had "prevented the group from settling upon a single list of demands to present to the public," underscoring the Big Media's inability to define the movement within a proper framework.[89] Additional AP reports published in the *CDT* declared that the movement's openness had attracted former criminals, homeless people, "hangers-on," and demonstrators against just about everything, bringing a variety of issues into the movement that threatened "to alter the message" against income inequality and corporate greed, the frame that the media had finally settled upon.[90]

In order to maintain this focus and remain inclusive, the movement adopted the slogan "We Are the 99 Percent." This also simplified matters for the media, but raised a long-standing taboo subject: the U.S. class structure. It suddenly broke the hegemonic mystification of class defined by the color of shirt collars, income levels, and self-identification with the "middle class." These sociological categories were supplanted by the economic categorization of class defined by ownership and control of the means of production—the one percent. The new slogan also underscored the fact that, as some columnists reluctantly acknowledged, capitalism is inherently based upon inequality. Reports on the growing disparity between the obscenely rich and everyone else became more numerous. News shapers became uncomfortable because having to discuss class meant debunking of the myth of classlessness. This in turn led the news media to accuse the Occupy movement of engaging in "class warfare." Meanwhile, they continued to refuse to acknowledge the reality that it was the ruling capitalist class that had, from the beginning of capitalism, declared war on the working class.

Much to the relief of Big Media and Big Money, the Occupy movement issued a list of demands on December 1, 2011. The headline on the second-to-last page of the *CDT*'s news section said it all: "Occupy Protesters Finally Present Specifics." The AP story that followed revealed that the movement was merely seeking to reform capitalism, not overthrow it.[91] Then media coverage of the movement shifted almost entirely to the systematic dismantling of Occupy camps around the United States. Without protesters in the streets, there was no longer anything tangible to report. The use of state force had effectively silenced the media and the movement. Nevertheless, the issue of inequality did remain within the realm of public discourse, and "occupiers" joined in protests against home foreclosures, voter identification laws, and union-busting efforts, for which they merited an occasional mention.

To question capitalism is to ask whether genuine democracy can exist within such an existing order. The answer, as McChesney has argued, is that "the relationship between capitalism and democracy is a rocky one."[92] A genuine democracy requires a degree of equality that permits all members of the citizenry to be involved in political and economic decision making. Under capitalism wealth is concentrated, giving a tiny minority the power and privilege it affords. A genuine democracy is based on communitarian values. Capitalism is based on possessive individualism that has become channeled into rabid consumerism. A genuine democracy requires an informed citizenry with access to a wide and diverse range of information and culture. Capitalism turns information and culture into commodities, products to be bought and sold in the marketplace rather than shared knowledge to enlighten or pose challenges to existing reality. The Big Media therefore inhibits citizens' ability to imagine alternative realities. It denies the history-making power of the people. It impedes the very concept that new forms of existence are possible—a concept that would enable the full development of human potential.

Notes

CHAPTER 1: INTRODUCTION

1. Clifford G. Christians and James W. Carey, "The Logic and Aims of Qualitative Research," in *Research Methods in Mass Communication*, ed. Guido H. Stempel and Bruce H. Westley (Englewood Cliffs, N.J.: Prentice-Hall, 1981), 342–62.

2. Christians and Carey, "The Logic and Aims of Qualitative Research," 353.

3. Elizabeth L. Eisenstein, *The Printing Revolution in Early Modern Europe* (Cambridge, U.K.: Cambridge University Press, 1983), 93.

4. George Farah and Justin Elga, "What's Not Talked About on Sunday Morning?" *Extra!* October 2001, 14–17.

5. John Nerone, *Violence against the Press: Policing the Public Sphere in U.S. History* (New York: Oxford University Press, 1994).

6. Jon Bekken, "The Working Class Press at the Turn of the Century," in *Ruthless Criticism: New Perspectives in U.S. Communication History*, ed. Bob McChesney and Bill Solomon (Minneapolis: University of Minnesota Press, 1993), 151–75; and Nerone, *Violence against the Press*, 265–95.

7. Sudarsan Raghavan and Sumana Chatterjee, "Child Slavery Persists on African Cocoa Farms," *State College (Pa.) Centre Daily Times*, 25 June 2001, A1, A7; Sudarsan Raghavan, "The Slavery Trap," *State College (Pa.) Centre Daily Times*, 26 June 2001, A1, A7; and Sumana Chatterjee, "Chocolate Companies React to Slavery Revelations," *State College (Pa.) Centre Daily Times*, 26 June 2001, A7.

8. Sumana Chatterjee, "Consumers: Why Not Boycott Chocolate?" *State College (Pa.) Centre Daily Times*, 26 June 2001, A7.

9. Sumana Chatterjee, "Chocolate Companies Fight 'Slave Free' Labels," *State College (Pa.) Centre Daily Times*, 1 August 2001, A4.

10. Sumana Chatterjee, "Chocolate Makers to Accept Responsibility for Cocoa Farm Practices," *State College (Pa.) Centre Daily Times*, 1 October 2001, A3.

11. Edward Herman, "Market System Constraints on Freedom of Expression," *Journal of Communication Inquiry* 15, no. 1 (Winter 1991): 45–53.

CHAPTER 2: MEDIA MERGER MANIA

1. Benjamin M. Compaine and Douglas Gomery, *Who Owns the Media? Competition and Concentration in the Mass Media Industry*, 3rd ed. (Mahwah, N.J.: Erlbaum, 2000).

2. Ben Bagdikian, *The New Media Monopoly* (Boston: Beacon, 2004).

3. "The National Entertainment State, 2006," *The Nation*, 3 July 2006, http://www.thenation.com/doc/20060703/intro (accessed 6 October 2006).

4. Bradley Johnson, "Special Report: 100 Leading Media Companies," *Advertising Age*, 1 October 2007, www.lexisnexis.com (accessed 8 December 2007). According to *Advertising Age*, the top ten media companies in terms of net U.S. media revenue in 2006 were Time Warner, Comcast Corp., Walt Disney Co., News Corp., DIRECTV Corp., NBC/Universal (General Electric), CBS Corp., Cox Enterprises, EchoStar Communications Corp., and Viacom.

5. Ronald V. Bettig, "Concentration in the Copyright Industries," in *Intellectual Property and Information Wealth: Issues and Practices in the Digital Age*, vol. 1, *Copyright and Related Rights*, ed. Peter Yu (Westport, Conn.: Praeger, 2007), 361–84.

6. "The Top 20 U.S. Media Owners," Media Owners, 2007, http://www.mediaowners.com/about/index.html (accessed 9 November 2007).

7. Center for Public Integrity, "Top Telecommunications, Media, and Technology Companies," 2006, http://www.publicintegrity.org/telecom/rank.aspx?act=industry#0 (accessed 3 March 2008).

8. *Time*, 27 June 1994, cover.

9. Edward S. Herman and Noam Chomsky, *Manufacturing Consent: The Political Economy of Mass Media* (New York: Pantheon, 1988), 26–28.

10. Ronald V. Bettig, "Who Owns Prime Time? Industrial and Institutional Conflict over Television Programming and Broadcast Rights," in *Framing Friction: Media and Social Conflict*, ed. Mary S. Mander (Urbana: University of Illinois Press, 1999), 125–60.

11. Douglas Gomery, "Radio Broadcasting and Music Industry," in Compaine and Gomery, *Who Owns the Media?* 298.

12. Stuart Elliot, "A Combined Viacom-CBS Would Cast an Awfully Large Shadow across a Wide Range of Ad Media," *New York Times*, 8 September 1999, C8.

13. Lawrie Mifflin, "Viacom to Buy CBS, Forming 2nd Largest Media Company," *New York Times*, 8 September 1999, A1, C15.

14. Elliot, "A Combined Viacom-CBS," C8.

15. Seth Sutel, "Giants of Media Join at the Hip," *State College (Pa.) Centre Daily Times*, 8 September 1999, 1A, 7A.

16. Sutel, "Giants of Media," 1A.

17. Forbes 400, "The 400 Richest People in America," *Forbes*, 8 October 2001, 127–298.

18. Sutel, "Giants of Media," 1A.

19. Charles Haddad, "CBS-Viacom Merger Further Narrows Media," *Atlanta Journal-Constitution*, 9 September 1999, F1, F3.

20. Charles Haddad, "CBS, Viacom Follow Trail Blazed by Disney, Time Warner," *State College (Pa.) Centre Daily Times*, 12 September 1999, 15B.

21. Haddad, "CBS-Viacom Merger," F1, F3.

22. *NBC Nightly News* with Tom Brokaw, National Broadcasting Company, 7 September 1999.

23. Edward Herman, "Media Mega-Mergers," *Dollars & Sense*, May 1996, 8–13.

24. Alex Kuczynski, "CBS Chief Wanted His MTV," *New York Times*, 8 September 1999, C1, C14; Floyd Norris, "The New, Improved Redstone Still Knows How to Get His Way," *New York Times*, 8 September 1999, C1, C13.

25. Felicity Barringer, "CBS News May Face More Cuts," *New York Times*, 9 September 1999, C8.

26. Lawrie Mifflin, "CBS-Viacom Deal Raises Competition Questions," *New York Times*, 9 September 1999, C1, C8.

27. Matt Richtel, "A New Force in Distributing Music across the Internet," *New York Times*, 8 September 1999, 14C.

28. Elliot, "A Combined Viacom-CBS," C8.

29. Veryln Klinkenborg, "The Vision behind the CBS-Viacom Merger," *New York Times*, 9 September 1999, A28.

30. Stephen Labaton, "Wide Belief U.S. Will Let a Vast Deal Go Through," *New York Times*, 8 September 1999, C14.

31. Labaton, "Wide Belief," C14.

32. Stephen Labaton, "Federal Regulators Give Approval to Viacom's Buyout of CBS," *New York Times*, 4 May 2000, C1.

33. "The 400 Richest People in America," 158, 170.

34. Frank Ahrens, "The Great Deregulator: Five Months into His Tenure as FCC Chairman, Michael Powell Is Coming Through Loud and Clear," *Washington Post*, 18 June 2001, C1.

35. Stephen Labaton, "Court Weighs Easing Limits on Big Media," *New York Times*, 8 September 2001, A1.

36. Stephen Labaton, "Appellate Court Eases Limitations for Media Giants: Rejects Longtime Rules," *New York Times*, 20 February 2002, A1, C6.

37. Labaton, "Appellate Court Eases Limitations," A1, C6.

38. "The 400 Richest People in America," 2001, 168.

39. Brett Pulley, "The Cable Capitalist," *Forbes*, 8 October 2001, 42–54.

40. Bill Carter, "Media Talk: An Executive with Synergistic Vision," *New York Times*, 11 September 2000, C17.

41. Frances Katz, "AOL, Time Warner Deal Sets the Tone," *State College (Pa.) Centre Daily Times*, 11 January 2000, 1A, 7A.

42. Marc Gunther, "Sumner of Love," *Fortune*, 2 May 2005, www.fortune.com (accessed 16 January 2008), 90.

43. Matthew Karnitschnig and Brooks Barnes, "Sins of the Parent: CBS and Viacom Find Life Tough after the Big Split," *Wall Street Journal*, 22 July 2006, www.proquest.com (accessed 1 October 2007).

44. Forbes 400, "The Richest People in America," *Forbes*, 8 October 2007, 72–346.

45. "Viacom Reports Third Quarter Results 2007," press release, 2 November 2007, www.viacom.com (accessed 15 January 2008).

46. "CBS Reports Third Quarter Results," 1 November 2007, www.cbscorpora tion.com (accessed 16 January 2008).

47. G. William Domhoff, "State and Ruling Class in Corporate America," *Insurgent Sociologist* 4, no. 3 (1974): 4.

48. "Viacom Inc.," OneSource Information Services, 27 July 2007, www.lexis nexis.com (accessed 16 January 2008).

49. Center for Public Integrity, *Networks of Influence: The Political Power of the Communications Industry* (Washington, D.C.: Center for Public Integrity, 2005), app. A, 188.

50. Michael A. Hiltzik and Claudia Eller, "Roots of Redstone Family's Bitter Rift," *Los Angeles Times*, 2 August 2007, www.proquest.com (accessed 19 January 2008).

51. Claudia Eller and Michael A. Hiltzik, "Redstone's Letter Takes Public Slap at Daughter," *Los Angeles Times*, 21 July 2007, www.proquest.com (accessed 19 January 2008).

52. Katz, "AOL, Time Warner Deal," 1A, 7A.

53. Katz, "AOL, Time Warner Deal," 1A.

54. Forbers 400, "The 400 Richest People in America," *Forbes*, 8 October 2001, 148.

55. Chris O'Brien, "AOL Merger May Fuel Silicon Valley Growth," *State College (Pa.) Centre Daily Times*, 13 January 2000, 6B.

56. *NewsHour with Jim Lehrer*, Public Broadcasting System, 10 January 2000.

57. Walter Goodman, "When Corporate Synergy Becomes Manifest Destiny," *New York Times*, 19 January 2000, E10.

58. Saul Hansell, "America Online Agrees to Buy Time Warner for $165 Billion: Media Deal is Richest Merger," *New York Times*, 11 January 2000, A1, C11.

59. Amy Harmon, "Exceptions Made for Dress Code, but Never for His Internet Vision," *New York Times*, 11 January 2000, A1, C12.

60. Steve Lohr, "Medium for Main Street," *New York Times*, 11 January 2000, A1, C10.

61. Amy Harmon and Alex Kuczynski, "A Bridge Builder for Corporate Culture," *New York Times*, 12 January 2000, C1, C7.

62. Harmon and Kuczynski, "A Bridge Builder," C7.

63. Lohr, "Medium for Main Street," A1.

64. Harmon, "Exceptions Made for Dress Code," A1.

65. Harmon and Kuczynski, "A Bridge Builder," C7.

66. Harmon and Kuczynski, "A Bridge Builder," C7.

67. Saul Hensel, "Not-So-Subtle Engine Drives AOL Profit Forecasts," *New York Times*, 31 January 2000, C1, C12.

68. Harmon and Kuczynski, "A Bridge Builder," C7.

69. Harmon and Kuczynski, "A Bridge Builder," C7.

70. Laura M. Holson, "The Online Generation Courts the Old Guard," *New York Times*, 11 January 2000, C1, C13.

71. Holson, "The Online Generation," C13.

72. Lohr, "Medium for Main Street," C10.

73. Alex Berenson, "Investors Seem to Want to Keep AOL–Time Warner Asunder," *New York Times*, 13 January 2000, C1, C6.

74. Berenson, "Investors," C1.

75. Goodman, "When Corporate Synergy," E10.

76. Goodman, "When Corporate Synergy," E10.

77. Denise Caruso, "If the AOL–Time Warner Deal Is about Proprietary Content, Where Does That Leave a Noncommercial Directory It Will Own?" *New York Times*, 17 January 2000, C5.

78. Stuart Elliot, "Advertising: The AOL–Time Warner Deal Changes Everything for Those Who Move, and Buy, in Media Circles," *New York Times*, 11 January 2000, C8.

79. Elliot, "Advertising," C8.

80. "The Biggest Media Merger Yet," *New York Times*, 11 January 2000, A30.

81. Dan Perkins, aka Tom Tomorrow, Op-Art, *New York Times*, 11 January 2000, A31.

82. Robert H. Frank, "A Merger's Message: Dominate or Die," *New York Times*, 11 January 2000, A31.

83. Kevin Siers, "Contents: Copyright AOL–Time Warner," *State College (Pa.) Centre Daily Times*, 16 January 2000, 9A.

84. Tom Toles, "Coming to a Screen near You," *State College (Pa.) Centre Daily Times*, 13 February 2000, 13A.

85. Henry Giroux, "Merger Mania Dazzles Eyes, but Imprisons You and Me," *State College (Pa.) Centre Daily Times*, 13 February 2000, 13A.

86. Felicity Barringer, "Does Deal Signal Lessening of Media Independence?" *New York Times*, 11 January 2000, C12; Laurence Zuckerman, "As Media Influence Grows for Handful, Can That Be a Good Thing?" *New York Times*, 13 January 2000, C6.

87. Zuckerman, "As Media Influence Grows," C6.

88. Zuckerman, "As Media Influence Grows," C6.

89. Zuckerman, "As Media Influence Grows," C6.

90. Joel Bleifuss, "Communication Breakdown: AOL–Time Warner Threatens Public Interest," *In These Times*, 21 February 2000, 2–3.

91. Bleifuss, "Communication Breakdown," 2.

92. "Rapid Media Consolidation Dramatically Narrows Number of Companies Controlling Time Spent Online," Jupiter Media Metrix, 4 June 2001, www.iup.com/company/ (accessed 7 January 2002).

93. Bleifuss, "Communication Breakdown," 2.

94. Pat Aufderheide, "Open Access or Else," *In These Times*, 26 June 2000, 2.

95. Brian Winston, *Misunderstanding Media*, Cambridge, Mass.: Harvard University Press, 1986.

96. Brian Stelter, "With Video Delivered by Web, the Desk Is a Hot Lunch Spot," *New York Times*, 5 January 2007, A1, B4.

97. David Carr, "Publishing That's All about Me," *New York Times*, 7 January 2008, C1, C11.

98. "AT&T to Exit Pay Phones as the Business Shrinks," *New York Times*, 4 December 2007, C11.

99. Jackie Crosby, "Electronic Waste to Follow iPhone Sales," *State College (Pa.) Centre Daily Times*, 6 July 2007, A9.

100. See, for example Brad Stone, "States Fault Myspace on Predator Issues," *New York Times*, 15 May 2007, C2; Jim Puzzanghera, "High-Tech TVs Could Become Low-Tech Trash," *State College (Pa.) Centre Daily Times*, 11 June 2007, C8; Tom

Zeller Jr., "AOL Acts on Release of Data," *New York Times*, 14 June 2007, C1, C7; Ken Belson, "At I.B.M., a Vacation Anytime, or Maybe No Vacation at All," *New York Times*, 31 August 2007, A1, A18; Bruce Lambert, "Craigslist Emerges as Resource for Both Prostitutes and Police," *New York Times*, 5 September 2007, A1, A22; Joseph A. Hirsch, letter to the editor, "Web Sites for Kids," *New York Times*, 9 September 2007, A24; James Gordon Meek and Bill Hutchinson, "Facebook under Fire by N.Y. Attorney General," *State College (Pa.) Centre Daily Times*, 28 September 2007; Laura M. Holson, "Verizon Letter on Privacy Stirs Debate," *New York Times*, 16 October 2007, C1, C8; "MP3 Player Came Preloaded with Porn," *State College (Pa.) Centre Daily Times*, 29 December 2007, A8.

101. "100 Leading National Advertisers Report 2010," *Advertising Age*, 28 December 2009, http://adage.com/marketertrees09update/ (accessed 25 March 2010).

102. Graham Murdock, "Programming: Needs and Answers," paper presented at New Dimensions in Television meeting, Venice, Italy, 15 March 1981.

103. "AOL's Big Byte," *The Nation*, 31 January 2000, 3.

104. Bagdikian, *The New Media Monopoly*; Herman, "Media Mega-Mergers," 11; James Ledbetter, "Merge Overkill: When Big Media Gets Too Big, What Happens to Open Debate?" *Village Voice*, 16 January 1996, 30–35.

105. Zuckerman, "As Media Influence Grows," C6.

106. "But a Survey," in *Special Report: News and Editorial Independence. A Survey of Group and Independent Editors* (Easton, Pa: Ethics Committee, American Society of Newspaper Editors, 1980).

107. Pew Research Center for the People and the Press, "Journalists Avoiding the News, Self-Censorship: How Often and Why," 30 April 2000, www.people-press.org/jour00rpt.htm (accessed 5 January 2002).

108. Pew Research Center for the People and the Press, "Bottom-Line Pressures Now Hurting Coverage, Say Journalists," 23 May 2004, http://people-press.org/reports/display.php3?ReportID=214 (accessed 26 January 2008).

109. Zuckerman, "As Media Influence Grows," C6.

110. Robert H. Lande, "Antitrust and the Media—II," *The Nation*, 22 May 2000, 5–6.

111. Forbes 400, "The Richest People in America," 30 September 2009, www.forbes.com (accessed 12 November 2009).

112. Benjamin M. Compaine, "Who Owns the Media Companies?" in *Who Owns the Media? Competition and Concentration in the Mass Media Industry*, ed. Benjamin M. Compaine and Douglas Gomery (Mahwah, N.J.: Erlbaum, 2000), table 8.5.

113. Thomas Guback, "Ownership and Control in the Motion Picture Industry," *Journal of Film and Video* 38, no. 1 (1986): 7–20.

114. Felicity Barringer, "Other Media Companies' Assets Tied to Those of Deal's Partners," *New York Times*, 13 January 2000, C6.

115. Time Warner, *Annual Report 2000*, 44.

116. Walt Disney Company, "Notice of Annual Meeting of Shareholders," 4 January 2002, 25–31.

117. Viacom, *Proxy Statement, 2007*, 76.

118. Daniel Fusfeld, *Economics: Principles of Political Economy*. 3rd ed. (Glenview, Ill.: Scott Foresman, 1988), 416.

119. Ben Bagdikian, *The Media Monopoly*, 6th ed. (Boston: Beacon, 2000), 9.

120. Jon Katz, "Invasion of the Billionaire," *The Netizen*, 30 May 1997, http://hotwired.lycos.com/netizen/97/21/index4a.html (accessed 21 September 2000).

121. Benjamin M. Compaine, "The Newspaper Industry," in *Who Owns the Media? Competition and Concentration in the Mass Media Industry*, ed. Benjamin M. Compaine and Douglas Gomery (Mahwah, N.J.: Erlbaum, 2000), 1–59.

122. David Barsamian, "Monopolies, NPR, and PBS: An Interview with Robert McChesney," *Z Magazine*, February 2000, 40–46.

123. Barsamian, "Monopolies," 42.

124. Katz, "Invasion of the Billionaire," 4.

125. Bagdikian, *The Media Monopoly*, 6th ed., 9.

126. Aimee Picchi, "AOL–Time Warner Too Optimistic?" *Philadelphia Enquirer*, 15 December 2000, C1, C7.

127. Patricia Horn and Akweli Parker, "AOL Merger Gets Key Approval," *Philadelphia Enquirer*, 15 December 2000, A1, A16.

128. Federal Communications Commission, "Subject to Conditions, Commission Approves Merger between America Online, Inc. and Time Warner, Inc.," 11 January 2001, www.fcc.gov/Bureaus/Cable/ (accessed 18 January 2002).

129. Stephen Labaton, "FCC Approves AOL–Time Warner Deal, with Conditions," *New York Times*, 12 January 2001, C11.

130. Labaton, "Federal Regulators Give Approval," C1.

131. "AOL–Time Warner Trims 2,000 from Its Workforce," *Philadelphia Inquirer*, 25 January 2001, www.lexisnexis.com (accessed 29 January 2008).

132. Floyd Norris, "Which Would Have Done Better without the Merger?" *New York Times*, 14 January 2003, C6.

133. Richard Morochove, "America Online Has Lost Its Edge," *Toronto Star*, 29 July 2002, D2, www.lexisnexis.com (accessed 28 January 2008).

134. David Kirkpatrick, "Question of New Chairman at Top of Board's Agenda," *New York Times*, 14 January 2003, C1, C7.

135. Aimee Picchi, "AOL Buys AT&T's Venture Stake for US$3.6 Billion," *Financial Post*, FP4, www.lexisnexis.com (accessed 26 January 2008).

136. Richard Siklos, "Icahn Group Steps Up Time Warner Proxy Fight," *New York Times*, 13 September 2005, C3.

137. Joe Nocera, "Running an Empire? No Sweat," *New York Times*, 25 August 2007, B1, B8.

138. Saul Hansell, "AOL to Cut 5,000 Jobs in Web Access Business," *New York Times*, 4 August 2007, C3.

139 Time Warner, *Annual Report 2006*, http://files.shareholder.com/downloads/TWX/229105524x0x154481/39d9368c-c6f8-4162-ab2e-30bdf6f8f21d/2006AR.pdf (accessed 17 January 2008).

140. Tim Arango, "What Would Henry Luce Do? Looking Forward at Time Warner," *New York Times*, 24 December 2007, C1, C4.

141. Time Warner News, "Time Warner Inc. Declares Spin-off Dividend of Time Warner Cable Inc." 26 February 2009, www.timewarner.com (accessed 15 May 2010).

142. Time Warner Cable Inc., *10-K Report*, 31 March 2010.

143. Time Warner Cable Inc., "Investor Relations: Board of Directors 2010," www.timewarner.com (accessed 16 May 2010).

144. Center for Public Integrity, *Networks of Influence*, app. A, 172, 173.

145. "Heavy Hitters: Top All-Time Donors, 1989–2012," Center for Responsive Politics, http://www.opensecrets.org/orgs/list.php?order=A (accessed 13 February 2012).

146. "Heavy Hitters: Time Warner Totals," Center for Responsive Politics, http://www.opensecrets.org/orgs/totals..phpcycle=2012&id=D0000... (accessed 13 February 2012).

147. "Lobbying: Time Warner," Center for Responsive Politics, http://www.opensecrets.org/lobby/clientsum.php?id=D0000... (accessed 13 February 2012).

148. "Lobbying: TV/Movies/Music (Industry Profile 2008)," Center for Responsive Politics, http://www.opensecrets.org/lobby/indus/clientphp?id=B02&year=2008 (accessed 13 February 2012).

149. Rolfe Winkler and Martin Hutchinson, "After the Divorce, AOL Faces Challenges," *New York Times*, 11 December 2009, B2, http://www.nytimes.com/2009/12/11/business/11views.html (accessed 15 May 2010).

150. Tim Arango, "In Retrospect: How It Went So Wrong," *New York Times*, 11 January 2010, B1, B1–11.

151. Arango, "In Retrospect," B10.

152. Arango, "In Retrospect," B10.

153. Arango, "In Retrospect," B11.

154. Arango, "In Retrospect," B11.

155. Ken Boettcher, "AOL–Time Warner Merger Makes Media Critics Nervous," *The People*, April 2000, 3.

CHAPTER 3: THE HOLLYWOOD MOVIE INDUSTRY

1. Benjamin M. Compaine and Douglas Gomery, eds., *Who Owns the Media? Competition and Concentration in the Mass Media Industry*, 2nd ed. (Mahwah, N.J.: Erlbaum, 2000).

2. Compaine and Gomery, *Who Owns the Media?* 515.

3. Ben Bagdikian, *The New Media Monopoly*, Boston: Beacon, 2004, 27–54.

4. "The National Entertainment State, 2006," *The Nation*, 3 July 2006, 25–28, http://www.thenation.com/doc/20060703/intro (accessed 6 October 2006).

5. Bradley Johnson, "Special Report: 100 Leading Media Companies," *Advertising Age*, www.lexisnexis.com (accessed 6 October 2006).

6. "The Top 20 U.S. Media Owners," Media Owners, 2009, http://www.mediaowners.com/about/index.html (accessed 9 November 2009).

7. Center for Public Integrity, "Top Telecommunications, Media, and Technology Companies, 2006," http://projects.publicintegrity.org/telecom/rank.aspx?act=industry (accessed 3 March 2008).

8. Bradley Johnson, "100 Leading Media Companies," *Advertising Age*, 3 October 2011, 44–50, 46.

9. Associated Press, "People in the News," 7 May 1999, a.m. cycle.

10. "Studio Market Share 2009," Box Office Mojo http://www.boxofficemojo.com/yearly/chart/?yr=2009&p=.htm (accessed 2 April 2010).

11. Carl DiOrio, "*Avatar* Eyeing Big Box Office Bow," *Hollywood Reporter*, 15 December 2009, www.hollywoodreporter.com (accessed 1 September 2010).

12. "Studio Market Share 2009."

13. Samuel Bowles and Richard Edwards, *Understanding Capitalism: Competition, Command, and Change in the U.S. Economy.* 2nd ed. (New York: HarperCollins, 1993), 229–38.

14. Janet Wasko, *How Hollywood Works* (Thousand Oaks, Calif.: Sage, 2007), 60.

15. "Fortune 500 2009," April 2009, http://money.cnn.com/magazines/fortune/fortune500/2009/index.html (accessed 7 June 2010).

16. "Fortune Global 500 2009," http://money.cnn.com/magazines/fortune/global500/2009/ (accessed 7 June 2010).

17. "Warner Bros. International Cinemas and Village Cinemas," Time Warner press release, 22 December 2004, http://www.timewarner.com/ (accessed 12 February 2008).

18. Eileen Meehan, "'Holy Commodity Fetish, Batman!': The Political Economy of a Commercial Intertext," in *The Many Lives of the Batman,* ed. Roberta Pearson and William Uricchio (New York: Routledge, 1991), 47–65.

19. Laura M. Holson and Rick Lyman, "In Warner Brothers' Strategy, a Movie Is Now a Product Line," *New York Times,* 2 November 2002, C1, C4.

20. "Franchise Index," Box Office Mojo, 6 June 2010, http://www.boxofficemojo.com/franchises/ (accessed 22 June 2010).

21. Holson and Lyman, "In Warner Brothers' Strategy," C1.

22. Holson and Lyman, "In Warner Brothers' Strategy," C4.

23. Holson and Lyman, "In Warner Brothers' Strategy," C4.

24. Henry A. Giroux, *Breaking In to the Movies: Film and the Culture of Politics* (Malden, Mass.: Blackwell, 2002), 3; emphasis ours.

25. "Fortune 500," April 2009; "Fortune Global 500 2009."

26. "Fortune 500 2010: Top 1000 American Companies—Walt Disney," http://money.cnn.com/magazines/fortune/fortune500/2010/snapshots/2190.html (accessed 25 June 2010).

27. The Walt Disney Company, *Proxy Statement,* 22 January 2010, http://media.disney.go.com/investorrelations/proxy/proxy_2010.pdf (accessed 2 February 2010) p. 81.

28. Forbes 400, "The 400 Richest Americans 2009," Forbes.com, http://www.forbes.com/lists/2009/54/rich-list-09_The-400-Richest-Americans_NameProper_7.html (accessed 22 February 2010).

29. The Walt Disney Company, *2007 Annual Report,* 16.

30. Bruce Westbrook, "Snow White to Make Digital Debut; Disney DVD Set Packed with Extras," *Houston Chronicle,* 7 October 2001, 8.

31. Dave Itzkoff, "Disney Looks Past the Mouse to a Ratings Record," *New York Times,* 20 August 2007, A1, A14.

32. Bill Gorman, "Disney Channel Breaks USA's Hold on Prime-time Cable Network Crown," 17 March 2009, www.indiewire.com (accessed 22 June 2010).

33. John Byrne, Ronald Grover, and Robert D. Hof, "Pay Stubs of the Rich and Corporate," *Business Week,* 7 May 1990, 56–64.

34. Del Jones, "82 Billionaires Did Not Make Forbes List," *USA Today,* 21 September 2007, 4B, www.lexisnexis.com (accessed 18 February 2008).

35. The Business Council, "About US," 2008, http://www.thebusinesscouncil.org/about/ (accessed 17 March 2009).

36. "The Richest People in America: Star Power," *Forbes*, 6 October 2003, http://www.forbes.com/forbes/2003/1006/164.html (accessed 11 September 2010).

37. The Walt Disney Company, *Notice of 2009 Annual Meeting and Proxy Statement*, January 2009.

38. The Walt Disney Company, "Institutional Ownership," 20 July 2010, http://www.dailyfinance.com/company/the-walt-disney-company/dis/nys/institutional ownership (accessed 22 June 2010).

39. "Walt Disney Company Lobbying 2008," Center for Responsive Politics, http://www.opensecrets.org/lobby/clientsum.php?year=2008&lname=Walt+Disney +Co (accessed 24 June 2010).

40. "Heavy Hitters: Walt Disney Co.," Center for Responsive Politics, www.opensecrects.org (accessed 24 June 2010)

41. Bernard Weinraub, "Disney Hires Kissinger," *New York Times*, 10 October 1997, E7.

42. Ronald V. Bettig, "Copyright and the Commodification of Culture," *Media Development* 52, no. 1 (2003): 25–37.

43. Brooks Barnes, "The Line between Homage and Parody," *New York Times*, 25 November 2007, Art 8.

44. Clair Cain Miller, "YouTube Ads Turn Piracy into Revenue," *New York Times*, 3 September 2010, B1, B4.

45. Christy Lemire, "Moore's Sept. 11 Film Loses Disney Backing," *State College (Pa.) Centre Daily Times*, 4 June 2004, A1, A6.

46. Lemire, "Moore's Sept. 11 Film," A6.

47. "Is News Corp. a Great Company, or What?" CNN.com, http://money.cnn.com/magazines/fortune/fortune500/2009/full_list/ (accessed 25 June 2010).

48. "The Global 2000," http://www.forbes.com/lists/2010/18/global-2000-10_The-Global-2000_Rank_2.html (accessed 25 June 2010).

49. News Corporation, *2009 Annual Report*, 18, 19, http://www.newscorp.com/Report2009/html/2.html (accessed 4 November 2011).

50. News Corporation, *2007 Annual Report*, 4, http://www.newscorp.com/Report2007/AR2007.pdf (accessed 4 November 2011).

51. Forbes 400, "The Richest People in America," 9 October 2009, http://www.forbes.com/lists/2009/54/rich-list-09_The-400-Richest-Americans_NamePro-per_11.html (accessed 12 November 2009).

52. "The World's Billionaires," *Forbes*, http://www.forbes.com/lists/2010/10/billionaires-2010_The-Worlds-Billionaires_NameProper_2.html (accessed 26 June 2010).

53. Ronald Grover, "Rupert Murdoch's Latest Deal with John Malone," *Bloomsberg Business Week*, 4 June 2009, http://www.businessweek.com/technology/content/jun2009/tc2009064_532827.htm (accessed 13 October 2009).

54. News Corporation, *U.S. Security and Exchange Commission Form 10K*, 30 June 2009, http://shareholder.com/ (accessed 28 June 2010), 55.

55. News Corporation, *2007 Annual Report*, 6.

56. News Corporation, *Form 10K*, 55.

57. Bagdikian, *The New Media Monopoly*, 38.

58. Eric Alterman, "The Liberal Media: All Rupert, All the Time," *The Nation*, 13 August 2007, 10.

59. Richard Perez-Pena and Andrew Ross Sorkin, "So Near, Yet So Far: Murdock Awaits Decision on His Dow Offer," *New York Times*, 31 July 2007, C1, C5.

60. Don Groves and Adam Dawtrey, "Hogwarts and Hobbits in Global Grab," *Variety*, 11 February 2002, 1.

61. Rebecca Keegan, "How Much Did *Avatar* Really Cost?" *Vanity Fair*, 22 December 2009, http://www.vanityfair.com/online/oscars/2009/12/how–much-did-avatar-really-cost (accessed 1 July 2010).

62. *Avatar*, www.boxofficemojo.com (accessed 28 June 2010).

63. "Allen and Company, Inc.: Overview," *Hoover's Fact Sheet*, 2005, http://hoovers.com/ (accessed 19 September 2005).

64. Joe Flint, "Mood is Dark at Sun Valley Business Meeting," *Los Angeles Times*, 11 July 2009, www.newsbank.com (accessed 3 July 2010).

65. David Carr, "Murdoch, a Folk Hero in Silicon," *New York Times*, 29 October 2007, C1, C5.

66. Ted Turner, "My Beef with the Big Media," *Washington Monthly*, July/August 2004, http://www.washingtonmonthly.com/features/2004/0407.turner.html (accessed 22 February 2007).

67. Paul Farhi, "Rupert Murdoch Empire Finds Business Not So Taxing Offshore," *Washington Post*, 7 December 1997, A1.

68. Center for Public Integrity, *Networks of Influence: The Political Power of the Communications Industry* (Washington, D.C.: Center For Public Integrity, 2005), app. A, 145.

69. David G. Savage, "Supreme Court Upholds Fine for TV Profanity," *Los Angeles Times*, 29 April 2009, http://articles.sfgate.com (accessed 3 July 2010).

70. "News Corporation: A Corporate Profile," Corporate Watch UK, May 2004, www.corporatewatch.org (accessed 26 February 2008).

71. Bernard Weinraub, "A Strained Relationship Turns Sour," *New York Times*, 18 October 1999, C18.

72. Bernard Weinraub, "A Strained Relationship," C18.

73. "Misperceptions, the Media, and the Iraq War," Program on International Policy Studies, 2 October 2003, http://www.worldpublicopinion.org/pipa/articles/international_security_bt/102.php?nid=&id=&pnt=102&lb=brus (accessed 26 September 2006).

74. "Iraq Dominates PEJ's First Quarterly NCI Report," Project for Excellence in Journalism, 25 May 2007, http://www.journalism.org/node/5719 (accessed 28 February 2008).

75. Paul Krugman, "The Murdoch Factor," *New York Times*, 29 June 2007, A27.

76. David Gunzerath, "Rupert K. Murdoch," Museum of Broadcast Communications, n.d., http://www.museum.tv/eotvsection.php?entrycode=murdochrupe (accessed 26 February 2008).

77. Viacom Inc., *Form 10-K*, 11 February 2010.

78. Viacom Inc., *Form 10-K*, 1.

79. Viacom Inc., *Form 10-K*, 1.

80. "Yearly Box Office: 2007 Domestic Grosses" and "Yearly Box Office: Overseas Total," www.boxofficemojo.com (accessed 12 February 2008).

81. Viacom Inc., *Form 10-K*, 3.

82. Ben Bagdikian, *The Media Monopoly*, 6th ed. (Boston: Beacon, 2000), 27–29.

83. Jennifer Thomas, "Heat on Video Rental Stores," *State College (Pa.) Centre Daily Times*, 5 July 2008, A1, A7.

84. Jonathan Stempel, "Carl Icahn Unwinding Blockbuster Stake," Reuters, 2 April 2010, http://www.reuters.com/article/idUSTRE63127T20100402 (accessed 13 September 2010).

85. Brooks Barnes, "The $1 Redbox Alarm," *New York Times*, 7 September 2009, B1, B5.

86. Michael Cieply and Brooks Barnes, "Chief of Universal Finds Success at the Back of the Pack," *New York Times*, 16 July 2007, C1, C7.

87. Viacom Inc., *Form 10-K*, 10.

88. "CBS Films and Simon & Schuster in Film and Publishing Deal for Best-Selling Author," *New York Times* Market Watch, 8 February 2008, http://www.mar ketwatch.com/news/story/cbs-films-simon--schuster/story.aspx?guid={5636B393-753E-4904-A3CC-CFBC5EF241A2}&dist=TQP_Mod_pressN (accessed 29 February 2008).

89. Brooks Barnes, "With New Films, CBS Charts Tough Middle Course," *New York Times*, 19 January 2010, C1, C4.

90. *Fortune 500* and *Fortune Global 500*, 2009.

91. NBC Universal, "Company Overview, Film," http://www.nbcuni.com/About_NBC_Universal/Company_Overview/Film.shtml (accessed 13 July 2010), 2.

92. Janet Wasko, *Hollywood in the Information Age* (Austin: University of Texas Press, 1994), 63.

93. Yumiko Ono, "Was Japan's Craze for Art Yen Motivated?" *Wall Street Journal*, 2 April 1991, C1.

94. "The Big Ten," *The Nation*, 7 January 2002, 27–30, especially 28.

95. "Forbes 400," 2001; Seth Schiesel, "Vivendi Is Said to Have Deal for Expansion in U.S. Media," *New York Times*, 17 December 2001, A16.

96. "The Big Ten," 28.

97. Bill Carter, "G.E. Finishes Vivendi Deal, Expanding Its Media Assets," *New York Times*, 9 October 2003, www.nytimes.com (accessed 2 March 2008).

98. General Electric Co., Bloomberg Businessweek, http://investing.business week.com/research/stocks/people/board.asp?ticker=ge:us (accessed 13 September 2010).

99. Bob Fernandez, "FCC Commissioner Is Skeptical over Comcast, NBC Universal Merger at Hearing," *Philadelphia Enquirer*, 13 July 2010, http://articles.philly.com/2010-07-13/news/24969209_1_comcast-spokeswoman-sena-fitzmaurice-nbc-universal-merger (accessed 19 September 2010).

100. Comcast, "Corporate Overview," 20 June 2010, htpp://www.comcast.com/corporate/about/pressroom/corporateoverview (accessed 18 September 2010.)

101. Comcast, *2009 Annual Report on Form 10-K*, 23 February 2010, http://files.shareholder.com/downloads/CMCSA/1482724372x0xS1193125%2D10%2D37551/1166691/filing.pdf (accessed 3 November 2011), 3.

102. Comcast, "Comcast Spotlight," 2010, http://www.comcast.com/corporate/about/pressroom/comcastspotlight (accessed 18 September 2010).

103. "Special Report: CEO Compensation," Forbes.com, 28 April 2010, http://www.forbes.com/lists/2010/12/boss-10_CEO-Compensation-Media_9Rank.html (accessed 19 September 2010).

104. "Heavy Hitters: Comcast Corp.," Center for Responsive Politics, 22 August 2010, http://www.opensecrets.org/orgs/summary.php?id=D000000461 (accessed 22 September 2010).

105. "Lobbying: General Electric," Center for Responsive Politics, 26 July 2010, http://www.opensecrets.org/lobby/clientsum.php?lname=General+Electric& year=2010 (accessed 22 September 2010).

106. Susan Crawford, "Comcast's NBC-U Dreams May Be Online Video's Nightmare," 11 September 2010, http://gigaom.com/2010/09/11/comcasts-nbc-u-dreams-may-be-online-videos-nightmare (accessed 14 September 2010); emphasis in the original.

107. "Free Press: Comcast-NBC Mega-Merger Must Be Stopped," 30 November 2009, http://www.freepress.net/node/74889 (accessed 14 September 2010).

108. "Fortune Global 500," CNNMoney.com, 26 July 2010, http://money.cnn.com/magazines/fortune/global500/2010/full_list/ (accessed 26 July 2010).

109. "Studio Market Share 2009," Box Office Mojo, http://www.boxofficemojo.com/studio/?view=company&view2=yearly&yr=2009&p=.htm (accessed 8 November 2010).

110. Sony Pictures, "Corporate Fact Sheet," 2010, www.sonypictures.com (accessed 14 July 2010).

111. Sony Corporation of America, "Senior Management," June 2010, http://www.sony.com/SCA/bios/stringer.shtml (accessed 26 September 2010).

112. "Sony Corp-Sponsored ADR, "Latest Proxy Reports 2009–2010," Bloomberg Businessweek, http://investing.businessweek.com/research/stocks/people/relationship.asp?personId=631152&ticker=SNE (accessed 27 September 2010).

113. "Lobbying: TV/Movies/Music," Center for Responsive Politics, 2010, http://www.opensecrets.org/lobby/indusclient.php?lname=B02&year=a (accessed 27 September 2010).

114. "National Donors Search: Sony, Sony Pictures Entertainment," Center for Responsive Politics, 2010, http://www.opensecrets.org/orgs/lookup_stfed.php (accessed 27 September 2010).

115. Tom Graves, "Movies and Home Entertainment: Current Environment," *Standard & Poor's Industry Surveys*, 2 October 1997, 7.

116. Graves, "Movies and Home Entertainment," 2.

117. Claudia Eller and James Bates, "Hollywood Box Office Is Boffo," *Los Angeles Times*, 11 November 2001, 1–4, www.latimes.com (accessed 3 February 2002); Paul M. Sherer, "Loews Cineplex to Be Acquired by Onex Group," *Wall Street Journal*, 16 February 2001, A4.

118. Carl DiOrio, "U Dumps Its Loews Shares," *Daily Variety*, 29 June 2001, 6.

119. "Onex Aiming to Acquire Loews Theatre Chain," *Toronto Star*, 14 November 2001, E11.

120. Forbes 400, "The 400 Richest People In America," *Forbes*, 8 October 2001, 142.

121. Forbes 400, 2001, 142.

122. Josh Friedman, "Box-Office Revenue Swings Up Even as Attendance Hits a Wall," *Los Angeles Times*, 4 January 2008, www.lexisnexis.com (accessed 12 February 2008), C1.

123. Brooks Barnes, "An Imax and AMC Venture Will Expand 3-D Theaters," *New York Times*, 12 July 2007, C8.

124. Ronald V. Bettig, *Copyrighting Culture: The Political Economy of Intellectual Property* (Boulder, Colo.: Westview Press, 1996), 217.

125. Matthew Jackson, "From Private to Public: Reexamining the Technological Basis for Copyright," *Journal of Communication* 52 (2002): 416–33, 418.

126. David Tetzlaff, "Yo-Ho-Ho and a Server of Warez: Internet Software Piracy and the New Global Information Economy," in *The World Wide Web and Contemporary Cultural Theory*," ed. A. Herman and T. Swiss (New York: Routledge, 2000), 99–126, 122.

127. Rick Lyman, "Coming to a Computer near You: Movie Rentals Direct from Five Studios," *San Diego Union-Tribune*, 17 August 2001, A1, A26.

128. "Mediaforce Announces Top Ten Pirated Movies for July; Pirates Using Internet to Grow Personal Bootlegged Movies Collections," *PR Newswire*, 16 August 2001.

129. "Tristar Strikes Deal with In-Demand," Associated Press Online, 28 August 2001.

130. Bettig, *Copyrighting Culture*.

131. Sallie Hofmeister, "Lights, Camera, Download? Studios Focus on the Web," *Los Angeles Times*, 30 November 2000, A1.

132. U.S. Department of Justice, "Department Closes Antitrust Investigation into the Movielink Movies-on-Demand Joint Venture," 3 June 2004, http://www.justice.gov/atr/public/press_releases/2004/203932.htm (access 2 October 2010).

133. Ronald V. Bettig, "Hollywood and Intellectual Property," in *The Contemporary Hollywood Film Industry*, ed. Paul MacDonald and Janet Wasko (Malden, Mass.: Blackwell, 2008), 195–205, 202–203.

134. Randall Stross, "Why Bricks and Clicks Don't Always Mix," *New York Times*, 10 September 2010, Sunday Business 3.

135. Brooks Barnes, "In This War, Movie Studios Are Siding with Your Couch," *New York Times*, 26 September 2010, Sunday Business 1, 6.

136. "Disney Buys Stake in YouTube Rival Hulu," AFP, 30 April 2009, www.google.com (accessed 4 October 2010).

137. Kristina Shevory, "Aiming to Stem Attendance Losses, More Cinemas Try a Full-Frills Model," *New York Times*, 20 February 2008, C6.

138. Brooks Barnes, "For Hollywood Producers, Is the Glamour Gone?" *New York Times*, 22 May 2010, http://www.nytimes.com/2010/05/23/business/media/23steal.html (accessed 5 October 2010).

139. "Yearly Box Office," Box Office Mojo, http://www.boxofficemojo.com/yearly/ (accessed 8 November 2010).

140. Paramount, *10-K Report*, 2006, especially 34.

141. Paramount, *10-K Report*, especially 34, 49.

142. Thomas R. King, "Mickey Mouse vs. Pearl Harbor—Hoping to Avoid a Costly Bomb," *Wall Street Journal*, 6 April 2001, W1.

143. Douglas Gomery, "The Hollywood Film Industry: Theatrical Exhibition, Pay TV, and Home Video," in *Who Owns the Media? Competition and Concentration in the Mass Media Industry*, ed. Benjamin Compaine and Douglas Gomery (Mahwah, N.J.: Erlbaum, 2000), 359–439, especially 375.

144. Tom Graves, "Movies and Home Entertainment: Industry Trends," *Standard and Poor's*, 10 May 2001, www.netadvantage.standardandpoors.com/netahtml/ind sur/mhe20501.htm (accessed 19 November 2001).

145. Graves, "Movies and Home Entertainment," 4.

146. "Star News and Gossip," *TV Guide Live*, 11 December 2001, www.tvguide live.com/newsgossip-archives/01-dec/12-11-01.html (accessed 28 January 2002).

147. David M. Halbfinger and Geraldine Fabrikiant, "Fired or Quit, Tom Cruise Parts Ways with Studio," *New York Times*, 22 August 2006, C1, C2, especially C1.

148. Richard Natale, "Company Town Film Profit Report," *Los Angeles Times*, 30 January 2001, C10.

149. Thomas Schatz, "Show Me the Money: In Search of Hits, the Industry May Go Broke," *The Nation*, 5 April 1999, 26–31.

150. "My Big Fat Greek Wedding," Box Office Mojo, http://www.boxofficemojo.com/movies/?id=mybigfatgreekwedding.htm (accessed 8 November 2010).

151. "Reese Witherspoon Tops Rich List," Hollywood.com, 30 November 2007, http://www.hollywood.com/news/Witherspoon_Tops_Rich_List/5005010 (accessed 5 October 2010).

152. "Will Smith Tops Highest-Earner List," Hollywood.com, 24 July 2008, http://www.hollywood.com/news/Will_Smith_Tops_Highest_Earner_Poll/5280730 (accessed 5 October 2010).

153. "Nicole Kidman and Russell Crowe Named Most Overpaid Stars," Hollywood.com, 13 December 2007, http://www.hollywood.com/news/Kidman_and_Crowe_Named_Most_Overpaid_Stars/5014730 (accessed 5 October 2010).

154. Stratford P. Sherman, "Ted Turner: Back from the Brink," *Fortune*, 7 July 1986, 25–31, 28.

155. Phyllis Furman, "MGM Buys Back Movie Rights to Launch TV Cable Channel," *State College (Pa.) Centre Daily Times*, 16 September 1999, 8C; "MGM Regains Rights to Films," *New York Times*, 16 September 1999, C23.

156. Rick Lyman, "Coming Soon: Harry Potter and Hollywood's Cash Cow," *New York Times*, 4 November 2001, A1, A31.

157. Don Groves and Adam Dawtrey, "Hogwarts and Hobbits in Global Grab," *Variety*, 11 February 2002, E1.

158. Rick Lyman, "Harry Potter and the Box Office of Gold," *New York Times*, 19 November 2001, E1.

159. Lyman, "Coming Soon," A1.

160. Lyman, "Coming Soon," A31.

161. Phil Kloer, "Poof! Harry Potter Is Visible: Movie, Hype Make Wizard Hard to Miss," *Atlanta Journal-Constitution*, 26 October 2001, 1A.

162. "Potter Proves Power of Cross-Marketing," *Investor's Business Daily*, 23 November 2001, A6.

163. "$25 Million Ad Blitz Planned for Potter Video," *Milwaukee Journal Sentinel*, 7 February 2002, 6B.

164. Jennifer Netherby and Scott Hettrick, "Warner Wild about Harry: Studio Reaches for Stratosphere," *Video Business*, 11 February 2002, 1.

165. "Rings Goes to WB for $160 Million," *St. Petersburg Times*, 5 February 2002, 5D.

166. "Box Office," Hollywood.com, 19 July 2009, http://cdn-images.hollywood.com/site/harry_potter_franchise.pdf (accessed 6 October 2010).

167. Claudia Eller, "DVD Slump Might Weaken 'Half-Blood' Sales," *Los Angeles Times*, 22 June 2009, http://articles.latimes.com/2009/jun/22/business/fi-ct-potter22/3 (accessed 11 October 2010).

168. "Yearly Box Office," Box Office Mojo, 2009, http://www.boxofficemojo.com/yearly/?vidw2=worldwide$view=re (accessed 16 October 2010).

169. *Variety Portable Movie Guide* (New York: Berkeley Boulevard Books, 1999), 979.

170. Max Horkheimer and Theodor W. Adorno, *Dialectic of Enlightenment*, trans. John Cumming (New York: Seabury, 1972), 124. Originally published in 1944.

171. Horkheimer and Adorno, *Dialectic*, 139.

CHAPTER 4: THE MUSIC INDUSTRY

1. Ed Christman, "UMVD Marks Third Straight Year as Top U.S. Music Distributor," *Billboard*, 26 January 2002, 51.

2. Forbes 400, "The 400 Richest People in America," *Forbes*, 8 October 2001, 127–298, 235.

3. "The Media Nation: Music," *The Nation*, 25 August 1997, centerfold.

4. "The Media Nation," centerfold.

5. Christman, "UMVD Marks," 51.

6. Time Warner Inc., *Annual Report 2000*, 48.

7. Christman, "UMVD Marks," 51.

8. "The Media Nation," centerfold.

9. Christman, "UMVD Marks," 51.

10. "The Big Ten," *The Nation*, 7 January 2002, 27–30, 27–28.

11. Christman, "UMVD Marks," 51.

12. Christman, "UMVD Marks," 51.

13. Andrew Pollack and Andrew Ross Sorkin, "Time Warner to Acquire Control of EMI Music," *New York Times*, 24 January 2000, C1, C12.

14. Robert G. Woletz, "A New Formula: Into the 'Bin,' Out Comes a Hit," *New York Times*, 2 August 1992, D1.

15. Michael Goldberg, "MTV's Sharper Picture," *Rolling Stone*, 8 February 1990, 61–64, 118.

16. Neil Strauss, "MTV Winner: Neither Rejected nor Censored," *New York Times*, 2 September 1995, C15.

17. International Federation of Phonographic Industries, "Digital Music Report," 2011, http://www.ifpi.org/content/library/DMR2011.pdf (accessed 19 May 2011).

18. "Worldwide Music Industry Revenues (2006–2011)," GrabStats.com, http://www.grabstats.com/statmain.aasp?StatID=71 (accessed 23 May 2011); "Worldwide Recorded Music Revenues (2006–2011)," GrabStats.com, http://www.grabstats.com/statmain.aasp?StatID=68 (accessed 5 May 2011).

19. "North American Recorded Music Revenues (2006–2011)," GrabStats.com, http://www.grabstats.com/statmain.asp?StatID=71 (accessed 23 May 2011).

20. "Worldwide Music Industry Revenues (2006–2011)."

21. Ed Christman, "UMG Is Market Leader in 2010," *Hollywood Reporter*, 1 May 2011, http://www.hollywoodreporter.com/news/umg-market-leader-2010-katy-68702 (accessed 23 May 2011).

22. "Fortune Global 500," CNNMoney.com, 26 July 2010, http://money.cnn.com/magazines/fortune/global500/2010/full_list/ (accessed 26 July 2010).

23. Vivendi, S.A., *Annual Financial Report*, 31 December 2010, http://www.vivendi.com/vivendi/IMG/pdf/03_01_2011_Annual_Report.pdf (accessed 23 May 2011), 21.

24. Vivendi, S.A. *Annual Financial Report*, 20.

25. Universal Music Group, "History: Labels," 2010, http://www.universalmusic.com/history (accessed 7 June 2011.

26. "Jean-Bernard Lévy: Executive Profile and Biography—BusinessWeek," Bloomberg, 5 May 2011, http://investing.businessweek.com/research/stocks/people/person.asp?personId=2879833&ticker=VIV:FP (accessed 24 May 2011).

27. Vivendi, S.A., "Shareholding Structure," 31 December 2010, http://www.vivendi.com/vivendi/shareholding-structure (accessed 24 May 2011).

28. Vivendi, S. A., *2010 Annual Report*.

29. Christman, "UMG Is Market Leader."

30. Brent Lang, "Sony Loses $3.2B for Fiscal Year on Earthquake Fallout—DVD Declines Didn't Help," *The Wrap*, 26 May 2011, http://www.thewrap.com/movies/article/sony-loses-32b-weak-earnings-partly-due-earthquake-27744 (accessed 26 May 2011).

31. Chris Lee, "Michael Jackson Estate, Sony Music Entertainment Strike Distribution Deal," *Los Angeles Times*," 16 March 2010, https://www.google.com/adsense/support/bin/request.py?contact=abg_afc&url=http://a (accessed 31 May 2011).

32. Sony Corporation of America, "Outline of Principal Operations: Sony/ATV Music Publishing," November 2010, http://www.sony.com/SCA/outline/atv.shtml (accessed 26 May 2011).

33. Peter Cohen, "EMusic-Sony Deal: One Step Forward, One Big Step Back," *Macworld*, 4 June 2009, http://www.pcworld.com/businesscenter/article/166117/emusicsony_deal_one_step_forward_one_big_step_back.html (accessed 31 May 2011).

34. Sony Corporation of America, "Outline of Principal Operations: Music Choice," November 2010, http://www.sony.com/SCA/outline/partnerships.shtml (accessed 26 May 2011).

35. Kristen Schweizer, "Sony, Record Labels to Take On iTunes by Offering Fee-Based Music Service," Bloomberg, 24 January 2011, http:www.bloomberg.com/news/print/2011-01-24/sony-record-labels-to-rival-apple-s-itunes-with-music-service-in-the-u-s-.html (accessed 31 May 2011).

36. "BMI Pacts with Sony's Qriocity Streaming Service," *Business Sense (BMI)*, 12 April 2011, http://www.bmi.com/news/entry/551226 (accessed 31 May 2001).

37. Schweizer, "Sony, Record Labels."

38. "100 Leading National Advertisers Report 2010," *Advertising Age*, 28 December 2009, http://adage.com/marketertrees09update/ (accessed 25 March 2010).

39. Warner Music Group, "Warner Music Group Corp. Reports Results for the Fiscal Fourth Quarter and Full Year Ended September 30, 2010," 17 November

2010, http://www.wmg.com/newsdetails/id/8a0af8122c353d41012c56ba06bf0f65 (accessed 2 June 2011).

40. Warner Music Group, "Recorded Music Overview," 2011, www.wmg.com (accessed 2 June 2011).

41. David D. Kirkpatrick, "Time Warner Sells Music Unit for $2.6 Billion," *New York Times*, 25 November 2003, C1.

42. Doug Henwood, "Take Me to Your Leader," *Left Business Observer* 115, 31 May 2007, 1–2, 2.

43. Henwood, "Take Me to Your Leader," 2.

44. Warner Music Group. *2009 Annual Report*, 31 September 2009, http://www. scribd.com/doc/48117825/WMG-2009-Annual-Report (accessed 26 July 2010).

45. Jeff Leeds, "A Music Stock Offering Turns Downbeat," *New York* Times, 11 May 2005, http://www.nytimes.com/2005/05/11/business/media/11place.html (accessed 6 July 2011), 3.

46. Swati Panday, "Warner Music Whittles Its Losses on Brisk Digital Sales," *Los Angeles Times*, 8 August 2008, http://articles.latimes.com/2008/aug/08/business/fi warner8 (accessed 8 November 2008).

47. The Forbes 400, "The Richest People in America," September 2010, http:// www.forbes.com/wealth/forbes-400/list (accessed 7 June 2011).

48. Christman, "UMG Is Market Leader."

49. EMI Music, "About," 2011, http://www.emimusic.com/about/ (accessed 8 June 2011).

50. Phil Gallo, "Restructuring Ahead for EMI," *Variety*, 17 September 2008, http://www.variety.com/article/VR1117972092.html (accessed 17 October 2007).

51. Dana Cimilluca and Ethan Smith, "Citigroup Takes Control of EMI," *WSJ. com*, 2 February 2011, http://online.wsj.com/article/SB1000142405274870344590 4576118083710352572.html (accessed 8 June 2011).

52. Forbes 400, "The Richest People in America," September 2011, http://www .forbes.com/forbes-400/list/ (accessed 12 February 2012).

53. EMI Music, "About."

54. Christman, "UMG Is Market Leader."

55. Andy Fixmer, "News Corp. Said to Approach Vevo.com about Myspace Joint Venture," 29 March 2011, Bloomberg, http://www.bloomberg.com/news/2011- 03-28/news-corp-said-to-approach-vevo-com-music-site-on-myspace-joint-venture. html (accessed 22 June 2011).

56. International Federation of Phonographic Industries, "New Report Shows How Much Record Companies are 'Investing in Music,'" 9 March 2010, http:// www.ifpi.org/content/section_news/investing_in_music.html (accessed 4 December 2010).

57. Recording Industry Association of America, *Let's Play: The American Music Business*, 2010, 6, http://www.ifpi.org/content/library/RIAA_Brochure_Final.pdf (accessed 4 November 2011).

58. International Federation of Phonograph Industries, "New Report."

59. Ed Christman, "U.S. Music Sales Hit a Wall," *Billboard*, 26 January 2002, 1, 76.

60. Neil Strauss, "Wal-Mart's CD Standards Are Changing Pop Music," *New York Times*, 12 November 1996, A1, C12.

61. Strauss, "Wal-Mart's CD Standards," A1.

62. NPD Group, "Amazon Ties Wal-Mart as Second-Ranked U.S. Music Retailer, Behind Industry-Leader iTunes," NDP Press Release, 26 May 2010, http://www.npd.com/press/releases/press_100526.html (accessed 31 May 2011).

63. "Music Stores: Overview," Hoovers, 2011, http://www.hoovers.com/industry/music-stores/1931-1.html (accessed 2 July 2011).

64. Melissa Allison and Amy Martinez, "Independent Record Shops Competing in Digital Age," *Seattle Times*, 8 April 2010, http://seattletimes.nwsource.com/html/retailreport/2011562280_retailreport09.html (accessed 2 July 2011).

65. Ed Christman, "Solutions for Sale," *Billboard*, 23 January 2010, 10–11, 11.

66. "Worldwide Live Music/Concert Revenues (2006–2011)," GrabStats.com, http://www.grabstats.com/statmain.asp?StatID=70 (accessed 9 July 2011).

67. Randy Lewis, "Bon Jovi Posts Highest Grossing Concert Tour of the Year," *Los Angeles Times*, 29 December 2010, http://articles.latimes.com/2010/dec/29/entertainment/la-et-pollstar-numbers-20101229 (accessed 10 July 2011).

68. Live Nation Entertainment, *10-K Report*, 28 February 2011, www.livenation.com (accessed 7 July 2011).

69. Live Nation, *10-K Report*, 2.

70. Live Nation, *10-K Report*, 17.

71. Live Nation, *10-K Report*, 6.

72. David Segal, "They're Calling Most Everyone's Tune," *New York Times*, 24 April 2010, BU1, BU6–7, BU6.

73. Segal, "They're Calling," 6.

74. Anschutz Company, "AEG Music," 2010, http://aegworldwide.com/music/music (accessed 10 July 2011).

75. Madison Square Garden Company, "MSG Entertainment," n.d., http://www.themadisonsquaregardencompany.com/our-company (accessed 10 July 2011).

76. Ben Sisario, "Front-Row Seat to Go? Rock Fans Pay for Perks with the Stars," *New York Times*, 23 May 2010, C1, C4.

77. Edna Gundersen, "U2 Turns 360 Stadium Tour into Attendance-Shattering Sellouts," *USA Today*, 5 October 2009, http://www.usatoday.com/life/music/news/2009-10-04-u2-stadium-tourN.html (accessed 16 July 2011).

78. Lewis, "Bon Jovi."

79. Georg Szlalai, "Record Industry Revenues Increased 6% in 2010," *Hollywood Reporter*, 18 February 2010, http://www.hollywoodreporter.com/news/radio-industry-revenue-increases-6-101551 (accessed 9 July 2011).

80. "Radio Broadcasting in the U.S: Current Performance," IBISWorld, 2010, http://clients.ibisworld.com/industryus/currentperformance.aspx (accessed 10 July 2011).

81. Georg Szlalai, "Radio Industry Continues to Grow Revenue in First Quarter," *Hollywood Reporter*, 20 May 2011, http://www.hollywoodreporter.com/news/radio-industry-continues-grow-revenue-190697 (accessed 11 July 2011).

82. "Radio Broadcasting in the U.S.: Major Companies," IBISWorld, 2010, http://www.ibisworld.com/ (accessed 10 July 2011), 1.

83. "Radio Broadcasting in the U.S.: Major Companies," 2.

84. Carlyle Adler, "Clear Channel, Incorporated," Portfolio.com, n.d., http://www.portfolio.com/resources/companyprofiles/1107?TID=rm/ys2/Company_Database (accessed 11 August 2008).

85. Meena Thiruvengadam, "Clear Channel Sells More Radio Stations," *Knight Ridder Tribune Business News*, 3 May 2007, 1.

86. David Lieberman, "Clear Channel Chief Loves Idea of Going Private," *USA Today*, 22 November 2006, B4.

87. "Radio Broadcasting in the U.S.: Major Companies," 2.

88. "Radio Broadcasting in the U.S.: Major Companies," 2.

88. "Radio Broadcasting in the U.S.: Major Companies," 2.

90. CBS Radio, "About Us: Corporate Profile," 2011, http://www.cbsradio.com/about/index.html (accessed 10 July 2011).

91. CBS Radio, "About Us."

92. CBS Corporation, *10-K Annual Report*, 25 February 2011, I-1.

93. CBS Corporation, *10-K Annual Report*, I-11, 1-12.

94. "Radio Broadcasting in the U.S.: Major Companies," 3.

95. Bryan F. Yurcan, "Radio Stations Dial in New Owner," *Westchester County Business Journal*, 30 July 2007, 3.

96. Cumulus Media Inc., "Company Profile," 2006, http://www.corporate-ir.net/ir_site.zhtml (accessed 19 October 2007).

97. Cumulus Media Inc., *110-K Report*, 2008, http://phx.corporate-ir-net/phoenix.zhtml (accessed 4 April 2009).

98. Amy Thomson, "Cumulus to Buy Citadel Broadcasting in $2.4 Billion Deal," Bloomberg, 10 March 2011, http://www.bloomberg.com/news/2011-03-10/cumulus-agrees-to-buy-citadel-broadcasting-in-deal-valued-at-2-4-billion.html (accessed 14 July 2011).

99. "Radio Broadcasting in the U.S.: Major Companies," 3.

100. Bradley Johnson, "100 Leading Media Companies," *Advertising Age*, 3 October 2011, 44–50, 46.

101. Cox Enterprises Inc., "Cox Companies," 2011, http://www.coxenterprises.com/cox-companies.aspx (accessed 14 July 2011).

102. Jenny Eliscu, "Why Radio Sucks," *Rolling Stone*, 3 April 2003, 22.

103. Jeff Leeds, "Universal Music Settles Big Payola Case," *New York Times*, 12 May 2006, http://www.nytimes.com/2006/05/12/business/12payola.html?scp=1&sq=Leeds,%20Universal%20music%20settles%20big%20payola%20case&st=cse (accessed 14 July 2011).

104. Eliscu, "Why Radio Sucks," 22.

105. Tom Samiljan, "I Want My MP3," *Rolling Stone*, 18 March 1999, 69.

106. John Markoff, "Bridging Two Worlds to Make On-Line Digital Music Profitable," *New York Times*, 13 September 1999, C1.

107. Sara Robinson, "Recording Industry Escalates Crackdown on Digital Piracy," *New York Times*, 4 October 1999, C5.

108. Jeff Goodell, "World War MP3," *Rolling Stone*, 8 July 1999, 43.

109. Eric Hellweg, "Down with MP3," *Spin*, October 1999, 57.

110. Eric Boehlert, "MP3.mess: Petty Single Pulled from Net," *Rolling Stone*, 29 April 1999, 40.

111. Boehlert, "MP3.mess."

112. Sue Cummings, "The Flux in Pop Music Has a Distinctly Download Beat to It," *New York Times*, 22 September 1999, G60.

113. Fred Schruers, "Tom Petty: The Rolling Stone Interview," *Rolling Stone*, 22 July 1999, 88–94, 92.

114. Robinson, "Recording Industry."

115. Goodell, "World War MP3."

116. International Federation of Phonographic Industries, "IFPI Publishes Digital Music Report 2011," 20 January 2011, http://www.ifpi.org/content/section_re sources/dmr2011.html (accessed 10 July 2011).

117. Recording Industry of America, "Music, Movie, TV and Broadband Leaders Team to Curb Online Content Theft," 2011, http://riaa.com/newsitem .php?content_selector=newsandviews&news_month_filter=7&news_year_filter= 2011&id=2DDC3887-A4D5-8D41-649D-6E4F7C5225A5 (accessed 10 July 2011).

118. Recording Industry Association of America, "U.S. Government Issues Annual Report Naming Foreign Countries with Worst IP Protections," 2 May 2011, http:// www.riaa.com/newsitem.php?content_selector=newsandviews&news_month_ filter=5&news_year_filter=2011&id=F4B3CD29-B810-CF82-0537-1855502021EA (accessed 10 July 2011).

119. Matthew David, *Peer to Peer and the Music Industry: The Criminalization of Sharing* (Thousand Oaks, Calif.: Sage, 2010), 9.

CHAPTER 5: THE NEWS AND ADVERTISING INDUSTRIES

1. Michael Schudson, *Discovering the News: A Social History of American Newspapers* (New York: Basic Books, Inc., 1978), 110–11.

2. Schudson, *Discovering the News*, 111–12.

3. Schudson, *Discovering the News*, 112–13.

4. *The Journalist*, 4 December 1897, 46, cited in Schudson, *Discovering the News*, 107.

5. Gerald J. Baldasty, "The Rise of News as a Commodity: Business Imperatives and the Press in the Nineteenth Century," in *Ruthless Criticism: Perspectives in U.S. Communication History*, ed. William S. Solomon and Robert W. McChesney (Minneapolis: University of Minnesota Press, 1993), 112–13.

6. *Rolling Stone* officially adopted the motto later, but the antiestablishment tone it embodies is evident from the first issue.

7. Jann Wenner, "A Letter from the Editor," *Rolling Stone*, 9 November 1967, 2.

8. *Rolling Stone*, 9 November 1967, 1–8.

9. "Help!" *Rolling Stone*, 20 January 1968, 3.

10. Tom Wolfe, "Preface," in *Rolling Stone: The Photographs*, ed. Laurie Kratochvil (New York: Simon & Schuster, 1989), ii.

11. Ronald V. Bettig, *Copyrighting Culture: The Political Economy of Intellectual Property* (Boulder, Colo.: Westview Press, 1996), 16.

12. Schudson, *Discovering the News*, 16–19.

13. Calvin F. Exoo, *The Politics of the Mass Media* (St. Paul, Minn.: West Publishing Company, 1994), 119.

14. Schudson, *Discovering the News*, 93.

15. Schudson, *Discovering the News*, 93.

16. Donald L. Shaw, "News Bias and the Telegraph: A Study of Historical Change," *Journalism Quarterly* 44 (Spring 1967): 3–12, 31. Cited in Schudson, *Discovering the News*, 4.

17. W. Ronald Lane and J. Thomas Russell, *Advertising: A Framework* (Upper Saddle River, N.J.: Prentice Hall, 2001), 1–3.

18. Lane and Russell, *Advertising*, 1–3.

19. Schudson, *Discovering the News*, 93.

20. Exoo, *The Politics of the Mass Media*, 120.

21. Exoo, *The Politics of the Mass Media*, 119.

22. Matt Carlson, "Boardroom Brothers: Interlocking Directorates Indicate Media's Corporate Ties," *Extra!* September/October 2001, 18.

23. "The National Entertainment State, 2006," *The Nation*, 3 July 2006 http://www.thenation.com/doc/20060703/intro (accessed 6 October 2006).

24. Ben H. Bagdikian, *The Media Monopoly*, 6th ed. (Boston: Beacon, 2000), 265.

25. Benjamin M. Compaine, "The Newspaper Industry," in *Who Owns the Media? Competition and Concentration in the Mass Media Industry*, ed. Benjamin M. Compaine and Douglas Gomery (Mahwah, N.J.: Erlbaum, 2000), 2–6.

26. Compaine, "The Newspaper Industry," 2–6.

27. "Industry Overview: Newspapers and News Organizations," Hoovers Inc., 2007, http://www.hoovers.com/ (accessed 9 November 2007).

28. "New York Times Co.," *Standard & Poor's Corporate Descriptions Plus News*, 29 January 2002, www.lexisnexis.com (accessed 1 February 2002).

29. "Fortune 500, 2007," CNNMoney.com, http://money.cnn.com/magazines/fortune/fortune500/2007/snapshots/1380.html.

30. Bradley Johnson, "The 100 Leading Media Companies," *Advertising Age*, 3 October 2011, 44–50, 46.

31. "The New York Times Company Reports December Revenues," 24 January 2006, http://advertise.about.com/newspress/news01_24_06.html (accessed 27 February 2008).

32. "The New York Times Company Reports December Revenues."

33. "*Rolling Stone*, Disney Join Forces for *US*," *State College (Pa.) Centre Daily Times*, 28 February 2001, B9.

34. Alex Kuczynski, "Disney to Take 50% Stake in *US Weekly* Magazine," *New York Times*, 28 February 2001, C1.

35. Jeff Leeds, "Disney Returns to Publishing with Stake in *US*," *Los Angeles Times*, 28 February 2001, C1.

36. "*Rolling Stone*," *Wikipedia*, http://en.wikipedia.org/wiki/Rolling_Stone (accessed 23 February 2008).

37. Steven Thomas, "White House Manages New Media, Stays on Message," *State College (Pa.) Centre Daily Times*, 16 May 2010, A3.

38. Justin Jones, "Young Adults Are Giving Newspapers Scant Notice," *New York Times*, 16 July 2007, C4.

39. The Pew Research Center for the People and the Press, "Summary of Findings: Public Knowledge of Current Affairs Little Changed by News and Information Revolutions," 15 April 2007, http://people-press.org/reports/display.php3?ReportID=319 (accessed 26 January 2008).

40. Pew Research Center, "Summary of Findings."

41. Frank Rich, *The Greatest Story Ever Sold: The Decline and Fall of Truth from 9/11 to Katrina* (New York: Penguin, 2006), 224–25.

42. "Data Center," *Advertising Age*, 25 June 2007, 5.

43. "Data Center," *Advertising Age*, 25 June 2007, 7.

44. Johnson, 52.

45. Exoo, *The Politics of the Mass Media*, 24.

46. Exoo, *The Politics of the Mass Media*, 25–27. Exoo draws data from three sources: Herbert McClosky and John Zaller, *The American Ethos* (Cambridge, Mass.: Harvard University Press, 1984); Sidney Verba and Gary R. Owen, *Equality in America* (Cambridge, Mass.: Harvard University Press, 1985); and Kay Schlozman and Sidney Verba, *Injury to Insult* (Cambridge, Mass.: Harvard University Press, 1979).

47. Exoo, *The Politics of the Mass Media*, 25–26.

48. Exoo, *The Politics of the Mass Media*, 26–27.

49. Michael F. Jacobson and Laurie Ann Mazur, *Marketing Madness: A Survival Guide for a Consumer Society* (Boulder, Colo.: Westview Press, 1995), 12.

50. Douglas Quenqua, "Upload a Prom Dress Photo, and Hope," *New York Times*, 13 May 2010, E8.

51. Exoo, *The Politics of the Mass Media*, 262.

52. Stuart Ewen, *Captains of Consciousness* (New York: McGraw-Hill, 1977), 58.

53. John Belton, *American Cinema/American Culture* (New York: McGraw-Hill, 1994), 234.

54. Exoo, *The Politics of the Mass Media*, 264.

55. Chuck Collins, "Horatio Alger, Where Are You?," *Dollars and Sense*, January/February 1997, 9.

56. "Fortune 500, 2007, Full List," CNNMoney.com, http://money.cnn.com/magazines/fortune/fortune500/2007/full_list/ (accessed 27 February 2008).

57. Alex Berenson, "Minky Viagra? Pfizer Doesn't Want You to Understand It, Just Buy It," *New York Times*, 30 April 2007, C1.

58. Paul Farhi, "Ad Trend on Radio: Hear Today, Gone in 2 Seconds," *San Diego Union Tribune*, 20 June 2007, A1.

59. Exoo, *The Politics of the Mass Media*, 258.

60. Lane and Russell, *Advertising*, 2.

61. Philip Gold, *Advertising, Politics, and American Culture* (New York: Paragon, 1987), 18.

62. Exoo, *The Politics of the Mass Media*, 266.

63. Marc Cooper, "*The Progressive* Interview: George Carlin," *The Progressive*, July 2001, 32–37.

64. Lane and Russell, *Advertising*, 15.

65. Naomi Klein, *No Logo: Taking Aim at the Brand Bullies* (New York: Picador USA, 1999), 17.

66. Bob Garfield, "Benetton on Death Row," *Advertising Age*, 10 January 2000, 45.

67. Jade Garrett, "Shock! Horror! New Benetton Ad Shows Clothes," *The Independent (London)*, 24 January 2001, 12.

68. Garfield, "Benetton on Death Row," 45.

69. Garrett, "Shock! Horror!" 12.

70. Bob Dart, "Denny's Begins TV Spots on Race Today," *Atlanta Journal and Constitution*, 13 January 1999, E10.

71. Dart, "Denny's Begins TV Spots," E10.

72. Dart, "Denny's Begins TV Spots," E10.

73. Todd Henneman, "Denny's Sued by Bay Area Latinos; Restaurant Announces Anti-Discrimination Ads on TV Same Day," *San Francisco Chronicle*, 13 January 1999, A4.

74. Tannette Johnson-Elie, "Denny's Turnabout Means Fair Play for Minority Employees," *Milwaukee Journal Sentinel*, 31 October 2000, D10.

75. Malone continued to run his programming company, Liberty Media, after the 1999 merger. Liberty split off from AT&T in August 2001, and the following December, it raised its stake in UnitedGlobalCom Inc., Europe's second-largest cable operator.

76. "Whither the Tube?" *New York Times*, 4 January 1999, 18A.

77. "Whither the Tube?" 18A.

78. Schudson, *Discovering the News*, 8.

79. Will Lester, "Poll: Democratic Voters Still Support Their Candidates," *State College (Pa.) Centre Daily Times*, 28 August 1998, 6A.

80. George Farah and Justin Elga, "What's Not Talked About on Sunday Morning?" *Extra!* October 2001, 14–17.

81. Farah and Elga, "What's Not Talked About," 14–17.

82. Pew Research Center for the People and the Press, "Too Much Celebrity News, Too Little Good News," 12 October 2007, http://people-press.org/reports/display.php3?ReportID=362 (accessed 22 February 2008).

83. Maureen Dowd, "America's Anchors," *Rolling Stone*, 16 November 2006, 54.

84. "Inside Politics, Wikipedia, http://en.wikipedia.org/wiki/Inside_Politics (accessed 22 February 2008).

85. "Microsoft's Illegal Monopoly," *New York Times*, 4 April 2000, A30.

86. Joel Brinkley, "U.S. Judge Says Microsoft Violated Antitrust Laws with Predatory Behavior," *New York Times*, 4 April 2000, A1, C12.

87. Herbert J. Gans, "The Messages behind the News," *Columbia Journalism Review*, January–February 1979, 40–45.

88. Gans, "The Messages," 40–45.

89. *The New Webster's Dictionary and Thesaurus of the English Language* (Danbury, Conn.: Lexicon, 1992), 1111.

90. Robert Parry, Sam Parry, and Nat Parry, "Journalists 'Humbled' but Unrepentent," *Extra!* November–December 2007, 22.

91. Edward Herman, "Market System Constraints on Freedom of Expression," *Journal of Communication Inquiry* 15, no. 1 (1991): 45–53.

92. Jon Bekken, "The Working-Class Press at the Turn of the Century," in *Ruthless Criticism: Perspectives in U.S. Communication History*, ed. William S. Solomon and Robert W. McChesney (Minneapolis: University of Minnesota Press, 1993), 151.

93. Schudson, *Discovering the News*, 100.

94. James Curran and Jean Seaton, *Power without Responsibility*, 3rd ed. (London: Fontana, 1988), 39.

95. Curran and Seaton, *Power without Responsibility*, 37–38.

96. Bagdikian, *The Media Monopoly*, 122–23.

97. Bagdikian, *The Media Monopoly*, 122.

98. Bagdikian, *The Media Monopoly*, 124.

99. Compaine, *"The Newspaper Industry,"* 8.

100. Compaine, *"The Newspaper Industry,"* 9–10.

101. U.S. Census Bureau, American Fact Finder, Concentration by Largest Firms, EC075155 Z6, 2007 Economic Census.

102. Bagdikian, *The Media Monopoly*, 177.

103. Bagdikian, *The Media Monopoly*, 192.

104. "When Being No. 1 Is Not Enough: The Impact of Advertising Practices on Minority-Owned and Minority-Formatted Broadcast Stations," www.fcc.gov/Bureaus/Media (accessed 29 December 2001).

105. "Kilpatrick Responds to FCC Minority Advertising Study," 13 January 1998, http://transition.fcc.gov/Bureaus/Mass_Media/Informal/ad-study/kilpatrick.html (accessed 30 December 2001).

106. Richard W. Pollay, Jung S. Lee, and David Carter-Whitney, "Separate, but Not Equal: Racial Segmentation in Cigarette Advertising," in *Gender, Race, and Class in Media*, ed. Gail Dines and Jean M. Humez (Thousand Oaks, Calif.: Sage Publications, 1995), 109–11.

107. Joanne Lipman, "Media Content Is Linked to Cigarette Ads," *Wall Street Journal*, 30 January 1992, B7.

108. "FCC Presented with Advertising Study Which Reveals a Tale of Two Systems: Study Shows Broadcasters Serving Minority Community Earn Less per Listener," www.fcc.gov/Bureaus/Media (accessed 28 December 2001).

109. David Handelman, "Without a Media Umbrella: Solo Magazines Must Scramble in Hard Times," *New York Times*, 10 December 2001, 9C.

110. Handelman, "Without a Media Umbrella," 9C.

111. Thomas R. King, "Time Warner Close to Big Cross-Media Ad Deal for Mazda," *Wall Street Journal*, 28 May 1991, C15.

112. "SoundBites: Ads Are Not Enough," *Extra! Update*, December 1999, 2.

113. "SoundBites: Ads Are Not Enough," 2.

114. "Advertising: G.M.'s Response to *Roger & Me*," *New York Times*, 31 January 1990, D23.

115. Doron P. Levin, "When Car Makers Retaliate against Critical Magazines," *New York Times*, 26 June 1992, D9.

116. Levin, "When Car Makers Retaliate," D9.

117. Bill Carter, "Few Sponsors for TV War News," *New York Times*, 7 February 1991, D1, D20.

118. Carter, "Few Sponsors for TV War News," D1, D20.

119. Carter, "Few Sponsors for TV War News," D1, D20.

120. Carter, "Few Sponsors for TV War News," D1, D20.

121. Carter, "Few Sponsors for TV War News," D1, D20.

122. Carter, "Few Sponsors for TV War News," D1, D20.

123. Seth Schiesel with Felicity Barringer, "News Media Risk Big Losses to Cover War," *New York Times*, 22 October 2001, C1.

124. Schiesel, "News Media Risk," C1.

125. Schiesel, "News Media Risk," C1.

126. "Antismoking Product's Ad Stirs Debate," *New York Times*, 11 November 1988, D17.

127. Lipman, "Media Content," B7.

128. Lipman, "Media Content," B7.

129. Joel Bleifuss, "It's a Mad Ad World," *In These Times*, 18–24 March 1992, 4–5.

130. Nancy Zuckerford, "Study: Ads Have Greater Effects Than Anti-Tobacco Efforts," *State College (Pa.) Centre Daily Times*, 12 June 2001, A4.

131. "Live Longer, Better, Wiser," *Parade*, 19 March 2000, 1.

132. Joan Tarshis, "Celebrities Reveal Their Secrets," *Parade*, 19 March 2000, 10.

133. Advertisement, Wyeth-Ayerst Laboratories, *Parade*, 19 March 2000, 15.

134. Sally Squires, "Experts Say Medicine Ads Often Omit Basics," *State College (Pa.) Centre Daily Times*, 18 December 2000, C1.

135. Breast cancer, for example, is known to be an estrogen-dependent disease. See Tom Monte, *Natural Healing* (New York: Berkeley Publishing Group, 1997), 60.

136. Connie Lauerman, "Aging Baby Boomers Fight War on Wrinkles," *State College (Pa.) Centre Daily Times*, 7 September 1998, C3.

137. "SoundBites: Buy One, Get One Free," *Extra! Update*, June 2000, 2.

138. Alex S. Jones, "Knight-Ridder Faces a Newspaper Puzzle," *New York Times*, 18 November 1991, D8.

139. Jones, "Knight-Ridder Faces," D8.

140. Schudson, *Discovering the News*, 93.

141. *New Webster's Dictionary*, 992.

142. Ann Marsh, "Meet the Class of 1996," *Forbes*, 14 October 1996, 100.

143. Collins, "Horatio Alger, Where Are You?" 9.

144. Eric R. Quinones, "Market Woes Lessen Ranks of Billionaires," *State College (Pa.) Centre Daily Times*, 28 September 1998, A1.

145. Alex E. Hill, letter to the editor: "Who Cares about the Depletion of Billionaires?" *State College (Pa.) Centre Daily Times*, 4 October 1998, A11; "Editor's Note," *State College (Pa.) Centre Daily Times*, 4 October 1998, A11.

146. "Cash Countesses," *Forbes*, 8 October 2007, 312–17, 312.

147. "Buffett Tops Gates as World's Richest," *State College (Pa.) Centre Daily Times*, 7 March 2007, A2.

148. R. C. Longworth, "CEOs' Average 531 Times the Salary of Workers," *State College (Pa.) Centre Daily Times*, 28 August 2001, B7.

149. "Measuring Privilege," *Left Business Observer*, July 1997, 3.

150. Barbara Crossette, "Experts Scaling Back Their Estimates of World Population Growth," *New York Times*, 20 August 2002, D8.

CHAPTER 6: AD CREEP

1. "Ad Creep," *Word Spy*, www.wordspy.com/words/adcreep.asp (accessed 2 January 2008).

2. "Ad Creep," *Wikipedia*, http://en.wikipedia.org/wiki/Ad_creep#_note-Macmillan (accessed 2 January 2008).

3. "Commercial Creep," *Word Spy*, http://www.wordspy.com/words/commercialcreep.asp (accessed 2 January 2008).

4. Robert W. McChesney, *The Problem of the Media* (New York: Monthly Review Press, 2004), 143.

5. Charles Eicher, "Disinfotainment: Product Placement Problems," http://weblog.ceicher.com/archives/2002/04/product_placement_problems.html (accessed 3 January 2008).

6. "Round Tables: Ad Creep," *MediaChannel.org*, 4 January 2000, http://www.mediachannel.org/views/oped/adcreep.shtml (accessed 3 January 2008).

7. McChesney, *The Problem of the Media*, 167.

8. Janet Wasko, *How Hollywood Works* (Thousand Oaks, Calif.: Sage, 2003), 155.

9. Kimbrew McLeod, *Freedom of Expression: Overzealous Copyright Bozos and Other Enemies of Creativity* (New York: Doubleday, 2005), 188–97, excerpted at http://www.brandhype.org/MovieMapper/Resources/ProductPlacementAndTheRealWorld.jsp (accessed 23 January 2008).

10. J. D. Rummel, "*You've Got Mail*: It's Okay," *Manly Men's Movie Reviews*, http://morpo.com/movies/?id=83&au=2 (accessed 30 September 2004).

11. Paul Farhi, "AOL Gets Message Out in *Mail*," *Washington Post*, 17 December 1998, http://www.washingtonpost.com/wp-srv/style/movies/features/aolinmail.htm (accessed 12 November 2007).

12. John Simons, "Big Pharma's Ready for Prime Time," *Fortune*, 28 September 2007, http://money.cnn.com/2007/09/28/magazines/fortune/simons_product-placement.fortune/index.htm (accessed 12 October 2007).

13. Joanne Weintraub, "TV Industry Oh So Flexible on Money," *Milwaukee Journal Sentinel*, cited in "The One with the Apothecary Table," *Wikipedia*, http://en.wikipedia.org/wiki/The_One_with_the_Apothecary_Table (accessed 28 February 2008).

14. Beth Negus Viveiros, *DirectMag.com*, cited in "The One with the Apothecary Table," *Wikipedia*, http://en.wikipedia.org/wiki/The_One_with_the_Apothecary_Table (accessed 28 February 2008).

15. Ira Tenowitz, "Congressmen Tackle Product Placement," *TV Week*, 26 September 2007, http://www.tvweek.com/news/2007/09/congressmen_tackle_product_pla.php (accessed 24 January 2008).

16. Mike Adams, "Pharmaceutical Television Advertising Is a Grand Hoax," NaturalNews.com, 30 January 2007, http://www.naturalnews.com/021526.html (accessed 13 January 2008).

17. Joel Rose, "Rock Artists Embrace TV Sales," *NPR Morning Edition*, 6 February 2007, http://www.npr.org/templates/story/story.php?storyId=7213219 (accessed 14 January 2008).

18. "Pete Townshend's Strongly Held Political Beliefs," NotBored.org, 18 July 2004, http://www.notbored.org/townshend.html (accessed 18 January 2008).

19. "Crumbelievable!!! The Ten Cheesiest Rock Commercials," *Spinner*, http://spinner.aol.com/photos/swiffer-commercial-song-devo (accessed 21 January 2008).

20. Theresa Howard, "Dylan Ad for Underwear Generates Lingering Buzz," *USA Today*, 16 May 2005, http://www.usatoday.com/money/advertising/adtrack/2004-05-16-victoria-secrets-dylan_x.htm (accessed 15 January 2008).

21. Alan Light, "Changes in Mellencamp Country," *New York Times*, 22 January 2007, http://www.nytimes.com/2007/01/22/arts/music/22mell.html?ex=1327122000&en=00271aa689653496&ei=5090&partner=rssuserland&emc=rss (accessed 21 January 2008).

22. Seth Stevenson, "Can Rosa Parks Sell Pickup Trucks?" *Slate*, 9 October 2006, http://www.slate.com/id/2151143/ (accessed 13 January 2008).

23. Austin Scaggs, "Q&A: The King of Heartland Returns with Renewed Optimism, a New Album, and a Chevy Ad," *Rolling Stone*, 8 February 2007, 28.

24. Light, "Changes in Mellencamp Country," (accessed 21 January 2008).

25. Jeff Chang, "Fight the Power: Can Hip-Hop Get Past the Thug Life and Back to Its Radical Roots?" *Mother Jones*, November–December 2007, 67.

26. McChesney, *The Problem of the Media*, 156–57.

27. "Blue Flame Marketing, a P. Diddy Owned Company, to Offer Corporations Partnership Opportunities with Bad Boy Entertainment," 14 January 2003, http://findarticles.com/p/articles/mi_m0EIN/is_2003_Jan_14/ai_96432192 (accessed 3 March 2008).

28. Jameel Spencer, quoted in Gil Kaufman, "Push the Courvoisier: Are Rappers Paid for Product Placement?" *MTV.com*, 9 June 2003, http://www.mtv.com/news/articles/1472393/20030606/puff_daddy.jhtml (accessed 3 March 2008).

29. "About Us," Rocawear.com, http://www.rocawear.com/shop/aboutus.php (accessed 3 March 2008).

30. Kaufman, "Push the Courvoisier."

31. Chang, "Fight the Power," 67.

32. Joanne Lipman, "Chrysler to Bring Splashy Ads to Stage," *Wall Street Journal*, 13 May 1992, B8.

33. Stuart Elliott, "On Broadway, Ads Now Get to Play Cameo Roles," *New York Times*, 22 April 2005, http://www.nytimes.com/2005/04/22/business/media/22adco.html (accessed 3 March 2008).

34. Rich Mintzer, "Product Placement Takes the Stage," Entrepreneur.com, 28 September 2007, http://www.entrepreneur.com/advertising/adsbytype/otherideas/article184830.html (accessed 3 March 2008).

35. Kurt Vonnegut, *Breakfast of Champions* (New York: Dial, 1973), 199–200.

36. David Kirkpatrick, "Now, Many Words from Our Sponsor," *New York Times*, 3 September 2001, http://query.nytimes.com/gst/fullpage.html?res=9F00E5D61F30F930A3575AC0A9679C8B63&sec=&spon=&pagewanted=all (accessed 3 March 2008).

37. Martin Plaut, "Ford Advertises the Literary Way," BBC News, 1 March 2004, http://news.bbc.co.uk/1/hi/business/3522635.stm (accessed 3 March 2008).

38. "New Product Placement: Best Selling Novels," *Kicking Tires*, 20 November 2006, http://blogs.cars.com/kickingtires/2006/11/patterson_merce.html (accessed 3 March 2008).

39. Vonnegut, *Breakfast of Champions*, 47.

40. Thomas Kostigan, "Novel Idea Is All Wet," MarketWatch, 14 July 2006, http://www.marketwatch.com/News/Story/Story.aspx?dist=newsfinder&siteid=google&guid=%7BC7B959C1-C8AC-4C0F-AAFA-F38FDD66CEE6%7D&keyword= (accessed 3 March 2008).

41. Motoko Rich, "Product Placement Deals Make Leap From Film to Books," *New York Times*, 12 June 2006, http://www.nytimes.com/2006/06/12/business/media/12book.html (accessed 3 March 2008).

42. Peter A. Maresco, "Using Teen Chick Lit Novels to Teach Marketing," Goliath, 22 March 2007, http://goliath.ecnext.com/coms2/gi_0199-6701070/Using-teen-chick-lit-novels.html (accessed 11 January 2008).

43. Motoko Rich, "In Books for Young, Two Views on Product Placement," *New York Times*, 19 February 2008, B1, B7, especially B7.

44. Juliet B. Schor, *Born to Buy* (New York: Scribner, 2004), 13.

45. Schor, *Born to Buy*, 19.

46. Schor, *Born to Buy*, 20.

47. Thomas N. Robinson, Dina L. G. Borzekowski, Donna M. Matheson, and Helena C. Kraemer, "Effects of Fast Food Branding on Young Children's Taste Preferences," *Archives of Pediatric & Adolescent Medicine* 161, no. 8, 8 August 2007, 792–97, http://www.google.com/search?hl=en&client=safari&rls=en&sa=X&oi=spell&resnum=0&ct=result&cd=1&q=Mcdonald%27s+Brand+Recognition+Kids&spell=1 (accessed 3 March 2008).

48. Roy F. Fox, "Warning: Advertising May Be Hazardous to Your Health," *Society for the Advancement of Education*, November 2001, http://findarticles.com/p/articles/mi_m1272/is_2678_130/ai_80533093/pg_3 (accessed 3 March 2008).

49. Lorne Manly, "The Goat at Saks and Other Marketing Tales," *New York Times*, 14 November 2005, cited by Commercial Alert, http://www.commercialalert.org/issues/culture/books/the-goat-at-saks-and-other-marketing-tales (accessed 3 March 2008).

50. Rich, "In Books for Young," B7.

51. Katherine Fordham Neer, "How Product Placement Works," http://money.howstuffworks.com/product-placement7.htm (accessed 3 March 2008).

52. "Playing with Product Placement," Blogspot.com, 17 April 2007, http://playproduct.blogspot.com/2007/04/board-games-galore.html (accessed 3 March 2008).

53. John Belton, *American Cinema/American Culture*, 2nd ed. (New York: McGraw-Hill, 2005), 4.

54. Henry Giroux, *The Mouse That Roared: Disney and the End of Innocence* (New York: Rowman & Littlefield, 1999): 93.

55. Wasko, *How Hollywood Works*, 171–73.

56. Jonathan Bing, "Marketing Is King for Disney's Princess Line," *Variety*, 12 December 2005, http://www.variety.com/article/VR1117934460.html?categoryid=1979&cs=1 (accessed 29 January 2008).

57. Peggy Orenstein, "What's Wrong with Cinderella?" *New York Times* 24 December 2006, http://www.nytimes.com/2006/12/24/magazine/24princess.t.html?pagewanted=4&ei=5088&en=8e5a1ac1332a802c&ex=1324616400&partner=rssnyt&emc=rss (accessed 3 March 2008).

58. Edward Wyatt, "SpongeBob SquareProfits: Nickelodeon Swears by Cartoons," *New York Times*, 12 December 2006, B1, B6.

59. Geraldine Fabrikant, "Nickelodeon Looks over Its Shoulder at Disney," *New York Times*, 14 October 2006, B1.

60. Wyatt, "SpongeBob," B6.

61. Kristen Mehler, "Montana Mania," *Wichita Eagle*, 29 January 2008, http://www.kansas.com/entertainment/story/293013.html (accessed 30 January 2008).

62. Mehler, "Montana Mania."

63. "Wal-Mart Teams with Disney to Be Hannah Montana™ Retail Headquarters," CNNMoney.com, http://money.cnn.com/news/newsfeeds/articles/prnewswire/LAW03630012008-1.htm (accessed January 30 2008).

64. Laura Petrecca, "Wal-Mart Joins Forces with *Hannah Montana*," *USA Today*, 29 January 2008, http://www.usatoday.com/money/industries/retail/2008-01-29-hannah-montana-walmart_N.htm (accessed 30 January 2008).

65. Jeremy Heron, "Disney Extends 'Hannah Montana' Run," *State College (Pa.) Centre Daily Times*, 7 February 2008, A2.

66. Heron, "Disney Extends 'Hannah Montana,'" A2.

67. "User Ratings for Hanna & Miley Cyrus: Best of Both Worlds," IMDb, http://www.imdb.com/title/tt1127884/ (accessed 5 February 2012).

68. Mike Reynolds, "Ratings Go Higher for Hannah," *Multichannel News*, 8 September 2008.

69. "Girls Intelligence Agency, LLC," Hoover's Profile, http://www.answers.com/topic/girls-intelligence-agency-llc?cat=biz-fin (accessed 3 March 2008).

70. Girls Intelligence Agency, "Research Services," http://www.girlsintelligenceagency.com/researchservices.htm

71. Schor, *Born to Buy*, 77.

72. Barbara F. Meltz, "Protecting Kids from Marketers' Clutches," *Boston Globe*, 30 September 2004, http://www.boston.com/yourlife/family/articles/2004/09/30/protecting_kids_from_marketers_clutches/?page=2? (accessed 3 March 2008).

73. "Big Money in the Cyber-Kid Stakes," *Sydney Morning Herald*, 10 August 2007, http://www.smh.com.au/news/technology/big-money-in-the-cyberkid-stakes/2007/08/09/1186530532698.html (accessed 3 March 2008).

74. "Big Money in the Cyber-Kid Stakes."

75. "Big Money in Cyber-Kid Stakes."

76. Ken Boettcher, "AOL-Time Warner Merger Makes Media Critics Nervous," *The People*, April 2000, 3.

77. Netmarketshare.com, 5 February 2012.

78. "Google Investor Relations, 2011 Financial Tables," http://investor.google.com/financial/tables.htlm (accessed 5 February 2012).

79. Leslie Marable, "False Oracles: Consumer Reaction to Learning the Truth about How Search Engines Work (Abstract)," Consumer Reports WebWatch, June 30, 2003, http://www.consumerwebwatch.org/dynamic/search-report-false-oracles-abstract.cfm (accessed 14 November 2011).

80. "Commercial Alert Files Complaint against Search Engines for Deceptive Ads," news release, July 16, 2001, Public Citizen's Commercial Alert, http://www.commercialalert.org/issues/culture/search-engines/commercial-alert-files-complaint-against-search-engines-for-deceptive-ads (accessed 14 November 2011).

81. U.S. Federal Trade Commission to Gary Ruskin, June 27, 2002, http://www.ftc.gov/os/closings/staff/commercialalertletter.shtm (accessed 14 November 2011).

82. Jergen J. Wouters, "Still in Search of Disclosure," Consumer Reports Web Watch, 9 June 2005, http://www.consumerwebwatch.org/dynamic/jorgen-wouters.cfm (accessed 3 March 2008).

83. Kevin Newcomb, "Study: Search Engines Still Fail to Disclose Ads," *ClickZ*, 9 June 2005, http://www.clickz.com/showPage.html?page=3511576 (accessed 3 March 2008).

84. Douglas Quenqua, "Saying 'Will You' for Prizes, on the Web," *New York Times*, 7 January 2008, C6.

85. Quenqua, "Saying 'Will You,'" C6.

86. "U.S. Cell-Phone Penetration Tops 82 Percent," Gearlog, http://www.gearlog.com/2007/11/us_cellphone_penetration_tops.php (accessed 3 March 2008).

87. "50 Wireless Quick Facts," CITA Advocacy, June 2011, http://www.cita.org/advocacy/research/index.cfm/aid/10323 (accessed 5 February 2012).

88. "Global Mobile Statistics," mobiThinking, January 2012, http://mobithinking.com/mobile-marketing-tools/latest-mobile/stats (accessed 5 February 2012).

89. "MIT Communications Forum," 17 November 2005, http://web.mit.edu/comm-forum/forums/cell_phone_culture.htm (accessed 3 March 2008).

90. "U.S. Mobile Ad Expenditures More than Double to $2.1 Billion in 2011, Google Dominates," mobiThinking, 20 December 2011, http://mobithinking.com/blog/mobile-ad-network-share-2011 (accessed 5 February 2012).

91. Louise Story, "Madison Avenue Calling," *New York Times*, 20 January 2007, B1.

92. "Do Not Call List Unites Politicians," *State College (Pa.) Centre Daily Times*, 7 February 2008, A5.

93. Jennifer C. Kerr, "Do Not Call List Set to Expire," *State College (Pa.) Centre Daily Times*, 22 September 2007, A2.

94. Miguel Helft, "Google to Sell Web-Page Ads Visible on Mobile Phones," *New York Times*, 18 September 2007, C5.

95. Louise Story, "A Company Will Monitor Phone Calls and Devise Ads to Suit," *New York Times*, 24 September 2007, C1.

96. Jon Swartz, "Widgets Make a Big Splash on the Net," *USA Today*, 27 January 2007, B1–B2.

97. Peter Eavis and Evelyn M. Rusli, "Investors Get the Chance to Assess Facebook's Potential," *New York Times*, 2 February 2012.

98. Mike Snider, "iPods Knock Over Beer Mugs," *USA Today*, 7 June 2006.

99. Richard Siklos, "A Virtual World but Real Money," *New York Times*, 19 October 2006, http://www.nytimes.com/2006/10/19/technology/19virtual.html?_r=1&oref=slogin (accessed 27 February 2008).

100. Siklos "A Virtual World."

101. Louise Story, "Coke Promotes Itself in a New Virtual World," *New York Times*, 7 December 2007.

102. Cynthia Heimel, "Love Stinks," *Premier*, 1999, 27–28.

103. Sherry Turkle interviewed by Liz Else, "Our Blackberries, Ourselves," *Utne Reader*, January–February 2007, 12.

CHAPTER 7: THE COMMERCIALIZATION OF EDUCATION

1. Daily Finance website, http://wwwdailyfinance.com/ (accessed 17 May 2010).

2. BabyPlus website, http://www.babyplus.com/ (accessed 18 February 2008).

3. Brainy Baby website, http://www.brainybaby.com/ (accessed 18 February 2008).

4. Baby Prodigy website, http://www.babyprodigy.com/ (accessed 18 February 2008).

5. "Nestlé Boycott," *Wikipedia*, http://en.wikipedia.org/wiki/Nestle_boycott (accessed 18 February 2008).

6. F. J. Zimmerman, D. A. Christakis, and A. N. Meltzoff, "Associations between Media Viewing and Language Development in Children under Age 2 Years," *Journal of Pediatrics*, August 2007, cited in "Baby Einstein," *Wikipedia*, http://en.wikipedia.org/wiki/Baby_Einstein (accessed 3 March 2008).

7. Jonathon Takiff, "What's Hot from the Toy Show," *State College (Pa.) Centre Daily Times*, 28 February 2008, B2.

8. Alissa Quart, "Extreme Parenting," *Atlantic Monthly*, 1 August 2006, Extreme%20Parenting%20(The%20Atlantic%20Monthly)%20%7C%20Alissa%20Quart.webarchive (accessed 16 February 2008).

9. "Warren Buffett Turns Toon," *New York Times*, 9 February 2006, B2.

10. "Unions Boycott Wal-Mart," *New York Times*, 11 August 2005, http://www.nytimes.com/2005/08/11/business/11walmart.html (accessed 2 March 2008).

11. Cynthia Peters, "Marketing to Teens," *Z Magazine*, April 1999, 23.

12. Ben Bagdikian, *The Media Monopoly*, 5th ed. (Boston: Beacon, 1997), 51.

13. Wayne Grytting, "Teach the Kids," *Z Magazine* (citing a *Clear View* story), May 1999, 6.

14. Alex Molnar and Jennifer Morales, "Commercialism@Schools," *Educational Leadership*, October 2000, 43.

15. "Marketing of Junk Food to School Children," Commercial Alert, www.essential.org/alert/junkfood/ (accessed 8 November 2001).

16. Ken Schroeder, "One-derful Channel One," *Education Digest* 66, no. 1 (September 2000): 72.

17. Mark Francis Cohen, "Must-See TV," *Washington Post*, 9 April 2000, 20W.

18. Lia Miller, "NBC to Provide Content for Channel One," *New York Times*, 9 July 2007, http://www.nyt.com (accessed 17 May 2010).

19. Mya Frazier, "Channel One: New Owner, Old Issues," *Advertising Age*, 26 November 2007, 10.

20. Wayne Grytting, "The New Math," *Z Magazine*, 27 March 1999, 5.

21. Caroline Terenzini, "Productive Tinkering," *State College (Pa.) Centre Daily Times*, 18 May 1999, C1.

22. Molnar and Morales, "Commercialism@Schools," 40.

23. Andrew Stark, "Taste: Let's Make a Deal—Commerce," *Wall Street Journal*, 31 March 2000, W17.

24. Stuart Elliott, "Straight A's, with a Burger as a Prize," *New York Times*, 6 December 2007, C4.

25. Stewart Elliott, "McDonald's Ending Promotion on Jackets of Children's Report Cards," *New York Times*, 18 January 2008, http://www.nytimes.com/2008/01/18/business/media/18card.html?_r=1&oref=slogin (accessed 16 February 2008).

26. Ryan Doherty, "State College Schools Weigh Soft-Drink Deal," *State College (Pa.) Centre Daily Times*, 5 May 2001, A5.

27. Carol Pogash, "Poor Students in High School Suffer Stigma from Lunch Aid," *New York Times*, 1 March 2008, A1, A14.

28. Mark Little, letter to the editor, *Adbusters* 34, March–April 2001, 6.

29. Constance L. Hayes, "District Rethinks a Soda-Pop Strategy," *New York Times*, 19 April 2000, A19.

30. Usha Lee McFarling, "Food Police: Teens Consume Too Much Soda," *State College (Pa.) Centre Daily Times*, 22 October 1998, A6.

31. Gina Kolata, "While Children Grow Fatter, Experts Search for Solutions," *New York Times*, 19 October 2000, A1.

32. "Childhood Obesity Facts," Centers for Disease Control and Prevention, 15 September 2011, http://www.cdc.gov/healthyyouth/obesity/facts.htm (accessed February 2012).

33. McFarling, "Food Police," A6.

34. "Corporate Spotlight," *Adbusters* 35, May–June 2001, 93.

35. Annys Shin, "Removing Schools' Soda Is Sticky Point: Bottlers' Contracts Limit Cash-Strapped Districts," *Washington Post*, 22 March 2007, D3, http://www.washingtonpost.com/wp-dyn/content/article/2007/03/21/AR2007032101966.html (accessed 1 March 2008).

36. Shin, "Removing Schools' Soda."

37. Sarah Gilbert, "Soda Makers Claim War on Sugary Drinks in Schools Is Won," 11 March 2010, http://www.dailyfinance.com (accessed 17 May 2010).

38. Natalie Zmuda, "Beverage Giants Team Up in Campaign to Remove Soda from Schools," *Advertising Age* 9, March 2010, http://adage.com (accessed 17 May 2010).

39. Sarah Gilbert, "Is Pepsi's Removal of Sodas from Schools Just a Publicity Stunt?" 18 March 2010, http://www.dailyfinance.com (accessed 17 May 2010).

40. Gilbert, "Soda Makers Claim ."

41. "TV News in Schools Costs $1.8 Billion in Class Time," *New York Times*, 1 April 1998, B11.

42. "School Questions Pepsi Contract," *State College (Pa.) Centre Daily Times*, 6 June 2001, A2; "School District Ponders Deal for Coke Products," *State College (Pa.) Centre Daily Times*, 2 July 1999, A11.

43. Hayes, "District Rethinks," A19.

44. Steve Manning, "Students for Sale," *The Nation*, 27 September 1999, 15.

45. Mary B. W. Tabor, "Schools Profit from Offering Students for Market Research," *New York Times*, 5 April 1999, A1.

46. Steve Manning, "Zapped," *The Nation*, 27 September 1999, 13.

47. "2008 State of the Union Address," White House press release, 28 January 2008, http://www.state.gov/r/pa/ei/wh/rem/99783.htm (accessed 4 March 2008).

48. "No Child Left Behind," *Wikipedia*, http://en.wikipedia.org/wiki/No_Child_Left_Behind (accessed 2 March 2008).

49. "No Child," *Wikipedia*.

50. "2008 State of the Union Address."

51. Anya Sostek, "Management Doctrines Hit Schools," *State College (Pa.) Centre Daily Times*, 24 February 2008, B3.

52. Sam Dillon, "Obama to Propose New Reading and Math Standards," *New York Times*, 20 February 2010, A13.

53. Dillon, "Obama to Propose," A13.

54. Jim Hightower, "No Enlightenment in Texas," *The Progressive*, May 2010, 46.

55. Hightower, "No Enlightenment," 46.

56. Eyal Press and Jennifer Washburn, "The Kept University," *Atlantic Monthly* 285, no. 3 (March 2000): 41.

57. Naomi Klein, *No Logo: Taking Aim at the Brand Bullies* (New York: Picador USA, 1999), 105.

58. Stanley Aronowitz, "The New Corporate University: Higher Education Becomes Higher Training," *Dollars & Sense* 216, March 1998, 32–35.

59. Press and Washburn, "The Kept University," 41.

60. Klein, *No Logo*, 98–101.

61. "GE Fund Awards Two Grants to Penn State," *State College (Pa.) Centre Daily Times*, 18 December 2000, A5.

62. Margaret Hopkins, "Six Companies Pledge $1.85 Million for e-Business Center," *State College (Pa.) Centre Daily Times*, 14 December 2000, B10.

63. Press and Washburn, "The Kept University," 41.

64. "GE Fund Awards Two Grants," A5.

65. Aronowitz, "The New Corporate University," 32.

66. Hopkins, "Six Companies Pledge $1.85 Million," B10.

67. "Local Hotel Group to Build on Delaware Campus," *State College (Pa.) Centre Daily Times*, 24 May 2001, A5.

68. Megan Novack, "Program Provides Disney Experience," *Penn State Daily Collegian*, 26 September 2000, 2.

69. Press and Washburn, "The Kept University," 39–40.

70. Press and Washburn, "The Kept University," 41–45. Figure is compared to 79 percent of papers based on research not funded by industry.

71. Press and Washburn, "The Kept University," 42.

72. Megan McKeever and Tiffany Peden, "PSU, Chevron to Work Together," *Penn State Daily Collegian*, 5 October 2007, 1.

73. Adam Smeltz, "Alliance to Study Coal Uses," *State College (Pa.) Centre Daily Times*, 4 October 2007, A1.

74. "Chevron Corporation," *Fortune 500*, 2007, http://money.cnn.com/magazines/fortune/fortune500/2007/snapshots/290.html (accessed 3 March 2008).

75. "Chevron Corporation," *Wikipedia*, http://en.wikipedia.org/wiki/Chevron_Corporation (accessed 3 March 2008).

76. Stephanie Saul, "Conflict on the Menu," *New York Times*, 16 February 2008, B1, B4.

77. Saul, "Conflict on the Menu," B4.

78. "Newsflashes," *Adbusters* 30, June–July 2000, 17.

79. Dick Cooper, "Saying 'No' to a Gift of Water," letter to the editor, *State College (Pa.) Centre Daily Times*, 5 July 2001, A6.

80. David Smith, "Nittany Lion Print Foots Too Many Toes," *Penn State Daily Collegian*, 29 January 1999, 8.

81. Janet Wasko, *Understanding Disney* (Cambridge, U.K.: Polity Press, 2001), 84.

82. Groucho Marx, *The Groucho Letters: Letters from and to Groucho Marx* (New York: DeCapo, 1994), 14.

83. Danielle Vickery, "Penn State Sees Copycat Logo for Second Time This Year," *Penn State Daily Collegian*, 4 October 2007, 1.

84. Marx, *The Groucho Letters*, 14.

85. "PSU Sues Over Football Rentals," *State College (Pa.) Centre Daily Times*, 11 January 2012.

86. Gilbert M. Gaul and Frank Fitzpatrick, "What Was Sacred Is Now Up for Sale," *Philadelphia Inquirer*, 14 September 2001, A1.

87. Gaul and Fitzpatrick, "What Was Sacred," A1.

88. Gaul and Fitzpatrick, "What Was Sacred," A1.

89. Gaul and Fitzpatrick, "What Was Sacred," A1.

90. National Collegiate Athletic Association (NCAA), "A Call to Action: Reconnecting College Sports to Higher Education," June 2001, www.ncaa.org/databases/knight_commission/2001_report/2001_knight_report.html (accessed 19 October 2001).

91. Douglas Braunsdorf, "Knight Commission Report Sparks Debate," *State College (Pa.) Centre Daily Times*, 29 June 2001, B1.

92. Braunsdorf, "Knight Commission Report," B1.

93. Darryl Leroux, "Who's Zooming Who?" *Adbusters* 34, March–April 2001, 47.

94. Leroux, "Who's Zooming Who?" 47.

95. "THON to Showcase Hilfiger Wear," *State College (Pa.) Centre Daily Times*, 12 February 2000, A5.

96. "Credit Card Usage Analysis," December 2000, www.nelliemae.com/shared/ccstat.htm (accessed 17 October 2001).

97. W. A. Lee, "Student Loan GSE Slams Card Company Marketing," *American Banker* 166, no. 42 (2 March 2001): 8.

98. Betty Lin-Fisher, "Credit Cards for Students Mean Big Business," *State College (Pa.) Centre Daily Times*, 26 August 2001, C8.

99. "Students Binge on Credit," *USA Today*, 14 September 2000, A26.

100. *Student Debt and the Class of 2010*, Institute for College Access and Success, 3 November 2001, 1, http://ticas.org/files/pub/classof2010.pdf (accessed 12 February 2012).

101. Manning, "Zapped," 13.

102. Jack Myers, *Adbashing: Surviving the Attacks on Advertising* (Parsippany, N.J.: American Media Council, 1993), 151.

103. Klein, *No Logo*, 88.

104. Lori Leibovich, "Choosing Quick Hits over the Card Catalog," *New York Times*, 10 August 2000, G1.

105. Katie Hafner, "Schools and Computers: Debate Heats Up," *New York Times*, 5 October 2001, E8.

106. Tom Zeller Jr., "Amid Clamor for Computer in Every Classroom, Some Dissenting Voices," *New York Times*, 17 March 2001, A3.

107. "Penn Staters Tinker with Computers," *State College (Pa.) Centre Daily Times*, 25 July 2000, A5.

108. "State High Teacher Awarded Palm Grant," *State College (Pa.) Centre Daily Times*, 10 September 2001, A5.

109. "Raytheon Grant Helps Endow State High Award," *State College (Pa.) Centre Daily Times*, 24 September 2001, A5.

110. Barbara Brueggebors, "'A Taste of Pennsylvania' Gives Governors a Flavor of High-Tech," *State College (Pa.) Centre Daily Times*, 11 July 2000, A7; Yuri Kageyama, "Mechanical Mutt: Sony Puppy Robot Good for Laughs, Still Far Call from Lovable Pet," *State College (Pa.) Centre Daily Times*, 24 December 2000, E3.

111. Ellen Goodman, "Technology Sets You Free . . . to Work All the Time," *State College (Pa.) Centre Daily Times*, 25 July 2000, A6.

112. Margaret Hopkins, "Greenspan Visit Caps NGA Event: Fed Chief Challenges States to Provide Training for Workers," *State College (Pa.) Centre Daily Times*, 12 July 2000, A1.

113. Zeller, "Amid Clamor for Computer," A3.

114. Manning, "Students for Sale," 12.

115. Christopher Carey, "Lisa MacFarlane's Story," *St. Louis Post-Dispatch*, 11 July 1999, B1.

116. Neil Postman, "Virtual Students, Digital Classrooms," *The Nation*, 9 October 1995, 377.

117. Manning, "Zapped," 13.

118. Aronowitz, "The New Corporate University," 32.

119. Press and Washburn, "The Kept University," 54.

120. *Business Week*, 22 December 1997, quoted in Klein, *No Logo*, 101.

121. Arthur Levine, "The Soul of a New University," *New York Times*, 13 March 2000, A25.

CHAPTER 8: MEDIA AND DEMOCRACY

1. Andrew Jacobs, "The Protesters: Mostly Pleased, but Knowing Few Heard Their Message," *New York Times*, 5 February 2002, A15.

2. "2008 State of the Union Address by President Bush," *White House Press Release*, 28 January 2008, http://www.state.gov/r/pa/ei/wh/rem/99783.htm (accessed 4 March 2008).

3. Terence Hunt, "A Sluggish State," *State College (Pa.) Centre Daily Times*, 29 January 2008, A1, A3.

4. Tom Raum and Emma Vandore, "World Leaders Dub Gathering a Success," *State College (Pa.) Centre Daily Times*, 26 September 2009, A1.

5. Sam Howe Verhovek, "Seattle Police Chief Resigns in Aftermath of Protests," *New York Times*, 8 December 1999, A13.

6. Timothy Egan, "Black Masks Lead to Pointed Fingers in Seattle," *New York Times*, 2 December 1999, A1.

7. Starhawk, "How We Shut Down the WTO," *Z Magazine*, February 2000, 18–19.

8. Paddy Agnew, "Genoa Braces for Disruption of G8 Summit," *Irish Times*, 14 July 2001, 11.

9. Agnew, "Genoa Braces," 11.

10. Jacobs, "The Protesters," A15.

11. Serge Schmemann, "The Meeting: Annan Cautions Business as Forum Ends," *New York Times*, 5 February 2002, A14; Dan Barry, "The Streets: So Long New York, and Thanks for a Mostly Well-Ordered Bash," *New York Times*, 5 February 2002, A14; Jacobs, "The Protesters," A15; William K. Rashbaum and Al Baker, "The Police: Shrewd Anticipation Helped Avert Trouble," *New York Times*, 5 February 2002, A15.

12. David Moberg, "Tear Down the Walls: The Movement Is Becoming More Global," *In These Times*, 28 May 2001, 11–14. Note that Moberg is a critical journalist whose tone here is ironic.

13. Agnew, "Genoa Braces," 11.

14. Moberg, "Tear Down the Walls," 11–14.

15. Dana Milbank, "Bush Greeted by Demonstrators, Critics," *State College (Pa.) Centre Daily Times*, 13 June 2001, A3.

16. Paul Ames, "Demonstrators Riot outside EU Conference," *State College (Pa.) Centre Daily Times*, 16 June 2001, A3.

17. Ames, "Demonstrators Riot," A3.

18. Forbes 400, "The Richest People in America," *Forbes*, 8 October 2001, 179; *Forbes*, 8 October 2007, 326.

19. Marsha Hill, "World Economic Summit Opens amid Anti-Globalization Protests," *State College (Pa.) Centre Daily Times*, 2 July 2001, B8.

20. Agnew, "Genoa Braces," 11.

21. Agnew, "Genoa Braces," 11.

22. Schmemann, "The Meeting," A14.

23. Schmemann, "The Meeting," A14.

24. David Moberg, "After Seattle," *In These Times*, 18 February 2002, 41.

25. Martin Grutsinger, "Protesters Aim at IMF Meeting," *State College (Pa.) Centre Daily Times*, 7 April 2000, B8.

26. Larry Margasak, "PETA Dumps Four Tons of Manure near World Bank," *State College (Pa.) Centre Daily Times*, 15 April 2000, A3.

27. Margasak, "PETA Dumps Four Tons," A3.

28. Ronald V. Bettig, *Copyrighting Culture: The Political Economy of Intellectual Property* (Boulder, Colo.: Westview Press, 1996), 191.

29. Bettig, *Copyrighting Culture*, 191.

30. Moberg, "Tear Down the Walls," 11–14.

31. "An Alternative History: Timeline," *The Nation*, 10 January 2000, 8–51.

32. Thomas L. Friedman, "Senseless in Seattle," *New York Times*, 1 December 1999, A31.

33. Seth Ackerman, "Prattle in Seattle," *Extra!* January–February 2000, 13–17.

34. Ackerman, "Prattle in Seattle," 13–17.

35. Jennifer Brown, "Protests Planned for GOP Convention," *State College (Pa.) Centre Daily Times*, 7 June 2000, D1.

36. Jacobs, "The Protesters," A15.

37. Agnew, "Genoa Braces," 11.

38. Milbank, "Bush Greeted," A3.

39. Jacobs, "The Protesters," A15.

40. Steven Greenhouse, "A Carnival of Derision to Greet the Princes of Global Trade," *New York Times*, 29 November 1999, A12.

41. "Trade Talks Begin," *State College (Pa.) Centre Daily Times*, 30 November 1999, A4.

42. Sam Howe Verhovek, "Trade Talks Start in Seattle Despite a Few Disruptions," *New York Times*, 30 November 1999, A14.

43. "WTO Protests Turn Violent," *State College (Pa.) Centre Daily Times*, 1 December 1999, A1.

44. "National Guard Is Called to Quell Trade-Talk Protests," *New York Times*, 1 December 1999, A1.

45. Derrill Holly, "DC Police Ready for IMF Duty," Associated Press, 7 April 2000, a.m. cycle; Larry Margasak, "Washington Braces for IMF Protesters," *State College (Pa.) Centre Daily Times*, 9 April 2000, A1.

46. Martin Crutsinger, "Protesters Aim at IMF Meeting," *State College (Pa.) Centre Daily Times*, 7 April 2000, B8.

47. "Trade Protest Roils Capital," *State College (Pa.) Centre Daily Times*, 17 April 2000, A1.

48. "Million Mom March a Personal Statement for Some," *State College (Pa.) Centre Daily Times*, 14 May 2000.

49. "Trade Protest Roils Capital," A1.

50. David Graeber, "The Riot That Wasn't," *In These Times*, 29 May 2000, 12.

51. "Protesters March, Fail to Block World Finance Meeting," *State College (Pa.) Centre Daily Times*, 17 April 2000, A7.

52. Larry Margasak, "IMF Protesters Try—and Fail—to Shut Down Meetings," *State College (Pa.) Centre Daily Times*, 18 April 2000, A1.

53. Erin R. Wengerd, "Protest Preparation Fails to Draw Crowd," *State College (Pa.) Centre Daily Times*, 25 May 2000, A1.

54. Graeber, "The Riot That Wasn't," 13.

55. "Trade Protest Roils Capital," A1.

56. Rashbaum and Baker, "The Police," A15.

57. Rashbaum and Baker, "The Police," A15.

58. Larry Margasak, "Protesters Disrupt Washington," *Penn State Daily Collegian*, 18 April 2000, 1.

59. Margasak, "Protesters Disrupt Washington," 1.

60. Margasak, "Protesters Disrupt Washington," 1.

61. John Kifner, "In This Washington, No 'Seattle' Is Found by Police and Protesters," *New York Times*, 19 April 2000, A12.

62. Rashbaum and Baker, "The Police," A15.

63. "Messages for the W.T.O.," *New York Times*, 2 December 1999, A30.

64. Sam Howe Verhovek, "Seattle Is Stung, Angry and Chagrined as Opportunity Turns to Chaos," *New York Times*, 2 December 1999, A14.

65. David Graeber, "Anarchy in the USA," *In These Times*, 10 January 2000, 18.

66. Egan, "Black Masks," A1, A14.

67. Edmund L. Andrews, "U.S. Stance on Trade Is Unclear at the G-20," *New York Times*, 25 September 2009, A4.

68. Mac Lojowsky, "Seattle to Pittsburgh," *Z Magazine*, December 2009, 14.

69. Lojowsky, "Seattle to Pittsburgh," 13.

70. Jerome L. Sherman, "Charges Dismissed against PG Reporter," *Pittsburgh Post-Gazette*, 15 October 2009, http://infoweb.newsbank.com (accessed 23 May 2010).

71. "Pittsburgh Steels Itself for G-20 Protests," *Wall Street Journal*, 11 September 2009, cited in Lojowsky, "Seattle to Pittsburgh," 12.

72. "G-20 Protest Plans Raise Alarm in City," *Pittsburgh Tribune Review*, 11 July 2009, cited in Lojowsky, "Seattle to Pittsburgh," 14.

73. "Hospital Coordinator Anticipates Unknown during G-20 Summit," *Pittsburgh Post-Gazette*, 10 September 2009, cited in Lojowsky, "Seattle to Pittsburgh," 14.

74. Ian Urbina, "Protesters at G-20 Meeting Are Met by Tear Gas," *New York Times*, 25 September 2009, A10.

75. *New York Times*, 25 September 2009, A1.

76. Urbina, "Protesters at G-20," A10.

77. Urbina, "Protesters at G-20," A10.

78. Urbina, "Protesters at G-20," A10.

79. "Summit Lesson: Pittsburgh Can Learn More about Police Response," *Pittsburgh Post-Gazette*, 11 March 2010, http://infoweb.newsbank.com,(accessed 23 May 2010).

80. Urbina, "Protesters at G-20," A10.

81. Scott King, "Businesses Caught in G-20 Crossfire," *State College (Pa.) Centre Daily Times*, 26 September 2009, http://www.centredaily.com (accessed 23 May 2010).

82. Jacobs, "The Protesters," A15.

83. Jacobs, "The Protesters," A15.

84. Jacobs, "The Protesters," A15.

85. "Messages for the W.T.O.," A30.

86. Jim Naureckas, "They Are the 1 Percent," *Extra!*, November 2011, http://www.fair.org/index.php?page=2265 (accessed 12 February 2012).

87. "Have Corporate Media Warmed to Occupy Wall Street?" *Media Advisory*, 18 October 2011, http://www.fair.org/index.php?page=4420 (accessed 12 February 2012).

88. Chris Hawley and David B. Caruso, "Protestors Push Ahead Even without Leaders," *State College (Pa.) Centre Daily Times*, A1, A3, A1.

89. Hawley and Caruso, A3.

90. Verana Dobnik, "As Protests Grow, So Do Funds," *State College (Pa.) Centre Daily Times*, 17 October 2011, A1, A3; Amy Westfeldt, "Protesters Embrace Variety of Messages," *State College (Pa.) Centre Daily Times*, 10 November 2011, A9.

91. Amy Westfeldt, "Occupy Protesters Finally Present Specifics," *State College (Pa.) Centre Daily Times*, 2 December 2011, A9.

92. Robert W. McChesney, "The Communication Revolution: The Market and the Prospect for Democracy," in *Democratizing Communication?* ed. M. Bailie and D. Winseck (Creskill, N.J.: Hampton Press, 1997), 57–78.

Bibliography

"About Us." Rocawear.com, http://www.rocawear.com/shop/aboutus.php (accessed 3 March 2008).

Ackerman, Seth. "Prattle in Seattle." *Extra!* January–February 2000, 13–17.

Adams, Mike. "Pharmaceutical Television Advertising Is a Grand Hoax." NaturalNews.com, 30 January 2007, http://www.naturalnews.com/021526.html (accessed 13 January 2008).

Adler, Carlyle. "Clear Channel, Incorporated." Portfolio.com, n.d., http://www.portfolio.com/resources/companyprofiles/1107?TID=rm/ys2/Company_Database (accessed 11 August 2008).

"Advertising: G.M.'s Response to *Roger & Me.*" *New York Times*, 31 January 1990, D23.

Agnew, Paddy. "Genoa Braces for Disruption of G8 Summit." *Irish Times*, 14 July 2001, 11.

Ahrens, Frank. "The Great Deregulator: Five Months into His Tenure as FCC Chairman, Michael Powell Is Coming Through Loud and Clear." *Washington Post*, 18 June 2001, C1.

"Allen and Company, Inc.: Overview." Hoover's Fact Sheet, 2005, http://hoovers.com/ (accessed 19 September 2005).

Allison, Melissa, and Amy Martinez. "Independent Record Shops Competing in Digital Age." *Seattle Times*, 8 April 2010, http://seattletimes.nwsource.com/html/retailreport/2011562280_retailreport09.html (accessed 2 July 2011).

Alterman, Eric. "The Liberal Media: All Rupert, All the Time." *The Nation*, 13 August 2007, 10.

"An Alternative History: Timeline." *The Nation*, 10 January 2000, 8–51.

Ames, Paul. "Demonstrators Riot outside EU Conference." *State College (Pa.) Centre Daily Times*, 16 June 2001, A3.

Andrews, Edmund L. "U.S. Stance on Trade Is Unclear at the G-20." *New York Times*, 25 September 2009, A4.

Anschutz Company. "AEG Music." 2010, http://aegworldwide.com/music/music (accessed 10 July 2011).

"Antismoking Product's Ad Stirs Debate." *New York Times*, 11 November 1988, D17.

"AOL's Big Byte." *The Nation*, 31 January 2000, 3.

"AOL–Time Warner Trims 2,000 from Its Workforce." *Philadelphia Inquirer*, 25 January 2001, www.lexisnexis.com (accessed 29 January 2008).

Arango, Tim. "What Would Henry Luce Do? Looking Forward at Time Warner." *New York Times*, 24 December 2007, C1, C4.

——. "In Retrospect: How It Went So Wrong." *New York Times*, 11 January 2010, B1, B1-11.

Aronowitz, Stanley. "The New Corporate University: Higher Education Becomes Higher Training." *Dollars & Sense* 216 (March 1998): 32-35.

Associated Press. "People in the News." 7 May 1999, a.m. cycle.

"AT&T to Exit Pay Phones as the Business Shrinks." *New York Times*, 4 December 2007, C11.

Aufderheide, Pat. "Open Access or Else." *In These Times*, 26 June 2000, 2.

Avatar. www.boxofficemojo.com (accessed 28 June 2010).

Bagdikian, Ben. *The Media Monopoly*. 5th ed. Boston: Beacon, 1997.

——. *The Media Monopoly*. 6th ed. Boston: Beacon, 2000.

——. *The New Media Monopoly*. Boston: Beacon, 2004.

Baldasty, Gerald J. "The Rise of News as a Commodity: Business Imperatives and the Press in the Nineteenth Century." In *Ruthless Criticism: Perspectives in U.S. Communication History*, edited by William S. Solomon and Robert W. McChesney, Minneapolis: University of Minnesota Press, 1993.

Barnes, Brooks. "An Imax and AMC Venture Will Expand 3-D Theaters." *New York Times*, 12 July 2007, C8.

——. "The Line between Homage and Parody." *New York Times*, 25 November 2007, Art 8.

——. "The $1 Redbox Alarm." *New York Times*, 7 September 2009, B1,B5.

——. "With New Films, CBS Charts Tough Middle Course." *New York Times*, 19 January 2010, C1, C4.

——. "For Hollywood Producers, Is the Glamour Gone?" *New York Times*, 22 May 2010, http://www.nytimes.com/2010/05/23/business/media/23steal.html (accessed 5 October 2010).

——. "In This War, Movie Studios Are Siding with Your Couch." *New York Times*, 26 September 2010, Sunday Business 1, 6.

Barringer, Felicity. "CBS News May Face More Cuts." *New York Times*, 9 September 1999, C8.

——. "Does Deal Signal Lessening of Media Independence?" *New York Times*, 11 January 2000, C12.

——. "Other Media Companies' Assets Tied to Those of Deal's Partners." *New York Times*, 13 January 2000, C6.

Barry, Dan. "The Streets: So Long New York, and Thanks for a Mostly Well-Ordered Bash." *New York Times*, 5 February 2002, A14.

Barsamian, David. "Monopolies, NPR, and PBS: An Interview with Robert McChesney." *Z Magazine*, February 2000, 40-46.

Bekken, Jon. "The Working-Class Press at the Turn of the Century." In *Ruthless Criticism: Perspectives in U.S. Communication History*, ed. William S. Solomon and Robert W. McChesney, 151–75. Minneapolis: University of Minnesota Press, 1993.

Belson, Ken. "At I.B.M., a Vacation Anytime, or Maybe No Vacation at All." *New York Times*, 31 August 2007, A1, A18.

Belton, John. *American Cinema/American Culture*. New York: McGraw-Hill, 1994.

———. *American Cinema/American Culture*, 2nd ed. New York: McGraw-Hill, 2005.

Berenson, Alex. "Investors Seem to Want to Keep AOL–Time Warner Asunder." *New York Times*, 13 January 2000, C1, C6.

———. "Minky Viagra? Pfizer Doesn't Want You to Understand It, Just Buy It." *New York Times*, 30 April 2007, C1.

Bettig, Ronald V. *Copyrighting Culture: The Political Economy of Intellectual Property*. Boulder, Colo.: Westview Press, 1996.

———. "Who Owns Prime Time? Industrial and Institutional Conflict over Television Programming and Broadcast Rights." In *Framing Friction: Media and Social Conflict*, edited by Mary S. Mander, 125–60. Urbana: University of Illinois Press, 1999.

———. "Copyright and the Commodification of Culture." *Media Development* 52, no. 1 (2003): 25–37.

———. "Concentration in the Copyright Industries." In *Intellectual Property and Information Wealth: Issues and Practices in the Digital Age*, vol. 1, *Copyright and Related Rights*, edited by Peter Yu, 361–84. Westport, Conn.: Praeger, 2007.

———. "Hollywood and Intellectual Property." In *The Contemporary Hollywood Film Industry*, edited by Paul MacDonald and Janet Wasko, 195–205. Malden, Mass.: Blackwell, 2008.

"The Biggest Media Merger Yet." *New York Times*, 11 January 2000, A30.

"Big Money in the Cyber-Kid Stakes." *Sydney Morning Herald*, 10 August 2007, http://www.smh.com.au/news/technology/big-money-in-the-cyberkid-stakes/2007/08/09/1186530532698.html (accessed 3 March 2008).

"The Big Ten." *The Nation*, 7 January 2002, 27–30.

Bing, Jonathan. "Marketing Is King for Disney's Princess Line." *Variety*, 12 December 2005, http://www.variety.com/article/VR1117934460.html?categoryid=1979&cs=1 (accessed 29 January 2008).

Bleifuss, Joel. "It's a Mad Ad World." *In These Times*, 18–24 March 1992, 4–5.

———. "Communication Breakdown: AOL–Time Warner Threatens Public Interest." *In These Times*, 21 February 2000, 2–3.

"Blue Flame Marketing, a P. Diddy Owned Company, to Offer Corporations Partnership Opportunities with Bad Boy Entertainment." 14 January 2003, http://findarticles.com/p/articles/mi_m0EIN/is_2003_Jan_14/ai_96432192 (accessed 3 March 2008).

"BMI Pacts with Sony's Qriocity Streaming Service." *Business Sense (BMI)*, 12 April 2011, http://www.bmi.com/news/entry/551226 (accessed 31 May 2001).

Boehlert, Eric. "MP3.mess: Petty Single Pulled from Net." *Rolling Stone*, 29 April 1999, 40.

Boettcher, Ken. "AOL–Time Warner Merger Makes Media Critics Nervous." *The People*, April 2000, 3.

Bowles, Samuel, and Richard Edwards. *Understanding Capitalism: Competition, Command, and Change in the U.S. Economy.* 2nd ed. New York: HarperCollins, 1993.

"Box Office." Hollywood.com, 19 July 2009, http://cdn-images.hollywood.com/site/harry_potter_franchise.pdf (accessed 6 October 2010).

Braunsdorf, Douglas. "Knight Commission Report Sparks Debate." *State College (Pa.) Centre Daily Times,* 29 June 2001, B1, B4.

Brinkley, Joel. "U.S. Judge Says Microsoft Violated Antitrust Laws with Predatory Behavior." *New York Times,* 4 April 2000, A1, C12.

Brown, Jennifer. "Protests Planned for GOP Convention." *State College (Pa.) Centre Daily Times,* 7 June 2000, D1.

Brueggebors, Barbara. "'A Taste of Pennsylvania' Gives Governors a Flavor of High-Tech." *State College (Pa.) Centre Daily Times,* 11 July 2000, A7.

"Buffett Tops Gates as World's Richest." *State College (Pa.) Centre Daily Times,* 7 March 2007, A2.

The Business Council. "About Us." 2008, http://www.thebusinesscouncil.org/about/ (accessed 17 March 2009).

"But a Survey." In *Special Report: News and Editorial Independence. A Survey of Group and Independent Editors.* Easton, Pa.: Ethics Committee, American Society of Newspaper Editors, 1980.

Byrne, John, Ronald Grover, and Robert D. Hof. "Pay Stubs of the Rich and Corporate." *Business Week,* 7 May 1990, 56–64.

Cain Miller, Clair. "YouTube Ads Turn Piracy into Revenue." *New York Times,* 3 September 2010, B1, B4.

Carey, Christopher. "Lisa MacFarlane's Story." *St. Louis Post-Dispatch,* 11 July 1999, B1.

Carlson, Matt. "Boardroom Brothers: Interlocking Directorates Indicate Media's Corporate Ties." *Extra!* September–October 2001.

Carr, David. "Murdoch, a Folk Hero in Silicon." *New York Times,* 29 October 2007, C1, C5.

———. "Publishing That's All about Me." *New York Times,* 7 January 2008, C1, C11.

Carter, Bill. "Few Sponsors for TV War News." *New York Times,* 7 February 1991, D1, D20.

———. "Media Talk: An Executive with Synergistic Vision." *New York Times,* 11 September 2000, C17.

———. "G.E. Finishes Vivendi Deal, Expanding Its Media Assets." *New York Times,* 9 October 2003, www.nytimes.com (accessed 2 March 2008).

Caruso, Denise. "If the AOL–Time Warner Deal Is about Proprietary Content, Where Does That Leave a Noncommercial Directory It Will Own?" *New York Times,* 17 January 2000, C5.

"Cash Countesses." *Forbes,* 8 October 2007, 312–17.

CBS Corporation. *10-K Annual Report.* 25 February 2011.

"CBS Films and Simon & Schuster in Film and Publishing Deal for Best-Selling Author." *New York Times* Market Watch, 8 February 2008, http://www.marketwatch.com/news/story/cbs-films-simon--schuster/story.aspx?guid={5636B393-753E-4904-A3CC-CFBC5EF241A2}&dist=TQP_Mod_pressN (accessed 29 February 2008).

CBS Radio. "About Us: Corporate Profile." 2011, http://www.cbsradio.com/about/index.html (accessed 10 July 2011).

"CBS Reports Third Quarter Results." 1 November 2007, www.cbscorporation.com (accessed 16 January 2008).

Center for Public Integrity. *Networks of Influence: The Political Power of the Communications Industry,* app. A. Washington, D.C.: Center for Public Integrity, 2005.

——. "Top Telecommunications, Media, and Technology Companies." 2006, http://projects.publicintegrity.org/telecom/rank.aspx?act=industry (accessed 3 March 2008).

Chang, Jeff. "Fight the Power: Can Hip-Hop Get Past the Thug Life and Back to Its Radical Roots?" *Mother Jones,* November–December 2007, 67.

Chatterjee, Sumana. "Chocolate Companies React to Slavery Revelations." *State College (Pa.) Centre Daily Times,* 26 June 2001, A7.

——. "Consumers: Why Not Boycott Chocolate?" *State College (Pa.) Centre Daily Times,* 26 June 2001, A7.

——. "Chocolate Companies Fight 'Slave Free' Labels." *State College (Pa.) Centre Daily Times,* 1 August 2001, A4.

——. "Chocolate Makers to Accept Responsibility for Cocoa Farm Practices." *State College (Pa.) Centre Daily Times,* 1 October 2001, A3.

"Chevron Corporation." *Fortune 500.* 2007, http://money.cnn.com/magazines/fortune/fortune500/2007/snapshots/290.html (accessed 3 March 2008).

"Childhood Obesity Facts." Centers for Disease Control and Prevention, 15 September 2011, http://www.cdc.gov/healthyouth/obesity/facts.htm (accessed 8 February 2012).

Christians, Clifford G., and James W. Carey. "The Logic and Aims of Qualitative Research." In *Research Methods in Mass Communication,* edited by Guido H. Stempel and Bruce H. Westley, 342–62. Englewood Cliffs, N.J.: Prentice-Hall, 1981.

Christman, Ed. "UMVD Marks Third Straight Year as Top U.S. Music Distributor." *Billboard,* 26 January 2002, 51.

——. "U.S. Music Sales Hit a Wall." *Billboard,* 26 January 2002, 1, 76.

——. "Solutions for Sale." *Billboard,* 23 January 2010, 10–11.

——. "UMG Is Market Leader in 2010." *Hollywood Reporter,* 1 May 2011, http://www.hollywoodreporter.com/news/umg-market-leader-2010-katy-68702 (accessed 23 May 2011).

Cieply, Michael, and Brooks Barnes. "Chief of Universal Finds Success at the Back of the Pack." *New York Times,* 16 July 2007, C1, C7.

Cimilluca, Dana, and Ethan Smith. "Citigroup Takes Control of EMI." *WSJ.com,* 2 February 2011, http://online.wsj.com/article/SB10001424052748703445904576118083710352572.html (accessed 8 June 2011).

Cohen, Mark Francis. "Must-See TV." *Washington Post,* 9 April 2000, 20W.

Cohen, Peter. "EMusic-Sony Deal: One Step Forward, One Big Step Back." *Macworld,* 4 June 2009, http://www.pcworld.com/businesscenter/article/166117/emusic-sony_deal_one_step_forward_one_big_step_back.html (accessed 31 May 2011).

Collins, Chuck. "Horatio Alger, Where Are You?" *Dollars & Sense,* January–February 1997, 9.

Comcast. "Comcast Spotlight." 2010, http://www.comcast.com/corporate/about/pressroom/comcastspotlight (accessed 18 September 2010).

——. *2009 Annual Report on Form 10-K.* 23 February 2010, http://files.shareholder.com/downloads/CMCSA/1482724372x0xS1193125%2D10%2D37551/1166691/filing.pdf (accessed 3 November 2011).

———. "Corporate Overview." 20 June 2010, htpp://www.comcast.com/corporate/about/pressroom/corporateoverview (accessed 18 September 2010).

"Commercial Alert Files Complaint against Search Engines for Deceptive Ads." News release, July 16, 2001, Public Citizen's Commercial Alert, http://www.commercialalert.org/issues/culture/search-engines/commercial-alert-files-complaint-against-search-engines-for-deceptive-ads (accessed 14 November 2011).

Compaine, Benjamin M. "The Newspaper Industry." In *Who Owns the Media? Competition and Concentration in the Mass Media Industry*, edited by Benjamin M. Compaine and Douglas Gomery, 1–59. Mahwah, N.J.: Erlbaum, 2000.

———. "Who Owns the Media Companies?" In *Who Owns the Media? Competition and Concentration in the Mass Media Industry*, edited by Benjamin M. Compaine and Douglas Gomery, 481–506. Mahwah, N.J.: Erlbaum, 2000.

Compaine, Benjamin M., and Douglas Gomery, eds. *Who Owns the Media? Competition and Concentration in the Mass Media Industry*. 2nd ed. Mahwah, N.J.: Erlbaum, 2000.

Cooper, Dick. "Saying 'No' to a Gift of Water." Letter to the editor, *State College (Pa.) Centre Daily Times*, 5 July 2001, A6.

Cooper, Marc. "*The Progressive* Interview: George Carlin." *The Progressive*, July 2001, 32–37.

"Corporate Spotlight." *Adbusters* 35 (May–June 2001): 93.

Cox Enterprises Inc. "Cox Companies." 2011, http://www.coxenterprises.com/coxcompanies.aspx (accessed 14 July 2011).

Crawford, Susan. "Comcast's NBC-U Dreams May Be Online Video's Nightmare." 11 September 2010, http://gigaom.com/2010/09/11/comcasts-nbc-u-dreams-may-be-online-videos-nightmare (accessed 14 September 2010).

"Credit Card Usage Analysis." December 2000. NellieMae, www.nelliemae.com/shared/ccstat.htm (accessed 17 October 2001).

Crosby, Jackie. "Electronic Waste to Follow iPhone Sales." *State College (Pa.) Centre Daily Times*, 6 July 2007, A9.

Crossette, Barbara. "Experts Scaling Back Their Estimates of World Population Growth." *New York Times*, 20 August 2002, D8.

"Crumbelievable!!! The Ten Cheesiest Rock Commercials." Spinner, http://spinner.aol.com/photos/swiffer-commercial-song-devo (accessed 21 January 2008).

Crutsinger, Martin. "Protesters Aim at IMF Meeting." *State College (Pa.) Centre Daily Times*, 7 April 2000, B8.

Cummings, Sue. "The Flux in Pop Music Has a Distinctly Download Beat to It." *New York Times*, 22 September 1999, G60.

Cumulus Media, Inc. "Company Profile." 2006, http://www.corporate-ir.net/ir_site.zhtml (accessed 19 October 2007).

———. *2008 110-K Report.* http://phx.corporate-ir-net/phoenix.zhtml (accessed 4 April 2009).

Curran, James, and Jean Seaton. *Power without Responsibility.* 3rd ed. London: Fontana, 1988.

Dart, Bob. "Denny's Begins TV Spots on Race Today." *Atlanta Journal and Constitution*, 13 January 1999, E10.

"Data Center." *Advertising Age*, 25 June 2007, 5.

David, Matthew. *Peer to Peer and the Music Industry: The Criminalization of Sharing.* Thousand Oaks, Calif.: Sage, 2010.

Dillon, Sam. "Obama to Propose New Reading and Math Standards." *New York Times,* 20 February 2010, A13.

DiOrio Carl. "U Dumps Its Loews Shares," *Daily Variety,* 29 June 2001, 6.

———. "*Avatar* Eyeing Big Box Office Bow." *Hollywood Reporter,* 15 December 2009, www.hollywoodreporter.com (accessed 1 September 2010).

"Disney Buys Stake in YouTube Rival Hulu." AFP, 30 April 2009, www.google.com (accessed 4 October 2010).

Dobnick, Verana. "As Protests Grow So Do Funds." *State College (Pa.) Centre Daily Times,* 17 October 2011, A1, A3.

Doherty, Ryan. "State College Schools Weigh Soft-Drink Deal." *State College (Pa.) Centre Daily Times,* 5 May 2001, A5.

Domhoff, G. William. "State and Ruling Class in Corporate America." *Insurgent Sociologist* 4, no. 3 (1974): 3–16.

"Do Not Call List Unites Politicians." *State College (Pa.) Centre Daily Times,* 7 February 2008, A5.

Dowd, Maureen. "America's Anchors." *Rolling Stone,* 16 November 2006, 54.

Eavis, Peter, and Evelyn M. Rusli, "Investors Get the Chance to Assess Facebook's Potential." *New York Times,* 2 February 2012, B1, B4.

"Editor's Note." *State College (Pa.) Centre Daily Times,* 4 October 1998, A11.

Egan, Timothy. "Black Masks Lead to Pointed Fingers in Seattle." *New York Times,* 2 December 1999, A1, A14.

Eicher, Charles. "Disinfotainment: Product Placement Problems." http://weblog.ceicher.com/archives/2002/04/product_placement_problems.html (accessed 3 January 2008).

Eisenstein, Elizabeth L. *The Printing Revolution in Early Modern Europe.* Cambridge, U.K.: Cambridge University Press, 1983.

Eliscu, Jenny. "Why Radio Sucks." *Rolling Stone,* 3 April 2003, 22.

Eller, Claudia. "DVD Slump Might Weaken 'Half-Blood' Sales." *Los Angeles Times,* 22 June 2009, http://articles.latimes.com/2009/jun/22/business/fi-ct-potter22/3 (accessed 11 October 2010).

Eller, Claudia, and James Bates. "Hollywood Box Office is Boffo." *Los Angeles Times,* 11 November 2001, 1–4, www.latimes.com (accessed 3 February 2002).

Elliot, Stuart. "A Combined Viacom-CBS Would Cast an Awfully Large Shadow across a Wide Range of Ad Media." *New York Times,* 8 September 1999, C8.

———. "Advertising: The AOL–Time Warner Deal Changes Everything for Those Who Move, and Buy, in Media Circles." *New York Times,* 11 January 2000, C8.

———. "On Broadway, Ads Now Get to Play Cameo Roles." *New York Times,* 22 April 2005, http://www.nytimes.com/2005/04/22/business/media/22adco.html (accessed 3 March 2008).

———. "Straight A's, with a Burger as a Prize." *New York Times,* 6 December 2007, C4.

———. "McDonald's Ending Promotion on Jackets of Children's Report Cards." *New York Times,* 18 January 2008, http://www.nytimes.com/2009/01/18/business/media/18card.html?_r=1&oref=slogin (accessed 16 February 2008).

Else, Liz. "Our Blackberries, Ourselves." *Utne Reader*, January–February 2007, 12.

EMI Music. "About." 2011, http://www.emimusic.com/about/ (accessed 8 June 2011).

Ewen, Start. *Captains of Consciousness*. New York: McGraw-Hill, 1977.

Exoo, Calvin F. *The Politics of the Mass Media*. Saint Paul, Minn.: West Publishing, 1994.

Fabrikant, Geraldine. "Nickelodeon Looks over Its Shoulder at Disney." *New York Times*, 14 October 2006, B1.

Farah, George, and Justin Elga. "What's Not Talked About on Sunday Morning?" *Extra!* October 2001, 14–17.

Farhi, Paul. "Rupert Murdoch Empire Finds Business Not So Taxing Offshore." *Washington Post*, 7 December 1997, A1.

———. "AOL Gets Message Out in *Mail*." *Washington Post*, 17 December 1998, http://www.washingtonpost.com/wp-srv/style/movies/features/aolinmail.htm (accessed 12 November 2007).

———. "Ad Trend on Radio: Hear Today, Gone in 2 Seconds." *San Diego Union Tribune*, 20 June 2007, A1.

"FCC Presented with Advertising Study Which Reveals a Tale of Two Systems: Study Shows Broadcasters Serving Minority Community Earn Less per Listener." www.fcc.gov/Bureaus/Media (accessed 28 December 2001).

Federal Communications Commission. "Subject to Conditions, Commission Approves Merger between America Online, Inc. and Time Warner, Inc." 11 January 2001, www.fcc.gov/Bureaus/Cable/ (accessed 18 January 2002).

Fernandez, Bob. "FCC Commissioner Is Skeptical over Comcast, NBC Universal Merger at Hearing." *Philadelphia Enquirer*, 13 July 2010, http://articles.philly.com/2010-07-13/news/24969209_1_comcast-spokeswoman-sena-fitzmaurice-nbc-universal-merger (accessed 19 September 2010).

"50 Wireless Quick Facts." CITA Advocacy, June 2011, http://www.cita.org/advocacy/research/index.cfm/aid/10323 (accessed 5 February 2012).

Fixmer, Andy. "News Corp. Said to Approach Vevo.com about Myspace Joint Venture." 29 March 2011, Bloomberg, http://www.bloomberg.com/news/2011-03-28/news-corp-said-to-approach-vevo-com-music-site-on-myspace-joint-venture.html (accessed 22 June 2011).

Flint, Joe. "Mood Is Dark at Sun Valley Business Meeting." *Los Angeles Times*, 11 July 2009, www.newsbank.com (accessed 3 July 2010).

Forbes 400. "The 400 Richest People in America," *Forbes*, 8 October 2011, 27–298.

Forbes 400. "The Richest People in America." *Forbes*. 8 October 2007, 72–346.

Forbes 400. "The Richest People in America." 9 October 2009, http://www.forbes.com/lists/2009/54/rich-list-09_The-400-Richest-Americans_NameProper_11.html (accessed 12 November 2009).

The Forbes 400. "The Richest People in America." September 2010, http://www.forbes.com/wealth/forbes-400/list (accessed 7 June 2011).

Forbes 400. "The Richest People in America," September 2011, http://www.forbes.com/forbes.400/list/ (accessed 12 February 2012).

The Forbes 400 2009. "The Richest People in America." 30 September 2009, www.forbes.com (accessed 12 November 2009).

Forbes, Steve. "Why the List." *Forbes*, 8 October 2001, 30.

Fortune 500. "Chevron Corporation." 2007, http://money.cnn.com/magazines/ fortune/fortune500/2007/snapshots/290.html (accessed 3 March 2008).

"Fortune 500, 2007." CNNMoney.com, http://money.cnn.com/magazines/fortune/ fortune500/2007/snapshots/1380.html.

"Fortune 500, 2007, Full List." CNNMoney.com, http://money.cnn.com/maga zines/fortune/fortune500/2007/full_list/

"Fortune 500 2009." April 2009, http://money.cnn.com/magazines/fortune/for tune500/2009/index.html (accessed 7 June 2010).

"Fortune 500 2010: Top 1000 American Companies—Walt Disney." http://money. cnn.com/magazines/fortune/fortune500/2010/snapshots/2190.html (accessed 25 June 2010).

"Fortune Global 500 2009." http://money.cnn.com/magazines/fortune/global500/ 2009/ (accessed 7 June 2010).

"The 400 Richest Americans 2009." Forbes.com, http://www.forbes.com/ lists/2009/54/rich-list-09_The-400-Richest-Americans_NameProper_7.html (ac cessed 22 February 2010).

"The 400 Richest People in America." *Forbes*, 8 October 2001, 127–298.

Fox, Roy F. "Warning: Advertising May Be Hazardous to Your Health." *Society for the Advancement of Education*, November 2001, http://findarticles.com/p/articles/ mi_m1272/is_2678_130/ai_80533093/pg_3 (accessed 3 March 2008).

"Franchise Index." Box Office Mojo, 6 June 2010, http://www.boxofficemojo.com/ franchises/ (accessed 22 June 2010).

Frank, Robert H. "A Merger's Message: Dominate or Die." *New York Times*, 11 Janu ary 2000, A31.

Frazier, Mya. "Channel One: New Owner, Old Issues." *Advertising Age*, 26 Novem ber 2007, 10.

Free Press. "Comcast-NBC Mega-Merger Must Be Stopped." 30 November 2009, http://www.freepress.net/node/74889 (accessed 14 September 2010).

Friedman, Josh. "Box-Office Revenue Swings Up Even as Attendance Hits a Wall." *Los Angeles Times*, 4 January 2008, www.lexisnexis.com (accessed 12 February 2008), C1.

Friedman, Thomas L. "Senseless in Seattle." *New York Times*, 1 December 1999, A31.

Furman, Phyllis. "MGM Buys Back Movie Rights to Launch TV Cable Channel." *State College (Pa.) Centre Daily Times*, 16 September 1999, 8C.

Fusfeld, Daniel. *Economics: Principles of Political Economy*. 3rd ed. Glenview, Ill.: Scott Foresman, 1988.

Gallo, Phil. "Restructuring Ahead for EMI." *Variety*, 17 September 2008, http:// www.variety.com/article/VR1117972092.html (accessed 17 October 2007).

Gans, Herbert J. "The Messages behind the News." *Columbia Journalism Review*, Janu ary–February 1979, 40–45.

Garfield, Bob. "Benetton on Death Row." *Advertising Age*, 10 January 2000, 45.

Garrett, Jade. "Shock! Horror! New Benetton Ad Shows Clothes." *The Independent (London)*, 24 January 2001, 12.

Gaul, Gilbert M., and Frank Fitzpatrick. "What Was Sacred Is Now Up for Sale." *Philadelphia Inquirer*, 14 September 2001, A1, A14.

"GE Fund Awards Two Grants to Penn State." *State College (Pa.) Centre Daily Times*, 18 December 2000, A5.

General Electric Co. Bloomsberg Businessweek, http://investing.businessweek.com/research/stocks/people/board.asp?ticker=ge:us (accessed 13 September 2010).

Gilbert, Sarah. "Soda Makers Claim War on Sugary Drinks in Schools Is Won." 11 March 2010, http://www.dailyfinance.com (accessed 17 May 2010).

———. "Is Pepsi's Removal of Sodas from Schools Just a Publicity Stunt?" 18 March 2010, http://www.dailyfinance.com (accessed 17 May 2010).

Girls Intelligence Agency. "Research Services." http://www.girlsintelligenceagency.com/researchservices.htm

"Girls Intelligence Agency, LLC." Hoover's Profile, http://www.answers.com/topic/girls-intelligence-agency-llc?cat=biz-fin (accessed 3 March 2008).

Giroux, Henry A. *The Mouse That Roared: Disney and the End of Innocence.* New York: Rowman & Littlefield, 1999.

———. "Merger Mania Dazzles Eyes, but Imprisons You and Me." *State College (Pa.) Centre Daily Times,* 13 February 2000, 13A.

———. *Breaking In to the Movies: Film and the Culture of Politics.* Malden, Mass.: Blackwell, 2002.

"The Global 2000." http://www.forbes.com/lists/2010/18/global-2000-10_The-Global-2000_Rank_2.html (accessed 25 June 2010).

"Global Mobile Statistics." mobiThinking, January 2012, http://mobithinking.com/mobile-marketing-tools/latest-mobile-statistics (5 February 2012).

Gold, Philip. *Advertising, Politics, and American Culture.* New York: Paragon, 1987.

Goldberg, Michael. "MTV's Sharper Picture." *Rolling Stone,* 8 February 1990, 61–64, 118.

Gomery, Douglas. "The Hollywood Film Industry: Theatrical Exhibition, Pay TV, and Home Video." In *Who Owns the Media? Competition and Concentration in the Mass Media Industry,* edited by Benjamin Compaine and Douglas Gomery, 359–439. Mahwah, N.J.: Erlbaum, 2000.

———. "Radio Broadcasting and Music Industry." In *Who Owns the Media? Competition and Concentration in the Mass Media Industry,* edited by Benjamin Compaine and Douglas Gomery. Mahwah, N.J.: Erlbaum, 2000.

Goodell, Jeff. "World War MP3." *Rolling Stone,* 8 July 1999, 43.

Goodman, Ellen. "Technology Sets You Free . . . to Work All the Time." *State College (Pa.) Centre Daily Times,* 25 July 2000, A6.

Goodman, Walter. "When Corporate Synergy Becomes Manifest Destiny." *New York Times,* 19 January 2000, E10.

"Google Investor Relations, 2011 Financial Tables." http://investor.google.com/financial/tables.html (accessed 5 February 2012).

"Google-Global Market Share on." Netmarketshare, 5 February 2012.

Gorman, Bill. "Disney Channel Breaks USA's Hold on Prime-time Cable Network Crown." 17 March 2009, www.indiewire.com (accessed 22 June 2010).

Graeber, David. "Anarchy in the USA." *In These Times,* 10 January 2000, 18.

———. "The Riot That Wasn't." *In These Times,* 29 May 2000, 12.

Graves, Tom. "Movies and Home Entertainment: Current Environment." *Standard & Poor's Industry Surveys,* 2 October 1997, 7.

———. "Movies and Home Entertainment: Industry Trends." *Standard & Poor's,* 10 May 2001, www.netadvantage.standardandpoors.com/netahtml/indsur/mhe20501.htm (accessed 19 November 2001).

Greenhouse, Steven. "A Carnival of Derision to Greet the Princes of Global Trade." *New York Times*, 29 November 1999, A12.

Grover, Ronald. "Rupert Murdoch's Latest Deal with John Malone." *Bloomsberg Business Week*, 4 June 2009, http://www.businessweek.com/technology/content/jun2009/tc2009064_532827.htm (accessed 13 October 2009).

Groves, Don, and Adam Dawtrey. "Hogwarts and Hobbits in Global Grab." *Variety*, 11 February 2002, 1.

Grutsinger, Martin. "Protesters Aim at IMF Meeting." *State College (Pa.) Centre Daily Times*, 7 April 2000, B8.

Grytting, Wayne. "The New Math." *Z Magazine*, 27 March 1999, 5.

———. "Teach the Kids." *Z Magazine*, May 1999, 6.

"G-20 Protest Plans Raise Alarm in City." *Pittsburgh Tribune Review*, 11 July 2009, cited in Mac Lojowsky, "Seattle to Pittsburgh," *Z Magazine*, December 2009, 14.

Guback, Thomas. "Ownership and Control in the Motion Picture Industry." *Journal of Film and Video* 38, no. 1 (1986): 7–20.

Gundersen, Edna. "U2 Turns 360 Stadium Tour into Attendance-Shattering Sellouts." *USA Today*, 5 October 2009, http://www.usatoday.com/life/music/news/2009-10-04-u2-stadium-tourN.html (accessed 16 July 2011).

Gunther, Marc. "Sumner of Love." *Fortune*, 2 May 2005, www.fortune.com (accessed 16 January 2008).

Gunzerath, David. "Rupert K. Murdoch." Museum of Broadcast Communications, n.d., http://www.museum.tv/eotvsection.php?entrycode=murdochrupe (accessed 26 February 2008).

Haddad, Charles. "CBS-Viacom Merger Further Narrows Media." *Atlanta Journal-Constitution*, 9 September 1999, F1, F3.

———. "CBS, Viacom Follow Trail Blazed by Disney, Time Warner." *State College (Pa.) Centre Daily Times*, 12 September 1999, 15B.

Hafner, Katie. "Schools and Computers: Debate Heats Up." *New York Times*, 5 October 2001, E8.

Halbfinger, David M., and Geraldine Fabrikiant. "Fired or Quit, Tom Cruise Parts Ways with Studio." *New York Times*, 22 August 2006, C1, C2.

Handelman, David. "Without a Media Umbrella: Solo Magazines Must Scramble in Hard Times." *New York Times*, 10 December 2001, 9C.

Hansell, Saul. "America Online Agrees to Buy Time Warner for $165 Billion: Media Deal Is Richest Merger." *New York Times*, 11 January 2000, A1, C11.

———. "Not-So-Subtle Engine Drives AOL Profit Forecasts." *New York Times*, 31 January 2000, C1, C12.

———. "AOL to Cut 5,000 Jobs in Web Access Business." *New York Times*, 4 August 2007, C3.

Harmon, Amy. "Exceptions Made for Dress Code, but Never for His Internet Vision." *New York Times*, 11 January 2000, A1, C12.

Harmon, Amy, and Alex Kuczynski. "A Bridge Builder for Corporate Culture." *New York Times*, 12 January 2000, C1, C7.

"Have Corporate Media Warmed to Wall Street?" *Media Advisory*, http://www.fair.org/index.php?page4420 (accessed 12 February 2012).

Hawley, Chris, and David B. Caruso. "Protests Push Ahead Even without Leaders." *State College (Pa.) Centre Daily Times*, 16 October 2011, A1, A3.

Hayes, Constance L. "District Rethinks a Soda-Pop Strategy." *New York Times,* 19 April 2000, A19.

"Heavy Hitters: Comcast Corp." Center for Responsive Politics, 22 August 2010, http://www.opensecrets.org/orgs/summary.php?id=D000000461 (accessed 22 September 2010).

"Heavy Hitters: Time Warner Totals." Center for Responsive Politics, http://www. opensecrets.org/orgs/totals.phpcycle=202&id=D0000... (accessed 13 February 2012).

"Heavy Hitters: Top All-Time Donors, 1989–2012." Center for Responsive Politics, http://www.opensecrets.org/orgs/list.php?order=A (accessed 13 February 2012).

"Heavy Hitters: Walt Disney Co." Center for Responsive Politic, 22 August 2010, www.opensecrets.org (accessed 24 June 2010).

Heimel, Cynthia. "Love Stinks." *Premier,* 1999, 27–28.

Helft, Miguel. "Google to Sell Web-Page Ads Visible on Mobile Phones." *New York Times,* 18 September 2007, C5.

Hellweg, Eric. "Down with MP3." *Spin,* October 1999, 57.

"Help!" *Rolling Stone,* 20 January 1968, 3.

Henneman, Todd. "Denny's Sued by Bay Area Latinos; Restaurant Announces Anti-Discrimination Ads on TV Same Day." *San Francisco Chronicle,* 13 January 1999, A4.

Hensel, Saul. "Not-So-Subtle Engine Drives AOL Profit Forecasts." *New York Times,* 31 January 2000, C1, C12.

Henwood, Doug. "Measuring Privilege." *Left Business Observer,* July 1997, 3.

———. "Take Me to Your Leader." *Left Business Observer 115,* 31 May 2007, 1–2.

Herman, Edward. "Market System Constraints on Freedom of Expression." *Journal of Communication Inquiry* 15, no. 1 (1991): 45–53.

———. "Media Mega-Mergers." *Dollars & Sense,* May 1996, 8–13.

Herman, Edward S., and Noam Chomsky. *Manufacturing Consent: The Political Economy of Mass Media.* New York: Pantheon, 1988.

Heron, Jeremy. "Disney Extends 'Hannah Montana' Run." *State College (Pa.) Centre Daily Times,* 7 February 2008, A2

Hightower, Jim. "No Enlightenment in Texas." *The Progressive,* May 2010, 46.

Hill, Alex E. "Who Cares about the Depletion of Billionaires?" Letter to the editor, *State College (Pa.) Centre Daily Times,* 4 October 1998, A11.

Hill, Marsha. "World Economic Summit Opens amid Anti-Globalization Protests." *State College (Pa.) Centre Daily Times,* 2 July 2001, B8.

Hiltzik, Michael A., and Claudia Eller. "Roots of Redstone Family's Bitter Rift." *Los Angeles Times,* 2 August 2007, www.proquest.com (accessed 19 January 2008).

Hirsch, Joseph A. "Web Sites for Kids." Letter to the editor, *New York Times,* 9 September 2007, A24.

Hofmeister, Sally. "Lights, Camera, Download? Studios Focus on the Web." *Los Angeles Times,* 30 November 2000, A1.

Holly, Derrill. "DC Police Ready for IMF Duty." Associated Press, 7 April 2000, a.m. cycle.

Holson, Laura M. "The Online Generation Courts the Old Guard." *New York Times,* 11 January 2000, C1, C13.

———. "Verizon Letter on Privacy Stirs Debate." *New York Times,* 16 October 2007, C1, C8.

Holson, Laura M., and Rick Lyman. "In Warner Brothers' Strategy, a Movie Is Now a Product Line." *New York Times*, 2 November 2002, C1, C4.

Hopkins, Margaret. "Greenspan Visit Caps NGA Event: Fed Chief Challenges States to Provide Training for Workers." *State College (Pa.) Centre Daily Times*, 12 July 2000, A1.

———. "Six Companies Pledge $1.85 Million for e-Business Center." *State College (Pa.) Centre Daily Times*, 14 December 2000, B10.

Horkheimer, Max, and Theodor W. Adorno. *Dialectic of Enlightenment.* Translated by John Cumming. New York: Seabury, 1972.

Horn, Patricia, and Akweli Parker. "AOL Merger Gets Key Approval." *Philadelphia Enquirer*, 15 December 2000, A1, A16.

"Hospital Coordinator Anticipates Unknown during G-20 Summit." *Pittsburgh Post-Gazette*, 10 September 2009, cited in Mac Lojowsky, "Seattle to Pittsburgh," *Z Magazine*, December 2009, 14.

Howard, Theresa. "Dylan Ad for Underwear Generates Lingering Buzz." *USA Today*, 16 May 2005, http://www.usatoday.com/money/advertising/adtrack/2004-05-16-victoria-secrets-dylan_x.htm (accessed 15 January 2008).

Hunt, Terence. "A Sluggish State." *State College (Pa.) Centre Daily Times*, 29 January 2008, A1, A3.

"Inside Politics." Wikipedia, http://en.wikipedia.org/wiki/Inside_Politics (accessed 22 February 2008).

International Federation of Phonographic Industries. "New Report Shows How Much Record Companies Are 'Investing in Music.'" 9 March 2010, http://www.ifpi.org/content/section_news/investing_in_music.html (accessed 4 December 2010).

———. "IFPI Publishes Digital Music Report 2011." 20 January 2011, http://www.ifpi.org/content/section_resources/dmr2011.html (accessed 10 July 2011).

"Iraq Dominates PEJ's First Quarterly NCI Report." Project for Excellence in Journalism, 25 May 2007, http://www.journalism.org/node/5719 (accessed 28 February 2008).

"Is News Corp. a Great Company, or What?" CNN.com, http://money.cnn.com/magazines/fortune/fortune500/2009/full_list/ (accessed 25 June 2010).

Itzkoff, Dave. "Disney Looks Past the Mouse to a Ratings Record." *New York Times*, 20 August 2007, A1, A14.

Jackson, Matthew. "From Private to Public: Reexamining the Technological Basis for Copyright." *Journal of Communication* 52 (2002): 416–33.

Jacobs, Andrew. "The Protesters: Mostly Pleased, but Knowing Few Heard Their Message." *New York Times*, 5 February 2002, A15.

Jacobson, Michael F., and Laurie Ann Mazur. *Marketing Madness: A Survival Guide for a Consumer Society.* Boulder, Colo.: Westview Press, 1995.

"Jean-Bernard Lévy: Executive Profile and Biography—BusinessWeek." Bloomberg, 5 May 2011, http://investing.businessweek.com/research/stocks/people/person.asp?personId=2879833&ticker=VIV:FP (accessed 24 May 2011).

Johnson, Bradley. "100 Leading Media Companies." *Advertising Age*, 3 October 2011, 44–50.

———. "Special Report: 100 Leading Media Companies." *Advertising Age*, 1 October 2007, www.lexisnexis.com (accessed 8 December 2007).

Johnson-Elie, Tannette. "Denny's Turnabout Means Fair Play for Minority Employees." *Milwaukee Journal Sentinel*, 31 October 2000, D10.

Jones, Alex S. "Knight-Ridder Faces a Newspaper Puzzle." *New York Times*, 18 November 1991, D8.

Jones, Del. "82 Billionaires Did Not Make Forbes List." *USA Today*, 21 September 2007, 4B, www.lexisnexis.com (accessed 18 February 2008).

Jones, Justin. "Young Adults Are Giving Newspapers Scant Notice." *New York Times*, 16 July 2007, C4.

Kageyama, Yuri. "Mechanical Mutt: Sony Puppy Robot Good for Laughs, Still Far Call from Lovable Pet." *State College (Pa.) Centre Daily Times*, 24 December 2000, E3.

Karnitschnig, Matthew, and Brooks Barnes. "Sins of the Parent: CBS and Viacom Find Life Tough after the Big Split." *Wall Street Journal*, 22 July 2006, www.prquest.com (accessed 1 October 2007).

Katz, Frances. "AOL, Time Warner Deal Sets the Tone." *State College (Pa.) Centre Daily Times*, 11 January 2000, 1A, 7A.

Katz, Jon. "Invasion of the Billionaire." *The Netizen*. 30 May 1997, http://hotwired.lycos.com/netizen/97/21/index4a.html (accessed 21 September 2000).

Kaufman, Gil. "Push the Courvoisier: Are Rappers Paid for Product Placement?" *MTV.com*, 9 June 2003, http://www.mtv.com/news/articles/1472393/20030606/puff_daddy.jhtml (accessed 3 March 2008).

Keegan, Rebecca. "How Much Did *Avatar* Really Cost?" *Vanity Fair*, 22 December 2009, http://www.vanityfair.com/online/oscars/2009/12/how-much-did-avatar-really-cost (accessed 1 July 2010).

Kerr, Jennifer C. "Do Not Call List Set to Expire." *State College (Pa.) Centre Daily Times*, 22 September 2007, A2.

Kifner, John. "In This Washington, No 'Seattle' Is Found by Police and Protesters." *New York Times*, 19 April 2000, A12.

"Kilpatrick Responds to FCC Minority Advertising Study." 13 January 1998, http://transition.fcc.gov/Bureaus/Mass_Media/Informal/ad-study/kilpatrick.html (accessed 30 December 2001).

King, Scott. "Businesses Caught in G-20 Crossfire." *State College (Pa.) Centre Daily Times*, 26 September 2009, http://www.centredaily.com (accessed 23 May 2010).

King, Thomas R. "Time Warner Close to Big Cross-Media Ad Deal for Mazda." *Wall Street Journal*, 28 May 1991, C15.

———. "Mickey Mouse vs. Pearl Harbor—Hoping to Avoid a Costly Bomb." *Wall Street Journal*, 6 April 2001, W1.

Kirkpatrick, David. "Now, Many Words from Our Sponsor." *New York Times*, 3 September 2001, http://query.nytimes.com/gst/fullpage.html?res=9F00E5D61F3 0F930A3575AC0A9679C8B63&sec=&spon=&pagewanted=all (accessed 3 March 2008).

———. "Question of New Chairman at Top of Board's Agenda." *New York Times*, 14 January 2003, C1, C7.

———. "Time Warner Sells Music Unit for $2.6 Billion." *New York Times*, 25 November 2003, C1.

Klein, Naomi. *No Logo: Taking Aim at the Brand Bullies*. New York: Picador USA, 1999.

Klinkenborg, Verlyn. "The Vision behind the CBS-Viacom Merger." *New York Times*, 9 September 1999, A28.

Kloer, Phil. "Poof! Harry Potter Is Visible: Movie, Hype Make Wizard Hard to Miss." *Atlanta Journal-Constitution*, 26 October 2001, 1A.

Kolata, Gina. "While Children Grow Fatter, Experts Search for Solutions." *New York Times*, 19 October 2000, A1.

Kostigan, Thomas. "Novel Idea Is All Wet." MarketWatch, 14 July 2006, http://www.marketwatch.com/News/Story/Story.aspx?dist=newsfinder&siteid=google&guid=%7BC7B959C1-C8AC-4C0F-AAFA-F38FDD66CEE6%7D&keyword= (accessed 3 March 2008).

Krugman, Paul. "The Murdoch Factor." *New York Times*, 29 June 2007, A27.

Kuczynski, Alex. "CBS Chief Wanted His MTV." *New York Times*, 8 September 1999, C1, C14.

———. "Disney to Take 50% Stake in *US Weekly* Magazine." *New York Times*, 28 February 2001, C1.

Labaton, Stephen. "Wide Belief U.S. Will Let a Vast Deal Go Through." *New York Times*, 8 September 1999, C14.

———. "Federal Regulators Give Approval to Viacom's Buyout of CBS." *New York Times*, 4 May 2000, C1.

———. "FCC Approves AOL–Time Warner Deal, with Conditions." *New York Times*, 12 January 2001, C1, C11.

———. "Court Weighs Easing Limits on Big Media." *New York Times*, 8 September 2001, A1.

———. "Appellate Court Eases Limitations for Media Giants: Rejects Longtime Rules." *New York Times*, 20 February 2002, A1, C6.

Lambert, Bruce. "Craigslist Emerges as Resource for Both Prostitutes and Police." *New York Times*, 5 September 2007, A1, A22.

Lande, Robert H. "Antitrust and the Media—II." *The Nation*, 22 May 2000, 5–6.

Lane, W. Ronald, and J. Thomas Russell, *Advertising: A Framework*. Upper Saddle River, N.J.: Prentice Hall, 2001.

Lang, Brent. "Sony Loses $3.2B for Fiscal Year on Earthquake Fallout—DVD Declines Didn't Help." *The Wrap*, 26 May 2011, http://www.thewrap.com/movies/article/sony-loses-32b-weak-earnings-partly-due-earthquake-27744 (accessed 26 May 2011).

Lauerman, Connie. "Aging Baby Boomers Fight War on Wrinkles." *State College (Pa.) Centre Daily Times*, 7 September 1998, C3.

Ledbetter, James. "Merge Overkill: When Big Media Gets Too Big, What Happens to Open Debate?" *Village Voice*, 16 January 1996, 30–35.

Lee, Chris. "Michael Jackson Estate, Sony Music Entertainment Strike Distribution Deal." *Los Angeles Times*, 16 March 2010, https://www.google.com/adsense/support/bin/request.py?contact=abg_afc&url=http://a (accessed 31 May 2011).

Lee, W. A. "Student Loan GSE Slams Card Company Marketing." *American Banker* 166, no. 42 (2 March 2001): 8.

Leeds, Jeff. "Disney Returns to Publishing with Stake in *US*." *Los Angeles Times*, 28 February 2001, C1.

———. "A Music Stock Offering Turns Downbeat." *New York Times*, 11 May 2005, http://www.nytimes.com/2005/05/11/business/media/11place.html (accessed 6 July 2011).

————. "Universal Music Settles Big Payola Case." *New York Times*, 12 May 2006, http://www.nytimes.com/2006/05/12/business/12payola.html?scp=1&sq=Leeds,%20Universal%20music%20settles%20big%20payola%20case&st=cse (accessed 14 July 2011).

Leibovich, Lori. "Choosing Quick Hits over the Card Catalog." *New York Times*, 10 August 2000, G1.

Lemire, Christy. "Moore's Sept. 11 Film Loses Disney Backing." *State College (Pa.) Centre Daily Times*, 4 June 2004, A1, A6.

Leroux, Darryl. "Who's Zooming Who?" *Adbusters* 34 (March–April 2001), 47.

Lester, Will. "Poll: Democratic Voters Still Support Their Candidates." *State College (Pa.) Centre Daily Times*, 28 August 1998, 6A.

Levin, Doron P. "When Car Makers Retaliate against Critical Magazines." *New York Times*, 26 June 1992, D9.

Levine, Arthur. "The Soul of a New University." *New York Times*, 13 March 2000, A25.

Lewis, Randy. "Bon Jovi Posts Highest-Grossing Concert Tour of the Year." *Los Angeles Times*, 29 December 2010, http://articles.latimes.com/2010/dec/29/entertainment/la-et-pollstar-numbers-20101229 (accessed 10 July 2011).

Lieberman, David. "Clear Channel Chief Loves Idea of Going Private." *USA Today*, 22 November 2006, B4.

Light, Alan. "Changes in Mellencamp Country." *New York Times*, 22 January 2007, http://www.nytimes.com/2007/01/22/arts/music/22mell.html?ex=1327122000&en=00271aa689653496&ei=5090&partner=rssuserland&emc=rss (accessed 21 January 2008).

Lin-Fisher, Betty. "Credit Cards for Students Mean Big Business." *State College (Pa.) Centre Daily Times*, 26 August 2001, C8.

Lipman, Joanne. "Media Content Is Linked to Cigarette Ads." *Wall Street Journal*, 30 January 1992, B7.

————. "Chrysler to Bring Splashy Ads to Stage." *Wall Street Journal*, 13 May 1992, B8.

Little, Mark. Letter to the editor. *Adbusters* 34 (March–April 2001): 6.

"Live Longer, Better, Wiser." *Parade*, 19 March 2000.

Live Nation Entertainment. *10-K Report*. 28 February 2011, www.livenation.com (accessed 7 July 2011).

"Lobbying: General Electric." Center for Responsive Politics, 26 July 2010, http://www.opensecrets.org/lobby/clientsum.php?lname=General+Electric&year=2010 (accessed 22 September 2010).

"Lobbying: Time Warner." Center for Responsive Politics, http://www.opensecrets.org/lobby/clientsum.php?id=D0000... (accessed 13 February 2012).

"Lobbying: TV/Movies/Music (Industry Profile 2008). Center for Responsive Politics, http://www.opensecrets.org/indus/clientphp?id=B02&years=2008 (accessed 13 February 2012).

"Lobbying: TV/Movies/Music." Center for Responsive Politics, 2010, http://www.opensecrets.org/lobby/indusclient.php?lname=B02&year=a (accessed 27 September 2010).

"Local Hotel Group to Build on Delaware Campus." *State College (Pa.) Centre Daily Times*, 24 May 2001, A5.

Lohr, Steve. "Medium for Main Street." *New York Times*, 11 January 2000, A1, C10.

Lojowsky, Mac. "Seattle to Pittsburgh." *Z Magazine*, December 2009.

Longworth, R. C. "CEOs' Average 531 Times the Salary of Workers." *State College (Pa.) Centre Daily Times*, 28 August 2001, B7.

Lyman, Rick. "Coming to a Computer near You: Movie Rentals Direct from Five Studios." *San Diego Union-Tribune*, 17 August 2001, A1, A26.

———. "Coming Soon: Harry Potter and Hollywood's Cash Cow." *New York Times*, 4 November 2001, A1, A31.

———. "Harry Potter and the Box Office of Gold." *New York Times*, 19 November 2001, E1.

Madison Square Garden Company. "MSG Entertainment." n.d., http://www.the madisonsquaregardencompany.com/our-company (accessed 10 July 2011).

Manly, Lorne. "The Goat at Saks and Other Marketing Tales." *New York Times*, 14 November 2005, cited by Commercial Alert, http://www.commercialalert.org/is sues/culture/books/the-goat-at-saks-and-other-marketing-tales (accessed 3 March 2008).

Manning, Steve. "Students for Sale." *The Nation*, 27 September 1999, 11–15.

———. "Zapped." *The Nation*, 27 September 1999, 13.

Marable, Leslie. "False Oracles: Consumer Reaction to Learning the Truth about How Search Engines Work (Abstract)." Consumer Reports WebWatch, June 30, 2003, http://www.consumerwebwatch.org/dynamic/search-report-false-oracles-abstract.cfm (accessed 14 November 2011).

Maresco, Peter A. "Using Teen Chick Lit Novels to Teach Marketing." Goliath, 22 March 2007, http://goliath.ecnext.com/coms2/gi_0199-6701070/Using-teen-chick-lit-novels.html (accessed 11 January 2008).

Margasak, Larry. "Washington Braces for IMF Protesters." *State College (Pa.) Centre Daily Times*, 9 April 2000, A1.

———. "PETA Dumps Four Tons of Manure near World Bank." *State College (Pa.) Centre Daily Times*, 15 April 2000, A3.

———. "IMF Protesters Try—and Fail—to Shut Down Meetings." *State College (Pa.) Centre Daily Times*, 18 April 2000, A1.

———. "Protesters Disrupt Washington." *Penn State Daily Collegian*, 18 April 2000, 1.

"Marketing of Junk Food to School Children." Commercial Alert. www.essential. org/alert/junkfood/ (accessed 8 November 2001).

Markoff, John. "Bridging Two Worlds to Make On-Line Digital Music Profitable." *New York Times*, 13 September 1999, C1.

Marsh, Ann. "Meet the Class of 1996." *Forbes*, 14 October 1996, 100.

Marx, Groucho. *The Groucho Letters: Letters from and to Groucho Marx*. New York: DeCapo, 1994.

McChesney, Robert W. "The Communication Revolution: The Market and the Prospect for Democracy." In *Democratizing Communication? Comparative Perspectives on Information and Power*, ed. M. Bailie and D. Winseck. Cresskill, N.J.: Hampton Press, 1997.

———. *The Problem of the Media*. New York: Monthly Review Press, 2004.

McClosky, Herbert, and John Zaller. *The American Ethos*. Cambridge, Mass.: Harvard University Press, 1984.

McFarling, Usha Lee. "Food Police: Teens Consume Too Much Soda." *State College (Pa.) Centre Daily Times*, 22 October 1998, A6.

McKeever, Megan, and Tiffany Peden. "PSU, Chevron to Work Together." *Penn State Daily Collegian*, 5 October 2007, 1.

McLeod, Kimbrew. *Freedom of Expression: Overzealous Copyright Bozos and Other Enemies of Creativity*. New York: Doubleday, 2005, excerpted at http://www.brandhype.org/MovieMapper/Resources/ProductPlacementAndTheRealWorld.jsp (accessed 23 January 2008).

"Measuring Privilege." *Left Business Observer*, July 1997, 3.

"Mediaforce Announces Top Ten Pirated Movies for July; Pirates Using Internet to Grow Personal Bootlegged Movies Collections." *PR Newswire*, 16 August 2001.

"The Media Nation: Music." *The Nation*, 25 August 1997, centerfold.

Meehan, Eileen. "'Holy Commodity Fetish, Batman!': The Political Economy of a Commercial Intertext." In *The Many Lives of the Batman*, edited by Roberta Pearson and William Uricchio, 47–65. New York: Routledge, 1991.

Meek, James Gordon, and Bill Hutchinson. "Facebook under Fire by N.Y. Attorney General." *State College (Pa.) Centre Daily Times*, 28 September 2007.

Mehler, Kristen. "Montana Mania." *Wichita Eagle*, 29 January 2008, http://www.kansas.com/entertainment/story/293013.html (accessed 30 January 2008).

Meltz, Barbara F. "Protecting Kids from Marketers' Clutches." *Boston Globe*, 30 September 2004, http://www.boston.com/yourlife/family/articles/2004/09/30/protecting_kids_from_marketers_clutches/?page=2? (accessed 3 March 2008).

"Messages for the W.T.O." *New York Times*, 2 December 1999, A30.

"MGM Regains Rights to Films." *New York Times*, 16 September 1999, C23.

"Microsoft's Illegal Monopoly." *New York Times*, 4 April 2000, A30.

Mifflin, Lawrie. "Viacom to Buy CBS, Forming 2nd Largest Media Company." *New York Times*, 8 September 1999, A1, C15.

———. "CBS-Viacom Deal Raises Competition Questions." *New York Times*, 9 September 1999, C1, C8.

Milbank, Dana. "Bush Greeted by Demonstrators, Critics." *State College (Pa.) Centre Daily Times*, 13 June 2001, A3.

Miller, Lia. "NBC to Provide Content for Channel One." *New York Times*, 9 July 2007, http://www.nyt.com (accessed 17 May 2010).

"Million Mom March a Personal Statement for Some." *State College (Pa.) Centre Daily Times*, 14 May 2000, A9.

Mintzer, Rich. "Product Placement Takes the Stage." Entrepreneur.com, 28 September 2007, http://www.entrepreneur.com/advertising/adsbytype/otherideas/article184830.html (accessed 3 March 2008).

"Misperceptions, the Media and the Iraq War." Program on International Policy Studies. 2 October 2003, http://www.worldpublicopinion.org/pipa/articles/international_security_bt/102.php?nid=&id=&pnt=102&lb=brus (accessed 26 September 2006).

"MIT Communications Forum," 17 November 2005, http://web.mit.edu/comm-forum/forums/cell_phone_culture.htm (accessed 3 March 2008).

Moberg, David. "Tear Down the Walls: The Movement Is Becoming More Global." *In These Times*, 28 May 2001, 11–14.

———. "After Seattle." *In These Times*, 18 February 2002, 41.

Molnar, Alex, and Jennifer Morales. "Commercialism@Schools." *Educational Leadership*, October 2000, 43.

Monte, Tom. *Natural Healing*. New York: Berkeley Publishing Group, 1997.

Morochove, Richard. "America Online Has Lost Its Edge." *Toronto Star*, 29 July 2002, D2, www.lexisnexis.com (accessed 28 January 2008).

"MP3 Player Came Preloaded with Porn." *State College (Pa.) Centre Daily Times*, 29 December 2007, A8.

Murdock, Graham. "Programming: Needs and Answers." Paper presented at New Dimensions in Television meeting, Venice, Italy, 15 March 1981.

"Music Stores: Overview." Hoovers. 2011. http://www.hoovers.com/industry/music-stores/1931-1.html (accessed 2 July 2011).

"My Big Fat Greek Wedding." Box Office Mojo. http://www.boxofficemojo.com/movies/?id=mybigfatgreekwedding.htm (accessed 8 November 2010).

Myers, Jack. *Adbashing: Surviving the Attacks on Advertising*. Parsippany, N.J.: American Media Council, 1993.

Natale, Richard. "Company Town Film Profit Report." *Los Angeles Times*, 30 January 2001, C10.

National Collegiate Athletic Association (NCAA). "A Call to Action: Reconnecting College Sports to Higher Education." June 2001. www.ncaa.org/databases/knight_commission /2001_report/2001 _knight_report.html (accessed 19 October 2001).

"National Donors Search: Sony, Sony Pictures Entertainment." OpenSecrets.org. 2010, http://www.opensecrets.org/orgs/lookup_stfed.php (accessed 27 September 2010).

"The National Entertainment State, 2006." *The Nation*, 3 July 2006. http://www.thenation.com/doc/20060703/intro (accessed 6 October 2006).

"National Guard Is Called to Quell Trade-Talk Protests." *New York Times*, 1 December 1999, A1.

Naureckas, Jim. "They Are the 1 Percent." *Extra!* November 2011, http://www.fair.org/index.php?page=4465 (accessed 12 February 2012).

NBC Nightly News with Tom Brokaw. National Broadcasting Company. 7 September 1999.

NBC Universal. "Company Overview, Film." http://www.nbcuni.com/About_NBC_Universal/Company_Overview/Film.shtml (accessed 13 July 2010).

Neer, Katherine Fordham. "How Product Placement Works." http://money.howstuffworks.com/product-placement7.htm (accessed 3 March 2008).

Nerone, John. *Violence against the Press: Policing the Public Sphere in U.S. History*. New York: Oxford University Press, 1994.

"Nestlé Boycott." *Wikipedia*, http://en.wikipedia.org/wiki/Nestle_boycott (accessed 18 February 2008).

Netherby, Jennifer, and Scott Hettrick. "Warner Wild about Harry: Studio Reaches for Stratosphere." *Video Business*, 11 February 2002, 1.

Newcomb, Kevin. "Study: Search Engines Still Fail to Disclose Ads." *ClickZ*, 9 June 2005, http://www.clickz.com/showPage.html?page=3511576 (accessed 3 March 2008).

"New Product Placement: Best Selling Novels." *Kicking Tires*, 20 November 2006, http://blogs.cars.com/kickingtires/2006/11/patterson_merce.html (accessed 3 March 2008).

News Corporation. *2007 Annual Report*. http://www.newscorp.com/Report2007/
AR2007.pdf (accessed 4 November 2011).
———. *2009 Annual Report*. http://www.newscorp.com/Report2009/html/2.html
(accessed 4 November 2011).
———. *Form 10-K*. 30 June 2009. http://shareholder.com/ (accessed 28 June 2010).
"News Corporation: A Corporate Profile." Corporate Watch UK, May 2004, www.
corporatewatch.org (accessed 26 February 2008).
"Newsflashes." *Adbusters* 30 (June–July 2000): 17.
News Hour with Jim Lehrer. Public Broadcasting System, 10 January 2000.
"Newspapers and News Organizations." Hoovers. 2007. http://www.hoovers.com/
(accessed 9 November 2007).
"New York Times Co." *Standard & Poor's Corporate Descriptions Plus News*, 29 January
2002, www.lexisnexis.com (accessed 1 February 2002).
"The New York Times Company Reports December Revenues." 24 January 2006,
C2. http://advertise.about.com/newspress/news01_24_06.html, (accessed 27
February 2008).
"Nicole Kidman and Russell Crowe Named Most Overpaid Stars." Hollywood.com,
13 December 2007, http://www.hollywood.com/news/Kidman_and_Crowe_
Named_Most_Overpaid_Stars/5014730 (accessed 5 October 2010).
Nocera, Joe. "Running an Empire? No Sweat." *New York Times*, 25 August 2007, B1, B8.
"No Child Left Behind." *Wikipedia*, http://en.wikipedia.org/wiki/No_Child_Left_
Behind (accessed 2 March 2008).
Norris, Floyd. "The New, Improved Redstone Still Knows How to Get His Way."
New York Times, 8 September 1999, C1, C13.
———. "Which Would Have Done Better without the Merger?" *New York Times*, 14
January 2003, C6.
"North American Recorded Music Revenues (2006–2011)." GrabStats.com. http://
www.grabstats.com/statmain.asp?StatID=71 (accessed 23 May 2011).
Novack, Megan. "Program Provides Disney Experience." *Penn State Daily Collegian*,
26 September 2000, 2.
NPD Group. "Amazon Ties Wal-mart as Second-Ranked U.S. Music Retailer, Behind
Industry-Leader iTunes." NPD Press Release. 26 May 2010. http://www.npd.com/
press/releases/press_100526.html (accessed 31 May 2011).
O'Brien, Chris. "AOL Merger May Fuel Silicon Valley Growth." *State College (Pa.)
Centre Daily Times*, 13 January 2000, 6B.
"100 Leading National Advertisers Report 2010." *Advertising Age*, 28 December
2009, http://adage.com/marketertrees09update/ (accessed 25 March 2010).
"Onex Aiming to Acquire Loews Theatre Chain." *Toronto Star*, 14 November 2001,
E11.
Ono, Yumiko. "Was Japan's Craze for Art Yen Motivated?" *Wall Street Journal*, 2
April 1991, C1.
Orenstein, Peggy. "What's Wrong with Cinderella?" *New York Times*, 24 December
2006, http://www.nytimes.com/2006/12/24/magazine/24princess.t.html?pagew
anted=4&ei=5088&en=8e5a1ac1332a802c&ex=1324616400&partner=rssnyt&e
mc=rss (accessed 3 March 2008).
Panday, Swati. "Warner Music Whittles Its Losses on Brisk Digital Sales." *Los Angeles Times*, 8 August 2008, http://articles.latimes.com/2008/aug/08/business/
fi-warner8 (accessed 8 November, 2008).

Paramount. *10-K Report*. 2006.

Parry, Robert, Sam Parry, and Nat Parry. "Journalists 'Humbled' but Unrepentent." *Extra!* November–December 2007, 22.

"Penn Staters Tinker with Computers." *State College (Pa.) Centre Daily Times*, 25 July 2000, A5.

Perez-Pena, Richard, and Andrew Ross Sorkin. "So Near, Yet So Far: Murdoch Awaits Decision on His Dow Offer." *New York Times*, 31 July 2007, C1, C5.

Perkins, Dan, aka Tom Tomorrow. Op-Art. *New York Times*, 11 January 2000, A31.

Peters, Cynthia. "Marketing to Teens." *Z Magazine*, April 1999, 23.

"Pete Townshend's Strongly Held Political Beliefs." NotBored.org, 18 July 2004, http://www.notbored.org/townshend.html (accessed 18 January 2008).

Petrecca, Laura. "Wal-Mart Joins Forces with *Hannah Montana*." *USA Today*, 29 January 2008, http://www.usatoday.com/money/industries/retail/2008-01-29-hannah-montana-walmart_N.htm (accessed 30 January 2008).

Pew Research Center for the People and the Press. "Journalists Avoiding the News, Self-Censorship: How Often and Why." 30 April 2000, www.people-press.org/jour00rpt.htm (accessed 5 January 2002).

———. "Bottom-Line Pressures Now Hurting Coverage, Say Journalists." 23 May 2004, http://people-press.org/reports/display.php3?ReportID=214 (accessed 26 January 2008).

———. "Summary of Findings: Public Knowledge of Current Affairs Little Changed by News and Information Revolutions." 15 April 2007. http://people-press.org/reports/display.php3?Report ID=319, (accessed 26 January 2008).

———. "Too Much Celebrity News, Too Little Good News." 12 October 2007. http://people-press.org/reports/display.php3?ReportID=362 (accessed 22 February 2008).

Picchi, Aimee. "AOL–Time Warner Too Optimistic?" *Philadelphia Enquirer*, 15 December 2000, C1, C7.

———. "AOL Buys AT&T's Venture Stake for US$3.6 Billion." *Financial Post*, FP4, www.lexisnexis.com (accessed 26 January 2008).

"Pittsburgh Steels Itself for G-20 Protests." *Wall Street Journal*, 11 September 2009, cited in Mac Lojowsky, "Seattle to Pittsburgh," *Z Magazine*, December 2009, 12.

Plaut, Martin. "Ford Advertises the Literary Way." BBC News, 1 March 2004, http://news.bbc.co.uk/1/hi/business/3522635.stm (accessed 3 March 2008).

"Playing with Product Placement." Blogspot.com, 17 April 2007, http://playproduct.blogspot.com/2007/04/board-games-galore.html (accessed 3 March 2008).

Pogash, Carol. "Poor Students in High School Suffer Stigma from Lunch Aid." *New York Times*, 1 March 2008, A1, A14.

Pollack, Andrew, and Andrew Ross Sorkin. "Time Warner to Acquire Control of EMI Music." *New York Times*, 24 January 2000, C1, C12.

Pollay, Richard W., Jung S. Lee, and David Carter-Whitney. "Separate, but Not Equal: Racial Segmentation in Cigarette Advertising." In *Gender, Race, and Class in Media*, edited by Gail Dines and Jean M. Humez, 109–111, Thousand Oaks, Calif.: Sage Publications, 1995.

Postman, Neil. "Virtual Students, Digital Classrooms." *The Nation*, 9 October 1995, 377–82.

"Potter Proves Power of Cross-Marketing." *Investor's Business Daily*, 23 November 2001, A6.

Press, Eyal, and Jennifer Washburn. "The Kept University." *Atlantic Monthly* 285, no. 3 (March 2000): 39–54.

"Protesters March, Fail to Block World Finance Meeting." *State College (Pa.) Centre Daily Times,* 17 April 2000, A7.

"PSU Sues Over Football Rentals." *State College (Pa.) Centre Daily Times,* 11 January 2012, A4.

Pulley, Brett. "The Cable Capitalist." *Forbes,* 8 October 2001, 42–54.

Puzzanghera, Jim. "High-Tech TVs Could Become Low-Tech Trash." *State College (Pa.) Centre Daily Times,* 11 June 2007, C8.

Quart, Alissa. "Extreme Parenting." *Atlantic Monthly,* 1 August 2006, Extreme%20 Parenting%20(The%20Atlantic%20Monthly)%20%7C%20Alissa%20Quart .webarchive (accessed 16 February 2008).

Quenqua, Douglas. "Saying 'Will You' for Prizes, on the Web." *New York Times,* 7 January 2008, C6.

———. "Upload a Prom Dress Photo, and Hope." *New York Times,* 13 May 2010, E8.

Quinones, Eric R. "Market Woes Lessen Ranks of Billionaires." *State College (Pa.) Centre Daily Times,* 28 September 1998, A1.

"Radio Broadcasting in the U.S: Current Performance." IBIS*World.* 2010, http://cli ents.ibisworld.com/industryus/currentperformance.aspx (accessed 10 July 2011).

"Radio Broadcasting in the U.S.: Major Companies." IBIS*World.* 2010. http://www. ibisworld.com/ (accessed 10 July 2011).

Raghavan, Sudarsan. "The Slavery Trap." *State College (Pa.) Centre Daily Times,* 26 June 2001, A1, A7.

Raghavan, Sudarsan, and Sumana Chatterjee. "Child Slavery Persists on African Cocoa Farms." *State College (Pa.) Centre Daily Times,* 25 June 2001, A1, A7.

"Rapid Media Consolidation Dramatically Narrows Number of Companies Controlling Time Spent Online." Jupiter Media Metrix. 4 June 2001. www.iup.com/ company/ (accessed 7 January 2002).

Rashbaum, William K., and Al Baker. "The Police: Shrewd Anticipation Helped Avert Trouble." *New York Times,* 5 February 2002, A15.

Raum, Tom, and Emma Vandore. "World Leaders Dub Gathering a Success." *State College (Pa.) Centre Daily Times,* 26 September 2009, A1.

"Raytheon Grant Helps Endow State High Award." *State College (Pa.) Centre Daily Times,* 24 September 2001, A5.

Recording Industry Association of America. *Let's Play: The American Music Business.* 2010, http://www.ifpi.org/content/library/RIAA_Brochure_Final.pdf (accessed 4 November 2011).

———. "Music, Movie, TV and Broadband Leaders Team to Curb Online Content Theft." 2011. http://riaa.com/newsitem.php?content_selector=newsandviews&news_ month_filter=7&news_year_filter=2011&id=2DDC3887-A4D5-8D41-649D- 6E4F7C5225A5 (accessed 10 July 2011).

———. "U.S. Government Issues Annual Report Naming Foreign Countries with Worst IP Protections." 2 May 2011. http://www.riaa.com/newsitem.php?content _selector=newsandviews&news_month_filter=5&news_year_filter=2011&id= F4B3CD29-B810-CF82-0537-1855502021EA (accessed 10 July 2011).

"Reese Witherspoon Tops Rich List." Hollywood.com. 30 November 2007. http:// www.hollywood.com/news/Witherspoon_Tops_Rich_List/5005010 (accessed 5 October 2010).

Reynolds, Mike. "Ratings Go Higher for Hannah." Multichannel News, http://www.multichannel.com/article/134294-Ratings_Go_Higher_For_Hannah_.php (accessed 8 September 2008).

Rich, Frank. *The Greatest Story Ever Sold: The Decline and Fall of Truth from 9/11 to Katrina.* New York: The Penguin Press, 2006.

Rich, Motoko. "Product Placement Deals Make Leap From Film to Books." *New York Times*, 12 June 2006, http://www.nytimes.com/2006/06/12/business/media/12book.html (accessed 3 March 2008).

———. "In Books for Young, Two Views on Product Placement." *New York Times*, 19 February 2008, B1, B7.

"The Richest People in America: Star Power." *Forbes*, 6 October 2003, http://www.forbes.com/forbes/2003/1006/164.html (accessed 11 September 2010).

Richtel, Matt. "A New Force in Distributing Music across the Internet." *New York Times*, 8 September 1999, 14C.

"Rings Goes to WB for $160 Million." *St. Petersburg Times*, 5 February 2002, 5D.

Robinson, Sara. "Recording Industry Escalates Crackdown on Digital Piracy." *New York Times*, 4 October 1999, C5.

Robinson, Thomas N., Dina L. G. Borzekowski, Donna M. Matheson, and Helena C. Kraemer. "Effects of Fast Food Branding on Young Children's Taste Preferences." *Archives of Pediatric & Adolescent Medicine* 161, no. 8 (8 August 2007): 792–97, http://www.google.com/search?hl=en&client=safari&rls=en&sa=X&oi=spell&resnum=0&ct=result&cd=1&q=Mcdonald%27s+Brand+Recognition+Kids&spell=1 (accessed 3 March 2008).

"Rolling Stone." *Wikipedia.* http://en.wikipedia.org/wiki/Rolling_Stone (accessed 23 February 2008).

"Rolling Stone, Disney Join Forces for US." *State College (Pa.) Centre Daily Times*, 28 February 2001, B9.

Rose, Joel. "Rock Artists Embrace TV Sales." *NPR Morning Edition*, 6 February 2007, http://www.npr.org/templates/story/story.php?storyId=7213219 (accessed 14 January 2008).

"Round Tables: Ad Creep." *MediaChannel.org*, 4 January 2000, http://www.mediachannel.org/views/oped/adcreep.shtml (accessed 3 January 2008).

Rummel, J. D. "*You've Got Mail*: It's Okay." *Manly Men's Movie Reviews*, http://morpo.com/movies/?id=83&au=2 (accessed 30 September 2004).

Samiljan, Tom. "I Want My MP3." *Rolling Stone*, 18 March 1999, 69.

Saul, Stephanie. "Conflict on the Menu." *New York Times*, 16 February 2008, B1, B4.

Savage, David G. "Supreme Court Upholds Fine for TV Profanity." *Los Angeles Times*, 29 April 2009, http://articles.sfgate.com (accessed 3 July 2010).

Scaggs, Austin. "Q&A: The King of Heartland Returns with Renewed Optimism, a New Album, and a Chevy Ad." *Rolling Stone*, 8 February 2007, 28.

Schatz, Thomas. "Show Me the Money: In Search of Hits, the Industry May Go Broke." *The Nation*, 5 April 1999, 26–31.

Schiesel, Seth. "A Rush to Provide High-Speed Internet Access." *New York Times*, 12 January 2000, C1, C6.

———. "Vivendi Is Said to Have Deal for Expansion in U.S. Media." *New York Times*, 17 December 2001, A16.

Schiesel, Seth, with Felicity Barringer. "News Media Risk Big Losses to Cover War." *New York Times*, 22 October 2001, C1.

Schlozman, Kay, and Sidney Verba. *Injury to Insult.* Cambridge, Mass.: Harvard University Press, 1979.

Schmemann, Serge. "The Meeting: Annan Cautions Business as Forum Ends." *New York Times*, 5 February 2002, A14.

"School District Ponders Deal for Coke Products." *State College (Pa.) Centre Daily Times*, 2 July 1999, A11.

"School Questions Pepsi Contract." *State College (Pa.) Centre Daily Times*, 6 June 2001, A2.

Schor, Juliet B. *Born to Buy* (New York: Scribner, 2004), 13.

Schroeder, Ken. "One-derful Channel One." *Education Digest* 66, no. 1 (September 2000): 72–73.

Schruers, Fred. "Tom Petty: The Rolling Stone Interview." *Rolling Stone*, 22 July 1999, 88–94.

Schudson, Michael. *Discovering the News: A Social History of American Newspapers.* New York: Basic Books, 1978.

Schweizer, Kristin. "Sony, Record Labels to Take On iTunes by Offering Fee-Based Music Service." Bloomberg. 24 January 2011. http://www.bloomberg.com/news/2011-01-24/sony-record-labels-to-rival-apple-s-itunes-with-music-service-in-the-u-s-.html (accessed 31 May 2011).

Segal, David. "They're Calling Most Everyone's Tune." *New York Times*, 24 April 2010, BU1, BU6–7.

Shaw, Donald L. "News Bias and the Telegraph: A Study of Historical Change." *Journalism Quarterly* 44 (Spring 1967): 3–12, 31.

Sherer, Paul M. "Loews Cineplex to Be Acquired by Onex Group." *Wall Street Journal*, 16 February 2001, A4.

Sherman, Jerome L. "Charges Dismissed against PG Reporter." *Pittsburgh Post-Gazette*, 15 October 2009, http://infoweb.newsbank.com (accessed 23 May 2010).

Sherman, Stratford P. "Ted Turner: Back from the Brink." *Fortune*, 7 July 1986, 25–31.

Shevory, Kristina. "Aiming to Stem Attendance Losses, More Cinemas Try a Full-Frills Model." *New York Times*, 20 February 2008, C6.

Shin, Annys. "Removing Schools' Soda Is Sticky Point: Bottlers' Contracts Limit Cash-Strapped Districts." *Washington Post*, 22 March 2007, D3, http://www.washingtonpost.com/wp-dyn/content/article/2007/03/21/AR2007032101966.html (accessed 1 March 2008).

Siers, Kevin. "Contents: Copyright AOL–Time Warner." *State College (Pa.) Centre Daily Times*, 16 January 2000, 9A.

Siklos, Richard. "Icahn Group Steps Up Time Warner Proxy Fight." *New York Times*, 13 September 2005, C3.

——. "A Virtual World but Real Money." *New York Times*, 19 October 2006, http://www.nytimes.com/2006/10/19/technology/19virtual.html?_r=1&oref=slogin (accessed 27 February 2008).

Simons, John. "Big Pharma's Ready for Prime Time." *Fortune*, 28 September 2007, http://money.cnn.com/2007/09/28/magazines/fortune/simons_productplacement.fortune/index.htm (accessed 12 October 2007).

Sisario, Ben. "Front-Row Seat to Go? Rock Fans Pay for Perks with the Stars." *New York Times*, 23 May 2010, C1, C4.

Smeltz, Adam. "Alliance to Study Coal Uses." *State College (Pa.) Centre Daily Times*, 4 October 2007, A1.

Smith, David. "Nittany Lion Print Foots Too Many Toes." *Penn State Daily Collegian*, 29 January 1999, 8.

Snider, Mike. "iPods Knock Over Beer Mugs." *USA Today*, 7 June 2006.

Sony Corporation of America. "Senior Management." June 2010. http://www.sony.com/SCA/bios/stringer.shtml (accessed 26 September 2010).

———. "Outline of Principal Operations: Music Choice." November 2010. http://www.sony.com/SCA/outline/partnerships.shtml (accessed 26 May 2011).

———. "Outline of Principal Operations: Sony/ATV Music Publishing." November 2010, http://www.sony.com/SCA/outline/atv.shtml (accessed 26 May 2011).

Sony Corp–Sponsored ADR. "Latest Proxy Reports 2009–2010." Bloomsberg Businessweek, http://investing.businessweek.com/research/stocks/people/relationship.asp?personId=631152&ticker=SNE (accessed 27 September 2010).

Sony Pictures. "Corporate Fact Sheet." 2010. www.sonypictures.com (accessed 14 July 2010).

Sostek, Anya. "Management Doctrines Hit Schools." *State College (Pa.) Centre Daily Times*, 24 February 2008, B3.

"SoundBites: Ads Are Not Enough." *Extra! Update*, December 1999, 2.

"SoundBites: Buy One, Get One Free." *Extra! Update*, June 2000, 2.

"Special Report: CEO Compensation." Forbes.com, 28 April 2010, http://www.forbes.com/lists/2010/12/boss-10_CEO-Compensation-Media_9Rank.html (accessed 19 September 2010).

Squires, Sally. "Experts Say Medicine Ads Often Omit Basics." *State College (Pa.) Centre Daily Times*, 18 December 2000, C1.

Starhawk. "How We Shut Down the WTO." *Z Magazine*, February 2000, 18–19.

Stark, Andrew. "Taste: Let's Make a Deal—Commerce." *Wall Street Journal*, 31 March 2000, W17.

"Star News and Gossip." *TV Guide Live*, 11 December 2001, www.tvguidelive.com/newsgossip-archives/01-dec/12-11-01.html (accessed 28 January 2002).

"State High Teacher Awarded Palm Grant." *State College (Pa.) Centre Daily Times*, 10 September 2001, A5.

Stelter, Brian. "With Video Delivered by Web, the Desk Is a Hot Lunch Spot." *New York Times*, 5 January 2007, A1, B4.

Stempel, Jonathan. "Carl Icahn Unwinding Blockbuster Stake." Reuters, 2 April 2010, http://www.reuters.com/article/idUSTRE63127T20100402 (accessed 13 September 2010).

Stevenson, Seth. "Can Rosa Parks Sell Pickup Trucks?" *Slate*, 9 October 2006, http://www.slate.com/id/2151143/ (accessed 13 January 2008).

Stone, Brad. "States Fault Myspace on Predator Issues." *New York Times*, 15 May 2007, C2.

Story, Louise. "Madison Avenue Calling." *New York Times*, 20 January 2007, B1.

———. "A Company Will Monitor Phone Calls and Devise Ads to Suit." *New York Times*, 24 September 2007, C1.

———. "Coke Promotes Itself in a New Virtual World." *New York Times*, 7 December 2007.

Strauss, Neil. "MTV Winner: Neither Rejected nor Censored." *New York Times*, 2 September 1995, C15.

———. "Wal-Mart's CD Standards Are Changing Pop Music." *New York Times*, 12 November 1996, A1, C12.

Stross, Randall. "Why Bricks and Clicks Don't Always Mix." *New York Times*, 10 September 2010, Sunday Business 3.

Student Debt and the Class of 2010. Institute for College Access and Success, 3 November 2011, http://ticos.org/files/pub/classof2010.pdf (accessed 12 February 2012).

"Students Binge on Credit." *USA Today*, 14 September 2000, A26.

"Studio Market Share 2009." Box Office Mojo, http://www.boxofficemojo.com/st udio/?view=company&view2=yearly&yr=2009&p=.htm (accessed 8 November 2010).

"Summit Lesson: Pittsburgh Can Learn More about Police Response." *Pittsburgh Post-Gazette*. 11 March 2010. http://infoweb.newsbank.com (accessed 23 May 2010).

Sutel, Seth. "Giants of Media Join at the Hip." *State College (Pa.) Centre Daily Times*, 8 September 1999, 1A, 7A.

Swartz, Jon. "Widgets Make a Big Splash on the Net." *USA Today*, 27 January 2007, B1–B2.

Szlalai, Georg. "Record Industry Revenues Increased 6% in 2010." *Hollywood Reporter*, 18 February 2010, http://www.hollywoodreporter.com/news/radio-indus try-revenue-increases-6-101551 (accessed 9 July 2011).

———. "Radio Industry Continues to Grow Revenue in First Quarter." *Hollywood Reporter*, 20 May 2011, http://www.hollywoodreporter.com/news/radio-industry-continues-grow-revenue-190697 (accessed 11 July 2011).

Tabor, Mary B. W. "Schools Profit from Offering Students for Market Research." *New York Times*, 5 April 1999, A1.

Takiff, Jonathan. "What's Hot from the Toy Show." *State College (Pa.) Centre Daily Times*, 28 February 2008, B2.

Tarshis, Joan. "Celebrities Reveal Their Secrets." *Parade*, 19 March 2000, 10.

Tenowitz, Ira. "Congressmen Tackle Product Placement." *TV Week*, 26 September 2007, http://www.tvweek.com/news/2007/09/congressmen_tackle_product_pla. php (accessed 24 January 2008).

Terenzini, Caroline. "Productive Tinkering." *State College (Pa.) Centre Daily Times*, 18 May 1999, C1.

Tetzlaff, David. "Yo-Ho-Ho and a Server of Warez: Internet Software Piracy and the New Global Information Economy." In *The World Wide Web and Contemporary Cultural Theory*, edited by A. Herman and T. Swiss, 99–126. New York: Routledge, 2000.

Thomson, Amy. "Cumulus to Buy Citadel Broadcasting in $2.4 Billion Deal." *Bloomberg*, 10 March 2011, http://www.bloomberg.com/news/2011-03-10/ cumulus-agrees-to-buy-citadel-broadcasting-in-deal-valued-at-2-4-billion.html (accessed 14 July 2011).

Thiruvengadam, Meena. "Clear Channel Sells More Radio Stations." *Knight Ridder Tribune Business News*, 3 May 2007, 1.

Thomas, Jennifer. "Heat on Video Rental Stores." *State College (Pa.) Centre Daily Times*, 5 July 2008, A1, A7.

Thomas, Steven. "White House Manages New Media, Stays on Message." *State College (Pa.) Centre Daily Times*, 16 May 2010, A3.

"THON to Showcase Hilfiger Wear." *State College (Pa.) Centre Daily Times*, 12 February 2000, A5.

Time Warner. *Annual Report 2000.*

Time Warner. *Annual Report 2006.* http://files.shareholder.com/downloads/TWX/229105524x0x154481/39d9368c-c6f8-4162-ab2e-30bdf6f8f21d/2006AR.pdf (accessed 17 January 2008).

Time Warner Cable Inc. "Investor Relations: Board of Directors 2010." www.timewarner.com (accessed 16 May 2010).

Time Warner Cable Inc. *10-K Report.* 31 March 2010.

Time Warner News. "Time Warner Inc. Declares Spin-off Dividend of Time Warner Cable Inc." 26 February 2009, www.timewarner.com (accessed 15 May 2010).

Toles, Tom. "Coming to a Screen near You." *State College (Pa.) Centre Daily Times*, 13 February 2000, 13A.

"The Top 20 U.S. Media Owners." Media Owners, 2009, http://www.mediaowners.com/about/index.html (accessed 9 November 2009).

"Trade Protest Roils Capital." *State College (Pa.) Centre Daily Times*, 17 April 2000, A1.

"Trade Talks Begin." *State College (Pa.) Centre Daily Times*, 30 November 1999, A4.

"Tristar Strikes Deal with In-Demand." Associated Press Online, 28 August 2001.

Turner, Ted. "My Beef with the Big Media." *Washington Monthly*, July–August 2004. http://www.washingtonmonthly.com/features/2004/0407.turner.html (accessed 22 February 2007).

"TV News in Schools Costs $1.8 Billion in Class Time." *New York Times*, 1 April 1998, B11.

"$25 Million Ad Blitz Planned for Potter Video." *Milwaukee Journal Sentinel*, 7 February 2002, 6B.

"2008 State of the Union Address." White House press release, 28 January 2008, http://www.state.gov/r/pa/ei/wh/rem/99783.htm (accessed 4 March 2008).

"Unions Boycott Wal-Mart." *New York Times*, 11 August 2005, http://www.nytimes.com/2005/08/11/business/11walmart.html (accessed 2 March 2008).

Universal Music Group. "History: Labels." 2010. http://www.universalmusic.com/history (accessed 7 June 2011).

Urbina, Ian. "Protesters at G-20 Meeting Are Met by Tear Gas." *New York Times*, 25 September 2009, A10.

"U.S. Cell-Phone Penetration Tops 82 Percent." Gearlog, http://www.gearlog.com/2007/11/us_cellphone_penetration_tops.php (accessed 3 March 2008).

U.S. Census Bureau. American Fact Finder. Concentration by Largest Firms. ECO 7515 Z6. 2007 Economic Census.

U.S. Department of Justice. "Department Closes Antitrust Investigation into the Movielink Movies-on-Demand Joint Venture." 3 June 2004, http://www.justice.gov/atr/public/press_releases/2004/203932.htm (accessed 2 October 2010).

U.S. Federal Trade Commission to Gary Ruskin. June 27, 2002, http://www.ftc.gov/os/closings/staff/commercialalertletter.shtm (accessed 14 November 2011).

"U.S. Mobile Ad Expenditures More Than Double to $2.1 Billion, Google Domi-
nates." mobiThinking, 20 December 2011, http://mobithinking.com/blog/
mobile-ad-network-share-2011 (accessed 5 February 2012).

"User Ratings for Hannah & Miley Cyrus: Best of Both Worlds." IMDb. http://www.
imdb.com/title/tt1127884/ratings (accessed 5 February 2012).

Variety Portable Movie Guide. New York: Berkeley Boulevard Books, 1999.

Verba, Sidney, and Gary R. Owen. *Equality in America.* Cambridge, Mass.: Harvard
University Press, 1985.

Verhovek, Sam Howe. "Trade Talks Start in Seattle Despite a Few Disruptions." *New
York Times,* 30 November 1999, A14.

———. "Seattle Is Stung, Angry, and Chagrined as Opportunity Turns to Chaos."
New York Times, 2 December 1999, A14.

———. "Seattle Police Chief Resigns in Aftermath of Protests." *New York Times,* 8
December 1999, A13.

Viacom. *Proxy Statement, 2007.*

"Viacom Inc." OneSource Information Services, 27 July 2007, www.lexisnexis.com
(accessed 16 January 2008).

Viacom Inc. *10-K Form.* 11 February 2010.

"Viacom Reports Third Quarter Results 2007." Press release, 2 November 2007,
www.viacom.com (accessed 15 January 2008).

Vickery, Danielle. "Penn State Sees Copycat Logo for Second Time This Year." *Penn
State Daily Collegian,* 4 October 2007, 1.

Vivendi, S.A. *Annual Financial Report.* 31 December 2010, http://www.vivendi.com/
vivendi/IMG/pdf/03_01_2011_Annual_Report.pdf (accessed 23 May 2011).

———. "Shareholding Structure." 31 December 2010, http://www.vivendi.com/
vivendi/shareholding-structure (accessed 24 May 2011).

Vonnegut, Kurt. *Breakfast of Champions.* New York: Dial, 1973.

"Wal-Mart Teams with Disney to Be Hannah Montana™ Retail Headquarters."
CNNMoney.com, http://money.cnn.com/news/newsfeeds/articles/prnewswire/
LAW03630012008-1.htm (accessed January 30 2008).

"Walt Disney Company. Lobbying 2008." Center for Responsive Politics, http://
opensecrets.org/lobby/clientsum.php?year=2008&lname=Walt+Disney+Co (accessed 24 June 2010).

Walt Disney Company. "Notice of Annual Meeting of Shareholders." 4 January
2002.

———. *2007 Annual Report.*

———. *Notice of 2009 Annual Meeting and Proxy Statement.* January 2009.

———. *Proxy Statement.* 22 January 2010, http://media.disney.go.com/investorrela
tions/proxy/proxy_2010.pdf (accessed 2 February 2010).

———. "Institutional Ownership." 20 July 2010, http://www.dailyfinance.com/
company/the-walt-disney-company/dis/nys/institutional-ownership (accessed 22
June 2010).

"Warner Bros. International Cinemas and Village Cinemas." Time Warner press
release, 22 December 2004, http://www.timewarner.com/ (accessed 12 February
2008).

Warner Music Group. *2009 Annual Report.* 31 September 2009, http://www.scribd.
com/doc/48117825/WMG-2009-Annual-Report (accessed 26 July 2010).

———. "Warner Music Group Corp. Reports Results for the Fiscal Fourth Quarter and Full Year Ended September 30, 2010." 17 November 2010, http://www.wmg.com/newsdetails/id/8a0af8122c353d41012c56ba06bf0f65 (accessed 2 June 2011).

———. "Recorded Music Overview." 2011, www.wmg.com (accessed 2 June 2011).

"Warren Buffett Turns Toon." *New York Times*, 9 February 2006, B2.

Wasko, Janet. *Hollywood in the Information Age*. Austin: University of Texas Press, 1994.

———. *Understanding Disney*. Cambridge, U.K.: Polity Press, 2001.

———. *How Hollywood Works*. Thousand Oaks, Calif.: Sage, 2003.

Weinraub, Bernard. "Disney Hires Kissinger." *New York Times*, 10 October 1997, E7.

———. "A Strained Relationship Turns Sour." *New York Times*, 18 October 1999, C18.

Wengerd, Erin R. "Protest Preparation Fails to Draw Crowd." *State College (Pa.) Centre Daily Times*, 25 May 2000, A1.

Wenner, Jann. "A Letter from the Editor." *Rolling Stone*, 9 November 1967, 2.

Westbrook, Bruce. "Snow White to Make Digital Debut: Disney DVD Set Packed with Extras." *Houston Chronicle*, 7 October 2001, 8.

Westfeldt, Amy. "Protesters Embrace Variety of Messages." *State College (Pa.) Centre Daily Times*, 10 November 2011, A9.

———. "Occupy Protesters Finally Present Specifics. *State College (Pa.) Centre Daily Times*, 2 December 2011, A9.

"When Being No. 1 Is Not Enough: The Impact of Advertising Practices on Minority-Owned and Minority-Formatted Broadcast Stations." www.fcc.gov/Bureaus/Media (accessed 29 December 2001).

"Whither the Tube?" *New York Times*, 4 January 1999, 18A.

"Will Smith Tops Highest-Earner List." Hollywood.com, 24 July 2008, http://www.hollywood.com/news/Will_Smith_Tops_Highest_Earner_Poll/5280730 (accessed 5 October 2010).

Winkler, Rolf, and Martin Hutchinson. "After the Divorce, AOL Faces Challenges." *New York Times*, 11 December 2009, B2, http://www.nytimes.com/2009/12/11/business/11views.html (accessed 15 May 2010).

Winston, Brian. *Misunderstanding Media*. Cambridge, Mass.: Harvard University Press, 1986.

Woletz, Robert G. "A New Formula: Into the 'Bin,' Out Comes a Hit." *New York Times*, 2 August 1992, D1.

Wolfe, Tom. "Preface." In *Rolling Stone: The Photographs*, edited by Laurie Kratochvil. New York: Simon & Schuster, 1989.

"The World's Billionaires." *Forbes*, http://www.forbes.com/lists/2010/10/billionaires-2010_The-Worlds-Billionaires_NameProper_2.html (accessed 26 June 2010).

"Worldwide Live Music/Concert Revenues (2006–2011)." GrabStats.com, http://www.grabstats.com/statmain.asp?StatID=70 (accessed 9 July 2011).

"Worldwide Music Industry Revenues (2006–2011)." GrabStats.com, http://www.grabstats.com/statmain.asp?StatID=71 (accessed 23 May 2011).

"Worldwide Recorded Music Revenues (2006–2011)." GrabStats.com, http://www.grabstats.com/statmain.aasp?StatID=68 (accessed 5 May 2011).

Wouters, Jergen J. "Still in Search of Disclosure." Consumer Reports WebWatch, 9 June 2005, http://www.consumerwebwatch.org/dynamic/jorgen-wouters.cfm (accessed 3 March 2008).

"WTO Protests Turn Violent." *State College (Pa.) Centre Daily Times*, 1 December 1999, A1.

Wyatt, Edward. "SpongeBob SquareProfits: Nickelodeon Swears by Cartoons." *New York Times*, 12 December 2006, B1, B6.

"Yearly Box Office." Box Office Mojo. 2009, http://ww.boxofficemojo.com/yearly/?vidw2=worldwide$view=re (accessed 16 October 2010).

"Yearly Box Office." Box Office Mojo, http://www.boxofficemojo.com/yearly/ (accessed 8 November 2010).

"Yearly Box Office: Overseas Total." Box Office Mojo. www.boxofficemojo.com (accessed 12 February, 2008).

"Yearly Box Office: 2007 Domestic Grosses." Box Office Mojo. www.boxofficemojo.com (accessed 12 February 27, 2008).

Yurcan, Brian F. "Radio Stations Dial in New Owner." *Westchester County Business Journal*, 30 July 2007, 3.

Zeller, Tom, Jr. "Amid Clamor for Computer in Every Classroom, Some Dissenting Voices." *New York Times*, 17 March 2001, A3.

———. "AOL Acts on Release of Data." *New York Times*, 14 June 2007, C1, C7.

Zimmerman, F. J., D. A. Christakis, and A. N. Meltzoff. "Associations between Media Viewing and Language Development in Children under Age 2 Years." *Journal of Pediatrics*, August 2007.

Zmuda, Natalie. "Beverage Giants Team Up in Campaign to Remove Soda from Schools." *Advertising Age*, 9 March 2010, http://adage.com (accessed 17 May 2010).

Zuckerford, Nancy. "Study: Ads Have Greater Effects Than Anti-Tobacco Efforts." *State College (Pa.) Centre Daily Times*, 12 June 2001, A4.

Zuckerman, Laurence. "As Media Influence Grows for Handful, Can That Be a Good Thing?" *New York Times*, 13 January 2000, C6.

Index

children: books for, 208–9, 210–11; brand loyalty in, 7, 209; films for, 211–13; product placement affecting, 208–18; slave labor by, 8–9, 68; television programs for, 212, 213–16; virtual and actual playmates of, 216–18, 222. *See also* education
Chile, coup in, 99
China: Disney in, 69; movie theaters in, 60; music piracy in, 154; News Corp. in, 86
Cho, Mildred, 246
chocolate, 8–9, 68
Chomsky, Noam, 16
Chris-Craft, 21
Christians, Cliff, 1
Chrysler Corp., 205
cigarettes. *See* tobacco
Cigarrest, 185
Cinderella franchise, 213
Citadel Broadcasting, 145, 146
Citigroup, 130, 131
Clairol, 198, 239
classlessness, myth of, 167, 188, 189, 190, 279
Clear Channel Communications, Inc., 141–43; advertising revenues of, 143; bullying of artists by, 148; dominance of, 16, 18, 57, 58, 141; market share of, 141; ownership of, 142; radio stations of, 18, 141–42
Clinton, Bill, 3, 173, 258, 264
Clinton, Hillary Rodham, 3, 80, 262
CMT, 18, 20
CNN: audience of, 31; gaps in news coverage of, 175; war coverage of, 87, 184
Coca-Cola: in children's lives, 209–10; in film industry, 99, 111, 195; in higher education, 249; in public schools, 237–39, 240; in virtual worlds, 223
Cohen, Jeff, 35
cola wars, 237–39, 240, 248–49
Colbert, Stephen, 176–77

The Colbert Report (television show), 163, 164, 175, 236
colleges. *See* universities
Colorado, education funding in, 258
Columbia Journalism Review, 40
Columbia Pictures, 59, 99
Comcast: and AOL–Time Warner, 47; board of directors of, 97; in book publishing, 3; dominance of, 16, 58, 96; NBC Universal merger with, 57–58, 94–97; organizational interlocks of, 97; subsidiaries of, 96–97
Comedy Central, 47, 161, 175
Commercial Alert, 198, 200, 209, 219
Compaigne, Benjamin M., 42, 44, 57, 162
competition: in advertising, 6; in media industry, lack of, 57–58; in news, 2; in radio, 5
concerts. *See* live music
Congress, U.S.: on copyright extension, 72; ruling elite's lobbying of, 29; on slave labor in chocolate manufacturing, 9, 68; and Sony Corporation, 99; on television station ownership limits, 22; and Walt Disney Company, 68, 72
Connery, Sean, 58–59
conservatism, 75–80
conspicuous consumption, 166
consultants, faculty as corporate, 247–48
consumerism: in advertising, 6, 161, 166–68; definition of, 166; in editorial content, 6, 161; history of promotion of, 6, 161, 166–68; shift in views of, 167
Consumer Reports, 219
Consumers Union, 45, 46
Cooke, Janet, 16
Copps, Michael, 96
copyright: as censorship, 72–73; expiration of, 72; extension of, 72; First Sale Doctrine of, 89; Hollywood's strategy for protecting, 102–4; in music industry, 151–55;

172, 175–78; structure of industry, 178–82. *See also specific media*

news, advertising in, 157–91; amount of, 158, 160, 161, 168; consumerism promoted through, 161; early history of, 159–61; effects on news content, 178, 182–91; effects on news structure, 178–82; ideology of, 159, 165–71; organizational interlocks in, 165; revenues from, 158, 161, 164–65. *See also* magazines; newspapers

News Corporation, 73–87; advertising by, 40; board of directors of, 81; in book publishing, 3, 74, 86; dominance of, 15, 16, 57; in film industry, 73–87 (*see also* Twentieth Century Fox); on Iraq War, 86–87; major shareholders in, 74–75; in music industry, 132; newspapers of, 74, 85; organization interlocks of, 81, 82–84; political influence of, 41, 75–80, 85–87; revenues of, 73–74, 75; structure of, 74; subsidiaries of, 21, 74, 75, 76–80; tax payments by, 85; in television, 16, 21, 74, 81–85; unprofitable operations of, 39

news coverage: advertising's effects on content of, 178, 182–91; of AOL-Time Warner merger, 12, 17, 31–36, 46, 54; authority figures controlling agenda of, 7–8, 9, 174, 177; of capitalism, 176, 267; of capitalist class, 187–88; competition in, 2; of distribution of wealth, 190–91, 279; of educational products for infants and toddlers, 230; of film industry, 58; gaps in, 8, 16–17, 174–75, 187–88; investigative, 7, 8–9, 86, 172; of Iraq War, 86–87, 262; of media concentration, 12, 16–17, 35–36; media concentration's effects on, 40–44; objectivity in, 160, 172–73; of Occupy Wall Street, 278–79; of presidential elections, 2, 262; pro-corporate bias in, 177–78; self-censorship by journalists in,

40–41, 45; self-criticism of, 16–17; in social change, 8–9; of Viacom-CBS merger, 17, 18–23; working the beat in, 7, 174–75. *See also* alternative news media; mainstream news media

NewsHour with Jim Lehrer, 31

newspapers: concentration of ownership of, 16, 58, 161, 162, 179–80; history of industry, 159–62; on Internet, 161; media concentration's impact on coverage of, 40–41; names of, 160; prices of, 160; revenues of, 5, 161, 162, 164–65; working-class, 6, 8, 178–79. *See also specific publications*

newspapers, advertising in: amount of, 158, 160, 168; classified section of, 187; content of, 157; effects on industry structure, 179–80; revenues from, 5, 161, 164; rise of, 160–61

Newsweek, 185

New York Daily News, 85

New York Herald, 160

New York Post, 39, 41, 74, 80, 85

New York Times: advertising in, 157; on advertising in news media, 183–84, 187; on antiglobalization protests, 263, 269, 270, 272–73, 275, 276, 277; on AOL-Time Warner merger, 31, 32–35, 46, 54; on cell phone tracking, 221; on children's television, 214; on consumerism, 166; on franchise films, 61; on global trade meetings, 266; on Iraq War, 262; on Microsoft antitrust suit, 176; mission of, 157, 162; motto of, 157, 158; on MP3, 150, 152; on product placement, 203, 207, 209, 210; on public education, 236, 242; reputation of, 162; revenues of, 162; on technology's impact, 38; on television audiences, 171; on Viacom-CBS merger, 20–23

Nice, Treaty of, 265

Nickelodeon, 58, 64, 213–14

Nike, 234, 240, 250–51

About the Authors

Ronald V. Bettig is an associate professor in the College of Communications at the Pennsylvania State University, where he teaches courses in the political economy of communications. He is the author of *Copyrighting Culture: The Political Economy of Intellectual Property* (1996), one of the first works published on copyright from a critical perspective. He has written numerous journal articles, book chapters, and conference papers on media ownership and control.

Jeanne Lynn Hall was an associate professor in the College of Communications at the Pennsylvania State University, where she taught courses in film history, theory, and criticism. A former editor of *Wide Angle*, she published essays in journals such as *Cinema Journal, Film Criticism, Film Quarterly,* and *Creative Screenwriting.* She was the recipient of numerous teaching awards, and she directed conferences for Ohio University and the Union for Democratic Communications. She passed away on 23 December 2011, and will be greatly missed by those who knew and loved her.

Made in the USA
San Bernardino, CA
01 March 2017